A·N·N·U·A·L E·D·I·T·I·O·N·S

Educational Psychology

Fourteenth Edition

99/00

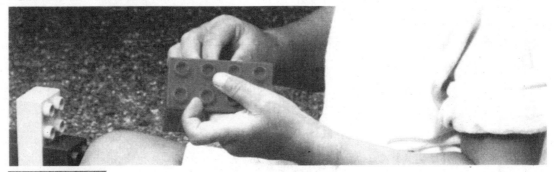

EDITORS

Kathleen M. Cauley
Virginia Commonwealth University

Kathleen M. Cauley received her Ph.D. in educational studies/human development from the University of Delaware in 1985. Her research interests center on applying cognitive developmental research to school learning. Currently, she is studying children's mathematical understanding.

Fredric Linder
Virginia Commonwealth University

Fredric Linder received an A.B. in American civilization from the University of Miami, Florida, an M.A. in psychology from the New School for Social Research, and a Ph.D. in educational psychology from the State University of New York at Buffalo. His research focuses on the values and cognitive learning styles of students.

James H. McMillan
Virginia Commonwealth University

James H. McMillan received his bachelor's degree from Albion College in 1970, an M.A. from Michigan State University in 1972, and a Ph.D. from Northwestern University in 1976. He has reviewed and written extensively in educational psychology.

Dushkin/McGraw-Hill
Sluice Dock, Guilford, Connecticut 06437

Visit us on the Internet
http://www.dushkin.com/annualeditions/

Credits

1. Perspectives on Teaching
Facing overview—© 1998 by PhotoDisc, Inc.
2. Development
Facing overview—© 1998 by PhotoDisc, Inc.
3. Exceptional and Culturally Diverse Children
Facing overview—© 1998 by PhotoDisc, Inc.
4. Learning and Instruction
Facing overview—© 1998 by PhotoDisc, Inc.
5. Motivation and Classroom Management
Facing overview—© 1998 CLEO Photography.
6. Assessment
Facing overview—© 1998 by CLEO Photography.

Copyright

Cataloging in Publication Data
Main entry under title: Annual Editions: Educational psychology. 1999/2000.
     1. Educational psychology—Periodicals. 2. Teaching—Periodicals. I. Cauley, Kathleen M., *comp.*; Linder, Fredric, *comp.*; McMillan, James H., *comp.* II. Title: Educational psychology.
ISBN 0-07-043513-8   370.15'05   82-640517   ISSN 0731-1141

Fourteenth Edition

Cover image © 1999 PhotoDisc, Inc.

Printed in the United States of America   1234567890BAHBAH5432109   Printed on Recycled Paper

To the Reader

In publishing ANNUAL EDITIONS we recognize the enormous role played by the magazines, newspapers, and journals of the public press in providing current, first-rate educational information in a broad spectrum of interest areas. Many of these articles are appropriate for students, researchers, and professionals seeking accurate, current material to help bridge the gap between principles and theories and the real world. These articles, however, become more useful for study when those of lasting value are carefully collected, organized, indexed, and reproduced in a low-cost format, which provides easy and permanent access when the material is needed. That is the role played by ANNUAL EDITIONS.

New to ANNUAL EDITIONS is the inclusion of related World Wide Web sites. These sites have been selected by our editorial staff to represent some of the best resources found on the World Wide Web today. Through our carefully developed topic guide, we have linked these Web resources to the articles covered in this ANNUAL EDITIONS reader. We think that you will find this volume useful, and we hope that you will take a moment to visit us on the Web at *http://www.dushkin.com* to tell us what you think.

Educational psychology is an interdisciplinary subject that includes human development, learning, intelligence, motivation, assessment, instructional strategies, and classroom management. The articles in this volume give special attention to the application of this knowledge to teaching.

Annual Editions: Educational Psychology 99/00 is divided into six units, and an overview precedes each unit, which explains how the unit articles are related to the broader issues within educational psychology.

The first unit, *Perspectives on Teaching,* presents issues that are central to the teaching role. The articles' authors describe the challenges of the teaching role at the secondary level, the role of research in meeting those challenges, and issues facing teachers in the twenty-first century.

The second unit, entitled *Development,* is concerned with child and adolescent development. It covers the cognitive, social, and emotional components of development. The essays in this unit examine the issues of parenting, moral development, the social forces affecting children and adolescents, as well as the personal and social skills needed to cope with school learning and developmental tasks.

The third unit, regarding exceptional and culturally diverse children, focuses on the learning disabled and the gifted, and on multicultural education. Diverse students require an individualized approach to education. The articles in this unit review the characteristics of these children and suggest programs and strategies to meet their needs.

In the fourth unit, *Learning and Instruction,* articles about theories of learning and instructional strategies are presented. The different views of learning, such as information processing, behaviorism, and constructivist learning, represent the accumulation of years of research on the way humans change in thinking or behavior due to experience. The principles generated by each approach have important implications for teaching. These implications are addressed in a section on instructional strategies, covering such topics as instructional methods, authentic instruction, and learning styles.

The topic of motivation is perhaps one of the most important aspects of school learning. Effective teachers need to motivate their students both to learn and to behave responsibly. How to manage children and what forms of discipline to use are issues that concern parents as well as teachers and administrators. The articles in the fifth unit, *Motivation and Classroom Management,* present a variety of perspectives on motivating students and discuss approaches to managing student behavior.

The articles in the sixth unit review assessment approaches that can be used to diagnose learning and improve instruction. The focus is on how alternative assessments, such as performance and portfolios, can be integrated with instruction to enhance student learning. Approaches to grading are also reviewed.

This edition also features selected *World Wide Web* sites, which can be used to further explore the articles' topics. These sites are cross-referenced by number in the *topic guide.*

This fourteenth edition of *Annual Editions: Educational Psychology* has been revised so as to present articles that are current and useful. Your responses to the selection and organization of materials are appreciated. Please complete and return the postage-paid *article rating form* on the last page of the book.

Kathleen M. Cauley

Fredric Linder

James H. McMillan

Editors

Contents

To the Reader — iv
Topic Guide — 2
○ Selected World Wide Web Sites — 4

Overview — 6

1. **How Novice Teachers Can Succeed with Adolescents,** — 8
   Robin L. Gordon, *Educational Leadership*, April 1997.
   Robin Gordon describes **social insight and "withitness"** as two critical aspects of the secondary **teacher's role.** Strategies for keeping in touch with the student culture and improving **student-teacher relationships** are listed.

2. **Using Action Research to Assess Instruction,** — 11
   Carole Schulte Johnson and Inga Kromann-Kelly, *Reading Horizons,* Volume 35, Number 3, 1995.
   Here are five basic steps teachers should take when **conducting an action research project,** a classroom inquiry to improve the learning environment in their classrooms.

3. **What Issues Will Confront Public Education in the Years 2000 and 2020? Predictions of Chief State School Officers,** Alan D. Morgan, Myrna Matranga, Gary L. Peltier, and George C. Hill, *The Clearing House,* July/August 1998. — 15
   Will students be educated in schools as we know them in 20 years? The authors of this article foresee shifts in **educational issues** as technology becomes more prevalent and as more students are educated at home or in the workplace.

UNIT 1

Perspectives on Teaching

Three selections discuss the importance of research and the value of scientific inquiry to the teaching process.

Overview — 18

A. CHILDHOOD

4. **New Brain Development Research—A Wonderful Window of Opportunity to Build Public Support for Early Childhood Education!** Julee J. Newberger, *Young Children,* May 1997. — 20
   Recent research on the structure and functioning of the brain sheds light on the importance of both nature and nurture regarding early infant and **child development.**

5. **The Moral Child,** *U.S. News & World Report,* June 3, 1996. — 26
   The cognitive, social, emotional, and biological underpinnings of **moral development** of children are examined here. Programs that enhance the moral skills of schoolchildren are also presented.

6. **Re-Evaluating Significance of Baby's Bond with Mother,** Sandra Blakeslee, *New York Times,* August 4, 1998. — 31
   Sandra Blakeslee discusses the role that early attachment between mother and infant contributes to later **child development.** Research is presented that contradicts the conclusions of earlier attachment studies.

UNIT 2

Development

Six articles examine how social interaction in the classroom influences child and adolescent development.

The concepts in bold italics are developed in the article. For further expansion please refer to the Topic Guide and the Index.

991101

v

7. **Helping Children Become More Prosocial: Ideas for** 34
   Classrooms, Families, Schools, and Communities,
   Alice S. Honig and Donna S. Wittmer, *Young Children,*
   January 1996.
   Techniques for parents and teachers on how to promote young
   children's **prosocial behaviors** are addressed in this article.
   Teachers should model these behaviors and create an atmosphere
   in the classroom that encourages prosocial deeds and attitudes.

B. ADOLESCENCE

8. **Developmental Tasks of Early Adolescence: How** 43
   Adult Awareness Can Reduce At-Risk Behavior,
   Judith L. Irvin, *The Clearing House,* March/April 1996.
   The personal, social, emotional, and cognitive **changes that
   confront early adolescents,** as well as the historical and cul-
   tural contexts within which they are maturing, are the focus here.

9. **Out of the Mouths of Babes: Voices of At-Risk** 47
   Adolescents, Korynne Taylor-Dunlop and Marcia M. Norton,
   The Clearing House, May/June 1997.
   A study of 11 at-risk young women finds that these **adolescent
   students** appreciate institutional caring, authentic learning, and
   attentive and helpful teachers.

Overview 52

A. EDUCATIONALLY DISABLED

10. **Where to Educate Rachel Holland? Does Least** 54
    Restrictive Environment Mean No Restrictions?
    Todd DeMitchell and Georgia M. Kerns, *The Clearing
    House,* January/February 1997.
    The authors provide an account of a controversial case involving
    a **special education** student and the services to which she is
    entitled under the federal **Individuals with Disabilities Educa-
    tion Act** (IDEA).

11. **Why Andy Couldn't Read,** Pat Wingert and Barbara 60
    Kantrowitz, *Newsweek,* October 27, 1997.
    Researchers have begun to unlock the puzzle of why bright students
    may have problems with learning. Millions of students have been
    labeled as **learning disabled,** but critics claim that these clas-
    sifications are vague and often misleading.

B. GIFTED AND TALENTED

12. **Is It Acceleration or Simply Appropriate Instruction** 65
    for Precocious Youth? John F. Feldhusen, Lanah Van
    Winkle, and David A. Ehle, *Teaching Exceptional Children,*
    Spring 1996.
    Acceleration is a term often used to describe appropriate practice
    for educating the **gifted child.** This is a call for new terminology
    and for providing individual children with higher-level learning
    opportunities.

UNIT 3

**Exceptional
and Culturally
Diverse Children**

Seven articles look at the problems
and positive effects of educational
programs for learning disabled,
gifted, and culturally diverse children.

The concepts in bold italics are developed in the article. For further expansion please refer to the Topic Guide and the Index.

13. **How All Middle-Schoolers Can Be "Gifted,"** Jay   **69**
A. McIntire, *The Education Digest*, May 1998.
Gifted education programs reward students with increased
academic excellence and help them develop positive attitudes about
their achievements and interpersonal relationships.

C. CULTURALLY AND ACADEMICALLY DIVERSE

14. **The Goals and Track Record of Multicultural**   **72**
Education, Rita Dunn, *Educational Leadership,* April
1997.
Rita Dunn reviews the ***multicultural education goals*** of
increasing academic achievement and promoting greater sensitivity
to cultural differences among students, but she believes that many
programs are misguided.

15. **Multiculturalism at a Crossroads,** John Gallagher,   **76**
The Education Digest, April 1998.
Author John Gallagher discusses some of the positive outcomes of
multicultural education in schools where content integration is
emphasized and racial prejudice is discouraged.

16. **Multiculturalism: Practical Considerations for**   **79**
Curricular Change, Tony R. Sanchez, *The Clearing
House,* January/February 1996.
Tony Sanchez describes ***the teacher's role*** in implementing a
multicultural curriculum. Sanchez provides guidelines to pro-
mote multicultural goals and objectives.

Overview   **82**

A. INFORMATION PROCESSING/COGNITIVE LEARNING

17. **Making Information Memorable: Enhanced**   **84**
Knowledge Retention and Recall through the
Elaboration Process, Donn Ritchie and Belinda Dunnick
Karge, *Preventing School Failure,* Fall 1996.
In this report, the authors suggest that strong ***memory skills*** that
enhance ***long-term memory*** will be facilitated through the use
of appropriate ***elaboration processes.***

18. **Brain Basics: Cognitive Psychology and Its Impli-**   **90**
cations for Education, Richard L. Bucko, *ERS Spectrum,*
Summer 1997.
Recent research on how the ***brain*** operates has provided educators
with principles for applying ***cognitive psychology*** to student
learning. In this article, Richard Bucko summarizes research on
how the brain works, levels of brain functions, and ***implications
for thinking skills and other learning and memory***
applications.

Learning and Instruction

Ten selections explore the important
types of student/teacher interaction.

19. **The First Seven . . . and the Eighth,** Kathy Checkley,   **96**
Educational Leadership, September 1997.
The theory of **multiple intelligences** (MI) has stirred controversy about the nature of the brain and the influence of culture on human performance. In this article, a conversation with Howard Gardner updates developments in MI and reviews implications of MI for **learning** and instruction.

20. **Styles of Thinking, Abilities, and Academic**   **101**
Performance, Elena L. Grigorenko and Robert J. Sternberg, *Exceptional Children,* Spring 1997.
This investigation shows how academic performance is affected by **styles of thinking.** The research is an effort to validate Robert Sternberg's **triarchic model of intelligence.**

B. LEARNING

21. **The Rewards of Learning,** Paul Chance, *Phi Delta*   **117**
Kappan, November 1992.
Paul Chance reviews important principles of **behaviorism,** such as **positive reinforcement** and **punishment.** He argues that there is an appropriate place in teaching for both **intrinsic** and **extrinsic rewards.**

22. **Rewards versus Learning: A Response to Paul**   **122**
Chance, Alfie Kohn, *Phi Delta Kappan,* June 1993.
Alfie Kohn challenges the notion that motivating students with artificial **incentives** is more effective than engaging students meaningfully in learning.

23. **Sticking Up for Rewards,** Paul Chance, *Phi Delta Kappan,* June 1993.   **126**
Psychologist Paul Chance stresses that it is a **teacher's responsibility** to become actively engaged in the educational process. A teacher must provide students with opportunities to perform within a framework that acknowledges consequences for that performance.

24. **The Tyranny of Self-Oriented Self-Esteem,** James   **129**
H. McMillan, Judy Singh, and Leo G. Simonetta, *Educational Horizons,* Spring 1994.
Healthy **self-esteem** develops as a result of the student's being occupied by interests and pursuits external to self and by **meaningful accomplishment of externally set standards of performance,** not from the self-preoccupation and selfism that are fostered by many self-esteem programs.

The concepts in bold italics are developed in the article. For further expansion please refer to the Topic Guide and the Index.

C. INSTRUCTIONAL STRATEGIES

25. Improving Student Thinking, Barry Beyer, *The Clear-* **133**
ing House, May/June 1998.
Student *thinking* can be enhanced by making the process more
visible in the *teaching-learning environment.* Barry Beyer
shows how several instructional techniques, including *scaffolding,*
meta-cognitive reflection, modeling, and cueing, can be
used to promote an environment in which thinking is explicit and
integrated with subject matter learning.

26. The Intelligence-Friendly Classroom: It Just **139**
Makes Sense, Robin Fogarty, *Phi Delta Kappan,* May
1998.
Based on recent theories of *intelligence,* including Vygotsky's
theory of *social mediation,* Gardner's theory of *multiple*
intelligences, and Sternberg's *successful intelligence,* among
others, Robin Fogarty explains how *constructivist classrooms*
can be created.

Overview **142**

A. MOTIVATION

27. A New Look at School Failure and School Success, **144**
William Glasser, *Phi Delta Kappan,* April 1997.
William Glasser argues that the root of poor student *motivation*
is problems in the *student-teacher relationship.* He suggests
that students who are destined to fail believe that no one cares
about them because teachers use coercive techniques promoted by
behaviorism. He describes the improvements in motivation and
achievement in schools that have adopted what he calls "choice
theory" as an alternative.

28. I Think I Can, I Think I Can: Understanding and **151**
Encouraging Mastery Motivation in Young Children,
Penny Hauser-Cram, *Young Children,* July 1998.
Penny Hauser-Cram describes mastery *motivation,* how it
changes in early childhood, and how parents and caregivers affect
it. She cautions us to guide children without being overly directive.

29. Using Motivational Theory with At-Risk Children, **156**
Rachel Buck Collopy and Theresa Green, *Educational Lead-*
ership, September 1995.
Rachel Collopy and Theresa Green describe how achievement goal
theory was implemented at one elementary school to create a
learner-centered environment. They also discuss the resulting
changes that teachers and parents see in the *motivation* of their
children.

UNIT 5

Motivation and Classroom Management

Eight selections discuss
student control and motivation in the classroom.

The concepts in bold italics are developed in the article. For further expansion please refer to the Topic Guide and the Index.

ix

B. CLASSROOM MANAGEMENT AND DISCIPLINE

30. Moving beyond Management as Sheer Compliance: Helping Students to Develop Goal Coordination Strategies, Mary McCaslin and Thomas L. Good, *Educational Horizons*, Summer 1998.   **159**

The authors describe several representations of **classroom management** that help us conceptualize classroom management goals and strategies. It is best, they say, to choose management strategies that fit instructional goals and students' needs and abilities. Ultimately they suggest that teachers should enable students to become self-regulating by learning to coordinate their multiple academic and social goals.

31. Connecting Instruction and Management in a Student-Centered Classroom, Nancy K. Martin, *Middle School Journal*, March 1997.   **167**

Nancy Martin asserts that **student-centered** instruction and teacher-centered **classroom management** do not mix. Instead, she suggests that teachers should encourage self-discipline and responsibility. These techniques nurture the **student-teacher relationship** that is crucial to student-centered instruction.

→ **32. How to Manage Disruptive Behavior in Inclusive Classrooms,** Vera I. Daniels, *Teaching Exceptional Children*, March/April 1998.   **174**

Vera Daniels maintains that teachers with inclusive classrooms can use many of the same strategies to **discipline students with disabilities** that they use with typical students. She poses 10 questions that teachers can use to analyze the situations that produce disruptive behavior and to select an appropriate disciplinary technique.

33. How to Defuse Defiance, Threats, Challenges, Confrontations . . . , Geoff Colvin, David Ainge, and Ron Nelson, *Teaching Exceptional Children*, July/August 1997.   **180**

Even teachers with a comprehensive **classroom management** system are sometimes challenged by students. The authors of this essay discuss five defusing tactics that minimize the likelihood that confrontational student behavior will escalate, including giving confrontational students a choice, reducing agitation, and disengaging and delaying a response.

34. Why Violence Prevention Programs Don't Work—and What Does, David W. Johnson and Roger T. Johnson, *Educational Leadership*, February 1995.   **185**

Arguing that implementing programs of conflict resolution will combat the growing violence in schools, the authors recommend that all students receive ongoing training in peer mediation. **The teacher's role in discipline** changes dramatically from manager of conflicts to supporter of peer mediation.

The concepts in bold italics are developed in the article. For further expansion please refer to the Topic Guide and the Index.

Overview   **190**

35. The Challenges of Assessing Young Children Appropriately, Lorrie A. Shepard, *Phi Delta Kappan*, November 1994.   **192**
Lorrie Shepard reviews issues and controversies in the assessment of young children, including **the impact of standardized tests,** how assessment must be matched to purpose, and how assessment should be different for screening, instruction, and monitoring of state and national trends.

36. Transforming Student Assessment, D. Monty Neill, *Phi Delta Kappan,* September 1997.   **199**
Monty Neill states that assessment should be transformed so that it is **integrated with, not separate from, curriculum and instruction.** This is best achieved by using multiple forms of assessments, including **performance assessments,** that provide the teacher and student with the best information to inform instruction.

37. Practicing What We Preach in Designing Authentic Assessments, Grant Wiggins, *Educational Leadership,* December 1996–January 1997.   **206**
Grant Wiggins, a leading authority on **alternative assessments,** points out the importance of designing credible **performance tasks,** establishing and maintaining standards for the **rubric and scoring criteria,** and using **peer review** in the development and implementation of authentic assessments. The assessment of student **understanding** is stressed.

38. What Happens between Assessments? Jay McTighe, *Educational Leadership,* December 1996–January 1997.   **213**
Jay McTighe describes **how instruction and assessment can be integrated.** Criteria that identify quality assessments, such as **clear performance targets, authenticity, and public criteria and standards,** are stressed.

39. Lessons Learned about Student Portfolios, Elizabeth A. Hebert, *Phi Delta Kappan,* April 1998.   **218**
Portfolios have become an increasingly popular kind of **alternative assessment.** In this article, principles for effective use of portfolios are based on 10 years of practical experience.

40. Grades: The Final Frontier in Assessment Reform, Gregory J. Cizek, *NASSP Bulletin,* December 1996.   **221**
Grading practices that enhance student learning and motivation are discussed by Gregory Cizek. Suggestions are made for **assigning grades** and producing helpful **report cards.**

Index   **225**
Article Review Form   **228**
Article Rating Form   **229**

UNIT 6

Assessment

Six articles discuss the implications of educational measurement for the classroom decision-making process and for the teaching profession.

This topic guide suggests how the selections and World Wide Web sites found in the next section of this book relate to topics of traditional concern to educational psychology students and professionals. It is useful for locating interrelated articles and Web sites for reading and research. The guide is arranged alphabetically according to topic.

The relevant Web sites, which are numbered and annotated on pages 4 and 5, are easily identified by the Web icon (◉) under the topic articles. By linking the articles and the Web sites by topic, this ANNUAL EDITIONS reader becomes a powerful learning and research tool.

TOPIC AREA	TREATED IN	TOPIC AREA	TREATED IN
Action Research	2. Using Action Research to Assess Instruction	**Disabilities**	10. Where to Educate Rachel Holland?
Alternative Assessment	36. Transforming Student Assessment		11. Why Andy Couldn't Read
	37. Practicing What We Preach in Designing Authentic Assessments		32. How to Manage Disruptive Behavior in Inclusive Classrooms
	39. Lessons Learned about Student Portfolios		◉ *17, 21, 31*
	◉ *32, 33, 34, 35*	**Discipline**	32. How to Manage Disruptive Behavior in Inclusive Classrooms
At-Risk Behavior	8. Developmental Tasks of Early Adolescence		34. Why Violence Prevention Programs Don't Work—and What Does
	9. Out of the Mouths of Babes: Voices of At-Risk Adolescents		◉ *29, 30, 31*
	29. Using Motivational Theory with At-Risk Children	**Diverse Students**	14. Goals and Track Record of Multicultural Education
	◉ *17, 30, 31*		15. Multiculturalism at a Crossroads
Behaviorism	21. Rewards of Learning		16. Multiculturalism: Practical Considerations for Curricular Change
	22. Rewards versus Learning: A Response to Paul Chance		◉ *17, 18, 19, 20, 22, 23, 24*
	23. Sticking Up for Rewards	**Early Childhood**	4. New Brain Development Research
	27. New Look at School Failure and School Success		7. Helping Children Become More Prosocial
	◉ *1, 13, 15, 16*		◉ *1, 11, 16*
Child/ Adolescent Development	4. New Brain Development Research	**Educational Issues**	3. What Issues Will Confront Public Education in 2000 and 2020?
	5. Moral Child		◉ *10*
	6. Re-Evaluating Significance of Baby's Bond with Mother	**Emotional Development**	4. New Brain Development Research
	7. Helping Children Become More Prosocial		◉ *1, 15, 16*
	8. Developmental Tasks of Early Adolescence	**Family Structure**	5. Moral Child
	◉ *13, 14, 15, 16*		6. Re-Evaluating Significance of Baby's Bond with Mother
Classroom Management	30. Moving beyond Management as Sheer Compliance		8. Developmental Tasks of Early Adolescence
	31. Connecting Instruction and Management in a Student-Centered Classroom		◉ *4*
	33. How to Defuse Defiance, Threats, Challenges, Confrontations . . .	**Gifted Children and Youth**	12. Is It Acceleration or Simply Appropriate Instruction for Precocious Youth?
	◉ *29, 30, 31*		13. How All Middle-Schoolers Can Be "Gifted"
Cognitive Development	4. New Brain Development Research		◉ *17*
	5. Moral Child		
	◉ *15, 16*		
Cognitive Learning	18. Brain Basics		
	◉ *24, 25, 26, 27, 28*		

TOPIC AREA	TREATED IN	TOPIC AREA	TREATED IN
Grading	40. Grades: The Final Frontier in Assessment Reform ◎ **8, 11, 12**	**Performance Assessment**	36. Transforming Student Assessment 37. Practicing What We Preach in Designing Authentic Assessments 38. What Happens between Assessments? ◎ **32, 33, 34, 35**
Humanistic Education	24. Tyranny of Self-Oriented Self-Esteem		
		Portfolio Assessment	39. Lessons Learned about Student Portfolios ◎ **33**
Information Processing	17. Making Information Memorable 18. Brain Basics ◎ **9, 26**		
		Positive Reinforcement/ Praise	21. Rewards of Learning 22. Rewards versus Learning: A Response to Paul Chance 23. Sticking Up for Rewards ◎ **27, 28**
Intelligence	19. First Seven . . . and the Eighth 20. Styles of Thinking, Abilities, and Academic Performance 26. Intelligence-Friendly Classroom: It Just Makes Sense ◎ **3, 5, 6, 24, 25, 26, 28**	**Self-Concept/ Self**	24. Tyranny of Self-Oriented Self-Esteem
		Social Development	7. Helping Children Become More Prosocial 8. Developmental Tasks of Early Adolescence ◎ **13, 14, 15, 16**
Mainstreaming	10. Where to Educate Rachel Holland? ◎ **15, 17, 21**		
Memory	17. Making Information Memorable 18. Brain Basics	**Standardized Tests**	35. Challenges of Assessing Young Children Appropriately 36. Transforming Student Assessment ◎ **3, 5**
Metacognition	25. Improving Student Thinking		
Minority Students	14. Goals and Track Record of Multicultural Education 15. Multiculturalism at a Crossroads ◎ **18, 19, 20, 22, 23, 24**	**Student- Centered Classroom**	29. Using Motivational Theory with At-Risk Children 31. Connecting Instruction and Management in a Student- Centered Classroom ◎ **17, 29, 30, 31**
Moral Development	5. Moral Child ◎ **13, 16**	**Student/ Teacher Relationships**	1. How Novice Teachers Can Succeed with Adolescents 27. New Look at School Failure and School Success 31. Connecting Instruction and Management in a Student- Centered Classroom ◎ **12, 27, 28**
Motivation	27. New Look at School Failure and School Success 28. I Think I Can, I Think I Can 29. Using Motivational Theory with At-Risk Children ◎ **29, 30, 31**		
		Teacher's Role	1. How Novice Teachers Can Succeed with Adolescents ◎ **12, 27, 28**
Multicultural Education	14. Goals and Track Record of Multicultural Education 15. Multiculturalism at a Crossroads 16. Multiculturalism: Practical Considerations for Curricular Change ◎ **18, 19, 20, 22, 23, 24**	**Thinking Skills**	18. Brain Basics 25. Improving Student Thinking ◎ **24, 25, 26, 27, 28**

AE: Educational Psychology

The following World Wide Web sites have been carefully researched and selected to support the articles found in this reader. If you are interested in learning more about specific topics found in this book, these Web sites are a good place to start. The sites are cross-referenced by number and appear in the topic guide on the previous two pages. Also, you can link to these Web sites through our DUSHKIN ONLINE support site at *http://www.dushkin.com/online/*.

The following sites were available at the time of publication. Visit our Web site—we update DUSHKIN ONLINE regularly to reflect any changes.

General Sources

1. American Psychological Association
http://www.apa.org/psychnet/
By exploring the APA's "PsychNET," you will be able to find links to an abundance of articles and other resources that are useful in the field of educational psychology.

2. Educational Resources Information Center
http://www.accesseric.org:81
This invaluable site provides links to all ERIC sites: clearinghouses, support components, and publishers of ERIC materials. Search the ERIC database for what is new.

3. National Education Association
http://www.nea.org
Something—and often quite a lot—about virtually every education-related topic can be accessed at or through this site of the 2.3-million-strong National Education Association.

4. National Parent Information Network/ERIC
http://npin.org
This is a clearinghouse of information on elementary and early childhood education as well as urban education. Browse through its links for information for parents.

5. U.S. Department of Education
http://www.ed.gov/pubs/TeachersGuide/
Government goals, projects, and grants are listed here plus many links to teacher services and resources.

Perspectives on Teaching

6. The Center for Innovation in Education
http://www.educenter.org
This is the main page of the Center for Innovation in Education, self-described as a "not-for-profit, non-partisan research organization" focusing on K–12 education reform strategies. Click on its links for information about and varying perspectives on school privatization and other reform initiatives.

7. Classroom Connect
http://www.classroom.net
This is a major Web site for K–12 teachers and students, with links to schools, teachers, and resources online. It includes discussion of the use of technology in the classroom.

8. Education World
http://www.education-world.com
Education World provides a database of literally thousands of sites that can be searched by grade level, plus education news, lesson plans, and professional-development resources.

9. EdWeb/Andy Carvin
http://edweb.cnidr.org
The purpose of EdWeb is to explore the worlds of educational reform and information technology. Learn about trends in education policy and information infrastructure development and examine success stories of computers in the classroom.

10. Goals 2000: A Progress Report
http://www.ed.gov/pubs/goals/progrpt/index.html
Open this site to survey a progress report by the U.S. Department of Education on the Goals 2000 reform initiative. It provides a sense of the goals that educators are reaching for as they look toward the future.

11. PREPnet
http://prep.net
This site contains Web sites for educators. It covers a wide range of topics dealing with K–12 resources and curricula. Its links will prove useful for examining issues ranging from school reform to teaching values.

12. Teacher Talk Forum
http://education.indiana.edu/cas/tt/tthmpg.html
Visit this site for access to a variety of articles discussing life in the classroom. Clicking on the various links will lead you to electronic lesson plans, covering a variety of topic areas, from Indiana University's Center for Adolescent Studies.

Development

13. Association for Moral Education
http://www.wittenberg.edu/ame/
AME is dedicated to fostering communication, cooperation, training, curriculum development, and research that links moral theory with educational practices. From here it is possible to connect to several sites on moral development.

14. Child Welfare League of America
http://www.cwla.org
The CWLA is the United States' oldest and largest organization devoted entirely to the well-being of vulnerable children and their families. This site provides links to information about issues related to morality and values in education.

15. Guidelines for Developmentally Appropriate Early Childhood Practice
http://www.newhorizons.org/naeyc.html
Here is a 23-page exerpt from a report, edited by Sue Bredekamp, that covers every aspect of appropriate programs that serve children from birth through age 8, published on the Web by the National Association for the Education of Young Children.

16. The National Academy for Child Development
http://www.nacd.org
This international organization is dedicated to helping children and adults reach their full potential. Its home page presents links to various programs, research, and resources into such topics as ADD/ADHD.

Exceptional and Culturally Diverse Children

17. ERIC Clearinghouse on Disabilities and Gifted Education
http://www.cec.sped.org/gifted/gt-faqs.htm
This page will give you access to information on identifying and teaching gifted children, attention-deficit disorders, and other topics in gifted education.

18. Global SchoolNet Foundation
http://www.gsn.org
Access this site for multicultural education information. The site includes news for teachers, students, and parents, as well as chat rooms, links to educational resources, programs, and contests and competitions.

19. International Project: Multicultural Pavilion
http://curry.edschool.virginia.edu/curry/centers/multicultural/papers.html
Here is a forum for sharing of stories and resources and for learning from the stories and resources of others, in the form of articles on the Internet that cover every possible racial, gender, and multicultural issue that could arise in the field of multicultural education.

20. Multicultural Publishing and Education Council
http://www.mpec.org
This is the main page of the MPEC, a networking and support organization for independent publishers, authors, educators, and librarians fostering authentic multicultural books and materials. It has excellent links to a vast array of resources related to multicultural education.

21. National Attention Deficit Disorder Association
http://www.add.org
This site, some of which is under construction, will lead you to information about ADD/ADHD. It has links to self-help and support groups, outlines behaviors and diagnostics, answers FAQs, and suggests books and other resources.

22. National MultiCultural Institute (NMCI)
http://www.nmci.org
NMCI is one of the major organizations in the field of diversity training. At this Web site, NMCI offers conference data, resource materials, diversity training and consulting service information, and links to other related sites.

23. Scholastic/Kristen Nelson
http://place.scholastic.com/instructor/curriculum/
Open this page for Kristen Nelson's discussion of ways in which teachers can help to nurture children's multiple intelligences. She provides a useful bibliography and resources.

Learning and Instruction

24. Celebrating Our Nation's Destiny
http://www.census.gov/ftp/pub/edu/diversity/
This teaching supplement has been designed to help teachers explore our nation's student diversity, working with real-world data. The site contains in-depth statistics on race and ethnicity in the United States.

25. Education Week on the Web
http://www.edweek.org
At this page you can open archives, read special reports, keep up on current events, and access a variety of articles in educational psychology. A great deal of material is helpful in learning and instruction.

26. Online Innovation Institute
http://www.oii.org
A collaborative project among Internet-using educators, proponents of systemic reform, content-area experts, and teachers who desire professional growth, this site provides a learning environment for integrating the Internet into educators' individual teaching styles.

27. Teachers Helping Teachers
http://www.pacificnet.net/~mandel/
This site provides basic teaching tips, new teaching-methodology ideas, and forums for teachers to share their experi-

ences. It features educational resources on the Web, with new ones added each week.

28. The Teachers' Network
http://www.teachnet.org
Bulletin boards, classroom projects, online forums, and Web mentors are featured on this site, as well as the book *Teachers' Guide to Cyberspace* and an online, 4-week course on how to use the Internet.

Motivation and Classroom Management

29. Canada's Schoolnet Staff Room
http://www.schoolnet.ca/home/e/
Here is a resource and link site for anyone involved in education, including special-needs educators, teachers, parents, volunteers, and administrators.

30. Early Intervention Solutions
http://www.earlyintervention.com
EIS presents this site to address concerns about children's stress and reinforcement. It suggests ways to deal with negative behaviors that may result from stress and anxiety among children.

31. National Institute on the Education of At-Risk Students
http://www.ed.gov/offices/OERI/At-Risk/
The At-Risk Institute supports a range of research and development activities designed to improve the education of students at risk of educational failure due to limited English proficiency, race, geographic location, or economic disadvantage. Access its work and links at this site.

Assessment

32. Awesome Library for Teachers
http://www.neat-schoolhouse.org/teacher.html
Open this page for links and access to teacher information on everything from assessments to child development topics.

33. Carfax
http://www.carfax.co.uk/subjeduc.htm
Look through this extensive index for links to education publications such as *Journal of Beliefs and Values*, *Educational Philosophy and Theory*, and *Assessment in Education*.

34. Phi Delta Kappa International
http://www.pdkintl.org
This important organization publishes articles about all facets of education. You can check out the online archive of the journal, *Phi Delta Kappan*, which has resources such as articles having to do with assessment.

35. Washington (State) Commission on Student Learning
http://csl.wednet.edu/
This Washington State CSL site is designed to provide access to information about the state's new academic standards, assessments, and accountability system. Many resources and Web links are included.

We highly recommend that you review our Web site for expanded information and our other product lines. We are continually updating and adding links to our Web site in order to offer you the most usable and useful information that will support and expand the value of your Annual Editions. You can reach us at: *http://www.dushkin.com/annualeditions/*.

Unit Selections

1. **How Novice Teachers Can Succeed with Adolescents,** Robin L. Gordon
2. **Using Action Research to Assess Instruction,** Carole Schulte Johnson and Inga Kromann-Kelly
3. **What Issues Will Confront Public Education in the Years 2000 and 2020? Predictions of Chief State School Officers,** Alan D. Morgan, Myrna Matranga, Gary L. Peltier, and George C. Hill.

Key Points to Consider

❖ Describe several of the roles teachers are expected to perform.

❖ As we move into the twenty-first century, what new demands will be placed on teachers and schools? What demands will fade?

❖ How does research, either teacher research or formal educational research, improve teaching?

 **Links** | **www.dushkin.com/online/**

6. **The Center for Innovation in Education**
   http://www.educenter.org
7. **Classroom Connect**
   http://www.classroom.net
8. **Education World**
   http://www.education-world.com
9. **EdWeb/Andy Carvin**
   http://edweb.cnidr.org
10. **Goals 2000: A Progress Report**
    http://www.ed.gov/pubs/goals/progrpt/index.html
11. **PREPnet**
    http://prep.net
12. **Teacher Talk Forum**
    http://education.indiana.edu/cas/tt/tthmpg.html

These sites are annotated on pages 4 and 5.

The teaching-learning process in school is enormously complex. Many factors influence pupil learning—such as family background, developmental level, prior knowledge, motivation, and, of course, effective teachers. Educational psychology investigates these factors to better understand and explain student learning. We begin our exploration of the teaching-learning process by considering the teaching role.

In the first article, Robin Gordon describes aspects of the secondary teacher's role that many beginning teachers may overlook. A less obvious aspect of the teaching role is the systematic effort to improve. In the second article, "Using Action Research to Assess Instruction," Carole Shulte Johnson and Inga Kromann-Kelly illustrate how teachers should conduct an action research project to improve the classroom learning environment. The authors describe five basic questions to guide the development of action research projects. The five questions determine (1) the question to answer in the study; (2) the data that are relevant; (3) how the data will be collected; (4) how the data will be analyzed; and (5) what implications can be drawn from the data. As the professional development schools envisioned by the Holmes partnership (a consortium of research universities and public schools) and others are established, teacher research may become a professional expectation.

Finally, we look toward the future and the educational issues that may ultimately change the teacher's role. The third article, "What Issues Will Confront Public Education in the Years 2000 and 2020? Predictions of Chief State School Officers," suggests dramatic changes in the way children will be educated by the year 2020. The authors suggest that technology will not only change what happens in classrooms but will enable more children to be educated at home or in the workplace.

Educational psychology is a resource for teachers that emphasizes disciplined inquiry, a systematic and objective analysis of information, and a scientific attitude toward decision making. The field provides information for decisions that are based on quantitative and qualitative studies of learning and teaching rather than on intuition, tradition, authority, or subjective feelings. It is our hope that this aspect of educational psychology is communicated throughout these readings and that, as a student, you will adopt the analytic, probing attitude that is part of the discipline.

While educational psychologists have helped to establish a knowledge base about teaching and learning, the unpredictable, spontaneous, evolving nature of teaching suggests that the best they will ever do is to provide concepts and skills that teachers can adapt for use in their classrooms. The issues raised in these articles about the impact of the reform movement on teachers help us understand the teaching role and its demands. As you read articles in other chapters, consider the demands they place on the teaching role as well.

Perspectives on Teaching

How Novice Teachers Can Succeed with Adolescents

Beginning secondary teachers need more than knowledge of content and teaching strategies. Insight into adolescent culture is critical to success in managing a classroom.

Robin L. Gordon

A student teacher was having serious problems managing the behavior of her 10th grade math students. When her students were not working well in their collaborative learning groups, she'd often ask them, "Can't we all just get along?" She could not understand why the students laughed when she used this phrase. The students, of course, immediately recognized it as Rodney King's plea during the 1992 Los Angeles uprising. The line was later incorporated into a song, displayed on T-shirts, and chanted by students. One of her students remarked to this confused teacher, "It just cracks me up when you say that!" Nevertheless, she did not comprehend the impact of what she was saying until her university observer explained.

This incident illustrates the need for beginning teachers to understand two critical teaching behaviors: social insight and what has been called "withitness." Such awareness can be the critical element in establishing an effective learning environment.

Social Insight

Waller asserted that teachers must learn "an elusive something which it is difficult to put between the covers of a book or to work up into a lecture. That elusive something is social insight" (1967, p. 1). Social insight can be described as an understanding of what is taking place in the classroom. That sounds rather simplistic at first. Yet, to accomplish this effectively, the teacher must have a sense of the students' culture as well as an understanding of student behavior.

Hall (1981) examined eight elements of culture that he defined generally as (1) verbal language, (2) nonverbal communication, (3) culture in general, (4) world view, (5) behavioral style, (6) values, (7) methods of reasoning, and (8) cultural and ethnic identification. Pennington adds a few more characteristics of culture: beliefs/values, sense of time, religion, and social relationships/communication networks (1985, pp. 30–39). Bennett notes that we often define culture as what shapes our thoughts and be-

havior. In line with this, multicultural education often concerns the development of multiple standards for perceiving, believing, doing, and evaluating (1990, p. 47).

These notions represent a sample of what some believe constitutes culture. The characteristics illustrate the fact that adolescent culture goes beyond ethnic or linguistic differences. Adolescents' speech patterns, popular music, styles of dress, favorite movies, and preferred places for recreation may either transcend or incorporate the political, religious, and social causes deemed important by adults. The requisite attribute is that adolescent culture belongs solely to the adolescent. Social insight is a vehicle that teachers can use to glimpse the meanings of the adolescent cultural milieu.

When a teacher lacks social insight, communication with students may be less effective, resulting in classroom management problems. In the case of the student teacher mentioned above, the students knew that their insults would not be understood. Their daily

From *Educational Leadership*, April 1997, pp. 56-58. © 1997 by the Association for Supervision and Curriculum Development. All rights reserved. Reprinted by permission.

behavior continued to disintegrate, and after six weeks the student teacher's assignment had to be terminated.

Helping preservice or beginning teachers develop social insight remains a critical challenge for the teacher educator. Although it might at first appear to be relatively insignificant when compared to the myriad learning and teaching theories new teachers must master, adolescent social development should be of paramount concern if for no other reason than its relationship to managing a classroom effectively. Assuming the lesson is appealing, teachers whom adolescents perceive as successful socially seem to experience less difficulty capturing the interest of their students. Their classrooms run more smoothly. The teacher educator will find it difficult to help the student teacher who lacks this "understanding of the social situation of the

more than one disturbance at a time and do so quickly. Beginning teachers too often focus on one disruption and miss the start of another. Students become adept at knowing when the teacher's attention is elsewhere and they may use the time for social interaction— chatting, flirting, making faces. Experienced teachers know this, address the behavior, and engender a modicum of respect by having "eyes in the back of their head."

Secondary students are particularly critical of any teacher who does not display social insight. The student teacher is especially fair game for the spunky adolescent and is a likely target of a certain degree of disdain and criticism. Thus, in a matter of days, the student teacher who lacks social insight and withitness can be reduced to emotional Jell-O.

A second anecdote involves a

A final example is more encouraging. A student teacher was discussing a particularly complex topic in genetics with a 10th grade ESL (English as a Second Language) class. The students were struggling with the content but were focused intently on the student teacher. She radiated warmth and professionalism, and she used a popular video game as an example to help the students remember the structure of a gene. Everything about her, including her body language, verbal expression, and even eye contact, communicated sensitivity and empathy with her students. They recognized that she understood them; she had encountered the same feelings they were experiencing. The teacher was familiar with their culture, and this familiarity laid the groundwork for mutual respect. Students did not need to act out with her. Additionally, if any disruption occurred, she spotted it immediately and acted accordingly.

> **Effective teachers understand the many behaviors taking place in the classroom and how to react appropriately. They learn their students' names and behavior patterns quickly.**

Acquiring Cultural Information

One of the teacher educator's goals is to expedite the development of classroom management skills. Expanding Waller's discussion of social insight to include Kounin's notion of withitness provides a useful tool for learning such skills. The teacher not only becomes aware of student behavior but understands what is current and meaningful in students' lives. I like to refer to the result as academic biculturalism. The withit and socially insightful teacher uses cultural information effectively.

classroom and the need to adapt his or her personality to the needs of that milieu" (Waller 1967, p. 1).

"Withitness"

Kounin (1993) introduces the term "withitness" in his discussion of classroom management (Charles 1989, p. 28). Teachers who demonstrate withitness understand the many behaviors taking place in the classroom and how to react appropriately. Kounin identifies two behaviors in particular that communicate to students that their teacher is aware of the classroom. The first is knowing who is causing a disturbance. Some students are brilliant at fomenting small classroom arguments and then fading into obscurity. Effective teachers learn their students' names and behavior patterns quickly. Second, withit teachers can handle

student teacher who was attempting to teach algebra to an uninterested group of 10th grade students. Solving for unknowns was not high on their list of priorities that day. Their questions began to veer from the mathematical to the personal: "Why do you perspire so much?" "Why does your shirt hang out?" "Why do you wear bow ties?" "Do you know what you are doing?" This student teacher had lost control of his class and had no clue about how to relate to 15-year-olds. The lesson here is that a teacher may have a thorough grasp of content, but without social insight, he or she will be perceived as being out of touch with what is happening in the students' culture. This particular teacher exacerbated the problem by displaying a seeming lack of withitness. He may actually have been conscious of the students' insults but took no action.

The question of how to develop social insight and withitness was posed to a group of secondary student teachers in their weekly seminar. The instructor's goal was twofold. First, she wanted students to realize that some of them might lack social insight by the very fact of their inability to address the question. Second, students who displayed social insight had the opportunity to share their knowledge with their peers.

The following list summarizes the strategies these student teachers used to ensure that they were in touch with their students' culture, thus facilitating

Photo courtesy of Robin Gordon

Megen O'Keefe, a student teacher in social studies at Hawthorne High School, shows confidence as she answers questions in the classroom.

their connection and rapport with students.

1. Expose yourself to adolescent culture. As painful as it may seem, watching MTV, listening to current music, and attending popular movies can help provide a connection to what is current in students' lives. This does not require teachers to participate in the latest fashions. For example, having an eyebrow pierced will not endear an adult to young people and can actually alienate them. Adolescents need to distinguish themselves from the adults who nurture them. Teachers can appreciate adolescent culture without embracing it as their own.

2. Affirm students' "weather." It can be helpful to express an understanding of why students have a high level of energy or are not interested in class on a particular day. For example, the school dance, Halloween, a lunch fight, or approaching vacations can all contribute to volatile student weather. Telling students it makes no difference that the prom is the next day is whistling in the wind.

3. Relate content to students' outside interests. Making abstract ideas more concrete by using examples that come from the students' adolescent world can be very effective. For example, in

one classroom, the teacher's explanation of why an oxygen atom attracts two hydrogen atoms did not seem relevant to Jesse; however, phrasing the concept in terms of the fact that two 7th grade girls were attracted to him hit closer to home. Teachers learn quickly that metaphors involving sex immediately pique adolescents' interest as long as the metaphors do not cross the invisible boundary of propriety.

4. Know your students. The secondary teacher has very little time to talk with students one-on-one, but it is important to find time for individual chitchat. Effective teachers use strategies such as greeting students at the door, referring to a student's interests in their lectures, or talking to students as they monitor classwork. Attending sporting events and school plays, reading the school paper, or being a club advisor are just a few ways teachers can connect with their students' educational and social loops.

5. Share your humanity with your students. Celebrate life with them. Successful teachers are not afraid to show their strengths and weaknesses to students in the proper context. The classroom is not a therapy group, but teachers can enjoy life along with their students.

Facilitating the beginning teacher's transition into the classroom is not a simple matter of presenting a list of do's and don'ts. As much as it may dismay the proponents of a technological model of teacher education, fledgling teachers can effectively process only a limited amount of information before facing students. New teachers enter the classroom armed with explicit class management plans, a firm belief about how students should act, and a strong grasp of content. However, if they cannot transport that arsenal of information and teacher tricks into the context of what is actually taking place in the classroom, their success will be hindered. Adding social insight and withitness to the arsenal makes it far more likely that the necessary connections will take place.

References

Bennett, C. (1990). *Comprehensive Multicultural Education: Theory and Practice.* 2nd ed. Boston: Allyn and Bacon.

Charles, C.M. (1989). *Building Classroom Discipline.* 3rd ed. New York: Longman.

Hall, E.T. (1981). *The Silent Language.* Garden City, N.Y.: Anchor Press.

Kounin, J.S. (November 1993). *Classrooms: Individuals or Behavior Setting.* Address sponsored by the Horizons of Knowledge Lecture Series, Indiana University, School of Education, Bloomington.

Pennington, D.L. (1985). "Intercultural Communication." In *Intercultural Communication: A Reader,* 4th ed., edited by L.A. Samovar and R.E. Porter. Belmont, Calif.: Wadsworth.

Waller, W.W. (1967). *The Sociology of Teaching.* New York: John Wiley and Sons.

Robin L. Gordon is Coordinator of Master of Arts of Teaching and Assistant Coordinator of Secondary Education at the School of Education, Loyola Marymount University, 7900 Loyola Blvd., Los Angeles, CA 90045.

Using Action Research To Assess Instruction

Carole Schulte Johnson and Inga Kromann-Kelly

Carole Schulte Johnson is a faculty member in the Department of Elementary and Secondary Education, at Washington State University, in Pullman, Washington. Inga Kromann-Kelly is a faculty member in the Department of Teaching and Learning, at Washington State University, in Pullman, Washington.

For years teachers have used self assessment as one way to improve the learning environment in their classrooms. Such assessment, however, tended to be of a private, nonsystematic nature and often was not clearly focused on a central question. Today more and more teachers are developing and experiencing an organized approach to classroom inquiry, known as action research, a concept which has evolved over the past several years. This approach entails stepping back from the immediate concern in order to gain a broader perspective on a problem; then collecting, analyzing, and interpreting data on the basis of a defined plan, and often sharing the results with professional colleagues.

Rather than formulating complex research procedures, perhaps best left to experts, we recommend beginning action research by answering these five basic questions: 1) What is the main question I am interested in pursuing? 2) What data are relevant? 3) What specific data will be collected, and how? 4) How will the data be analyzed? 5) What interpretations or implications can be drawn from the data?

THE QUESTION

Teachers often have several questions they wish to explore; however, in order to keep the research manageable you as a teacher embarking on action research need to decide your basic or most important question. Limited questions related to what you are doing in your classroom, such as "Are my students learning from this strategy?" or "What strategies do students use most successfully in perform-

ing some particular task?" work well for action research. For example, suppose we are interested in learning more about our students' attitude toward reading. We realize that various elements of the literacy program probably affect those attitudes so our basic question could be "How do the students feel about the different methods and materials used in the literacy program?"

COLLECTING DATA

Data can be gathered from transactions/interactions, products and cued or structured responses. Figure 1, while not all inclusive, suggests various sources of data within each category.

Triangulation of data (using at least three different data sources) is recommended. The value of using triangulation is in analyzing the question from several different viewpoints. For instance, one data set could be from each of the three categories on the chart or from two of the three categories. If only three data sources are used, it is recommended that no more than one cued or structured response source be included since these data usually are collected only at specific points of time, thus limiting the information to the context of those times.

When the different data sources are congruent, the acceptance of the results is strengthened. Conflicting data raise questions such as: Should other types of data sets have been used? Should some data sources carry more weight—for example, were the cued responses too structured or answered to please the teacher? Would it be valuable to refine or do additional research on this question?

We make decisions regarding the specific data to collect on the basis of its importance in seeking answers to the question and also the feasibility of collecting and analyzing it. In general, quantifiable data take less time to collect and analyze; however, meaningful data are not always readily quantifiable. While importance and feasibility are basic, other aspects are considered. Using excessive class, student and/or teacher time is avoided by collecting data from ongoing class activities such as journals and portfo-

---

Figure 1
Data Sources

	From Teacher	*From Students*
Transactions/ Interactions	Field/observation/anecdotal notes	Video/audio tapes
	Video/audio tapes	
Products		Written products
		Artifacts
		Open-ended interviews
		Open-ended conferences
Cued/Structured Responses	Ratings	Tests
	Checklists	Questionnaires
	Tally of behaviors	Attitude measures
		Structured interviews
		Structured conferences
		Writing/work samples
		Checklists
		Ratings
		Logs

---

lios, the taping of class or small group activities as well as from brief cued or structured responses.

Unless individual conferences are part of the ongoing program and the data to be collected a normal part of the conferences, they may not be a feasible source of information. However, if a second person is available or only a small subset of students is involved, individual conferences become a possibility.

Another consideration is that students may tell teachers what they think the teacher wants to hear when cued or structured responses are obtained face-to-face. Responses on paper may be similarly biased, but such data-gathering instruments are generally viewed as providing a degree of anonymity.

When teacher observations are used, consideration is given to how structured and systematic they will be. Ways to provide structure include using a checklist of behaviors (e.g., answering, volunteering, getting out of seat) and keeping a tally of the number of times a behavior occurs, or by describing behavior at set time intervals. Audio/videotaping of an on-going class activity is an example of an unstructured observation. Systematic observations are made on a regular basis such as daily or weekly. The data can be taped; however, if teacher notes

are used, it is recommended they be written daily. Less systematic observations are those noted occasionally, when the teacher has time or when something strikes the teacher as important to note.

When writing notes, we need to remind ourselves that we see what we expect, so there is danger of bias. For example, as teachers, we know that certain of our students love to read while others do not. Thus, in examining attitudes, we are more inclined to note student behaviors which confirm what we already believe than those which conflict with our expectations.

Each source of data requires decisions on the part of the teacher. With materials such as journals, portfolios, or tapes, you decide what data to include and then structure the class or group so it can be collected. When a checklist or questionnaire is involved, you decide its content and how students (or teacher) will respond. Among the possibilities for such instruments are open ended questions or statements, items for the respondent to check off, or some type of rating system.

If you use a rating scale, you need to decide whether it will be an even numbered scale, thus avoiding a neutral position, or an odd numbered one which includes it. A two or three point scale is simpler for students in the primary grades; a five to seven point scale is common in upper grades and has the advantage of identifying subtle differences. Common terms for labeling points on a scale are *agree/disagree, like most/like least,* or 1 *(very low)* to 5 *(highest).*

A simple format is helpful. Present the ratings at the top of the page; then list the items below with a blank for the number rating in front of each item. With instruments such as this, it is important to remind the students that you really want to know what they think so their opinions can be considered in making decisions about materials or procedures. From whom will student data be collected—the entire class, a small group or groups of students, individuals or some combination? For our research on student attitudes, we prefer information from the class rather than from selected representative students. The latter may well provide the spectrum of attitudes regarding reading, but not its strength related to specific methods or materials.

In examining student attitudes toward reading, the feelings of students constitute important and relevant data. To collect such information, we might use informal teacher observations, preferably collected on a regular basis, and student records of books and pages read daily and brief comments or reactions to what they have read. All of these items are easily obtained as a normal part of classroom activity.

Additionally, we would include a questionnaire asking students to rate what they think about each of the different literacy materials and activities used in the program. If many items are included, the questionnaire can be divided into several parts. Class discussion of the results would provide a useful source of additional information. Neither activity would take an inordinate amount of time and the findings could result in an improved curriculum. Our questionnaire requires limited teacher preparation time since it only involves developing a list of the materials and activities used, deciding their order as well as the kind of rating scale to use, and formatting the instrument.

ANALYZING AND INTERPRETING DATA

When analyzing data, teachers may want information about the class as a whole, about individual children, or about certain subgroups. Subgroups might include students at certain achievement levels, such as above grade level, at grade level, students with special needs, boys at different achievement levels, or girls at different ones. When data are kept for each student, teachers can decide at any time what individuals or subgroups they may wish to study.

Some of the data teachers gather are quantifiable and can be analyzed without the use of statistics. Under some circumstances, statistical analyses show significance with only small differences in raw data, and such results may not be particularly useful. For example, knowing the percent of the class rating an item *very low* or *highest* may be more important for your consideration in curriculum change. Again, it is the teacher who must interpret the data and decide what is meaningful. What do the results mean in your classroom? How do they answer your original question? Were they what you expected? Any surprises? What was successful or not successful?

Our questionnaire regarding student opinion about materials and activities can best be summarized with tables for the class and for each subgroup. We would list the materials and activities in a column with the ratings listed across the top. Then for each item, the percent choosing the rating is listed.

To interpret the tables, we would consider the class or group distribution across the continuum: Were responses concentrated at one end of the continuum? Were there gross differences such as a large group at each end of the continuum, or was there a fairly even distribution across it? If the distribution is mainly at one end, we would decide what percent of the class or group to consider significant in our decision making: it might be 40 percent, $1/3$, $1/4$ or whatever we feel is appropriate. For example, if 40 percent of students rate something *very low* while few or no students rate it *highest*, or the reverse, that clearly is important information.

Data which are not readily quantifiable, such as that from logs, journals, informal observations, conferences or tapes of class activities, are usually reviewed by teachers so they can pull out what appear to be trends, major ideas, or important elements related to the question at hand. If these data are collected over a period of time, or if the material is extensive, it will need to be reviewed periodically, and preferably over a time frame which allows for reflection. This is an important and valuable process because it often leads to further insights and refinements. In general, for non-quantified data, we would review all the categories and subcategories and draw conclusions related to the original question. The conclusions may be firm or tentative. In either case, it is important to consider whether data from other sources agree with it. Informal observations, anecdotal notes, and class discussion of results are used to confirm, disconfirm or raise questions about findings from the rest of the data.

In the case of our question about students' attitudes, we would review teacher observations and anecdotal notes as well as student logs for indication of feelings about reading, positive, negative, or general reactions indicating that students are or are not involved with their reading. While we would start with categories such as *positive* and *negative*, as the data collection grows we would expect subcategories to develop. For example, we might subcategorize aspects related to writing, to self-selected reading, to assigned reading, or to informational reading. Categories are flexible and can change as we continue to review the data. Which categories make sense and help answer the question? How do these data fit with the results of the questionnaire?

Finally, we would review the data as a whole. What is supported by all data sources? What is partially supported? Is anything not supported? What conclusions do you draw?

We piloted a questionnaire in a fourth grade class which used both trade books and children's literature. The results indicated that boys and girls were quite similar in their high and low ratings, as were the readers who were mature, on-grade level or special needs readers. However, when we looked at the groups of items rated *high* or *low,* we noticed those rated *low* tended to be the type of activities associated with the basal while those rated *high* were those traditionally considered enrichment activities. In terms of materials, with the exception of the special needs readers, all rated using literature books higher than using basals. The students in the class willingly informed us why they responded as they did. In general, the special needs readers felt they could handle the grade level basal but with literature books they had trouble keeping pace with others in their groups, and in some cases with the vocabulary as well.

Since there was nothing in teacher notes or student logs to contradict this, we would use literature books as the core of the literacy program, avoiding "basalizing" them by incorporating writing and enrichment activities similar to those suggested by Yopp and Yopp (1992). In selecting and gathering books related to themes or units, we would seek to include books special needs readers would feel successful in using. Then while implementing this program, we'd probably start a new action research project concentrating on the special needs readers.

CONSIDERATIONS FOR INVOLVEMENT IN ACTION RESEARCH

There are four important factors to consider in planning action research. First, action research requires additional planning time. However, useful and successful projects can be accomplished without consuming an inordinate amount of additional time. Second, action research is improved when teachers discuss the five questions with colleagues because the interaction provides a supportive environment which helps clarify and solidify thinking regarding the project. Sharing ideas and suggestions, whether for the same question or different ones, can be valuable. Colleagues not involved in action research also can provide helpful insights.

Third, teachers undertaking action research should be aware that expectations affect what we see and how we interpret data. Triangulation of data is helpful as are our awareness of this effect, discussion with others as the research evolves, and an effort on our part to be open to alternative explanations as well as to surprises in the data. Finally, teachers can use the results of action research in their classrooms. Action research can improve the teaching/learning process in classrooms by reinforcing, modifying and/or changing perceptions based solely on more informal techniques such as non-systematic observations.

REFERENCES

Yopp, R. H., & Yopp, H. K. (1992). *Literature-based reading activities.* Boston: Allyn and Bacon.

What Issues Will Confront Public Education in the Years 2000 and 2020? Predictions of Chief State School Officers

ALAN D. MORGAN, MYRNA MATRANGA, GARY L. PELTIER, and GEORGE C. HILL

National education goals notwithstanding, public education remains a state-level responsibility by virtue of the Tenth Amendment to the U. S. Constitution. Specifically, state education systems must ensure access to a free public education for every citizen.

To carry out that responsibility, the average state spends over 45 percent of its general fund budget to educate children in our elementary and secondary schools (NEA 1994). Thus, public education commands a greater proportion of state funds than that appropriated for highways, corrections, or even public health services. Although it is true that the percentage assigned for public education from state-level budgets has declined in the past decade, actual total appropriations for public education have steadily increased during the period. Despite that increased expenditure, however, the public perception is that "public schools have frittered away vast sums without much visible improvement in student performance" (Mandel 1995, 64).

From the perspective of professional educators, there are many reasons for the lackluster performance of public education, ranging from low expectations to inadequate financial support. Whatever the reason, however, one overlooked strategy to *improve* school performance is to emphasize goal setting and long-range planning, especially by anticipating the future needs of, and demands upon, the public education system. In the face of a current lack of information regarding those future needs and demands, we sur-

veyed the chief state school officer (CSSO) in each state to determine what he or she saw as the critical issues that will confront public education in the future. The chief state school officer—known as commissioner, state superintendent, or director of education—is the person in each state who oversees and administers the state education system and so is in a particularly advantageous position to predict what the education issues of the future will be.

A questionnaire was mailed to all 51 CSSOs. Forty-eight returned the data collection instrument (for a response rate of 94 percent). In the questionnaire, we asked the CSSOs to rank the level of importance of eleven critical issues of public education policy for the years 2000 and 2020; the issues were as follows: utilization of technology in instruction, site-based decision making, equity in funding school operations, equity in funding capital projects, student preparation for the workplace, services for special populations, educator preparation and licensure, preschool and early childhood education, assessment of student progress, safe environment for learning, and adult learning.

Results

The three most frequently chosen public education issues perceived as likely to be very important in the year 2000 (of the eleven given) were (1) student preparation for the workplace (81 percent), (2) utilization of technology in instruction (79 percent), and (3) providing a safe environment for learning (79 percent). The three issues perceived most often as not likely to be important or not likely to be very important for the year 2000 were (1) equity in funding capital projects, (2) educator preparation and licensure, and (3) services for special populations.

The predictions for the year 2020 were somewhat different. The three most frequently chosen were (1) utilization of technology in instruction (73 percent), (2) student preparation for the workplace (71 percent), and (3) preschool and early childhood education (58 percent). Four of the eleven

Alan D. Morgan, formerly the New Mexico superintendent of public instruction, is executive vice president for governmental relations, Voyager Expanded Learning, Inc., in Albuquerque, New Mexico. Myrna Matranga is the chair of the Department of Educational Leadership, Gary L. Peltier is a professor of educational leadership, and George C. Hill is an associate professor of educational leadership, all in the College of Education, University of Nevada, Reno.

From *The Clearing House*, July/August 1998, pp. 339-341. Reprinted with permission of the Helen Dwight Reid Educational Foundation. Published by Heldref Publications, 1319 Eighteenth St., NW, Washington, DC 20036-1802. © 1998.

public education policy issues were rated by 30 percent or more of the respondents as not likely to be important or not likely to be very important in 2020: (1) equity in funding of capital projects, (2) site-based decision making, (3) equity in funding school operations, and (4) educator preparation and licensure.

The questionnaire also invited respondents to make written comments regarding public education policy issues of the future. Among the issues identified in those narrative responses were the following: (1) concern over the potential withdrawal of public support, and funding, of public institutions such as local schools; (2) a vision of schools becoming the primary architects of societal values in ways not thought of in the twentieth century, such as through genetic engineering and the creation of new life forms; (3) the burgeoning of individual and self-paced learning, at home or in the workplace, coupled with currently unknown technologies, thus eliminating the need for school buildings, school campuses, and traditional school-funding mechanisms; and (4) the possibility that society will put an increased value on education, as seen in the increasing support for lifelong learning and intergenerational partnerships.

Regional differences. The only issue regarding which statistically significant differences existed between the responses from CSSOs of different regions in the country was preschool and early childhood education as seen for the year 2000. Specifically, the CSSOs of the Pacific West perceived the issue of pre-school and early childhood education as being considerably more important than did their counterparts in the other four regions of the country.

Selection differences. Each respondent had been asked to indicate the method by which he or she was selected to the position of chief state school officer. (Responses indicated that 27 percent of the CSSOs were elected by popular vote, 58 percent were appointed to their positions by state boards of education, and 15 percent were appointed by the governors of their states.) Based on the method of selection, the only issue for which a statistically significant difference existed (identified at the .05 level) was "safe environment for learning" in the year 2020. Elected CSSOs viewed a safe environment as being of much greater importance than did the chief state school officers who had been appointed by governors or state boards of education.

Gender differences. This study found a statistically significant difference (at the .01 level) between male respondents and female respondents with regard to the perceived importance of site-based decision making in the year 2000. Female CSSOs were far more certain than their male counterparts that site-based decision making would continue to be an important issue. Several male respondents, on the other hand, shared the perception that, in the future, schooling would not happen in discrete school buildings and on campuses but rather would occur through a more eclectic arrangement, one tailored to the needs of individual students in the workplace, home, and other physical settings—thus obviating the need for school site-based decision making. Both males and females perceived site-based decision making as likely to be less important by the year 2020 than it is now.

Implications

Most respondents availed themselves of the opportunity to add comments to the survey. (A total of eighty-six individual comments were received from the forty-eight respondents.) The comments suggested that a wide variety of public education policy issues await communities and states in the relatively near future:

1. By the year 2000, as much as 75 percent of the present teaching force will still be on the job. Therefore, the greatest pending policy issue requiring attention in and before the year 2000, as noted in the comments, will be continuous professional development of teachers and professional staff to improve student learning.

2. No policy dilemma will exceed that of governance. Respondents observed that by the year 2000 a clear indication must be evident to answer the question of who controls the education of children. With the advent of charter schools, vouchers, and privatization of services, local school boards may be a fading memory in the governance schema of the future.

3. One chief state school officer provided insight, and qualified pessimism, by noting that the age wave and global competitiveness are likely to be the driving forces behind the changes in schools by the year 2000. The baby boomers, now 35 to 50 years of age, will represent 76 million persons ages 40 to 55 by 2000. Equity will be of less concern than it has been, given the heightened emphasis on achievement. Also, the children of 2000 will be considerably more economically and linguistically diverse, and born to less-well-paid parents, than children in the past; families, therefore, will require more day care for the youngest children and more job training and retraining for the adults. Finally, greater achievement will be required to re-establish America's pre-eminence in the global marketplace. It is likely that schools will be the governmental entities with the breadth and depth of experience and the human resources—as well as the public confidence—to meet these changing priorities.

In regard to the year 2020, comments included the following:

> Public schools will not likely exist as known in 1995. School-aged students may participate in a government-sponsored and publicly funded range of experiences. A child's early years may include more structured group processes. As children age, they may more likely be tutored, guided, and instructed through new partnerships representing the home, a work sponsor, and an educational liaison utilizing new technologies and advanced applications of learning theories.

America's new demographics warrant a new vision of public education. By the year 2020, almost 50 percent of the population under seventeen years of age will be composed of ethnic minority children. This trend suggests the projected change in composition will result in a substantial increase in the proportion of educationally disadvantaged children, thus requiring an unparalleled commitment to new teaching techniques, new technologies, new efficiencies, and new resources.

The Future

The results of the study lead us to speculate about emerging or continuing demands within education. For example, it is possible that, by 2020,

- the use of technology will not be seen to be as critical an issue as it is today because technology will be so pervasive as to be institutionalized;
- equity in funding capital projects will diminish in import because students will be learning at home and in other community environments;
- adult learning will gain increased attention as the population grows older overall and demands lifelong opportunities for learning and an extended work life; and
- site-based decision making will be less of an issue in the future because school "sites" as we know them today will no longer exist.

Studies such as this one rely on the knowledge, insight, and "connectedness" of the respondents. The country's chief state school officers have given us a look with a special lens into the future of public education policy issues.

REFERENCES

Mandel, J. M. 1995. Will schools ever get better? *Business Week* 41(17 April): 64–68.
National Education Association. 1994. *Ranking of the states.* Washington, D.C.: NEA Research Division.

Unit 2

Unit Selections

Childhood

4. **New Brain Development Research—A Wonderful Window of Opportunity to Build Public Support for Early Childhood Education!** Julee J. Newberger
5. **The Moral Child,** *U.S. News & World Report*
6. **Re-Evaluating Significance of Baby's Bond with Mother,** Sandra Blakeslee
7. **Helping Children Become More Prosocial: Ideas for Classrooms, Families, Schools, and Communities,** Alice S. Honig and Donna S. Wittmer

Adolescence

8. **Developmental Tasks of Early Adolescence: How Adult Awareness Can Reduce At-Risk Behavior,** Judith L. Irvin
9. **Out of the Mouths of Babes: Voices of At-Risk Adolescents,** Korynne Taylor-Dunlop and Marcia M. Norton

Key Points to Consider

❖ How can parents and teachers provide children and adolescents with experiences that promote their cognitive, moral, social, and emotional development?

❖ Describe the developmental tasks adolescents face. What are the historical and cultural changes that may put some youth at risk?

❖ What can at-risk adolescents tell us about their perceptions of caring?

 **Links**   **www.dushkin.com/online/**

13. **Association for Moral Education**
    http://www.wittenberg.edu/ame/
14. **Child Welfare League of America**
    http://www.cwla.org
15. **Guidelines for Developmentally Appropriate Early Childhood Practice**
    http://www.newhorizons.org/naeyc.html
16. **The National Academy for Child Development**
    http://www.nacd.org

These sites are annotated on pages 4 and 5.

The study of human development provides us with knowledge of how children and adolescents mature and learn within the family, community, and school environments. Educational psychology focuses on description and explanation of the developmental processes that make it possible for children to become intelligent and socially competent adults. Psychologists and educators are presently studying the idea that biology as well as the environment influences cognitive, personal, social, and emotional development and involves predictable patterns of behavior.

Jean Piaget's theory regarding the cognitive development of children and adolescents is perhaps the best known and most comprehensive. According to this theory, the perceptions and thoughts that young children have about the world are often quite different when compared to adolescents and adults. That is, children may think about moral and social issues in a unique way. Children need to acquire cognitive, moral, and social skills in order to interact effectively with parents, teachers, and peers. If human intelligence encompasses all of the above skills, then Piaget may have been correct in saying that development is the child's intelligent adaptation to the environment.

Today the cognitive, moral, social, and emotional development of children takes place in a rapidly changing society. A child must develop positive conceptions of self within the family as well as at school in order to cope with the changes and become a competent and socially responsible adult. In "New Brain Development Research—A Wonderful Window of Opportunity to Build Public Support for Early Childhood Education!" Julee Newberger discusses the importance of both nature and nurture in early development, while the articles "The Moral Child" and "Helping Children Become More Prosocial: Ideas for Classrooms, Families, Schools, and Communities" discuss the moral and social skills of children.

Adolescence brings with it the ability to think abstractly and hypothetically and to see the world from many perspectives. Adolescents strive to achieve a sense of identity by questioning their beliefs and tentatively committing to self-chosen goals. Their ideas about the kinds of adults they want to become and the ideals they want to believe in sometimes lead to conflicts with parents and teachers. Adolescents are also sensitive about espoused adult values versus adult behavior. The articles in this unit discuss the cognitive, social, and emotional changes that confront adolescents and also suggest ways in which the family and school can help meet their needs.

Development

New Brain Development Research— A Wonderful Window of Opportunity to Build Public Support for Early Childhood Education!

Julee J. Newberger

More than 20 years of brain development research is finally making news. Articles have appeared recently in *Time* (see Nash 1997), *Working Mother* (see Jabs 1996), *The Chicago Tribune, Newsweek* (see Begley 1996), and *The Washington Post*. A special edition of *Newsweek* focusing on learning in the early years is on the newsstands this spring in conjunction with the April 28, ABC-TV special "I Am Your Child." Receiving unprecedented attention, they kick off a massive three-year campaign to engage the public. What is the significance of this new research on the brain, and what does it mean for early childhood professionals?

New brain-imaging technologies have enabled scientists to investigate how the brain develops and works. Stimulated in part by growing concern about the overall well-being of children in America, the findings affirm what many parents and caregivers have known for years: (1) good prenatal care, (2) warm and loving attachments between young children and adults, and (3) positive, age-appropriate stimulation from the time of birth really do make a difference in children's development for a lifetime.

In addition to giving us a glimpse of the complex activity that occurs in the brain during infancy, the new research tools have stimulated dialogue between scientists and educators. In June 1996 Families and Work Institute sponsored a conference, "Brain Development in Young Children: New Frontiers for Research, Policy, and Practice," at the University of Chicago (see Families and Work Institute 1996). Convening professionals from the media, human services, business, and public policy, the conference explored how knowledge about the brain can inform our efforts to make better beginnings for

Just as experts agree that we have only begun to understand the complexities of the growing brain, so we have only begun to bridge the gap between neuroscience and education. The question for early childhood professionals is, How can we take advantage of the public interest that these stories and events have sparked to build support for high-quality early childhood education?

children and families. One month later, a workshop sponsored by the Education Commission of the States and the Charles A. Dana Foundation brought together 74 neuroscientists, cognitive psychologists, and education researchers and practitioners to foster communication and bridge a "historical communications gap" (ECS 1996). Similar events have followed, such as President Clinton's White House Conference on Early Childhood Development and Learning on April 17, 1997.

Just as experts agree that we have only begun to understand the complexities of the growing brain, so we have only begun to bridge the gap between neuroscience and education. The question for early childhood professionals is, How can we take advantage of the public interest that these stories and events have sparked to build support for high-quality early childhood education?

Julee J. Newberger, M.F.A., is a communications specialist in the NAEYC public affairs division. She is the primary author of "Early Years Are Learning Years" news releases.

What we know about how children learn

Although the scientists of all varieties who have been researching biology-versus-environment issues for much of this century have long agreed that both are enormously important influences on growth and development, only about 20 years ago neuroscientists believed that the genes we are born with determine the structure of our brains. They held that this fixed structure determines the way we develop and interact with the world. But recent brain research, enabled by new technologies, disproves this notion. Heredity may determine the basic number of neurons (brain cells) children are born with, and their initial arrangement, but this is merely a framework. A child's environment has enormous impact on how the circuits of the brain will be laid. Nature and nurture together—not nature or nurture alone—determine the outcome of our lives.

Beginning even before birth, the kind of nourishment and care a child receives affects not only the "wiring" of her brain but also the qualities of her experiences beyond the first few years of life. Many parents and caregivers have understood intuitively that warm, everyday interaction—cuddling infants closely or singing to toddlers—actually helps prepare children for learning throughout life. More and more we begin to understand the biological reasons behind this.

When a child is born, the brain produces trillions more neurons and synapses (connections between the brain cells) than she will ultimately need. Positive interactions with caring adults stimulate a child's brain profoundly, causing synapses to grow and existing connections to be strengthened. Those synapses in a child's brain that are used tend to be-

© The Growth Program

Many parents and caregivers have understood intuitively that warm, everyday interaction—cuddling infants closely or singing to toddlers—actually helps prepare children for the learning they will do throughout life. More and more we begin to understand the biological reasons behind this.

come permanent fixtures; those that are not used tend to be eliminated. If a child receives little stimulation early on, synapses will not sprout or develop, and the brain will make fewer connections. Therefore, a child's experiences during the first few days, months, and years may be more decisive than scientists once believed.

We now know that during the early years the brain has the greatest capacity for change. Neural plasticity, the brain's ability to adapt with experience, confirms that early stimulation sets the stage for how children will continue to learn and interact with others throughout life.

Neural plasticity: The brain's ability to adapt

Particularly during the first three years of life, brain connections develop quickly in response to outside stimulation. A child's experiences—good or bad—influence the wiring of his brain and the connections in his nervous system. Thus, when we snuggle a baby or talk to him in a singsong, undulating rhythm, we are contributing to the growth of his brain. How do we know this?

Recent research examining one of the body's "stress-sensitive" systems demonstrates how outside experiences shape a child's developing brain (Gunnar et al. 1996). One stress-sensitive system in particular is activated when children are faced with physical or emotional trauma. Activation of this system produces a steroid hormone called *cortisol*. High levels of cortisol cause the death of brain cells and a reduction in connections between the cells in certain areas of the brain. Research in adults who have experienced chronic or intense activation of the system that produces cortisol shows shrinkage

Particularly during the first three years of life, brain connections develop quickly in response to outside stimulation. Thus, when we snuggle a baby or talk to him in a singsong, undulating rhythm, we are contributing to the growth of his brain.

of a certain brain region that is important in learning and memory. Clearly, a link exists between physical or emotional trauma and long-term impairments to learning and development.

But nature has provided a way of buffering the negative effects of these stress systems in the brain: strong attachments between children and their parents or caregivers. Studies measuring the levels of cortisol in children's saliva showed that those who received warm and responsive care were able to turn off this stress-sensitive response more quickly and efficiently. Babies with strong emotional bonds to their caregivers showed consistently lower levels of cortisol in their brains.

While positive, nurturing experiences can help brighten a child's future, negative experiences can do the opposite. Children who are emotionally neglected or abandoned early in life not only are more likely to have difficulty in learning but also may have more trouble experiencing empathy, attachment, and emotional expression in general. An excess of cortisol in the brain is linked to impaired cognitive ability and difficulty in responding appropriately or productively in stressful situations. Healthy relationships during the early years help children create a framework for interactions with others throughout life.

Windows of opportunity

Studies have increased our understanding of "windows of opportunity" or critical periods in children's lives when specific types of learning take place. For instance, scientists have determined that the neurons for vision begin sending messages back and forth rapidly at two to four months of age, peaking in intensity at eight months. It is no coincidence that babies begin to take notice of the world during this period. A well-known experiment conducted in the 1970s prompted research on the window of opportunity in development of vision in children. The original study demonstrated that sewing shut

one eye of a newborn kitten caused the kitten's brain to be "rewired." Because no synapses were created in the brain to allow the kitten to see with the eye that had been closed, the kitten was blind in that eye even after scientists reopened it. The results could not be repeated in adult cats, whose brains were already wired for sight in both eyes. We now know that by the age of two these synapses in the human brain have matured as well. The window of opportunity for vision has already closed.

Scientists believe that language is acquired most easily during the first decade of life. Infants under six months respond with equal interest to the sounds of all languages, but they soon develop "perceptual maps" that direct them toward the sounds of the language they hear most frequently and away from the sounds of other languages. They start by forming connections for specific vowel sounds they hear repeatedly. The circuits in children's brains then become wired for those sounds that are significant in their own language, diminishing their ability to discern sounds that are not. As a result, the brains of babies in Japan, for example, begin to develop differently than those of babies in the United States. These perceptual maps eventually account for regional accents—and the increasing difficulty in acquiring new languages as we grow older.

Studies well-known to early childhood educators make one thing clear: Talking to an infant increases the number of words she will recognize and eventually come to understand. She also will learn better when spoken to in brief phrases, preferably in singsong tones. Researchers report that infants whose parents and caregivers frequently speak to them recognize far more words later on than do infants whose parents are less vocal or less engaged. An infant's repeated exposure to words clearly helps her brain build neural circuitry that will enable her to learn more words later on. For infants, individual attention and responsive, sensitive care-giving are critical for later language and intellectual development.

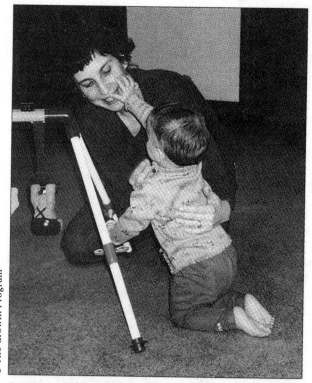

© The Growth Program

Studies make one thing clear: Talking to an infant increases the number of words she will recognize and eventually come to understand. She also will learn better when spoken to in brief phrases, preferably in singsong tones.

Children who are emotionally neglected or abandoned early in life not only are more likely to have difficulty in learning but also may have more trouble experiencing empathy, attachment, and emotional expression in general. An excess of cortisol in the brain is linked to impaired cognitive ability and difficulty in responding appropriately or productively in stressful situations.

Many reports on brain research point to the implications for the introduction of second-language learning during the early years (ECS 1996). We now know that if children are to learn to speak a second language like a native, they should be introduced to the language by age ten. Mastering an additional language is still possible after this point, but the window of opportunity for easy acquisition is gone.

Research does not suggest drilling children in alphabet songs from different languages or using flash cards to promote rote memorization of letters and numbers. Rather, it reinforces the principles of developmentally appropriate practice. Children learn any language best in the context of meaningful, day-to-day interactions with adults or other children who speak the language.

More windows of opportunity in children's learning may exist. Studies show that the most effective time to begin music lessons, for instance, is between the ages of three and ten. Few professional musicians began later in life. Music also seems to be linked to spatial orientation, so providing a child with the opportunity to play an instrument and using basic music education to spark her interest may do more than help her become musically inclined. With such knowledge, scientists and educators can work together to create the best plans for developing the whole child during the early years of life.

Implications for early care and education programs

Now that scientific research has reinforced what many already knew about early childhood education, what impact will this knowledge have on programs and centers across the country? We know that enriched home and school environments can help make the most of children's mental capacities. We also know that when we bring an understanding of child development to our interactions with children, we can meet their developmental needs more than just adequately. Parents and the general public, having children's best interests in mind, may raise issues about early education practices. Here are some questions that are likely to arise.

1. Should new parents put off employment and stay at home?

The relationship between secure attachment and healthy brain development makes this a reasonable question, although working parents should not be blamed for any and every developmental obstacle their children encounter. At a time when 55% of women provide about half or more of their families' income, decisions as to whether parents should put off employment remain a personal, family matter (Families and Work Institute 1996). Research shows that the best scenario for children and families if child care is used involves high-quality parenting and access to high-quality, affordable child care and early education that enhances—not disrupts—attachments between parents and children. Flexible workplace policies can help accommodate and support modern family life.

2. Is it too late for children to develop cognitive skills after the early years?

While scientists have found that the early years may be even more important than anticipated, human development continues throughout the life span. It may not be as easy to acquire a second language at the age of fifty, but learning new skills is always possible. A meaningful context and the desire to develop new skills make learning more likely at any age.

The significance of this new research, according to Harry Chugani (1997) of Wayne State University, is for all of us to "be aware and take advantage of these critical periods nature has provided us with." Chugani says, "We must create innovations to make learning fun." Parents and educators should focus on ways to take advantage of windows of opportunity that remain open.

Research does not suggest drilling children in alphabet songs from different languages or using flash cards to promote rote memorization of letters and numbers. Rather, it reinforces the principles of developmentally appropriate practice. Children learn any language best in the context of meaningful, day-to-day interactions with adults or other children who speak the language.

3. To take advantage of the early years of learning, should I invest more in toys and new products for my child?

New developments in research may prompt manufacturers to market products that claim to make the most of children's learning potential. Remember that scientific evidence does not change the fundamental principles of developmentally appropriate practice. In fact, research supports the theory that learning must take place in a meaningful context and in an environment of love and support. A developing brain doesn't know the difference between an inexpensive set of measuring cups and a pricey set of stackables purchased at a toy store.

The key to fostering early childhood learning is understanding that there will be a range in the amount of stimulation children are comfortable with and can tolerate. Before children can move on to new skills, they must have time to practice and master those they have already learned. Parents or caregivers who push children too fast or too hard can do as much damage as those who do not challenge children at all. Chugani recommends, "Be rigorous, but be aware of early signs of overload" (1997). Continue to respect the child as a human being and use common sense in determining when he enjoys what he is learning and when he is resistant.

Bridging the gaps

The ECS workshop on neuroscience and education outlined the following conflicts between research and current education practice (ECS 1996):
• While we know that development of children's capacity to learn is crucial in the first few years of life, children during these years receive the least attention from the educational world.
• Interactive environments enhance development, but many children are in child care programs today with staff who are underpaid, lack training in early childhood and brain development, and may be responsible for too many children.

• Although some adverse effects can be reversed or prevented for much less than it costs to provide special services later on, our educational system waits for children to fall behind, then places them in special education programs at high costs to states.

In light of this research, shouldn't parents have more options to stay home with children during the years in which this critical learning takes place? Parental leave policies must be put on the table for discussion. And what about new welfare reform policies that push single mothers into the workforce without guaranteeing high-quality child care to promote children's optimum development and learning? The concerns raised and the dialogue generated at this workshop and other conferences may be timely in preventing more children from growing up without the benefit of the kind of education that early childhood professionals, utilizing years of research and practice, can provide.

Where we go from here

The Families and Work Institute conference on brain development offered the following recommendations for parents, caregivers, policymakers, and the public to institute policies and practices that improve the day-to-day experiences of all young children and families.

First, do no harm.

• Allow parents to fulfill their all-important role in providing and arranging sensitive, predictable care for their children.

Parents or caregivers who push children too fast or too hard can do as much damage as those who do not challenge children at all.

• Work to reform policies that prevent parents from forming strong, secure attachments with their infants in the first months of life.

• Mount intensive efforts to improve the quality of child care and early education so that families can be sure their young children's learning and emotional development are being fostered while parents are at work.

Prevention is best, but when a child needs help, intervene quickly and intensively.

• Ensure consistent and responsive care to help cushion children against the stresses of everyday life.

• Provide timely, intensive, sustained assistance to help children recover from serious trauma or overcome developmental problems.

Promote healthy development and learning for every child.

• Be aware that missed opportunities to promote healthy development may result later on in more expensive and less effective attempts at remediation.

• Support ongoing efforts to enhance the cognitive, emotional, and social development of children and adults in every phase of the life cycle.

Improve health and protection by providing health care coverage for expectant and new parents and their young children.

• Medical care, including preventive health screening, well-baby care, timely immunization, and attention to children's emotional and physical development, is cost-effective and provides a foundation for lifetime development.

Promote responsible parenthood by expanding proven approaches.

• Identify parent education and family support programs that promote the healthy development of children, improve the well-being of parents, and are cost-effective.

Safeguard children in early care and education from harm and promote their learning and development.

• Ensure that children will learn and thrive by improving the quality of early childhood programs and centers.

> **While we know that development of children's capacity to learn is crucial in the first few years of life, children during these years receive the least attention from the educational world.**

Enable communities to have the flexibility and resources they need to mobilize on behalf of young children and their families.

• Bring together leaders from business, media, community organizations, and religious institutions to develop goals and strategies for achieving the kind of community that supports all children and families.

* * *

Increased public awareness prompted by news-breaking reports on brain research may represent a window of opportunity in the early childhood field. With plans to make further links between science and education, early childhood professionals and advocates may find increased support for our cause— public understanding and support for child care that guarantees proper nutrition, well-planned physical environments, and developmentally appropriate practices to ensure the most promising future for all young children and families. The window of opportunity is open and the time for action is now.

References

Begley, S. 1996. I am your child. *Newsweek*, 19 February, 55–61.

Chugari, H. 1997. Personal communication, 21 March.

ECS (Education Commission of the States). 1996. *Bridging the gap between neuroscience and education: Summary of the workshop co-sponsored by Education Commission of the States and the Charles A. Dana Foundation.* Denver: Author.

Families and Work Institute. 1996. Rethinking the brain: New insights into early development. Executive summary of the Conference on Brain Development in Young Children: New frontiers for Research, Policy, and Practice. University of Chicago, June.

Gunnar, M. R., L. Brodersen, K. Krueger, & R. Rigatuso. 1996. Dampening of behavioral and adrenocortical reactivity during early infancy: Normative changes and individual differences. *Child Development* 67 (3): 877–89.

Jabs, C. 1996. Your baby's brain power. *Working Mother*, November, 24–28.

Nash, M. 1997. Fertile Minds. *Time,* 3 February, 48–56.

THE MORAL CHILD

We're at ground zero in the culture wars: how to raise decent kids when traditional ties to church, school and community are badly frayed

Only in contemporary America could selecting a family anthology be considered a political act. On one cultural flank is famous Republican moralist William Bennett's bestselling *Book of Virtues,* a hefty collection of tales, fables and poems celebrating universal virtues such as courage, compassion and honesty. Side by side with the Bennett tome in many bookstores is Herbert Kohl and Colin Greer's *A Call to Character,* a similar assemblage of proverbs and stories organized around equally cherished values. No one could blame the casual browser for arbitrarily grabbing one or the other. But it's not a casual choice. These two volumes represent a fundamental and acrimonious division over what critics call the most pressing issue facing our nation today: how we should raise and instruct the next generation of American citizens.

The differences between the two volumes of moral instruction aren't even that subtle, once you're familiar with the vocabulary of America's culture war. Both agree on qualities of character like kindness and responsibility. But look deeper: Is unwavering patriotism more desirable than moral reasoning? Does discretion trump courage, or the

other way around? Read the *Book of Virtues* to your children and they'll learn about valor from William Tell and Henry V at Agincourt. Read from *A Call to Character* and their moral instructors will be Arnold Lobel's decidedly unheroic but very human Frog and Toad. The former has sections devoted to work, faith and perseverance; the latter, playfulness, balance and adaptability. It's not just semantics or moral hairsplitting. These dueling miscellanies symbolize a much wider struggle for the hearts and minds of America's kids.

Beyond the hearth. Child rearing has always been filled with ambiguities. But while parents once riffled through their Dr. Spock and other how-to manuals for helpful perspectives on toilet training and fussy eaters, today the questions and concerns seem to have moved beyond the scope of child psychology and the familiar hearthside dilemmas. The issue for today's parents is how to raise decent kids in a complex and morally ambiguous world where traditional tethers to church, school and neighborhood are badly frayed. Capturing the heightened concerns of thousands of parents from around the country gathering at the Lincoln Memorial for this week's Stand for Children, one 41-year-old mother ob-

WIMP OR BULLY?

Your 5-year-old has been in a fistfight. Although another child was clearly the aggressor, your son dominated the older boy in the end. You experience mixed feelings: pride that your son is not a wimp, but concern about the escalating use of violence to resolve childhood disputes.

EXPERTS' VIEW

This is a common dilemma, experts say, and one that genuinely has two sides. Parents should always try first to teach a child that there are lots of ways to resolve conflict harmoniously and that reason and compromise are more effective than duking it out. Kids should also be taught that the distinction between wimp and aggressor is a false one. But if the choice is being a victim or not, children need to learn to stand up for themselves. Says psychologist William Damon: "Even young children can handle some complexity. You may not use the words 'justifiable self-defense,' but kids can grasp the idea."

serves about raising her teenage daughter: "It's not just dealing with chores and curfews. That stuff's easy. But what do you do when the values you believe in are being challenged every day at the high school, the mall, right around the corner in your own neighborhood?"

It is a sign of how high the stakes have risen that both first lady Hillary Rodham Clinton and former Vice President Dan Quayle weighed in this year with new books on proper moral child rearing. Both are motivated by fear that the moral confusion of today's youth could be deleterious to our democracy, which draws its sustenance and vitality from new generations of competent and responsible citizens. There's a sense of desperation in current writing about moral parenting, a sense that, as one psychologist puts it, improper child rearing has become a "public health problem" requiring urgent attention. Some lawmakers and public officials are even agitating for creation of a national public policy on the cultivation of private character.

The perceived threat to the commonwealth varies, of course, depending on one's political perspective. Critics on the right view moral relativity and indulgent parenting as the cause of today's moral confusion and call for the rediscovery of firmness, regimentation, deference and piety to counter our culture's decline. Those on the left are alarmed at what they see as a wave of simplistic nostalgia gaining force in the country: In their view, it is a bullying reformation designed to mold moral automatons incapable of genuine judgment or citizenship.

Morality's bedrock. The split is political, not scientific. Psychological understanding of moral development is actually quite sophisticated and consistent. For example, decades of research leave little doubt that empathy—the ability to assume another's point of view—develops naturally in the first years of life. Parents, of course, know this just from casual observation. Even infants show unmistakable signs of distress when another child is hurt or upset, and rudimentary forms of sympathy and helping—offering a toy to a distraught sibling, for example—can be observed in children as young as 1. Most psychologists who study empathy assume that the basic skill is biologically wired, probably created along with the bonds of trust that an infant forms with a caretaker, usually the mother. The task for parents is not so much a matter of teaching empathy as not quashing its natural flowering.

Building blocks. Empathy is the bedrock of human morality, the emotional skill required for the emergence of all other moral emotions—shame, guilt, pride

and so forth. Almost every form of moral behavior imaginable—from doing chores responsibly to sacrificing one's life for a cause—is inconceivable without it. Yet empathy is not enough. A second crucial building block of morality is self discipline, and psychologists have some solid evidence about how this moral "skill" is nurtured.

Most parents tend to adopt one of three general "styles" of interacting with their kids, each style a different combination of three basic factors: acceptance and warmth (vs. rejection), firmness (vs. leniency) and respect for autonomy (vs. control). How parents combine these traits sends very different messages to their children, which over time are "internalized" in such character traits as self-esteem, self-control, social competence and responsibility—or, of course, in the absence of those traits.

There is little doubt about what works and what doesn't. In fact, says Temple University child psychologist Laurence Steinberg, author of a new study called *Beyond the Classroom*, extensive research over many years shows that parents who are more accepting and warm, firmer about rules and discipline and more supportive of their child's individuality produce healthier kids: "No research has ever suggested that children fare better when their parents are aloof than when they are accepting, when their parents are lenient rather than firm, or when their parents are psychologically controlling, rather than supportive of their psychological autonomy."

Psychologists call this ideal parenting style "authoritative" parenting, a middle ground between "autocratic" and "permissive" parenting, both of which tend to produce untoward consequences for children in terms of both competence and integrity. The need to control children appears to be especially damaging to self-discipline. "Parents who are high in control," Steinberg says, "tend to value obedience over independence. They are likely to tell their children that young people should not question adults, that their opinions count less because they are children, and so on. Expressions of individuality are frowned upon in these families and equated with signs of disrespect."

The best con men, of course, combine self-discipline with a keen ability to read others' thoughts and feelings. Morality requires more—specifically, the ability to think about such things as justice and fairness and ultimately to act on those thoughts. According to the late psychologist Lawrence Kohlberg of Harvard Uni-

versity, people pass through six fairly inflexible "stages" or moral reasoning, beginning with a childlike calculation of self-interest and ending with the embodiment of abstract principles of justice. The ability to think logically about right and wrong, Kohlberg believed, was essential to the development of complete moral beings: Moral habits and emotions alone, he argued, were inadequate for dealing with novel moral dilemmas or when weighing one value against another, as people often must do in real life.

Moral identity. Psychologists emphasize the importance of young children's "internalizing" values, that is, absorbing standards that are then applied in different times, places or situations. In a recently published study called *Learning to Care*,

---

SHAME AND RIDICULE

Your 6-year-old's teacher punishes him by making him wear a dunce cap. That strikes you as archaic and severe, but the teacher insists a bit of shame helps teach old-fashioned manners.

EXPERTS VIEW

Psychologists no longer believe that shame and guilt are the stuff of neurosis. In fact, most now are convinced that morality cannot develop without these fundamental moral emotions. But public ridicule is more likely to produce humiliation and anger than healthy contrition. Parents should talk privately with the teacher to see if there are gentler and less demeaning ways to make misbehaving children feel shame.

Princeton sociologist Robert Wuthnow argues that teenagers basically need to go through a second experience of internalization if they are to become caring adults. Just as young children absorb and integrate a rudimentary understanding of kindness and caring from watching adult models, adolescents need to witness a more nuanced form of caring, to absorb "stories" of adult generosity and self-sacrifice. That way, they see that involvement is a real possibility in a world where so much caring has been institutionalized.

Similarly, a recent study suggests that people who have chosen lives of lifelong, passionate commitment have had more opportunities than most people to develop appropriate trust, courage and responsible imagination. There is no such thing as a "Gandhi pill," Lesley College Prof. Laurent Parks Daloz and his colleagues write in the new book *Common Fire,* but there are commonly shared experiences: a parent committed to a cause, service opportunities during adolescence, cross-cultural experiences, a rich mentoring experience in young adulthood. Often, the authors conclude, the committed differ from the rest of us only by having more of these experiences, and deeper ones.

Force of habit. Of course, cultural battles rarely reflect the complexity of human behavior, and the current debate about proper moral child rearing has a black-and-white quality. As Bennett writes in his introduction to the *Book of Virtues,* moral education involves "explicit instruction, exhortation, and training. Moral education *must* provide training in good habits." But critics charge that such preoccupation with drill and habit suggests a dark and cynical view of human nature as a bundle of unsavory instincts that need constant squelching and reining in. In theology, it's called original sin; in psychological terms, it's a "behaviorist" approach, conditioning responses—or habits—which eventually become automatic and no longer require the weighing of moral options. The opposing philosophy—drawing from the romanticism of Jean Jacques Rousseau, psychology's "human potential" movement and the "constructivist" movement in education—emphasizes the child's natural empathy and untapped potential for reasoning.

The Clinton and Quayle volumes show how simplistic psychology can make for unsophisticated public philosophy. There's no question that the first lady's *It Takes a Village* is informed by an overriding respect for children as essentially competent beings who need nurturance to blossom. But critics see Clinton's optimism as dewy eyed and unrealistic, too much akin to the self-esteem movement and a "child centered" parenting style that allows kids to become morally soft. Quayle's *The American Family,* by contrast, endorses control and punishment as "a way to shape behavior toward respect and obedience." He notes approvingly that the five healthy families he studied reject the counsel of "prominent child experts," including the well-documented finding that spanking and other forms of physical coercion teach violence rather than values.

Quayle's analysis is only one of many calls to return to a time when children knew their proper place and society was not so disorderly. Perhaps the strongest prescription is *The Perversion of Autonomy* by psychiatrist Willard Gaylin and political theorist Bruce Jennings, both of New York's Hastings Center for Bioethics. The book is a gleeful celebration of the value of coercion. In the view of these authors, the manifest vulgarities of liberal society justify and demand a serious rollback of the civil rights era; for the good of society, it follows, children require early and decisive flattening.

There is little question that the worst of New Age gobbledygook makes the cultural left an easy target for attack. One parent tells the story of when her 6-year-old was caught stealing at school. She met with the teacher, hoping together they could come up with a strategy to make it clear that stealing was unacceptable. But the teacher's response astonished her: "We don't use the word *stealing* here," she said. "We call it *uncooperative behavior.*" Few defend such foolish excesses of the self-esteem movement. But progressives argue they are aberrations used to attack liberal parenting and pedagogy. It's naive to focus on examples of indulgence, they argue, when if anything our culture is a child-hating culture, with family policies to match.

Classroom politics. This same ideological tug of war can be observed in the nation's schools, specifically in battles over the so-called character education movement. Only a few years old, the movement is fairly diverse, in some schools involving a specific packaged curriculum and reading materials, in others more of a philosophy or administrative style. But the general idea has captured the attention of the White House and Congress, both of which are searching for an appropriate federal role in promoting basic decency. Lawmakers have lent their symbolic support by endorsing "National Character Counts Week." The Department of Education has funded a few pilot programs and will soon fund a few more. And next week, President Clinton will address a joint White House-congressional conference on character building, the third such meeting sponsored by this administration.

Many states have also created character education requirements, and by conservative estimate, hundreds of schools and districts have adopted strategies for addressing morals and civic virtue. Precisely because of the diversity of philosophies that fall under the rubric "character education," experts say, parents need to be aware of what the term means in their own child's classroom.

For example, some schools have adopted conservative models that tend to emphasize order, discipline and courage—what Boston University educator Kevin Ryan labels the "stern virtues," as opposed to "soft" or easy virtues like compassion and self-esteem. Such programs don't shy away from unfashionable ideas like social control and indoctrination, says University of Illinois sociologist Edward Wynne, a guiding light of this approach and coauthor, with Ryan, of *Reclaiming Our Schools.*

ORDER AND SQUALOR

Your 12-year-old daughter's bedroom is a pigsty. You worry that a disorderly room means a disorderly mind, but your husband says it's more important not to violate her personal space.

EXPERTS VIEW

Experts are divided. Some come down firmly on the side of orderliness as an important habit and a lesson in family obligation. They dismiss the personal space argument as New Age nonsense. Others do not consider it a moral issue at all but an aesthetic one. Even adults differ: Some don't bother to make their beds, while others are fastidious. It's an issue for negotiation, which is a life skill that teenagers should learn.

Wynne calls for a return to the "great tradition in education," that is, the transmission of "good doctrine" to the next generation. Because of the "human propensity for selfishness," Wynne encourages schools to use elaborate reward systems, including "ribbons, awards and other signs of moral merit." The model also emphasizes group sports and pep rallies as effective ways to elevate school spirit. Variations of this reward-and-discipline model emphasize drilling in a prescribed set of values, often focusing on a "virtue of the month." Programs based on the stern virtues also tend to emphasize institutional loyalty and submission of the individual to the larger community. Ryan points to Roxbury Latin, a 350-year-old private boys' school in Boston, as an example of this approach. The school subscribes to an unambiguous set of Judeo-Christian values—honesty, courtesy and respect for others, according to the catalog. It attempts to inculcate these values through a classical curriculum, through mandatory, sermonlike "halls" and

CODES AND CREATIVITY

Your son is dismissed from school because his pierced ear violates the dress code. You argue with the principal that the earring is a form of self-expression, but he insists societies need rules.

EXPERTS VIEW

Some psychologists consider it unconscionable to place a child in the center of a culture war. The most crucial issue, they argue, is for parents and other authority figures to present kids with a united moral front. But psychologist Michael Schulman disagrees: "It could be an opportunity for a valuable lesson in choosing life's battles: Is this an important one? If so, what's the most effective strategy for social change?"

through formal and casual interactions between teachers (called "masters") and students. No racial, ethnic or religious student organizations are permitted, in order to encourage loyalty to the larger school community. According to Headmaster F. Washington Jarvis, an Episcopal priest, Roxbury Latin's view of human nature is much like the Puritan founders': "mean, nasty, brutish, selfish, and capable of great cruelty and meanness. We have to hold a mirror up to the students and say, 'This is who you are. Stop it.' "

Roxbury Latin teaches kids to rein in their negative impulses not with harsh discipline, however, but with love and security of belonging. Displays of affection are encouraged, according to Jar-

vis, and kids are disciplined by being made to perform (and report) good deeds—a powerful form of behavior modification. Students are rebuked and criticized when they stray, but criticism is always followed by acts of caring and acceptance. Whenever a student is sent to Jarvis's office for discipline, the headmaster always asks as the boy leaves, "Do I love you?"

Ethical dilemmas. At the other end of the spectrum are character education programs that emphasize moral reasoning. These, too, vary a great deal, but most are derived at least loosely from the work of Kohlberg and other stage theorists. Strict Kohlbergian programs tend to be highly cognitive, with students reasoning through hypothetical moral dilemmas and often weighing conflicting values in order to arrive at judgments of right and wrong. A classic Kohlbergian dilemma, for example, asks whether it's right for a poor man to steal medicine to save his dying wife. Even young children tend to justify dishonesty in this situation, but only adults do so based on a firmly held principle of what's unchallengeably right. Kohlbergian programs are also much more likely to have kids grapple with controversial social dilemmas, since it's assumed that the same sort of moral logic is necessary for citizens to come to informed decisions on the issues of the day—whether gay lifestyles ought to be tolerated in the U.S. Navy, for example.

Variations in programs on strict moral reasoning are generally based on a kind of "constructivist" model of education, in which kids have to figure out for themselves, based on real experiences, what makes the other person feel better or worse, what rules make sense, who makes decisions. Kids actively struggle with issues and from the inside out "construct" a notion of what kind of moral person they want to be. (Advocates of moral reasoning are quick to distinguish this approach from "values clarification," a 1960s educational fad and a favorite whipping boy of conservative reformers. Values clarification consisted of a variety of exercises aimed at helping kids figure out what was most important to them, regardless of how selfish or cruel those "values" might be. It's rarely practiced today.)

The Hudson school system in Massachusetts is a good example of this constructivist approach. The program is specifically designed to enhance the moral skills of empathy and self-discipline. Beginning in kindergarten, students participate in role-playing exercises, a series of readings about ethical

dilemmas in history and a variety of community service programs that have every Hudson student, K through 12, actively engaged in helping others and the community. Environmental efforts are a big part of the program: Kindergartners, for instance, just completed a yearlong recycling project. The idea, according to Superintendent Sheldon Berman, is for children to understand altruism both as giving to the needy today and as self-sacrifice for future generations. By contrast, the conservative "Character Education Manifesto"

MEDIA AND MORES

You allow your kids to watch certain R-rated videos, but you can't preview each one. Your 13-year-old argues: "I'm not going to become an ax murderer just because I watch a movie, Dad."

EXPERTS' VIEW

It's true he won't become an ax murderer, but he might absorb some distorted lessons about uncaring sexuality—if you're not around to discuss the differences between fantasy and reality. It's OK to question and reject social codes like movie ratings, psychologists say, but if you do, you must substitute meaningful discussion of sex, violence and censorship.

states explicitly: "Character education is *not* about acquiring the right *views*," including "currently accepted attitudes about ecology."

Needless to say, these philosophical extremes look very different in practice. Parents who find one or the other more appealing will almost certainly have different beliefs about human behavior. But the best of such programs, regardless of ruling philosophy, share in one crucial belief: that making decent kids requires constant repetition and amplification of basic moral messages. Both Roxbury Latin and Hudson, for example, fashion themselves as "moral communities," where character education is woven into the basic fabric of the school and reflected in every aspect of the school day.

Community voices. This idea is consistent with the best of moral development theory. According to Brown University developmental psychologist William Damon, author of *Greater Expectations,* "Real learning is made up of a thousand small experiences in a thousand different relationships, where you see all the facets of courage, caring and respect." Virtue-of-the-week programs will never work, Damon contends, because they lack moral dimension and trivialized moral behavior. Children can handle moral complexity, he says, and sense what's phony. "Kids need a sense of purpose, something to believe in. Morality is not about prohibitions, things to avoid, be afraid of or feel guilty about."

Building this sense of purpose is a task beyond the capacity of most families today. The crucial consistency of a moral message requires that kids hear it not only from their parents but from their neighbors, teachers, coach, the local policeman. Unfortunately, Damon says, few do. The culture has become so adversarial that the important figures in a child's life are more apt to be at one another's throats than presenting a unified moral front. Litigiousness has become so widespread that it even has a name, the "parents' rights movement." More than ever before, parents see themselves primarily as advocates for their children's rights, suing schools over every value conflict. In a New York case now making its way through the courts, for example, parents are suing because they object to the school district's community service requirement.

Moral ecology. The irony of postmodern parenting, writes sociologist David Popenoe in *Seedbeds of Virtue,* is that just when science has produced a reliable body of knowledge about what makes decent kids, the key elements are disintegrating: the two-parent family, the church, the neighborhood school and a safe, nurturing community. Popenoe and others advocate a much broader understanding of what it means to raise a moral child today—what communitarian legal theorist Mary Ann Glendon calls an "ecological approach" to child rearing, which views parents and family as just one of many interconnecting "seedbeds" that can contribute to a child's competency and character.

Hillary Clinton borrowed for her book title the folk wisdom, "It takes a village to raise a child." It's an idea that seems to be resonating across the political spectrum today, even in the midst of rough cultural strife. Damon, for example, ended his book with the inchoate notion of "youth charters," an idea that he says has taken on a life of its own in recent months. He has been invited into communities from Texas to New England to help concerned citizens identify shared values and develop plans for modeling and nurturing these values in newly conceived moral communities.

Americans are hungry for this kind of moral coherence, Damon says, and although they need help getting past their paralysis, it's remarkable how quickly they can reach consensus on a vision for their kids and community. He is optimistic about the future: "My great hope is that we can actually rebuild our com-

SMOKE AND MIRRORS

Despite your own youthful experimentation with drugs, you're worried about your teenager's fascination with today's drug culture. He claims he's embracing the values of the '60s.

EXPERTS' VIEW

This comes up a lot, now that children of the '60s are raising their own teenagers. It's crucial to be honest, but it's also fair to explain the social context and the spirit in which drugs were being used at the time. And it's OK to say it was a mistake—it wasn't the key to nirvana. Most experts suggest focusing on health effects and illegality rather than making it a moral issue.

munities in this country around our kids. That's one great thing about America: people love their kids. They've just lost the art of figuring out how to raise them."

BY WRAY HERBERT WITH
MISSY DANIEL IN BOSTON

Re-evaluating Significance of Baby's Bond With Mother

By SANDRA BLAKESLEE

Challenging a popular belief about human development, a researcher claims to have found that the security of a baby's attachment to its mother does not influence how well-adjusted that child will be later in life.

Events like divorce, disease and accidents are far more important in shaping a child's well-being at age 18 than any early bonding with its mother, said the researcher, Dr. Michael Lewis, a professor of pediatrics and psychiatry at the University of Medicine and Dentistry of New Jersey and director of the Institute for the Study of Child Development at the Robert Wood Johnson Medical School in New Brunswick.

The study is one of a number of research projects on attachment, a field that is gaining attention as experts debate what happens to infants and children when both mother and father work outside the home.

Dr. Lewis based his conclusion on a study of 84 children who were examined at age 1 in terms of maternal

An attack on the gold standard for understanding how babies and children develop

attachment—a popular measure of social adjustment and mental health—and again at age 18 in terms of adult attachment to family and friends.

Secure attachment in infancy did not protect children from being maladjusted at age 18, Dr. Lewis said, nor did insecure attachment in infancy predict trouble in adolescence. He reported his findings at a recent meeting of the International Society on Infant Studies in Atlanta and in a book "Altering Fate—Why the Past Does Not Predict the Future,"

published last year by the Guilford Press.

The new finding attacks the gold standard for understanding how babies and children develop: the so-called infant maternal attachment measure, which infers well-being from the reactions of babies who are temporarily separated then reunited with their mothers.

According to many experts in child development, how the baby reacts to the mother's return each time is critically important. In general, if the baby cries, goes to the mother and is comforted, the child is securely attached. If the baby ignores the mother and is ambivalent to her return or if the baby cries but refuses to be consoled, the baby is insecurely attached.

To the adherents of attachment theory, this little mini-drama speaks volumes about the child's psychological health and profoundly influences that child's developmental course.

Attachment theory is an offshoot of psychoanalysis and carries many of Sigmund Freud's ideas into modern practice, said Dr. Robert Cairns, director of the Center for Developmental Science at the University of North Carolina in Chapel Hill. It argues that early mother-infant relationships create "internal representations" in the baby's brain and that these shadows lay the foundation for psychological well-being and human personality throughout life. The mother is the critical figure. Early events are more primary than later events. Given these beliefs, the challenge became how to measure these "internal representations" in babies who cannot talk, Dr. Cairns said.

Figuring that behavior might imply something important about a baby's mind, researchers in the early 1970's devised a test called the Strange Situation. The test has many permutations but basically a mother and her 12-month-old baby enter a room in which they meet a stranger and find many interesting toys. After a few minutes, the mother leaves and the stranger plays with the baby.

After two minutes, the mother returns and the baby's behavior is observed. A little later, the mother leaves the child alone again, waits two minutes and comes back in.

The original goal was to find a measure that would, in five minutes, identify the structure of the course of human personality development, he said. The infant's external behavior is said to capture his or her internal model of the attachment relationship, Dr. Lewis said, "even though neglected and abused children often show secure attachment." Moreover, the nature of this early attachment emerges later in life, especially during stressful times.

A good attachment will protect you while a poor attachment will make you more vulnerable, he said.

This view now dominates infant and child psychiatry. The cardinal rule is that the mother-child relationship is vital for early life and determines subsequent social adjustment.

Psychiatric literature on adolescence treats attachment as a stable individual characteristic, like brown eyes. Some theorists claim that adults choose mates based on infant attachment status; insecurely attached individuals will seek securely attached people to balance out their weakness.

But life is not so simple, Dr. Lewis said. What happens to infants is important but the notion that our early reactions are frozen into the brain, unmalleable by later experience, is open to question. To see if early attachment correlates with later adjustment, Dr. Lewis found 84 children who had been evaluated at age 1—49 securely attached, 35 insecurely attached—and who were now seniors in high school. Each person was interviewed for an hour at home to measure adult attachment. Among other things, the teen-agers were asked to describe early relationships with their parents, to generate adjectives for each parent and provide memories to support the adjectives.

Interviews were scored by trained observers who examined how specific memories were integrated into a general understanding of the parent-child relationship. A teen-ager was deemed securely attached if he presented a coherent story about his relationship with his parents. A teenager was considered insecurely attached if that story was fragmented, ambivalent or incoherent.

Among securely attached infants, 57 percent were considered well-adjusted at age 18 and 43 percent were found to be maladjusted, Dr. Lewis said. Among insecure infants, 74 percent were considered secure at age 18 and 26 percent were believed to have remained insecure.

Dr. Lewis asserts that the critical factor in human development is not security of attachment at age 1 but subsequent experiences in family life. There are many critical periods in every child's life. Divorce played a primary role in their adjustment and "to understand a child's emotional and social development, you have to look at his current life," he

said. He added: "We don't so much remember the past as we reconstruct it in the light of present events. Accidents and chance encounters are a major part of life. The task is always adaptation to the present."

The proponents of attachment theory, however, are not ready to give up on a method that in their view works. For example, Dr. Alan Sroufe, a leading attachment expert at the University of Minnesota in Minneapolis, conducted a long-term study several years ago and found that, in his sample, infant attachment can predict psychopathology at age 17. "I disagree with Mike Lewis," Dr. Sroufe said, "His study is weaker than ours and he used fewer children. I'm not surprised he didn't find correlations. I also disagree with him on logical grounds. Your behavior is always a product of your history and your present circumstances."

Do life's dramas at 1 play out at 18?

Similarly, Dr. Jay Belsky, a professor of human development at Pennsylvania State University in University Park and another well-known proponent of attachment theory, argues that infant day care can disrupt attachment and may harm children in the long run. "To understand the present, you have to understand what the child brings to the circumstances," Dr. Belsky said. "Of course it matters how development proceeds, but what happens early in life makes a difference."

The debate is over how much of a difference. Critics of attachment theory, including Dr. Lewis, say that most researchers place far too much importance on what happens in the first year or two of life.

Some proponents of the theory even argue that critical mother- infant bonding begins at birth. "Years ago, I visited a program in Philadelphia to foster the social and emotional development of children of teen-aged inner-city mothers," Dr. Lewis said. "The program consisted of placing the naked newborn child on the naked belly of the mother, as if early bonding would somehow inoculate the child against all future problems."

Dr. Irving Lazar, a professor emeritus of child development at Vanderbilt University in Nashville, is even more critical of attachment theorists. "Of course babies need good mothers," he said.

"It's important to feel loved and secure. But the so-called attachment measure is ludicrous. The one-time observation of a baby's reaction to its mother's return has no meaningful consequences." All it does is make mothers feel guilty, he said.

Dr. Cairns said that animal studies mostly supported Dr. Lewis.

Studies of other mammals separated from their mothers, including the monkey experiments of Dr. Harry Harlow in which babies were raised without mothers, show no permanent damage to the deprived animals, he said. Dr. Harlow's monkeys treated their first-born babies "like basketballs" and that is what got reported, Dr. Cairns said, but babies born later to those same mothers were well-cared for.

The mothers adapted.

When pressed, people on both sides of the debate will say "of course both past and present are important," Dr. Cairns said, "but they really don't mean it." Many have entrenched ideological positions which, if confined to an ivory tower, might be amusing. These arguments, though, have important policy consequences for American society, he said.

If the first year of life is all-important, then why bother investing huge sums in later intervention programs? But if the first year of life is not that important, and it is the quality of your whole childhood that matters, how could we possibly change things?

Helping Children Become More Prosocial: Ideas for Classrooms, Families, Schools, and Communities

Alice S. Honig and Donna S. Wittmer

***Alice Sterling Honig**, Ph.D., professor of child development at Syracuse University in Syracuse, New York, was program director for the Family Development Research Program and has authored numerous books, including* Parent Involvement in Early Childhood Education *and* Playtime Learning Games for Young Children. *She directs the annual Syracuse Quality Infant/Toddler Caregiving Workshop.*

***Donna Sasse Wittmer**, Ph.D., is assistant professor in early childhood education at the University of Colorado in Denver. She has had extensive experience directing, training in, and conducting research in early childhood care and education programs.*

P art 1 of this review of strategies and techniques to enhance prosocial development focused on techniques that teachers and parents can use with individual children or small groups of children (see Wittmer & Honig, Encouraging Positive Social Development in Young Children, *Young Children* 49 [5]: 4–12). Part 2 offers suggestions for involving whole classrooms, entire school systems, parents, and communities in creating classroom and home climates for kindness, cooperation, generosity, and helpfulness.

Child-sensitive, high-quality care in classrooms promotes prosocial behaviors

If you thought so, you were right. Here is more information to back you up. Peaceful play and cooperation are more likely to occur when teachers set up developmentally appropriate classrooms (Bredekamp & Rosegrant 1992). Staff competence and years of teacher experience are significant factors in ensuring such quality care. In one research study the more highly trained and stable the preschool staff were, the *lower* were teacher-rated and observed preschool aggression scores, despite children's varying histories of full-time or part-time nonparental care during infancy and toddlerhood (Park & Honig 1991). In another study 4-year-olds in a constructivist classroom, given many opportunities for choices and autonomous construction of attitudes, principles, and social problem-solving strategies, showed higher social-cognitive skills than their peers from another preschool program with whom they played board games (DeVries & Goncu 1990).

Children in strongly adult-directed preschool classrooms engage in less prosocial behavior than do children in classrooms that encourage more child-initiated learning and interactions (Huston-Stein, Friedrich-Cofer, & Susman 1977). In a longitudinal study of 19-year-olds who had attended either a highly adult-directed preschool or a program

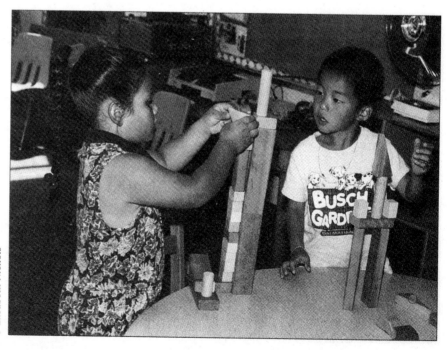

© Elisabeth Nichols

From *Young Children*, January 1996, pp. 62-70. © 1996 by the National Association for the Education of Young Children. Reprinted by permission.

that emphasized child initiations much more, the teenagers who had been in the latter program were more socially competent and had fewer juvenile delinquency convictions (Schweinhart, Weikart, & Larner 1986).

Howes and Stewart (1987) discovered that children who experience high-quality child care and supportive parents acquire the *ability to decode and regulate emotional signals in peer play.* Social sensitivity to others' cues and needs is a good predictor of positive peer relations. Unfortunately, the researchers also found that families who are the most stressed choose the lowest quality child care arrangements, are the most likely to change arrangements, and have children with the lowest levels of competence during social play with peers. A community resource-and-referral agency may be the best source of materials and information to help families recognize and choose high-quality child care and to inform parents about NAEYC accreditation.

Emphasize cooperation rather than competition

Every experienced preschool teacher surely wants young children to be prepared to succeed in their school learning careers. Competitive classrooms result in some children becoming tense, fearing failure, and becoming less motivated to persist at challenging tasks. In a cooperative-interaction classroom, the emphasis is on children working together to accomplish mutual goals (Aronson, Bridgeman, & Geffner 1978). Even toddlers can work together in cooperative play. For example, if each grasps the opposite end of a towel and both coordinate efforts, they can keep a beach ball bouncing on the towel.

Every child has an essential and unique contribution to make to class learning. One teaching tool has been called the "jigsaw technique" because the teacher provides each child with one piece of information about a lesson; then the children must work cooperatively with each other to learn all the material and information necessary for a complete presentation by the group (Aronson et al. 1978).

We have referred here only to a few studies emphasizing the positive outcomes of cooperative learning environments, but surely our readers have read about this in numerous books and articles in recent years!

Teach cooperative and conflict-resolution games and sports

Caregiver creativity in initiating group games and in devising conflict-resolution games promotes peace in the classroom (Kreidler 1984). New games and variations of traditional children's games and sports that encourage cooperation rather than competition facilitate prosocial interactions (Orlick 1982, 1985; Prutzman et al. 1988). When Musical Chairs is played so that each time a chair is taken away, the "leftover" child must find a lap to sit on rather than be forced out of the game, no child feels left out or a failure. Bos (1990) provides examples of such games. In Spider Swing one child sits on the lap of another, with legs hanging out the back of the swing. Bos calls games in which children play cooperatively together to create pleasure and fun "coaction." Why not try these and invent some of your own?

Of course, even more important than an occasional game is helping children live cooperatively in the classroom every day and resolve personal conflicts peaceably.

Set up classroom spaces and play materials to facilitate cooperative play

Arrangements of space and varieties of toys and learning materials affect whether children act more aggressively or cooperate more peacefully. A small, cluttered play area can lead to more tension and fights. A group seesaw, a tire-bouncer, or a nylon parachute encourage group cooperation because the children *need* each other to maximize their enjoyment.

In the research we reviewed, more prosocial responses were given by young children attending child care or nursery school programs when (1) a variety of age-appropriate materials were available and (2) space was arranged to accommodate groups of varying sizes (Holloway & Reichhart-Erickson 1988). Children who played with large hollow blocks and unit blocks in a large block area of their preschool learned and practiced positive social problem-solving skills rather than aggression (Rogers 1987). Yet, where preschoolers are crowded together in a narrow area with large blocks, there is greater pressure to use the blocks as missiles or pretend guns.

Classroom layout affects children's emotional security and sense of free choice in play. Combine your environmental design skills with your expertise in early childhood education to arrange class traffic patterns that maximize peaceful interactions. Think through the placement of clearly defined and well-supplied interest centers; provide unobstructed access to materials; give aesthetic attention to color and wall decorations; and decrease clutter. Arrange inviting spaces with soft cushions for children to nestle on when they need to calm down or rest when distressed.

Your executive space-planning skills can promote more comfortable feelings conducive to a more harmonious, cooperative classroom climate.

Use bibliotherapy: Incorporate children's literature to enhance empathy and caring in daily reading activities

A growing number of preschool and primary teachers do use bibliotherapy. If you do not, you may find this a good time to begin!

Choose children's literature for prosocial themes and characters that provide altruistic models. *Two Good Friends* (by Judy Delton) is the charming story of how two friends—Bear, who is messy but a fine cook, and Duck, who is tidy but a poor cook—care for each other lovingly and generously. Dr. Seuss's Horton the Elephant is that kind of prosocial character in the books *Horton Hears a Who* and *Horton Hatches an Egg*. So is the king's young page boy in Seuss's *The King's Stilts*. And so is *The Little Engine That Could*, as she chugs courageously up and over a very tall mountain to bring toys to boys and girls. Sucking his thumb vigorously, one little boy listened enraptured as his caregiver read the story of the brave little engine who did not want to disappoint the children. The child kept nodding his head and whispering to himself, "That was very nice of her! That was very nice of her!"

McMath (1989) suggests asking open-ended questions that help children think about and understand the motives and actions of storybook characters. When skilled adults read stories that feature altruistic characters, they promote children's ability to grasp socioemotional motivations and motivate children to imitate empathic and helpful responses (Dreikurs, Grunwald, & Pepper 1982). Many publishers, such as the Albert Whitman Company, provide children's books that adults can read to young children to help them cope with and find adaptive solutions to disturbing personal concerns, such as living with family alcoholism, parental divorce, or domestic violence.

Actively lead group discussions on prosocial interactions

Some teachers focus on developing supportive classroom communities. Discussion of social interactions within the group is usually a central part of the curriculum in this kind of classroom.

Sharing increases among preschool children whose teachers give them explanations as to *why* sharing is important and *how* to share (Barton & Osborne 1978). Some second-grade teachers daily set aside brief classroom time to encourage children to discuss specific incidents in which they and their classmates were helpful and kind with one another. After one month, prosocial interactions increased about twofold among these children, compared with a randomly assigned group of control children (Honig & Pollack 1990).

As a teacher, you have learned a great deal about the individual interests and talents of your children. During show-and-tell circle times you can extend group discussion to increase children's awareness of *distributive justice*—how goods and benefits are distributed justly among people with varying needs, temperaments, talents, and troubles. Lively discussions can center around what is "fair" or not so fair. Children between 4 and 8 years old are busy learning rules for games and rules for social relations, and they are often concerned about fairness and who gets advantages. Yet, preschoolers are capable of realizing, for example, that at meal and snack times, rigid equality in distributing food would not be the best plan if one child habitually comes to school without breakfast and is very hungry.

Young children often protest if there is not strict equality in distributing goodies. Many a teacher or parent has heard the protest, "That's not fair. He got more than me!" Through discussions, children can move from a position of belief in strict equality in treat or toy distribution toward awareness of the concepts of *equity and benevolence*—that is, the idea that the special needs of others must be taken into account (Damon 1977).

Talk about taking turns and about *different* ways each child gets some special time or privilege, although not exactly the same as another receives. These talks can be especially helpful for preschoolers who are distressed because Mama is now nursing a new baby and seemingly gives lots more time and attention to the tiny new stranger. Caregiver kindness lies not only in providing extra nurturing for that preschooler during this difficult time but also in assisting all the children to think through issues of neediness and fairness. As you help children to learn about "turn taking" through group discussions, you increase their understanding of fairness. Although in some families it may be a new baby's turn to get special attention, such as nursing, preschoolers now get other kinds of special attention from parents, such as a story reading at bedtime or a chance to help with cooking, a household repair job, or some other special activity in which a baby cannot participate.

Encourage social interaction between normally developing children and children with special needs

Teachers must initiate specific friendship-building strategies when atypical children in an inclusive classroom exhibit low-level prosocial skills. Activities to promote classroom friendship are available (Fox 1980; Smith 1982; Edwards 1986; Wolf 1986). Children with disabilities need your inventive interventions to learn how to make a friend, use positive and assertive techniques to enter a play group, and *sustain* friendly play bouts with peers (Honig & Thompson 1994). Promotion of specific friendship skills to enhance the social integration of typical and atypical children requires well-planned teacher strategies and initiatives. Prosocial interactions of children with disabilities may need a boost. Some typical preschoolers also may need a boost in their sensitivity to others' difficulties *and* competencies (Gresham 1981; Honig & McCarron 1990).

More than other children, a child with a disability may need help from classmates and the teacher or extra time to finish a project. If you are making preparations to create an inclusive classroom that integrates atypical and typical children, then class discussions about fairness become particularly urgent. Children will need to talk about and struggle with a new idea: strict equal apportionment according to work done may not be the kindest or most prosocial decision in special cases. If a child with cerebral palsy and marked difficulties in hand coordination finishes far fewer placemats than the other children in a class project, she or he has tried just as hard as the others and should receive the same share of any "profits" from the class craft sale.

Develop class and school projects that foster altruism

With the help of a caring teacher, children can think about and decide on a class project to help others (Solomon et al. 1988). Some classes prominently label and display a jar in which they put pennies to donate to hungry children or to families in need at holiday time. When the jar is full, children count the money and compose a joint class letter to the organization to which they are contributing. Other class projects can arise from children's suggestions during group discussion times about troubles that faraway or nearby children are having. Prosocial projects include cleaning up the schoolyard, writing as pen pals to children in troubled lands, collecting toys or food for individuals in need, and making friends with older people during visits to a home for the aged.

Your perceptive knowledge about individuals in the class is especially useful when you encourage each child to generate personal ideas for sharing kindness and caring in her or his own family. As a group, the children may decide to draw their own "helping coupons." Each child creates a gift book with large, hand-drawn coupons. Every coupon promises a helpful act to a parent or family member. Some of the coupons could be "reading my baby sister a story," "setting the table," "sorting socks from the laundry basket into pairs," "sharing my toy cars with my brother," and "brushing my teeth all by myself while Papa puts the baby to bed." Young children dictate their helpful offers for you to write down and then illustrate the coupons with signs and pictures that remind them of what sharing or caring action their coupon represents. Children generously give the coupons to family members as personal gifts—promises of help.

Encourage cooperative in-classroom activities that require several children's joint productive efforts. Ideas include drawing a group mural, building a large boat or space station with blocks and Tinkertoys, planning and producing a puppet show, and sewing a yarn picture that has been outlined on both sides of burlap.

Move very young children with peers to the next age group

Toddlers adjust more positively to movement from one group to a slightly older group in center care when they move with peers. Howes (1987) found that children who stayed in the same child care center with the same peer group increased their proportion of complementary and reciprocal peer play more than did children who changed peer groups within their center. Continuity of quality child care and continuity of peer group relationships are important in the development of a child's feelings of security and social competence. Consider security needs and friendship patterns rather than rigid age criteria in moving young children to a new classroom.

Arrange regular viewing of prosocial media and videogames

Viewing prosocial videos and television programs increases children's social contacts as well as fosters smiling, praising, hugging (Coates, Pusser, & Goodman 1976), sharing, cooperating, turn taking, positive verbal/physical contact (Forge & Phemister 1987), and willingness to help puppies in need (Poulds, Rubinstein, & Leibert 1975). Regular viewing of prosocial television, particularly *Mister Rogers' Neighborhood*, has resulted in higher levels of task persistence, rule obedience, and tolerance of delayed gratification. Children from low-socioeconomic families who watched this program daily showed increased cooperative play, nurturance, and verbalization of feelings (Friedrich & Stein 1973). In contrast, children who were exposed to aggressive videogames donated less to needy children than did children who played prosocial videogames (Chambers 1987).

Invite moral mentors to visit the class

Damon (1988) urges teachers actively to recruit and involve *moral mentors* in the classroom. Invite individuals who have contributed altruistically to better the lives of others in the community to come in and talk about their lives and experiences. Children may be eager to nominate someone in their own family to tell about how they help others. Perhaps Aunt Esther visits a nursing home and livens up senior citizens' days. Perhaps Uncle Irving outfitted the family station wagon with a ramp so he can take people in wheelchairs to weekend ball games. Children learn to reframe their ideas about community helpfulness and personal generosity toward others in trouble if a special guest—a high school swimming star who volunteers as a coach for children with physical impairments, for example—comes to visit and talks about her or his experiences helping others.

Work closely with families for prosocial programming

Families need to know that prosocial interactions are an integral curriculum component of your child care program. As a practicing professional, you use your prosocial skills to support and affirm family members of each child in your classroom. And, of course, you know how your close contact with parents provides you with insight and more sensitive understanding of each child. Parents also need you to share your concern for and emphasis on prosocial classroom activities and goals. During informal greetings at the beginning of the day or at end-of-day pickup times, you may want to affirm how special each parent's role is

in promoting care and concern for others at home (Barnett et al. 1980). Yarrow and colleagues (in Pines 1979) revealed that parents who exhibit tender concern when their very young children experience fright or upset and who firmly discourage aggressive actions to solve squabbles have children who show very early signs of concern and empathy for others' troubles. These personal examples of "baby altruism" persist into elementary school (Pines 1979).

In interviews 10 years after graduation from a program that emphasized caring and prosocial development in outreach with families as well as in high-quality group care, teenagers and their families reported that they felt more family support, closeness, and appreciation than did control youth. Compared with members of the control group, the adolescents also had far lower rates of juvenile delinquency (Lally, Mangione, & Honig 1988).

Establish a parent resource lending library

Interested parents will appreciate being able to browse through prosocial articles in your child care facility. For example, make available a copy of Kobak's (1979) brief article on how she embeds caring and awareness of positive social interactions in all classroom activities, dialogues, and projects. Her concept of a *caring quotient* (CQ) classroom emphasizes the importance of children learning positive social interaction skills as well as intellectual (IQ) skills. Social problem solving by a class must take into consideration that the child whose problem is being brainstormed has to feel that the class members *care* about him or her as they explore ways to resolve a problem, such as chronic truancy or a book borrowed from a teacher and never returned.

Convince parents of the importance of a specific focus on prosocial as well as cognitive curriculum through displays of brief, easy-to-read reports of research articles. The Abecedarian program provides powerful research findings (Finkelstein 1982). Children who had attended this infant and preschool program that emphasized cognitive development were 15 times more aggressive with kindergarten peers than a control group of children who had not been in child care or who had attended community child care. A prosocial curriculum was then instituted for future waves of children in the program; the difference in aggression between program children and their peers in kindergarten subsequently disappeared, according to later evaluations.

Promote a bias-free curriculum

A bias-free curriculum promotes more prosocial interactions among children despite multicultural differences in ethnicity, language, or family background (Derman-Sparks & the A.B.C. Task Force 1989). Emphasize how all children and adults feel better and get a fairer chance when others treat them courteously and kindly. Children who feel that others are *more,* rather than less, similar to themselves behave more prosocially toward them (Feshbach 1978). During class meeting times, children discover how much alike they are—in having special family members they feel close to, in enjoying a picnic or an outing with family, in playing with friends, and in wanting to feel safe, well-loved, and cared about.

Require responsibility: Encourage children to care for younger children and classmates who need extra help

Anthropologists, studying six different cultures, noted that when children help care for younger siblings and interact with a cross-age variety of children in social groups in nonschool settings, then children feel more responsible for the welfare of the group and gain more skills in nurturing (Whiting & Whiting 1975).

Children should be given responsibility, commensurate with their abilities, to care for and help teach younger children or children who may need extra personal help in the classroom. In a long-term study of at-risk infants born on the island of Kauai, children who carried out such caring actions of *required helpfulness* were more likely 32 years later to be positively socially functioning as family members and as community citizens (Werner 1986).

Become familiar with structured curriculum packages that promote prosocial development

Complete program packages are available with materials and specific ideas as well as activities for enhancing prosocial behaviors in the classroom. Shure's (1992) daily lesson plans give step-by-step techniques for teaching how the feelings or wishes of one child may be the same or different from those of another child and how to challenge children to think of the consequences of their behaviors and to think up alternatives to inappropriate or hurtful behaviors in solving their social problems. *Communicating to Make Friends* (Fox 1980) provides 18 weeks of planned activities to promote peer acceptance. Dinkmeyer and Dinkmeyer's *Developing Understanding of Self and Others* (1982) provides puppets, activity cards, charts, and audiocassettes to promote children's awareness of others' feelings and social skills. The Abecedarian

program instituted *My Friends and Me* (Davis 1977) to promote more prosocial development.

Arrange Bessell and Palomares's (1973) Magic Circle lessons so that children, each day during a safe, nonjudgmental circle time, feel *secure enough to share* their stories, feelings, and memories about times they have had troubles with others, times when they have been helped by others, and times when they have been thoughtful and caring on behalf of others.

Commercial sources also provide some materials that directly support teacher attempts to introduce peace programs and conflict-resolution programs in their classrooms (e.g., Young People's Press, San Diego). Sunrise Books (Provo, Utah) is a commercial source of book and video materials for teachers and parents to promote positive discipline and conflict resolution. One book by Nelson (n.d.) features the use of class meetings, a technique that builds cooperation, communication, and problem solving so that classmates' mutual respect and accountability increase.

Watkins and Durant (1992) provide pre-K to second-grade teachers with specific classroom techniques for prevention of antisocial behaviors. They suggest the right times to *ignore* inappropriate behavior and specify other situations when the teacher must use *control*. Teachers are taught to look for signs that they may actually be rewarding socially inappropriate behavior by their responses. The use of subtle, nonverbal cues of dress, voice control, and body language are recommended in order to promote children's more positive behaviors.

Implement a comprehensive school-based prosocial program that emphasizes ethical teaching

John Gatto, a recipient of the

New York City Teacher of the Year award in 1990, admitted, "The children I teach are cruel to each other, they lack compassion for misfortune, they laugh at weakness, they have contempt for people whose need for help shows too plainly" (Wood 1991, 7).

Wood urges teachers to conceptualize a more ethical style of teaching that he calls " maternal teaching." He suggests that teachers develop a routine of morning meetings that involve greetings and cooperation, as in singing together. Children feel personally valued when they are greeted by name as they enter a school. Classes can create rules of courtesy for and with each other, and the rules should be prominently posted. Wood urges teachers to "figure out a way to teach recess and lunch . . . . When children come in from recess, the teacher often can spend another half hour of instructional time sorting out the hurt feelings and hurt bodies and hurt stories she wasn't even there to see or hear" (1991, 8). Children can be taught the power of "please" and "thank you." Role playing helps them become aware of how hurtful name-calling and verbal put-downs are. You, of course, are a powerful positive model of social courtesies as you listen to each child's ideas and give each a turn to talk at mealtime and grouptime. Help children feel all-school ownership. Flowers and tablecloths in school lunchrooms can be incentives for making lunchtime a friendly and positive experience.

Brown and Solomon (1983) have translated prosocial research for application throughout school systems. In the California Bay Area, they implemented a comprehensive program in several elementary schools to increase prosocial attitudes and behavior among the children and their families. In the program the following occur:

Suggested Books for Classroom Parents' Library

Bos, B. 1990. *Together we're better: Establishing a coactive learning environment.* Roseville, CA: Turn the Page Press.

Briggs, D. 1975. *Your child's self-esteem.* New York: Dolphin.

Crary, E. 1990. *Kids can cooperate: A practical guide to teaching problem solving.* Seattle, WA: Parenting Press.

Damon, W. 1988. *The moral child: Nurturing children's natural moral growth.* New York: Free Press.

Feshbach, N., & S. Feshbach. 1983. *Learning to care: Classroom activities for social and affective development.* Glenview, IL: Scott Foresman.

Finkelstein, N. 1982. Aggression: Is it stimulated by day care? *Young Children* 37 (6): 3–13.

Gordon, T. 1975. *Parent effectiveness training.* New York: Plume.

Honig, A. 1996. *Developmentally appropriate behavior guidance for infants and toddlers from birth to 3 years.* Little Rock, AR: Southern Early Childhood Association.

Kobak, D. 1970. Teaching young children to care. *Children Today* 8 (6–7): 34–35.

Orlick, T. 1985. *The second cooperative sports and games book.* New York: Pantheon.

Shure, M. 1994. *Raising a thinking child: Help your young child to resolve everyday conflicts and get along with others.* New York: Henry Holt.

Smith, C. 1993. *The peaceful classroom: 162 easy activities to teach preschoolers compassion and cooperation.* Mount Rainier, MD: Gryphon House.

Wolf, P., ed. 1986. *Connecting: Friendship in the lives of young children and their teachers.* Redmond, WA: Exchange Press.

Train older children as peer mediators

In some New York City schools and elsewhere in the United States, the Resolving Conflict Creatively Program (RCCP) trains fifth-graders as peer mediators to move to situations of social conflict, such as a playground fight, and help the participants resolve their problems. RCCP rules mandate that each child in a conflict be given a chance by the peer mediators to describe and explain the problem from her or his viewpoint and to try to agree on how to settle the problem. Peer mediators are trained in nonviolent and creative ways of dealing with social conflicts (RCCP, 163 Third Avenue # 239, New York, NY 10003).

Teachers of kindergarten and primary children may want to look into this. Think how much influence the "big kids" would have on *your* children!

1. Children from about age 6 onward, with adult supervision, take responsibility for caring for younger children.

2. Cooperative learning requires that children work with each other in learning teams within classes.

3. Children are involved in structured programs of helpful and useful activities, such as visiting the elderly or shut-ins, making toys for others, cleaning up or gardening in nearby parks and playgrounds.

4. Children of mixed ages engage in activities.

5. Children help with home chores on a regular basis with parental approval and cooperation.

6. Children regularly role-play situations in which they can experience feelings of being a victim *and* a helper.

7. The entire elementary school recognizes and rewards caring, helping, taking responsibility, and other prosocial behaviors, whether they occur at home or at school.

8. Children learn about prosocial adult models in films, television, and their own community. The children watch for such models in the news media and clip newspaper articles about prosocially acting persons. They also invite such models to tell their stories in class.

9. Empathy training includes children's exposure to examples of animals or children in distress, in real life or staged episodes. They hear adults comment on how to help someone in trouble, and they watch examples of helpfulness.

10. Continuity and total saturation in a school program create a climate that *communicates prosocial expectations and supports children's learning and enacting prosocial behaviors* both at home and in school.

Cherish the children: Create an atmosphere of affirmation through family/classroom/ community rituals

Loving rituals—such as a group greeting song that names and welcomes each child individually every morning, or leisurely and soothing backrubs given at naptime in a darkened room—establish a climate of caring in the child care classroom.

College students who scored high on an empathy scale remembered their parents as having been empathic and affectionate when the students were younger (Barnett et al. 1980). Egeland and Sroufe (1981), in a series of longitudinal research studies, reported devastating effects from the lack of early family cherishing of infants and young children. (Of course, therapists' offices and prisons are full of people who were not loved in their early years.)

A warm smile or an arm around the shoulder lets a child know he or she is valued and cared for. Encourage children to tell something special about their relationship to a particular child on that child's birthday. Write down these birthday stories in a personal book for each child. An attitude of affirmation creates an environment in which children feel safe, secure, accepted, and loved (Salkowski 1991). Special holiday celebration times, such as Thanksgiving, Abraham Lincoln's birthday, Father's Day, and Mother's Day, offer opportunities to create ritual class activities and to illustrate ceremonies and appropriate behaviors for expressing caring and thankfulness.

Teachers are bombarded with books and articles about the importance of developing positive self-esteem in each child and how to attempt to instill it. Many of these sources contain important and helpful ideas (see Honig & Witt-mer 1992).

Sometimes children come into care from such stressful situations that it is hard for them to control their own sadness and anger. One teacher uses a "Magic Feather Duster" to brush off troubles and upsets from children. A preschooler arriving in child care aggravated and upset announces, "Teacher, I think you better get the Magic Feather Duster to brush off all the 'bad vibes'!" After the teacher carefully and tenderly uses her magic duster, the child sighs, relaxes, and feels ready to enter into the atmosphere of a caring and peaceful classroom. Each teacher creates her or his own magic touches to help children feel secure, calm, and cooperative.

The more cherished a child is, the less likely he or she is to bully others *or* to be rejected by other children. The more nurturing parents and caregivers are—the more positive affection and responsive, empathic care they provide—the more positively children will relate in social interactions with teachers, caring adults, and peers and in coooperating with classroom learning goals, as well.

References

Aronson, E., D. Bridgeman, & R. Geffner. 1978. Interdependent interactions and prosocial behavior. *Journal of Research and Development in Education* 12 (1): 16–27.

Aronson, E., C. Stephan, J. Sikes, N. Blaney, & M. Snapp. 1978. *The jigsaw classroom.* Beverly Hills, CA: Sage.

Barnett, M., J. Howard, L. King, & G. Dino. 1980. Empathy in young children: Relation to parents' empathy, affection, and emphasis on the feelings of others. *Developmental Psychology* 16: 243–44.

Barton, E.J., & J.G. Osborne. 1978. The development of classroom sharing by a teacher using positive practice. *Behavior Modification* 2: 231–51.

Bessell, H., & U. Palomares. 1973. *Methods in human development: Theory manual.* El Cajun, CA: Human Development Training Institute.

Bos, B. 1990. *Together we're better: Establishing a coactive learning environment.* Roseville, CA: Turn the Page Press.

Bredekamp, S., & T. Rosegrant, eds. 1992. *Reaching potentials: Appropriate curriculum and assessment for young children.* Vol. 1. Washington, DC: NAEYC.

Brown, D., & D. Solomon. 1983. A model for prosocial learning: An in-progress field study. In *The nature of prosocial development: Interdisciplinary theories and strategies,* ed. D.L. Bridgeman. New York: Academic.

Chambers, J. 1987. The effects of prosocial and aggressive videogames on children's donating and helping. *Journal of Genetic Psychology* 148: 499–505.

Coates, B., H. Pusser, & I. Goodman. 1976. The influence of "Sesame Street" and "Mr. Rogers' Neighborhood" on children's social behavior in the preschool. *Child Development* 47: 138–44.

Damon, W. 1977. *The social world of the child.* San Francisco, CA: Jossey-Bass.

Damon, W. 1988. *The moral child: Nurturing children's natural moral growth.* New York: Free Press.

Davis, D.E. 1977. *My friends and me.* Circle Pines, MN: American Guidance Service.

Derman-Sparks, L., & the A.B.C. Task Force 1989. *Anti-bias curriculum: Tools for empowering young children.* Washington, DC: NAEYC.

DeVries, R., & A. Goncu. 1990. Interpersonal relations in four-year-old dyads from constructivist and Montessori programs. In *Optimizing early child care and education,* ed. A.S. Honig, 11–28. London: Gordon & Breach.

Dinkmeyer, D., & D. Dinkmeyer, Jr. 1982. *Developing understanding of self and others (Rev. DUSO-R).* Circle Pines, MN: American Guidance Service.

Dreikurs, R., B.B. Grunwald, & F.C. Pepper. 1982. *Maintaining sanity in the classroom: Classroom management techniques.* New York: Harper & Row.

Edwards, C.P. 1986. *Social and moral development in young children: Creative approaches for the classroom.* New York: Teachers College Press.

Egeland, B., & A. Sroufe. 1981. Developmental sequelae of maltreatment in infancy. *Directions for Child Development* 11: 77–92.

Feshbach, N. 1978. Studies of empathetic behavior in children. In *Progress in experimental personality research,* Vol. 8, ed. B. Maher, 1-47. New York: Academic Press.

Finkelstein, N. 1982. Aggression: Is it stimulated by day care? *Young Children* 37 (6): 3–13.

Forge, K.L., & S. Phemister. 1987. The effect of prosocial cartoons on preschool children. *Child Study Journal* 17: 83–88.

Fox, L. 1980. *Communicating to make friends.* Rolling Hills Estates, CA: B.L. Winch.

Friedrich, L.K., & A.H. Stein. 1973. *Aggressive and prosocial television programs and the natural behavior of preschool children.* Monographs of the Society for Research in Child Development, vol. 38, issue 4, no. 151. Chicago: University of Chicago Press.

Gresham, F. 1981. Social skills training with handicapped children: A review. *Review of Educational Research* 51: 139–76.

Holloway, S.D., & M. Reichhart-Erickson. 1988. The relationship of day care quality to children's free-play behavior and social problem-solving skills. *Early Childhood Research Quarterly* 3: 39–53.

Honig, A., & P. McCarron. 1990. Prosocial behaviors of handicapped and typical peers in an integrated preschool. In *Optimizing early child care and education,* ed. A.S. Honig. London: Gordon & Breach.

Honig, A., & B. Pollack. 1990. Effects of a brief intervention program to promote prosocial behaviors in young children. *Early Education and Development* 1: 438–44.

Honig, A.S., & A. Thompson. 1994. Helping toddlers with peer entry skills. *Zero to Three* 14 (5): 15–19.

Honig, A.S., & D.S. Wittmer. 1992. *Prosocial development in children: Caring, sharing, and cooperating: A bibliographic resource guide.* New York: Garland Press.

Howes, C. 1987. Social competence with peers in young children: Developmental sequences. *Developmental Review* 7: 252–72.

Howes, C., & P. Stewart. 1987. Child's play

with adults, toys, and peers: An examination of family and child care influences. *Developmental Psychology* 23 (8): 423–30.

Huston-Stein, A., L. Friedrich-Cofer, & E. Susman. 1977. The relation of classroom structure to social behavior, imaginative play, and self-regulation of economically disadvantaged children. *Child Development* 48: 908–16.

Kobak, D. 1979. Teaching children to care. *Children Today* 8 (6/7): 34–35.

Kreidler, W. 1984. *Creative conflict resolution.* Evanston, IL: Scott Foresman.

Lally, J.R., P. Mangione, & A.S. Honig. 1988. The Syracuse University Family Development Research Program: Long range impact of an early intervention with low-income children and their families. In *Parent education as early childhood intervention: Emerging directions in theory, research, and practice,* ed. D. Powell, 79–104. Norwood, NJ: Ablex.

McMath, J. 1989. Promoting prosocial behaviors through literature. *Day Care and Early Education* 17 (1): 25–27.

Nelson, J. n.d. *Positive discipline in the classroom featuring class meetings.* Provo, UT: Sunrise.

Orlick, T. 1982. *Winning through cooperation: Competitive insanity—cooperative alternatives.* Washington, DC: Acropolis.

Orlick, T. 1985. *The second cooperative sports and games book.* New York: Pantheon Press.

Park, K., & A. Honig. 1991. Infant child care patterns and later teacher ratings of preschool behaviors. *Early Child Development and Care* 68: 80–87.

Pines, M. 1979. Good samaritans at age two? *Psychology Today* 13: 66–77.

Poulds, R., E. Rubinstein, & R. Leibert. 1975. Positive social learning. *Journal of Communication* 25 (4): 90–97.

Prutzman, P., L. Sgern, M.L. Burger, & G. Bodenhamer. 1988. *The friendly classroom for a small planet: Children's creative response to conflict program.* Philadelphia: New Society.

Rogers, D. 1987. Fostering social development through block play. *Day Care and Early Education* 14 (3): 26–29.

Salkowski, C.J. 1991. Keeping the peace: Helping children resolve conflict through a problem-solving approach. *Montessori Life* (Spring): 31–37.

Schweinhart, L.J., D.P. Weikart, & M.B. Larner. 1986. Consequences of three curriculum models through age 15. *Early Childhood Research Quarterly* 1: 15–45.

Shure, M. 1992. *I can problem solve: An interpersonal cognitive problem-solving pro-*

gram. Champaign, IL: Research Press.

Smith, C.A. 1982. *Promoting the social development of young children: Strategies and activities.* Palo Alto, CA: Mayfield.

Solomon, D., M.S. Watson, K.L. Delucci, E. Schaps, & V. Battistich. 1988. Enhancing children's prosocial behavior in the classroom. *American Educational Research Journal* 25 (4): 527–54.

Watkins, K.P., & L. Durant. 1992. *Complete early childhood behavior management guide.* West Nyack, NY: Center for Applied Research in Education.

Werner, E. 1986. Resilient children. In *Annual editions: Human development,* eds. H.E. Fitzgerald & M.G. Walraven. Sluice-Dock, CT: Dushkin.

Whiting, B., & J. Whiting. 1975. *Children of six cultures: A psychocultural analysis.* Cambridge, MA: Harvard University Press.

Wittmer, D., & A. Honig. 1994. Encouraging positive social development in young children, Part 1. *Young Children* 49 (5): 4–12.

Wolf, P., ed. 1986. *Connecting: Friendship in the lives of young children and their teachers.* Redmond, WA: Exchange Press.

Wood, C. 1991. Maternal teaching: Revolution of kindness. *Holistic Education Review* (Summer): 3–10.

Developmental Tasks of Early Adolescence: How Adult Awareness Can Reduce At-Risk Behavior

JUDITH L. IRVIN

Judith L. Irvin is an associate professor in the College of Education, Florida State University, Tallahassee. This article is drawn from her book, Reading and the Middle Level Student: Strategies to Enhance Learning *(Allyn and Bacon, 1997).*

At any inservice session for middle level educators, the first topic generally is "Characteristics of Young Adolescents," having to do with the physical, social, emotional, and intellectual growth and development of ten to fourteen year olds.

Although such information is important, it is somewhat incomplete. What needs to be explored in greater depth in those sessions—and by all middle level educators—are the developmental tasks of adolescence. A characteristic of early adolescents, for example, is defiance—not a pleasant trait. If looked at in broader terms, however, we see that defiance is a vehicle for the developmental task of personal autonomy.

Thus, although the developmental tasks of early adolescence more often than not are accompanied by obnoxious behaviors, it is how adults respond to those behaviors that can trigger a smooth or rocky transition into adulthood. And given that many "at risk" behaviors, such as drug and alcohol abuse and early sexual experiences, begin during early adolescence, it seems logical that success in developmental tasks and positive interactions with adults may reduce the need that some adolescents feel to engage in those behaviors.

In this article, I present a historical and cultural perspective of adolescence and discuss the developmental tasks at this period and the negative behaviors that can result from tackling those tasks. I believe that educators who understand the place of adolescence in history and society and who appreciate the behavior normally associated with the developmental tasks of that time in life will be in a good position to form positive relationships with young adolescents.

Background

Historical Perspectives

During the colonial days, the family formed the main social and economic unit of society; older children had an important and highly visible role in society and in the family. Young people were often farmed out to apprenticeships or boarding schools, and they generally functioned as adults at the tender age of fifteen or so (Modell and Goodman 1990).

In the next century, mass immigration and industrialization required keeping young people out of the labor force because of the need to provide sufficient employment for adult workers. Young people were obliged to remain in school for a longer period of time and were encouraged to attend college or vocational training beyond high school. That move had dire consequences for the teenager who, lacking an interest in formal education and biologically

From *The Clearing House*, March/April 1996, pp. 222-225. Reprinted with permission of the Helen Dwight Reid Educational Foundation. Published by Heldref Publications, 1319 Eighteenth St., NW, Washington, DC 20036-1802. © 1996.

ready to assume a productive adult role in society, now was forced to continue in school or to become a "dropout" and face many negative consequences as a result. Thus prolonged formal schooling, together with a lack of adequate vocational training, appears to put non–college-bound young people at risk, as they are underprepared to assume a role in adult society.

Cultural Perspectives

Families, neighborhoods, economic conditions, and our historical era are all factors that influence a gracious or awkward transition into adulthood. Because adolescence is closely tied to the structure of and condition of adult society (Modell and Goodman 1990), many of the factors that put students at risk, in reality, reflect larger societal problems.

Family conditions, socioeconomic status, and ethnicity are all important factors in adolescent development (Feldman and Elliott 1990). Minority youth, in particular, have difficulty in school for two reasons. First, "minority youth are well aware of the values of the majority culture and its standards of performance, achievement, and beauty" (Spencer and Dornbusch 1990, 131). "Minorities whose cultural frames of reference are oppositional to the cultural frame of reference of American mainstream culture have greater difficulty crossing cultural boundaries at school to learn" (Ogbu 1992, 5). Second, the conflict between the majority culture and their own often creates tension for minority students working on the developmental task of identity.

The Myth of Storm and Stress

Perhaps because of the cumulative physical, social, and psychological changes experienced by young adolescents, adults have traditionally viewed early adolescence as a time of turbulence and disruption (Hill 1980). Recent information, however (Brooks-Gunn and Reiter 1990; Hauser and Bowlds 1990; Hillman 1991; Offer, Ostrov, and Howard 1989; Scales 1991; Steinberg 1990), clearly indicates that only a small percentage of students (less than 20 percent) exhibit signs of serious disturbance and need adult intervention. Although the changes experienced are stressful for most young people, Dorman and Lipsitz (1981) argued, adults should "distinguish between behavior that is distressing (annoying to others) and behavior that is disturbed (harmful to the young person exhibiting the behavior)" (4). When adults expect and reinforce irresponsible behavior, they may, indeed, exacerbate the occurrence.

Developmental Tasks

If most teenagers pass through adolescence relatively problem free, then why does such a negative stereotype of that age exist? It may be that parents and teachers see only the narrow picture of sometimes irritating behavior. "Even well-adjusted, intelligent, and reasonable adolescents do, on occasion, exhibit truly obnoxious behavior. . . . [T]hey are not like this all of the time, but probably all adolescents

behave this way some of the time. They can be exasperating, and adult reaction can lead to more serious problems" (Newman 1985, 636). Viewing young adolescent development from a broader perspective may help the adults who share their lives to accept, if not condone, the behaviors that result from working on the tasks before them.

Some of the most obvious developmental tasks are learning how to handle a more mature body, forming a sexual identity, continuing to progress with such abilities as reading and writing, and beginning to explore career options. Of course, developmental tasks begin in early childhood and continue through adulthood. Unique to early adolescence, however, are the new cognitive abilities of dealing with problems in more abstract ways and of considering multiple perspectives. Students are moving from the "concrete" stage (able to think logically about real experiences) to the "formal" stage (able to consider "what ifs," think reflectively, and reason abstractly). This intellectual change is gradual and may occur at different times for different students. They may even shift back and forth from the concrete to the abstract, although it is important to remember that not all young adolescents, not even all adults, achieve this capacity.

These new abilities for young adolescents represent "*potential* accomplishments rather than typical everyday thinking" (Keating 1990, 65). Most students begin the process at about age twelve and display formal thinking consistently at age fifteen or sixteen. Until that time, during early adolescence, students are practicing this new ability. Like any new skill, formal reasoning must be practiced repeatedly in a safe, encouraging environment.

Young adolescents are egocentric. But, the emerging formal thinker is, for the first time, able to consider the thoughts of others and perceive him- or herself as the object of attention of others; in fact, adolescents "assume themselves to be a focus of *most* other people's perspective *much* of the time" (Keating 1990, 71). "As adolescents develop the capacity to think about their own thoughts, they become acutely aware of themselves, their person, and ideas. As a result they become egocentric, self-conscious, and introspective" (Rice 1990, 183). As students become accustomed to that new ability, they outgrow the egocentrism so characteristic of early adolescence.

Cognitive growth and development regulate the success of the four other major developmental tasks that I will discuss here: (1) forming a personal identity or self-concept, (2) acquiring social skills and responsibility, (3) gaining personal autonomy, and (4) developing character and a set of values.

Personal Identity/Self-Concept

The development of a personal identity is not really possible until children move beyond concrete levels of thinking, enabling them to be self-conscious and introspective. The development of positive self-esteem takes reflection, introspection, comparisons with others, and a sensitivity to the opinions of other people. Those processes only become possible with the advent of formal thinking.

Self-esteem declines at age eleven and reaches a low point between twelve and thirteen (Brack, Orr, and Ingersoll 1988; Harter 1990). Students, especially girls, making the shift to large, impersonal junior high schools at grade seven seem to experience long-term negative effects on their self-esteem (Simmons and Blyth 1987), particularly because of the interruption of peer groups. "Schools that emphasize competition, social comparison, and ability self-assessment" can cause students' academic motivation and self-esteem to deteriorate (Wigfield and Eccles 1995).

Minority youth have an especially difficult time forming an identity because the values of their culture may clash with the values and standards of the dominant culture. Minority youth, however, who have successful role models and who can learn to negotiate a balance between the two value systems will develop self-esteem (Spencer and Dornbusch 1990).

In a thorough review of literature on self-esteem, Kohn (1994) questioned the value of programs designed to enhance self-esteem. Educators would do better to treat students with "respect [rather] than shower them with praise" (282) "When members of a class meet to make decisions and solve problems, they get the self-esteem building message that their voices count, they experience a sense of belonging to a community, and they hone their ability to reason and analyze" (279). A meaningful curriculum (Beane and Lipka 1986), a safe and intellectually challenging environment (Wigfield and Eccles 1995), and meaningful success experiences (Kohn 1994) lead to the long-lasting development of self-identity and positive self-esteem.

Social Skills

Socialization is an important developmental task. Savin-Williams and Berndt (1990) concluded that "students who have satisfying and harmonious friendships typically report positive self-esteem, a good understanding of other people's feelings, and relatively little loneliness" (288). Additionally, those students with harmonious friendships "tend to behave appropriately in school, are motivated to do well, and often receive high grades" (290). Adults often ridicule the time and intensity of phone conversations, frenzied note passing, and frequent broken hearts, but those interactions are "critical interpersonal bridges that move [adolescents] toward psychological growth and social maturity" (277).

A myth about the negative influence of peer groups has developed over the years. Recent research shows that young adolescents "do not routinely acquiesce to peer pressure. In fact, they are more likely to follow the advice of adults rather than peers in matters affecting their long-term future and they actually rely on their own judgment more often than that of either peers or parents" (Brown 1990, 174). Peer groups usually reinforce rather than contradict the values of parents. It is not surprising that young adolescents tend to form friendships similar to the relationships they have with their families. Brown (1990) further concluded that students "seek out the peer group best suited to

meeting their needs for emotional support and exploration or reaffirmation of their values and aspirations" (180).

Students do not select a crowd as much as they are thrust into one by virtue of their personalities, backgrounds, interests, and reputations among peers (Brown 1990). A peer group is a place for trying out roles and ideas and serves as a validation of one's value within a social unit beyond the family. Young adolescents need many opportunities to experience success in socially acceptable ways so that the peer group reinforces prosocial activities.

Autonomy

Another developmental task that sometimes leads to emotional trauma is a young adolescent's need to establish autonomy. The onset of adolescence is, no doubt, a time for major realignments in relationships with adults both at home and at school. Steinberg (1990) took a sociobiological perspective of "intergenerational conflict" (family fighting). He suggested that "bickering and squabbling at puberty is an atavism that ensures that adolescents will spend time away from the family of origin and mate outside the natal group" (269). Disagreement becomes a vehicle to inform parents about changing self-conceptions and expectations and an opportunity to shed the view that parents can do no wrong. Of course, this low-level conflict must begin with an already strong emotional bond between parents and

---

A
lthough much young adolescent behavior appears rejecting, this is not the time for adults to alienate themselves from their children.

---

children. If relationships are not strong before puberty (and often stepchildren and stepparents have a particularly rough time), this fighting can become destructive.

We tend to treat young adolescents like children one minute, adults another. Their ambiguous status in society and their new powers of reasoning cause them frustration, which occasionally leads to their lashing out at adults. Although much young adolescent behavior appears rejecting, this is not the time for adults to alienate themselves from their children. Early separation from adults may result in an increased risk of susceptibly to negative peer influences and participation in unhealthy, even risky, behaviors.

Moral/Character Development

The development of character is intricately linked to socioemotional and cognitive growth. A new capacity for abstract thinking allows adolescents to ask the "what ifs"; social and emotional growth provide the context for the answers. "Character develops within a social web or environment" (Leming 1993, 69). Reference groups such as families, peer groups, and television are particularly important as students seek to understand their place in the world (Rice 1990). "Middle school students can be helped to think about who they are and who they want to be, to form identities as self-respecting, career minded persons" (Davis 1993, 32).

Young adolescents will acquire a value system with or without the help of parents and teachers. At a stage of development when students are emerging as reflective citizens, educators can help them to be consciously aware of constructive values, to think logically about consequences, to empathize with others, and to make personal commitments to constructive values and behavior (Davis 1993).

All young adolescents are "at risk" of not successfully completing developmental tasks and of bearing the emotional scars of inappropriate and negative interactions with adults. The socioeconomic condition of society partially shapes the experiences of youth, but societal norms and economic conditions change slowly.

Educators do, however, have control over their interactions with young adolescents. By understanding and appreciating the normal behaviors necessary to accomplish developmental tasks, they have the power to eliminate or at the very least reduce the "risk" for many young people.

REFERENCES

Beane, J. A., and R. P. Lipka. 1986. *Self-concept, self-esteem, and the curriculum*. New York: Teachers College Press.

Brack, C. J., D. P. Orr, and G. Ingersoll. 1988. Pubertal maturation and adolescent self-esteem. *Journal of Adolescent Health Care* 9: 280-85.

Brooks-Gunn, J., and E. O. Reiter. 1990. The role of pubertal processes. In *At the threshold: The developing adolescent*, edited by S. S. Feldman and G. R. Elliott, 16-53. Cambridge, Mass.: Harvard University Press.

Brown, B. B. 1990. Peer groups and peer cultures. In *At the threshold: The developing adolescent*, edited by S. S. Feldman and G. R. Elliott, 171-96. Cambridge, Mass.: Harvard University Press.

Davis, G. A. 1993. Creative teaching of moral thinking: Fostering awareness and commitment. *Middle School Journal* 24(4): 32-33.

Dorman, G., and J. Lipsitz. 1981. Early adolescent development. In *Middle grades assessment program, 4-8*, edited by G. Dorman. Carrboro, N.C.: Center for Early Adolescence.

Feldman, S. S., and G. R. Elliott. 1990. *At the threshold: The developing adolescent*. Cambridge, Mass.: Harvard University Press.

Harter, S. 1990. Self and identity development. In *At the threshold: The developing adolescent*, edited by S. S. Feldman and G. R. Elliott, 388-413. Cambridge, Mass.: Harvard University Press.

Hauser, S. T., and M. K. Bowlds. 1990. Stress, coping, and adaptation. In *At the threshold: The developing adolescent*, edited by S. S. Feldman and G. R. Elliott, 388–413. Cambridge, Mass.: Harvard University Press.

Hill, J. P. 1980. *Understanding early adolescence: A framework*. Carrboro, N.C.: Center for Early Adolescence.

Hillman, S. B. 1991. What developmental psychology has to say about early adolescence. *Middle School Journal* 23(1): 3-8.

Keating, D. P. 1990. Adolescent thinking. In *At the threshold: The developing adolescent*, edited by S. S. Feldman and G. R. Elliott, 54-90. Cambridge, Mass.: Harvard University Press.

Kohn, A. 1994. The truth about self-esteem. *Phi Delta Kappan* 76(4): 272-83.

Leming, J. S. 1993. Synthesis of research: In search of effective character education. *Educational Leadership* 51(3): 63-71.

Modell, J., and M. Goodman. 1990. Historical perspectives. In *At the threshold: The developing adolescent*, edited by S. S. Feldman, and G. R. Elliott, 93-122. Cambridge, Mass.: Harvard University Press.

Newman, J. 1985. Adolescents: Why they can be so obnoxious. *Adolescence* 10(79): 636-46.

Offer, D., E. H. Ostrov, and K. I. Howard. 1989. Adolescence: What is normal? *American Journal of Diseases of Children* 143: 731-36.

Ogbu, J. G. 1992. Understanding cultural diversity and learning. *Educational Researcher* 21(8): 5-14.

Rice, F. P. 1990. *Adolescent development: Relationships, and culture*. Boston: Allyn and Bacon.

Savin-Williams, R. C., and T. J. Berndt. 1990. Friendship and peer relations. In *At the threshold: The developing adolescent*, edited by S. S. Feldman and G. R. Elliott, 277-307. Cambridge, Mass.: Harvard University Press.

Scales, P. C. 1991. *A portrait of young adolescents in the 1990s*. Carrboro, N.C.: Center for Early Adolescence.

Simmons, R. G., and D. A. Blyth. 1987. *Moving into adolescence: The impact of pubertal change and school context*. Hawthorne, N.Y.: Aldine De Gruyter.

Spencer, M. B., and S. M. Dornbusch. 1990. Challenges in studying minority youth. In At the Threshold: The developing adolescent, edited by S. S. Feldman and G. R. Elliott, 123-46. Cambridge, Mass.: Harvard University Press.

Steinberg, L. 1990. Autonomy, conflict, and harmony in the family. In *At the threshold: The developing adolescent*, edited by S. S. Feldman, and G. R. Elliott, 255-76. Cambridge, Mass.: Harvard University Press.

Wigfield, A., and J. S. Eccles. 1995. Middle grades schooling and early adolescent development. *Journal of Early Adolescence* 15(1): 5-8.

Out of the Mouths of Babes

Voices of At-Risk Adolescents

KORYNNE TAYLOR-DUNLOP and MARCIA M. NORTON

Professional educators and public figures have had much to say in an attempt to educate us in the dynamics of family systems, addiction, and abuse and their impact on the group identified as "at-risk adolescents." The media has been quite graphic in its depiction of children who rear themselves when parents fail them. Newspapers, television, and radio outlets are frequently consumed with stories of crime, disease, poverty, loss of hope, and the absence of heroes.

In the past, dropout theory has linked dropping out with student's background. Over time, the concept of dropping out has evolved into the concept of at-risk, which focuses on the *potential* for dropping out. Dropping out is an event in a long series of life stresses. All students are at risk, but for some students, at a certain point, the risk becomes simply too high.

In addition to being confronted with background obstacles, students experience negative forces in the schools themselves. Those forces or impediments include the lack of intrinsic rewards, teacher obsession with covering curriculum, technical definitions of knowledge, mechanical perceptions of success, and a lack of variety in teaching styles.

Nearly everyone, from politicians to teaching professionals, has had something to say about how to help those students walk across "the bridge to the twenty-first century," but the voice that has consistently been missing from the dialogue is that of the adolescents. An in-depth ethnographic study of eleven at-risk young women, aged 15 to 17, was recently conducted at a high school in a middle class neighborhood in New York State. Two of the girls were in an alternative education program; the remainder were students in the regular program. The three Latino, two

Korynne Taylor-Dunlop is an assistant professor in the Division of Education, Department of Counseling and Human Services, at Indiana University–South Bend. Marcia M. Norton is a professor in the Department of Educational Administration at the State University of New York at New Paltz.

Caucasian, and six African American students participated in focus groups, individual interviews, and small group meetings. Data collection included school profile information and shadowing.

Three primary themes emerged: the young women's desire to have adults communicate with them in a non-hurtful way, to have what they learned be meaningful, and to be talked *with* instead of *at*. The intended outcomes of the study were (1) to develop recommendations that would guide school officials in building and sustaining a caring school community and (2) to develop a program that promoted self-esteem.

Persons Perceived as Caring

When the eleven young women were asked whom they turn to when they have a problem and why they turn to that person, they identified remarkably few people. That was also true when they were asked who keeps them in school. The school security guards, a guidance counselor, a female in the community who once had been at risk and since has "made it," a best friend, and a few professional staff members were perceived as the students' primary sources of support. That finding is in accord with Goodman (1995): "For all the reams of research and the endless social jargon, the current troubled state of children in America can be summed up pretty much in one sentence. There aren't enough caring adults in their lives. Most of the adults that children now see live inside of a television set" (79).

When probed, some of the students identified peers and cousins as the caring persons in their lives, primarily because those persons listened and could relate to them:

My cousin. My cousin can relate to it. She listens and gives good advice, even if I don't like to hear it.

Friends, no adults, I can't talk to my parents, they don't listen, their way that's it. They throw things back in my face. Friends give good advice. Friends understand more—like about a guy, they are going through the same thing.

The school security guards are often the first person to whom the girls turn:

From *The Clearing House*, May/June 1997, pp. 274-275. Reprinted with permission of the Helen Dwight Reid Educational Foundation. Published by Heldref Publications, 1319 Eighteenth St., NW, Washington, DC 20036-1802. © 1997.

Last week I was so upset, Alvin, the security guard, took me to Claire [a female security guard]. My best friend, she is in the hospital for depression [for the third time]. I can talk to Claire, and she can relate. She has good advice.

A few students perceived one counselor, one administrator, and a few teachers to be the persons they turn to when they have a problem:

Mr. Manilow [a counselor]—I'm cool with him. Dr. Angelou [the assistant principal], she tells me education is important, she helps me out. She wants me to write a book about my life and having babies.

The counselor had been instrumental in acquiring baby clothes for that student, giving her a car seat, and enrolling her in a parenting program. He has also begun researching colleges that have accommodations for teen parents so that she can consider going to college.

In another case, caring behavior on the part of an administrator was interpreted by a student as noncaring. The student had been sexually abused by various family members. She told the assistant principal about the abuse; the assistant principal, together with a counselor, then filed the mandated report to Child Protective Services and attempted to get the student to agree to counseling. She refused. The student commented:

My English teacher. I just feel close to her. She's always asking me if I'm O.K. Dr. Angelou—I used to like her. But, I told her about a big problem. She told the school, I didn't like that. She betrayed me. I didn't know she'd tell.

Sadly, there were a few students who felt there was no one they either would or could turn to:

Nobody. I don't trust nobody. I mostly leave it inside. I'm never going to change.

Myself. I keep problems for myself or write in my journal. Myself is the one person I can trust. You never know who will turn on you.

Uncaring People and Situations

When asked to describe noncaring behaviors exhibited by adults in the school, the students engaged in various nonverbal behavior that indicated their stress or upset. They hugged their bodies, rocked rhythmically, rubbed their eyes, twirled their hair, or put an arm on the chair or around the shoulder of the person who was speaking. A few students engaged in inappropriate laughter due to their lack of comfort. Finally, one said,

Mr. Godfrey, I hate him so much. He says he can't help you. I went to him the other day and cried and cried. He said nothing, didn't even give me a tissue. My friend was treated the same way. The school has the attitude of "why do I have to bother with them [us]?" It's easier that way for them. The security guards are caring and friendly, they say go to class, stay out of trouble.

A few students focused on teachers in general:

Teachers should act like they care. But they just want you in and out.

Everybody should get together. Like the Alternative Education program. Because it's a small group, the teachers have you deal with your problems in small group. Everybody is a friend. I really like it. Teachers have you make all the decisions.

They should talk to you more and try to help you more.

We should get equal attention but they make no effort. They focus on the good kids, they don't reach out. My math teacher treats me like dirt. I'm either embarrassed or ignored. I was told in front of the whole class that I failed my test. There should be more respect. Don't throw it in my face.

The students were sensitive to adult attitudes and the ways they are expressed:

People catch an attitude. The security guard, Delila, is always angry. I can't stand her. She's always talking about people, she's a phony.

People who scream at me. It's their attitude, tone of voice. Their tone of voice says they are looking down at you.

In response to a question about how the school could become more like a family, one student said,

The school is so segregated. It bothers me. I want everyone to get along. It is impossible for it to happen. Everyone doesn't want to listen.

Race and ethnicity were considered of major importance to the at-risk students. "It's the real issue," said one. Other students elaborated on how deep the feelings go:

Black, white and Spanish don't mix much. Black don't mix much. Black don't mix at all. You only stay with non-blacks if they are from when you were a little kid. The white kids in class say they can't do the work with these kids [us] in the class.

There are lots of racial fights. Latin, African American. The school is not really trying to make it come together. If anything they try to keep everyone separate. There is a lot of animosity and they do nothing about it.

Racism! I was shocked when I moved here. The whites are favored, the blacks and Hispanics are always wrong.

Supportive Links

Sykes (1990) pointed out that a personality, rather than a technique, a skill, or knowledge, was most important in touching the lives of students. Students remembered teachers' human qualities—their "personality and style, passion and caring, even their eccentricities" (79–80).

Supportive adult links were described in the following ways:

Teachers who care tell me not to go to the Alternative Education Program, that I am too bright. They tell me I can do a lot better. Some teachers really help you.

My counselor calls me down, checks in with me, takes me out to lunch. He says, "How are you doing, how's my daughter?" He knows it's hell with my schoolwork.

They talk to you seriously. They don't yell, like some do. They reach you.

They ask if I'm O.K., they conference with you. They say, "Is your homework done?" They let you know they really want you to pass.

When we asked the students to describe a time that they needed help or information and to whom they went, one student responded:

> I need help every day with my work. I ask people at home. There is an older lady, and sometimes I stay at her house. She helps me with my work.

The student had developed a relationship with a neighbor while baby-sitting for the woman's child. The woman serves as both a role model and a safe haven for the student, who lives with her grandfather and mother. The student's mother spends most of her time on the street and the grandfather sexually abused the mother. The student intimated that she is able to fend off her grandfather by escaping to her neighbor's house. The student continued:

> No one at school helps me. There are places to get help in school but I have no off periods to go there.

Spending time with friends, which is age appropriate, seemed to be the preferred activity of the young women in the study. Activities centered around going to each other's houses, talking on the phone, talking about their lives. Some spent time at the local teen center; others went to the local ice cream store and to the mall. Sports, which play a major role for some, represent both a skill and a way to pay for college.

Destructive Links

Those people whom the young women perceive as destructive links were described by them as lacking maturity and creating fear in the student. There was a consensus of opinion that one female security guard was a destructive link:

> There is one security guard, Delila. The things she says to you! Delila doesn't like [a female student]. Delila should be more mature, but instead she wants to fight [the student]. Delila, her attitude is bad, she should know [the student] is a little girl. Delila has her own kids and she is twenty-eight to thirty years old. She shouldn't be like that.

Some teachers were cited as failing to be supportive links:

> They tell me to come for extra help, and when I get there no one is there and they change the room around and don't tell you where it is.
> Teachers have a bad attitude, they say, "I get paid if you pass or don't pass."
> They don't pay attention to me, so I don't pay attention to them. I can see through them.

The guidance office received mixed reviews. Only one of the counselors was seen as consistently helpful, approachable, and available to the students:

> Mr. Manilow is very helpful. He is looking for colleges where I can bring my daughter. He has helped me realize I can go far away to school even though I have a baby.
> I needed information about the Alternative Education program. Mr. Manilow got me the application. He told me I had to wait until January. Working in the Alternative Education Program you do better, there are smaller classes. They pay attention to me individually. Not like here where there are about 120 kids in some classes.

One of the students responded very negatively about the guidance office:

> They are no help. It's the last place I'd go for anything. I hate going there.

When we asked her why, she responded:

> Most of the black students are told as freshmen that it's hopeless, helpless for college. That they should just hold on to staying in high school.

Another student had a different reason for not going to the guidance office:

> Mainly because of Mr. Godfrey. The secretaries have an attitude. Mr. Godfrey is always in a power struggle. He needs everything his own way. He talks down to me and my parents. He is negative in general, talks down to all the parents. You won't believe what he said to my parents when they talked to him about putting me in the Alternative Education program. He said, "Well, that is mostly for the minorities in this school."

When the students were asked what single thing they would change to improve the school's culture and strengthen the sense of caring, their responses were expressed in a variety of ways, but the message remained the same:

> More black kids, teachers. More kids I can relate to.
> Get everybody together whether Spanish or black. Do something that everyone participates in.

To determine if a sense of membership exists in the school, we asked if the school is like a family.

> No, it's little families—of kids.
> Not to me, not a family but different levels of work areas, houses.
> It's not like a family because of the cafeteria. Spanish are in one door, black in another door, white on the other side of the cafeteria. If you go out with a black guy, Spanish guys mind that. They talk about you if you do. If you are hanging out with a white person, they talk about you. They say you are turning white... a wannabe.

When we asked if there were celebrations or activities that attempted to bring the various cultures together, the uniform answer was no.

Adults Who Help Keep At-Risk Adolescents in School

The at-risk young women at this high school are staying in school by various means of support—role models, heroes, a significant teacher or counselor, and each other. In some cases, they attribute their ability to stay in school solely to their own determination.

Keeping an at-risk student in school sometimes requires the intervention of adults who have skills in networking, exploring resources, and putting strategies in place:

> I was pregnant eight months ago. I asked the nurse what to do. She suggested child development classes. Mr. Manilow enrolled me in the Teen Pregnancy Program at another school. We [the student, the nurse, and Mr. Manilow] and a

person at the Teen Pregnancy Program discussed how to be a responsible mother, how having to raise a child is, protective sex, labor.

The questions pertaining to whom students saw as successful or as heroes yielded disturbing results. Several students responded in a similar way to this one:

I have no heroes, not even when I was little.

On the brighter side:

Bill Cosby, he's a black person, he made it, rich, stayed together, no one put him down, he's very intelligent.

An older woman I know, she's a teacher, she went to school, supports herself, nobody to help.

Role of the Family and Home

Thirty years of research show that 90 percent of school achievement is determined by how often a child attends school, how much reading is done at home, and how much television a child watches. Studies also show that parental involvement is more important to academic success that the family's income level. Some of the barriers to involvement by parents at the school in this study were described by Boger (1989):

Parents who are underinvolved in their child's education do not lack interest. They have not been afforded the appropriate opportunities, encouragement and support. For many parents, there are several factors that present barriers to involvement in traditional home-school activities: school practices that do not accommodate the growing diversity of the families they serve; parent time and child care constraints; negative experience with schooling; lack of support for cultural diversity; and primacy of basic survival needs. (3)

For some students, school was a safe haven from the psychological and physical harm found at home. We spent many hours with one student before she shared that

I don't tell anyone my problems. I'll only tell you what I want you to know.

After several probes and a lengthy silence, she continued,

[Kids should] ask for help. Try to get someone. Encourage them. Talk to them, ask how they are doing in school. There is no one in my house. I live with my grandfather. *There is no one* there to say, Lucinda, go to school! My grandfather is seventy-four. No one says, go to school, I am on my own. Sometimes I think about moving in with a neighbor, but I don't know, I can't leave my grandfather by himself. But I need someone to take care of *me!* Things are not working out. If it wasn't for [an older woman], I wouldn't be in school.

A few responses indicated that the family system was a weak link in the lives of the young women, particularly with regard to spending time together. One student saw her father once a month, and another student reported that the family members were home at the same time but they did not really sit and talk:

Dinner is the only time I spend with my family. Watching T.V. during dinner.

There were similar responses to the question of what the students would tell families whose children were having difficulty in school. The responses centered on the importance of asking an adolescent why she said or did this or that, being involved, knowing what is going on at school, and talking to the teachers and counselors as well as to the student:

Work with the children. Don't let go. Have hope that they will do well. Help them, talk to them, talk to someone, if they are messing up. Don't say, "I'll forget about you." There is hope.

Pay more attention, ask how is she doing once in a while. Spend more time with her.

See what the problem is. Is something bothering her? Like me, my parents didn't even know I was doing bad. Ask are the kids trying to do what should be done.

One student cited her mother's words of wisdom as a positive influence on a sibling:

My sister was having trouble, my mother did good for her. My mother helped her and said, "You have to learn, it's important or you won't get anywhere." You have to keep reminding the person. Homework, do your homework all the time.

A few students admitted that their parents exhibited a lack of interest in the success or failure of them or a sibling:

My mother is sick and tired of going through problems with my brother. It is up to us to make it. Whether we do or we don't.

My mother doesn't even care. When I show her that I got good grades she says, "Yeah, O.K." If I come home and leave my bookbag on the floor and never move it, she doesn't say, "Did you do your homework?"

[Parents need to] see what's wrong with school. Why doesn't the student like going? Fix the problem. No matter what, fix it. Parents need to find out about homework, but don't pressure too much. My mother nags me sometimes. Parents need to find out about why that specific class is the problem.

In some cases, what may actually be parents' cultural and language barriers to helping students were perceived as evidence of parents not caring for the student:

If you want success, support them totally. My parents don't even know the school curriculum, they are Spanish. So I am by myself. I'm the mother and the father. Mine don't know what's going on. It's always been that way.

Why Students Say They Stay in School

Students reported coming to school for their favorite courses (art and math were the most popular). The students' criteria for a favorite course appeared to depend on the amount of self-expression they could achieve in the class, whether it offered practical application, and whether the subject matter came to them easily, giving them a feeling of mastery or being smart.

One of the impediments to keeping these students in school seems to be the school's revolving door detention/suspension policy. Mann (1986) asserted that the most difficult of the high school's clientele "serendipitously solve the institution's problem by disappearing" (314). A student demonstrated familiarity with this practice:

At [the high school] you cut, you get suspended, you cut, you get suspended. Soon you get so far away from the work that you can't pass. Then you are sixteen and you are dropped out. You're not doing nothing, you're failing, there's no point, you drop out.

The nature, enormity, and tension of the problems with which these students cope make it surprising that they actually come to school and that any learning occurs at all. They named the problems that work against their staying in school, such as:

My brother is in jail.

How problems at home affect school work. I don't want to do nothing. I can see.

Whether or not to be in school. I get lazy and don't go. I need someone to attach to, someone my age, older, black.

Boys. I love my baby's father. We went through a lot of fighting. He hit me while I was pregnant. But we are still together. I was mean when I was pregnant. I hit him, I spit on him. He went to jail after the baby was born. He stole a car. He's out and things are much better now. Babies, sex, relationships.

The students' consensus was that there should be more of what we were doing during the study, that is, meeting with students to discuss their feelings and opinions. One student seemed to speak for the others when she said

I like this group. It helps my feelings inside. I don't like to keep feelings inside, otherwise I blow up.

Summary

Research on successful secondary schools cites four characteristics of such schools: shared values, a sense of belonging, a sense of school membership, and academic engagement (Goodlad 1984; Wehlage 1989). Engagement requires intention, concentration, and commitment by students and staff. As with school membership, the degree of engagement is highly dependent on the institution's contribution to the equation that produces learning. Engagement is a result of interaction between the students, teachers, and curriculum.

Above all, the young women in the study sought and appreciated institutional caring and authentic learning. Students in the Alternative Education Program, who had self-selected into the program, seemed to be more secure in the feeling that teachers saw them as persons, made time for them, and in general, cared for them as people. Overall, the students perceived teachers who were attentive, respectful, helpful, and good at listening as being caring and concerned about the students' social and academic welfare.

Racism was a major theme for the black, Latino, and Caucasian students. The students indicated through their responses that they felt bias from adults as well as from the various ethnic groups of students in the school. Female students did not seem to perceive distinctions or discrimination based on gender.

Achieving understanding and reaching constructive solutions requires putting aside "if only" thinking: if only the kids were the way they used to be, if only families were intact, if only there were more money to hire counselors (Paterson, Purky, and Parker 1986). Schools need to help at-risk students interpret the life they are living. Decisions must be made on how schools are going to teach students the competencies they want them to have, the roles the students can play in reconstructing their neighborhoods, and how the students can change their community. Parallel to this must be the reconstructing of the educational delivery system to meet the needs of all students.

REFERENCES

Boger, J. 1989. The school development program's parents' program: An ecological approach to parent involvement. (Unpublished training material)

Ekstrom, R. B., M. E. Goertz, J. M. Pollack, and D. A. Rock. 1986. Who drops out of high school and why? Findings from a national study. *Teachers College Record* 87(3): 356-73.

Goodlad, J. I. 1984. *A place called school: Prospects for the future.* New York: McGraw-Hill.

Mann, D. 1986a. Can we help dropouts? Thinking about doing the undoable. *Teachers College Record* 87(3): 307-23.

———. 1986b. Dropout prevention: Getting serious about programs that work. *NASSP Bulletin* 70(489): 66-73.

Newmann, F. M., and G. G. Wehlage. 1993. Five standards of authentic instruction. *Educational Leadership* 50 (7): 8-12.

Sykes, G. 1990. Fostering teacher professionalism in schools. In *Restructuring schools: The next generation of educational reform,* edited by R. F. Elmore et al., 59-96. San Francisco: Jossey-Bass.

Wehlage, G. G. 1983. *Effective programs for the marginal high school student.* Bloomington, Ill.: Phi Delta Educational Foundation.

Wehlage, G. G., R. A. Rutter, N. Lesko, and R. R. Fernandez. 1989. *Reducing the risk: Schools as communities of support.* Philadelphia: Falmer Press, Taylor and Francis.

Unit 3

Unit Selections

Educationally Disabled 10. **Where to Educate Rachel Holland? Does Least Restrictive Environment Mean No Restrictions?** Todd DeMitchell and Georgia M. Kerns
11. **Why Andy Couldn't Read,** Pat Wingert and Barbara Kantrowitz

Gifted and Talented 12. **Is It Acceleration or Simply Appropriate Instruction for Precocious Youth?** John F. Feldhusen, Lanah Van Winkle, and David A. Ehle
13. **How All Middle-Schoolers Can Be "Gifted,"** Jay A. McIntire

Culturally and Academically Diverse 14. **The Goals and Track Record of Multicultural Education,** Rita Dunn
15. **Multiculturalism at a Crossroads,** John Gallagher
16. **Multiculturalism: Practical Considerations for Curricular Change,** Tony R. Sanchez

Key Points to Consider

❖ What are some issues regarding the Public Law 94-142 provision called "least restrictive environment"? What are the pros and cons of mainstreaming?

❖ Who are the gifted and talented? How can knowledge of their characteristics and learning needs help to provide them with an appropriate education?

❖ What cultural differences exist in our society? How can teacher expectations affect the culturally or academically diverse child? How would multicultural education help teachers deal more effectively with these differences?

❖ What are some of the criticisms concerning multicultural programs?

 **Links**   **www.dushkin.com/online/**

17. **ERIC Clearinghouse on Disabilities and Gifted Education**
http://www.cec.sped.org/gifted/gt-faqs.htm
18. **Global SchoolNet Foundation**
http://www.gsn.org
19. **International Project: Multicultural Pavilion**
http://curry.edschool.virginia.edu/curry/centers/multicultural/papers.html
20. **Multicultural Publishing and Education Council**
http://www.mpec.org
21. **National Attention Deficit Disorder Association**
http://www.add.org
22. **National MultiCultural Institute (NMCI)**
http://www.nmci.org
23. **Scholastic/Kristen Nelson**
http://place.scholastic.com/instructor/curriculum/

These sites are annotated on pages 4 and 5.

The Equal Educational Opportunity Act for All Handicapped Children (Public Law 94-142) gives disabled children the right to an education in the least restrictive environment, due process, and an individualized educational program that is specifically designed to meet their needs. Professionals and parents of exceptional children are responsible for developing and implementing an appropriate educational program for each child. The application of these ideas to classrooms across the nation at first caused great concern among educators and parents. Classroom teachers whose training did not prepare them for working with the exceptional child expressed negative attitudes about mainstreaming. Special resource teachers also expressed concern that mainstreaming would mitigate the effectiveness of special programs for the disabled and would force cuts in services. Parents feared that their children would not receive the special services they required because of governmental red tape and delays in proper diagnosis and placement.

It has been more than two decades since the implementation of P.L. 94-142, which was amended by the Individuals with Disabilities Education Act (IDEA) in 1991, which introduced the term "inclusion." Inclusion tries to ensure that disabled children will be fully integrated within the classroom. Many of the above concerns have been studied by psychologists and educators, and their findings have often influenced policy. For example, research has indicated that mainstreaming is more effective when regular classroom teachers and special resource teachers work cooperatively with disabled children.

The articles concerning the educationally disabled confront many of these issues. Todd DeMitchell and Georgia Kerns, in "Where to Educate Rachel Holland? Does Least Restrictive Environment Mean No Restrictions?" discuss a controversial case involving special education and IDEA. The next essay, by Pat Wingert and Barbara Kantrowitz, looks at children who have been labeled as learning disabled.

Other exceptional children are the gifted and talented. These children are rapid learners who can absorb, organize, and apply concepts more effectively than the average child. They often have IQs of 140 or more and are convergent thinkers (i.e., they give the correct answer to teacher or test questions). Convergent thinkers are usually models of good behavior and academic performance, and they respond to instruction easily; teachers generally value such children and often nominate them for gifted programs. There are other children, however, who do not score well on standardized tests of intelligence because their thinking is more divergent (i.e., they can imagine more than one answer to teacher or test questions). These gifted divergent thinkers may not respond to traditional instruction. They may become bored, respond to questions in unique and disturbing ways, and appear

uncooperative and disruptive. Many teachers do not understand these unconventional thinkers and fail to identify them as gifted. In fact, such children are sometimes labeled as emotionally disturbed or mentally retarded because of the negative impressions they make on their teachers. Because of the differences between these types of students, a great deal of controversy surrounds programs for the gifted. Such programs should enhance the self-esteem of all gifted and talented children, motivate and challenge them, and help them realize their creative potential. The two articles in the subsection on gifted children consider the characteristics of giftedness, and they explain how to identify gifted students and provide them with an appropriate education.

The third subsection of this unit concerns student diversity. Just as labeling may adversely affect the disabled child, it may also affect the child who comes from a minority ethnic background where the language and values are quite different from those of the mainstream culture. The term "disadvantaged" is often used to describe these children, but it is negative, stereotypical, and apt to result in a self-fulfilling prophecy whereby teachers perceive such children as incapable of learning. Teachers should provide academically and culturally diverse children with well-rounded experiences that expose them to aspects of American life and language not available to them at home or in their neighborhoods. Rita Dunn, in "The Goals and Track Record of Multicultural Education," takes issue with some aspects of multicultural programs, while other articles in this section address these individual differences and suggest strategies for teaching these diverse children.

Where to Educate Rachel Holland?
Does Least Restrictive Environment Mean No Restrictions?

TODD DeMITCHELL and GEORGIA M. KERNS

What shall be taught? How shall it be taught? Who shall teach our children? Those three critical questions have long been a part of the discussion about the appropriate role of public education in our society. Since the rise of the "one best system" of public education, the questions have been the subject of much dialogue, debate, and policy making. During the last fifty years, a fourth question has been added to those three: *Where* shall the student be educated? Separate but equal schools, desegregated schools, neighborhood schools, special schools, and magnet schools have been some of the answers to that question.

In the past, that matter of where a child will be educated has been a civil rights issue. Recently, a new dimension of the issue has emerged—that is, whether to include students with disabilities in the regular class or to educate them in a more restricted environment. This question has divided the educational community as well as the broader community. As with other important questions, the debate has produced much heat and has seen the various antagonists turn to the courts for support of their positions.

Determining the appropriate educational environment for students with special education needs can be problematic. Consider the case of Rachel Holland, who has a tested IQ of 44. Rachel was born in 1982, and from 1985 to 1989, she attended a variety of special education programs in the Sacramento City School District in California. Dur-

ing these four years, Rachel spent approximately one hour a day in a regular classroom. Her parents constantly tried to convince the school district to increase the amount of time that Rachel spent in regular classrooms. In the fall of 1989, Rachel's parents requested that their daughter be placed full-time in a regular classroom for the 1989–1990 school year. The district rejected their request and instead offered a placement that divided Rachel's time between a regular education class for nonacademic subjects—art, music, lunch, and recess—and a special education class of children with disabilities for all academic subjects. This placement would have required that Rachel move six times a day between the two classes. Rachel's parents rejected the district's proposal and enrolled Rachel in a regular kindergarten class at Shalom School, a private school. Her parents decided to fight the Sacramento City School District's stance on what education was appropriate for Rachel. The odyssey of where to educate Rachel had now truly begun.

Appropriateness and Special Education

The issue of what constitutes an appropriate educational environment for a special education student is not unique to Rachel. How much to include or mainstream a special education student into a regular education classroom as part of a legal mandate is a matter that has received a lot of attention lately. The National Association of State School Boards of Education (1992) has endorsed full inclusion, as has the Council for Exceptional Children (1993). On the other hand, the Learning Disabilities Association of America (1993) has taken a stand against full inclusion, as has the National Joint Committee on Learning Disabilities (1993). The American Federation of

---

Todd DeMitchell is associate chair and an associate professor and Georgia M. Kerns is an assistant professor and program coordinator of special education—both in the Department of Education, University of New Hampshire, Durham.

From *The Clearing House,* January/February 1997, pp. 161-166. Reprinted with permission of the Helen Dwight Reid Educational Foundation. Published by Heldref Publications, 1319 Eighteenth St., NW, Washington, DC 20036-1802. © 1997.

Teachers (Richardson 1994) has called for a moratorium on the placement of children with disabilities in regular classrooms.[1]

The matter of how to appropriately educate students who qualify for special education is of large consequence to education in general. In the 1991–1992 school year, 4,994,169 students received special education services in the regular classroom and via other service modalities. Almost three and one-half million of those students (69.3 percent) spent more than 40 percent of their instructional day in a general classroom while 25.1 percent, just over 1.2 million students, received services in a separate class for at least 60 percent of the day. Only 5.7 percent of the students received special education services in a separate school or other location (Ayers 1994).

Rachel Holland is and was one of these students who is entitled to special education services under the federal Individuals with Disabilities Education Act (IDEA). IDEA is predicated on the assumption that all children are capa-

---

" **T**he mainstreaming issue imposes a difficult burden on the district court. Since Congress has chosen to impose that burden, however, the courts must do their best to fulfill their duty."

---

ble of benefiting from an education. The corollary is that all identified special education children can be educated. As the Rochester School District in New Hampshire found out in the *Timothy W.* (1989) case, a school district does not have the authority to withhold services if it deems a special education student is not capable of benefiting from an education. The court characterized IDEA as a "zero reject" of services for an identified student. In other words, any student who is entitled to special education services must receive an appropriate education. A school district may not impose a litmus test of whether it believes a child can benefit from services as a pre-condition for receiving educational services.

IDEA requires that a state that accepts federal IDEA funds must meet three basic requirements in order to comply with the law. First, it must provide a free appropriate public education (FAPE) to qualified students, and second, to the "maximum extent appropriate," a child with a disability must be educated in the least restrictive environment. This last requirement is often called the mainstreaming mandate. The underlying rationale for this mandate is found in the *Brown v. Board of Education* (1954) desegregation case, which embraced the concept that separate is not equal. A third principle of IDEA is that education is to be individualized and appropriate to the child's needs. This is usually

accomplished through the formulation of an individualized educational plan (IEP). All three of these components are important, but the one that has received the most attention lately, and maybe the least understood of the three, is the least restrictive environment (LRE) requirement. Because the issue of Rachel Holland's education turns on what the appropriate environment for Rachel is, we will explore this requirement in a little more depth.

Least Restrictive Environment: Case Law

The IDEA provides that each state must establish

> procedures to assure that, to the maximum extent appropriate, children with disabilities . . . are educated with children who are not disabled, and that special classes, separate schooling, or other removal of children with disabilities from the regular educational environment occurs only when the nature or severity of the disability is such that education in regular classes with the use of supplementary aids and services cannot be achieved satisfactorily. (20 U.S.C. 1412(5)(B))

Also, IDEA regulations require schools to educate children with disabilities together with children who do not have disabilities (34 C.F.R. Sect. 300.500). According to the regulations, when selecting the least restrictive environment, school authorities should give consideration to any potential harmful effect on the child or on the quality of services that he or she needs; consideration should also be given to any potential harmful effect on the education of the other students (34 C.F.R. Sect. 300.522).

The courts have likewise underscored the importance of the LRE mandate. For example, the Sixth Circuit Court of Appeals in *Roncker v. Walter* (1983) wrote, "We recognize that the mainstreaming issue imposes a difficult burden on the district court. Since Congress has chosen to impose that burden, however, the courts must do their best to fulfill their duty" (1063).

Prior to 1994, two LRE tests were devised by the federal circuit courts of appeal to ascertain if the defendant school district had met its burden of compliance under IDEA. The first LRE test was devised by the Sixth Circuit in *Roncker*, mentioned above. The test looked at three areas:

1. Comparison of educational benefits in the restricted setting with educational benefits in a regular setting
2. Degree to which the student will disrupt the regular classroom
3. Cost of the regular classroom placement

The *Roncker* test was adopted by the Eighth Circuit (*A. W. v. Northwest R-1 School District* (1987)) and the Fourth Circuit (*DeVries v. Fairfax County School Board* (1989)).

A second appellate LRE test was devised by the Fifth Circuit in *Daniel RR v. State Board of Education* (1989). In establishing a new test, the *Daniel RR* court wrote as follows:

> We respectfully decline to follow the Sixth Circuit's analysis. Certainly the *Roncker* test accounts for factors that are

important in any mainstreaming case. We believe, however, that the test necessitates too intrusive an inquiry into educational policy choice that Congress deliberately left to state and local officers. Whether a particular service feasibly can be provided in a regular or special educational setting is an administrative determination that state and local officials are far better qualified and situated than we are to make. (1046)

The court's reluctance to substitute its judgment on policy matters for that of professional educators is consistent with the Supreme Court's decision in *Board of Education v. Rowley* (1982). In that case, the High Court reminded the lower courts not to second-guess school leaders on matters relating to educational methodology.[2]

The Fifth Circuit in *Daniel RR* started its LRE inquiry by examining whether the school district had "taken steps to accommodate the handicapped child in regular education" (1048). The IDEA, according to the court, requires school districts to provide supplementary aids and services and to modify the regular education program when they mainstream children with disabilities. This is similar to the Supreme Court's FAPE decision in *Rowley*, in which the Court stated that an appropriate education is "personalized instruction with sufficient support services that will permit the child to benefit educationally from instruction" (203). Whether education in a regular classroom with the use of supplemental aids and services is appropriate for a given child involves the following three-part inquiry:

1. Will the child receive an educational benefit, both nonacademic and academic, from the regular education placement?
2. What is the child's overall educational experience in the mainstreamed environment, balancing the benefits of regular and special education?
3. What effect does the special education child's presence have on the regular classroom environment and the education that the other students are receiving?

The Fourth, Fifth, Sixth, and Eighth Circuit Courts of Appeal have construed the least restrictive environment requirement of the IDEA as a presumption in favor of mainstreaming or educating children with disabilities in regular classrooms alongside their fellow students. For example, citing the *Daniel RR* test of the Fifth Circuit, the Third Circuit Court of Appeals in *Oberti v. Board of Education of Borough of Clementon School District* (1993) ruled that school districts have an obligation to consider placing students with disabilities in regular education classes with supplementary aids and services before they explore other alternatives. "The court stressed that in passing the IDEA, Congress recognized the fundamental right of students with disabilities to associate with nondisabled peers" (Osborne 1994, 548-49). Therefore, the starting place for any inquiry into what the appropriate least restrictive environment for a student is must be inclusion as a regular member of a regular education classroom; the inquiry can then move to the matter of a more restrictive environment if it is found that that environment is not appropriate.

This view is consistent with the Rehabilitation Act of 1973, which calls for placing a person with a disability in the regular education environment unless it is demonstrated that the education received in the regular classroom along with supplementary aids and services is inadequate. Thus, although the starting point for a least restrictive environment inquiry is the regular classroom, that does not mean that there can be no restrictions on what environment is appropriate for any given student. The decision as to whether a particular child should be educated in a regular classroom setting all of the time, part of the time, or none of the time is predicated on an inquiry into the needs and abilities of the child. The issue is not cast as the best academic setting possible for the student; rather, the presumption of the IDEA's least restrictive environment mandate in favor of mainstreaming is that the student receive a satisfactory education.

For example, in *Greer v. Rome City School District in Georgia* (1991), mainstreaming was emphasized over special education services.[3] This ruling allowed a nine-year-old student with Down's syndrome to be placed in a regular education kindergarten class rather than in the substantially separate special education class recommended by the school district. The court found that the student had made some progress in kindergarten with supplemental aids and services and was not disruptive. *Greer* also added "cost" to the *Daniel RR* test. The Eleventh Circuit in *Greer* stated that "[i]f the cost of educating a handicapped child in a regular classroom is so great that it would significantly impact upon the education of other children in the district, then education in a regular classroom is not appropriate" (697).

However, the LRE mandate does not require school districts to place students in their neighborhood schools, let alone in the regular classroom, in all situations. In *Barnett v. Fairfax County School Board* (1991), the Court of Appeals for the Fourth Circuit upheld a centralized program for high school students with hearing impairments, even though the parents of a student objected to busing their child several miles from home and requested that a similar program be established in the neighborhood school. The Tenth Circuit in *Murray by and through Murray v. Montrose County School District, RE-1J* (1995) held that a twelve year old with multiple disabilities was not entitled to an education in the neighborhood school because the child's needs could not be met in that setting. The court stated that while IDEA "clearly commands schools to include mainstreamed disabled children as much as possible, it says nothing about where, within a school district, that inclusion shall take place" (928-29). A federal district court in Colorado (*Urban v. Jefferson County School District, R-1* (1994)) reached a similar conclusion when it found that "the statutory preference for placement at a neighborhood school is only that—and it does not amount to a mandate" (1568).

Similarly, in Nebraska (*French v. Omaha Public Schools*) and in Pennsylvania (*Johnson v. Lancaster-Lebanon Intermediate Unit 13*) in 1991, two different federal district courts upheld the decision not to mainstream students who had profound hearing loss, severe language delays, and no meaningful communicative interaction with the hearing world. In those two cases, a more restricted environment more appropriately met the needs of the student than the less restrictive environment of the regular education classroom.

In *DeVries v. Fairfax County School Board* (1989), which adopted the *Roncker* test, the mother of a child with autism (who had depressed cognitive functioning, exhibited immature behavior, and needed a predictable environment) contested the school district's proposed placement in a vocational center. The mother wanted the child educated in the local public high school. The district court and the court of appeals found that the vocational center placement was appropriate because the student could not be educated satisfactorily, even with supplementary aids. The disparity

---

A hard-and-fast rule that all children will be mainstreamed irrespective of their needs and abilities . . . runs counter to the IDEA, judicial decisions, and good sense.

---

between the cognitive levels of the seventeen-year-old student and his non-disabled peers was so great that the court was concerned that the student would be simply "monitoring" the regular class.

From a different perspective, the Ninth Circuit in *Clyde K. and Sheila K. v. Puyallup School District* (1994) supported the transfer of a student with a special education designation from a regular classroom setting to a more self-contained setting. The student had Tourette's syndrome and attention-deficit/hyperactivity disorder. The behavior on his part that precipitated an emergency suspension and then placement in the restricted environment (a placement to which the parents initially agreed but one that they later rejected) included vulgar and profane comments, class disruptions, sexual harassment of female students, and the assault of a staff member and students.

The Case of Rachel Holland

We have briefly reviewed several court cases that found that the least restrictive environment for a student was one in which there were restrictions. What we have not looked at in depth is how that determination is made. For that part of the discussion, we return to the case of Rachel Holland to see how it was resolved. Should Rachel be educated in a special education classroom or should there be full inclusion?

The parents of Rachel Holland wanted Rachel to be educated full-time in a regular education classroom; the school district wanted her to be educated in a more restrictive environment. Rachel's parents appealed the Sacramento City School District's placement. Following a two-week hearing, the hearing officer, in a lengthy opinion dated August 15, 1990, found that the school district had failed to make an adequate effort to educate Rachel in a regular education class as required by the IDEA. The hearing officer found that Rachel had benefited from her year of kindergarten in a regular class at Shalom School, that Rachel was motivated to learn, and that she learned from imitation and modeling and thus would benefit from a regular education classroom setting with nondisabled peers. The hearing officer also found that Rachel would not be disruptive and that her IEP was consistent with the first-grade curriculum. The hearing officer ordered the district to place Rachel in a regular education classroom with appropriate support services, including a part-time special education consultant and a part-time classroom aide.

The school district appealed the decision of the hearing officer to the federal district court (*Sacramento City Unified School District v. Holland* (1992)). During the judicial proceedings, Rachel stayed put, completing first grade and half of second grade before the district court handed down its decision. The court fashioned a four-factor balancing test that was adapted from the *Daniel RR* test and the *Greer* addition of cost as a factor. The Rachel Holland court's four factors are (1) the educational benefits of placement in a regular class; (2) the nonacademic benefits of interaction with children who were not disabled; (3) the effect that Rachel had on the teacher and children in the regular class; and (4) the costs of mainstreaming Rachel. The school district lost and appealed the decision (*Sacramento City Unified School District v. Rachel H.* (1994)).

The court of appeals approved the district court's four-part test and adopted it and used it several months later in *Clyde K. and Sheila K. v. Puyallup School District* (1994) mentioned above. The court of appeals also accepted the findings of fact of the district court. The appellate court decided that the school district carried the burden of proof that its placement for Rachel provided mainstreaming to "the maximum extent appropriate."[4] Thus, the school district had to show that the four factors favored its preferred placement. The court found as to the first factor that, if a child's disabilities were so severe that he or she would receive little or no academic benefit from placement in a regular education class, then inclusion may not be appropriate. The experts for both sides provided conflicting evidence. The bulk of the evidence offered by the district related to Rachel's performance on achievement and aptitude tests. By contrast, Rachel's witnesses, who had observed her for extended periods of time in her classroom at Shalom School, testified that she had made significant academic strides there. The court, while acknowledging that the expert witnesses brought their own points of view to the case, gave great weight to the testimony of Rachel's second-grade teacher, Ms. Crone, who was characterized as experienced and skillful (and who was not a partisan to the controversy). Ms. Crone noted that Rachel was in many ways a typical second grader, eager to participate and very motivated. The district did not meet its burden of establishing that Rachel would not receive academic benefits in regular classes and failed to demonstrate that placement in special education classes would provide equal or greater educational benefit to Rachel.

The analysis of the second factor, nonacademic benefits to Rachel, centered on Rachel's attitude, her social communication skills, and her self-confidence. The school district's experts from the state's Diagnostic Center testified that Rachel was making little progress on her IEP goals and was isolated from her classmates. The school district's standardized testing techniques and results in this area were not persuasive to the court, however. The strongest evidence, according to the court, was Rachel's excitement about her class and her improved self-confidence. The district court concluded that the differing evaluations in large part reflected the predisposition of the evaluators. The testimonies of the classroom teacher and Rachel's mother were considered more credible by the district court.

The third factor, effect on the teacher and students, has two aspects. The first is whether there is a detriment to the other students because the child with the disability is disruptive, distracting, or unruly. There was no evidence that Rachel was a discipline problem at Shalom School; in fact, all parties agreed that Rachel was well-behaved. The second aspect is whether the child with special education needs would take up so much of the teacher's time that the other students would suffer from lack of attention. On this point, Rachel's second-grade teacher testified that Rachel's presence did not interfere with her ability to teach the other children in the class.

The fourth and last factor is cost. The court found that the school district had painted an exaggerated picture of what it would cost to educate Rachel in a regular classroom with appropriate services. For example, the district claimed that it would cost over $80,000 to provide schoolwide sensitivity training and another $29,000 for a full-time aide. Yet the district did not establish that such training was necessary. Further, much to the displeasure of the court, the district did not provide a cost comparison between placing Rachel in a special education class with a full-time teacher and two aides and the cost of placing her in a regular class with one part-time aide. The court found that the district did not offer any credible or persuasive evidence that educating Rachel in a regular classroom would be significantly more expensive than educating Rachel in a special classroom. The school district lost on all four factors of the test.

Conclusion

Where best to educate a child has emerged as one of the perennial questions of education. To include or not to include

is an important part of the question. It is a question that must be answered based on the individual needs and abilities of the child. We start from the proposition that the regular classroom is the appropriate setting; if through an analysis, such as Holland's four-factor analysis test, it is found to be inappropriate, then we must restrict the environment accordingly. A hard-and-fast rule that all children will be mainstreamed irrespective of their needs and abilities and the best interests of the other students without doing an analysis runs counter to the IDEA, judicial decisions, and good sense. Similarly, a rule that automatically places a student in a special restricted environment without an analysis is just as wrong. An appropriate analysis is crucial to meeting the needs of our students. The Holland analysis of educational benefit, noneducational benefit, effect on the teacher and other students, and cost is a fair and defensible test to use when we are deciding where best to educate a student.

NOTES

1. While much has been made of the difference between the terms *inclusion* and *mainstreaming*, we will not wade into that battle. The issue we are exploring here is that of determining a starting point for a special education student, regardless of what educators call it. McCarthy (1995) distinguished between the two terms as follows: "*inclusion* [consists of] bringing support services to the child rather than moving the child to a segregated setting to receive services" and *mainstreaming* means "integrating children with disabilities and nonhandicapped children for a portion of the day, usually at times when the regular education program does not have to be significantly modified to accommodate children with disabilities" (824). Yell (1995) asserted that while "mainstreaming refers to placement in regular education, LRE is a principle stating that students with disabilities are to be educated in settings as close to regular classes as appropriate for the child" (193, f.n. 7). Both terms refer to a special education student's receiving a meaningful education in a regular classroom with appropriate support services for as long as practical; therefore, we will use the terms interchangeably to avoid the definitional debate.

2. The Supreme Court in *Rowley* stated the following: "In assuring that the requirements of the Act have been met, courts must be careful to avoid imposing their view of preferable educational methods upon the States" (207).

3. The Eleventh Circuit Court of Appeals (950 F.2d 688 (11th Cir. 1991)) affirmed the judgment of the district court (762 F.Supp. 936 (N.D. Ga. 1990)), but withdrew its opinion (956 F.2d 1025 (11th Cir. 1992)) when the issue of jurisdiction arose. It reinstated its opinion (967 F.2d 470 (11th Cir. 1992)) supporting the district court except for Part 2 on jurisdiction, when the two parties signed a consent decree.

4. The court did not resolve the conflict of which party bears the burden of proof. The Third Circuit has held that the school district has the initial burden of justifying its placement decision at the administrative-hearing level and the trial level if the student challenges the placement (*Oberti v. Board of Education*, 995 F.2d 1204 (3rd Cir. 1993)). Also, the court in *Mavis and Mavis on behalf of Emily Mavis v. Sobol*, 839 F. Supp. 968 (N.D. N.Y. 1994) held that in mainstreaming cases, the burden is on the school district to establish compliance with the LRE mandate. Other courts of appeal have held that the burden of proof at the trial level rests with the party challenging the agency decision (*Roland M. v. Concord School Committee*, 910 F.2d 983 (1st Cir. 1990)). Either way, the school district in the Holland case carried the burden of proof, because the district was challenging the agency decision.

REFERENCES

A. W. v. Northwest R-1 School District, 813 F.2d 158 (8th Cir. 1987).
Ayers, G. E. 1994. Statistical profile of special education in the United

States, 1994. Supplement to *TEACHING Exceptional Children* 26(3): 1-4.

Barnett v. Fairfax County School Board, 927 F.2d 146 (4th Cir. 1991).

Board of Education v. Rowley, 458 U.S. 176 (1982).

Brown v. Board of Education, 47 U.S. 483 (1954).

Clyde K. and Sheila K. v. Puyallup School District, 35 F.3d 1396 (9th Cir. 1994).

Council for Exceptional Children. 1993. *Policy on Inclusive Schools and Community Settings.* Adopted by the Council for Exceptional Children Delegate Assembly, San Antonio (April).

Daniel RR v. State Board of Education, 874 F.2d 1036 (5th Cir. 1989).

DeVries v. Fairfax County School Board, 882 F.2d 876 (4th Cir. 1989).

French v. Omaha Public Schools, 766 F.Supp. 765 (D. Neb. 1991).

Greer v. Rome City School District, 950 F.2d 688 (11th Cir. 1991).

Johnson v. Lancaster-Lebanon Intermediate Unit 13, 757 F. Supp. 606 (E.D. Pa. 1991).

Learning Disabilities Association. 1993. Position paper on full inclusion of all students with learning disabilities in the regular education classroom. *Journal of Learning Disabilities* 26(9): 594.

McCarthy, M. M. 1995. Inclusion of children with disabilities: Is it required?" *95 Ed. Law Rep.* [823] (9 Feb).

Murray by and through Murray v. Montrose County School District, RE-1J, 51 F.3d 921 (10th Cir. 1995).

National Association of State Boards of Education. 1992. *Winners all: A call for inclusive schools.* Washington D.C. : National Association of State Boards of Education.

The National Joint Committee on Learning Disabilities. 1993. A reaction to full inclusion: A reaffirmation of the right of students with learning disabilities to a continuum of services. *Journal of Learning Disabilities* 26(9): 596.

Oberti v. Board of Education of Borough of Clementon School District, 995 F.2d 1204 (3rd Cir. 1993).

Osborne, A. G. Jr. 1994. The IDEA's least restrictive environment mandate: A new era. *88 Ed. Law Rep.* [541] (24 March).

Richardson, J. 1994. A.F.T. says poll shows many oppose 'inclusion'. *Education Week* (3 August): 14.

Roncker v. Walter, 700 F.2d 1058 (6th Cir. 1983).

Sacramento City Unified School District v. Holland, 786 F. Supp. 874 (E.D. Cal. 1992).

Sacramento City Unified School District v. Rachel H., 14 F.3d 1398 (9th Cir. 1994).

Timothy W. v. Rochester School District, 875 F.2d 954, cert. denied, 493 U.S. 983 (1989).

Urban v. Jefferson County School District, R-1, 870 F. Supp. 1558 (D. Colo. 1994).

Yell, M.L. 1995. Judicial review of least restrictive environment disputes under the IDEA. *Illinois School Law Quarterly* 15(4): 176-95.

Millions of kids have been labeled learning disabled. Critics smell a scam here, but researchers say they've begun to unlock the puzzle of bright kids who can't learn.

WHY ANDY COULDN'T READ

By Pat Wingert and Barbara Kantrowitz

ANDREW MERTZ WAS A very unhappy little boy in 1995. Third grade was a disaster, the culmination of a crisis that had been building since he entered kindergarten in suburban Maryland. He couldn't learn to read, and he hated school. "He would throw temper tantrums in the morning because he didn't want to go," recalls his mother, Suzanne. The year before, with much prodding from Suzanne, the school had authorized diagnostic tests for Andrew. The results revealed a host of brain processing problems that explained why he kept mixing up letters and sounds. Andrew's problem now had a label—he was officially classified as learning disabled—and he was legally entitled to help. But school officials, claiming bureaucratic delays, didn't provide any extra services.

In desperation, Suzanne, a trained reading specialist, pulled Andrew out of school and taught him at home for 10

Reading was especially hard for me because the teachers did not teach me what I needed to know about reading.   by: Andrew Mertz months. It was an awesome task. To Andrew, lowercase p, q, b and d all looked like sticks with circles attached. Suzanne taught through touch and sound. She spent hours helping him make letters out of Play-Doh, shaving cream, sand and rice while exaggerating the sounds that went with them. The next year the district agreed to place him in a high-quality program for "gifted" children with learning disabilities. Teachers there continued many of the same practices. Now, at 10, Andrew is still struggling, but at least he can finally read.

Just about every teacher knows students like Andrew Mertz, bright kids who can't learn—no matter how hard they try. They are a painful puzzle to their parents and the subject of an intense educational controversy. In the last few years, researchers have made great strides in identifying and treating learning problems. But the explosion in knowledge has also led to what some say is an epidemic of diagnoses. According to 1996 figures, 2.6 million kids (4.36 percent of the nation's students) were in publicly funded learning-disabilities programs. In 1977, about 800,000 (1.8 percent of the student body) had been diagnosed. And this may only be the beginning. In an astonishing estimate, some researchers now say that as many as 20 percent of schoolchildren may have a neurological deficit, ranging from mild to severe, that makes it hard for them to read and write.

That's a lot of kids—and trying to help them is expensive. Largely as a result of lobbying by parents, federal law now mandates a "free and appropriate education" for the learning disabled; districts even have to pay tuition at private schools if they can't provide appropriate services. Teachers and clinicians have devised a wide range of techniques—from having kids write letters in sandboxes to using tape recorders, computers and other special equipment—to combat specific disabilities. The price tag: $8.12 billion last year, according to the Center for Special Education Finance.

This revolution has bred a new wave of critics who sneer at the learning-disabilities "epidemic." Some say many students labeled learning disabled are just lazy and looking for an easy way out. Other critics blame bad teaching for kids' reading problems and claim that school officials are inflating the number of disabled kids in order to wrest more money from the government. Still others contend that overly pushy parents—stereotypical hyperambitious Yuppie strivers—are behind the dramatic increase in the numbers of learning-disabled students. These parents, the critics say, need a scientific excuse to explain why Jason or Jennifer isn't Harvard med-school material. The skeptics include prominent educators, like Boston University president Jon Westling, who was sued by students after he clamped down on accommodations for learning-disabled students.

But to parents whose children are struggling in school, the "epidemic" is real and heartbreaking. Learning disorders are often hard to accept because they afflict kids who appear perfectly healthy. It's easy to grasp the problems encountered by a child with a physical incapacity, such as blindness or paralysis. Yale University pediatrician and neuroscientist Sally Shaywitz, who studies the complex of reading problems called dyslexia, says a learning problem is a "hidden disability." In fact, learning-disabled kids often display talent in other areas—perhaps art or science—while failing in one or more of the three R's.

Tammy Hollingsworth of suburban Dallas was optimistic when Joey, the oldest of her four children, entered kindergarten 15 years ago. Teachers had told her the boy was a genius. "His IQ was over 150 and he had a photographic memory," she recalls. But as he grew older and schoolwork became harder, he ran into serious problems. "Any assignment that required a transfer from the brain to paper, forget it. He couldn't do it." Over the years, teachers told Hollingsworth that Joey was just lazy and a discipline problem. He was 15 years old before he was tested for learning disabilities. Although the results showed he had real problems expressing his thoughts in writing (a disorder technically known as dysgraphia), it was too late to save his school career. Years of frustration and failure had taken their toll, and he dropped out at 17. Joey eventually earned a high-school-equivalency diploma; he is now enrolled in a local police academy.

If Joey were entering kindergarten today, he might have a better chance. The term "learning disabilities" is relatively new. It was introduced in 1963, when parents and educators from around the country organized the nonprofit group now known as the Learning Disabilities Association. Until then, children with learning problems were generally classified as "perceptually handicapped," "brain injured" or "neurologically impaired." Many were turned away from public schools as uneducable, and if they couldn't afford private-school tuition, they just stayed home; some were even labeled mentally retarded. One advantage of combining the old diagnoses under a single new term was that it enabled educators to distinguish between children with below-average IQs (who were then put into classes for the mentally retarded) and kids of average or above-average intelligence who had trouble learning in specific areas but otherwise functioned normally.

More than three decades later, there is still no universal agreement about how to classify the constellation of problems that fall under this umbrella diagnosis. Medical doctors tend to accentuate differences in genetics, as well as brain organization and function. Psychologists focus on dysfunctions in areas like perception, processing, memory and attention. Teachers zero in on the specific areas of academic difficulty.

But researchers are getting closer to some concrete answers. The most tantalizing clues are coming from brain research that is still in the early stages, which is very promising. Using state-of-the-art functional magnetic resonance imaging (fMRI)—machines that take pictures of the brain in action—scientists are investigating disruptions in specific neurosystems. And they're learning even more from examining children and adults with brain injuries, says Martha Bridge Denckla, a neuropsychologist with the Kennedy Krieger Institute in Baltimore. "Some of these traumatic brain cases simulate the exact picture we see all the time in learning-disabled cases where we don't know the cause," Denckla says. "These experiences make me very confident that what is causing LD affects the brain." But there's a long way to go. It was only four years ago that Shaywitz's team took one of the first fMRI pictures of a brain caught in the act of reading.

This is the most critical area of research because the most common learning disabilities relate to language—reading, writing and spelling. Some children have trouble comprehending words or letters in sequence. Others read words but don't understand the content. Still others are dyslexics, children and adults who have trouble naming letters and sounding out words, despite the fact that they often have large vocabularies and reason well.

Because dyslexia seems to run in families, scientists think that it is often inherited. For years, researchers suspected it was caused by vision problems, and a stereotype developed that dyslexics commonly reverse letters (reading d's as b's, for example). Today, researchers like Yale's Shaywitz say dyslexics are not more likely to reverse letters than anyone else. Instead, Shaywitz and other researchers theorize that dyslexia is linked to a glitch in the brain's wiring that interferes with the ability to translate a written word into units of sound, of phonemes. Scientists have found that dyslexics often cannot recognize and break down spoken words into their phonetic segments or slice off one phoneme from a word—for example, they cannot figure out that "bat" without the b is "at." Technically, this problem is known as a "phonological awareness" deficit.

Researchers have identified four distinct steps in learning to read; breakdowns anywhere in this process can explain severe reading problems. G. Reid Lyon, acting chief of the child-development and behavior branch of the National Institutes of Child and Human Development, says that reading for all children begins with phonological awareness. Combinations of just 44 phonemes produce every English word. "Children who will be good readers," Lyon says, "just have a knack for understanding that words are made up of different sounds before they learn anything about the alphabet." The next step is linking these sounds with specific letters. This can be confusing because most letters—in English and many other languages—can have more than one sound. The reading-instruction methods known as linguistics (sound to letters) and phonics (letters to sound) focus on this part of the process by having kids sound out words. The third step, Lyon says, is for a child to become a fast reader—to make the association between symbol and sound virtually automatic so that the child can move on to the final step, concentrating on the meaning of the words. (Researchers around the country are testing ways to put these findings into reading programs for all kids, not just learning-disabled children.)

Some children also have spoken-language problems, which are often ignored because parents are told kids will "grow out of it." Kids with this disorder might mispronounce words because they're not processing sounds correctly. For example, they might call animals "aminals." They may also confuse specific sounds (thumb could become "fum") well after their peers are speaking clearly. School is a frustrating experience because they can't demonstrate what they know. They may, for example, recognize colors but not be able to name them. And their school troubles don't stop there. Studies indicate that preschoolers with oral-language problems often have difficulty later learning to read and write.

ANOTHER GROUP OF LEARNING disorders revolves around difficulties in learning to compute or reason mathematically. In severe cases, these problems are called dyscalculia. Sometimes math difficulties appear without any other learning problems. At other times, these are the same children who have difficulty learning to speak and read. Janet Lerner, professor of education at Northeastern Illinois University and the author of the classic textbook for teachers of learning-disabled children, says some kids with math disabilities may suffer from "visual motor" problems that may make it difficult for them to count objects without physically touching them. They also have trouble adding one group of objects to another without counting them out, one by one. Others may have "visual perception" problems that, for example, render them unable to see a triangle as anything but three unrelated lines. They find it very arduous to copy letters and numbers and align numbers properly for computation.

Complicating the picture is the fact that many learning-disabled children also have a variety of motor, social, memory, organizational and attention problems that affect their schoolwork, such as attention deficit disorder (ADD). Researchers estimate that up to 30 percent of children with learning disabilities may have ADD, which makes it even harder for them to focus. Children humiliated by their inability to overcome their learning problems also tend to develop behavioral and emotional disorders. Kids with learning problems are twice as likely to drop out of school; a disturbingly high number end up with criminal records.

Even after they learn to read, write and add, many learning-disabled people don't find these basic skills easy. That's why educators believe early intervention is critical. "If we do not identify children early, by the end of second grade, the majority of them will have difficulty reading for the rest of their lives," says Lyon. "What we're finding is that there are sensitive periods when children can learn to read more easily, just like there are windows when children learn foreign language easier."

In many clinics and hospitals around the country, such as Evanston Northwestern Healthcare's Evanston Hospital north of Chicago, babies and toddlers who had a traumatic birth are regularly checked for signs of developmental delays—significant lags in reaching the milestones of smiling, sitting, walking and talking. "We know problems at birth, including prematurity, increase the chances of developing learning problems later in childhood," says Joanne Bregman, director of Evanston's child-development clinic. "All the research says that the first three years of life are critical. The sooner a problem is identified, the sooner it can be treated and the better the outcome is likely to be." Early intervention usually consists of speech, occupational or physical therapy. Every state has outreach programs that funnel children exhibiting significant delays in development into specialized public preschools.

A few nursery schools formally screen all children for early signs of learning problems. In Washington, D.C., Lynn A. Balzer-Martin, a pediatric occupational therapist, begins her multipart screening with a thorough questionnaire to parents and teachers about a child's health history, behavior and activities. Then she observes the child's movements, taking note of balance, positioning and coordination. Brain research has shown that the way a child

The Language of Learning Disability

The parents of a child with a learning disability may be bombarded with Greek-rooted words that may confuse rather than clarify. Disabilities don't fit into neat categories; they are more likely to be a cocktail of disability types and associated problems.

Types of learning disabilities

Dyslexia Unusual difficulty sounding out letters and confusing words that sound similar. The most common form of disability.

Treatment: The latest techniques help students distinguish the different sounds that make up language and teach through touch (e.g., writing letters in sand). Word processors with spell-checking and speech-recognition software can help.

Dysgraphia Difficulty expressing thoughts on paper and with the act of writing itself. Characterized by problems gripping a pencil and unreadable penmanship.

Treatment: Students learn to describe thoughts orally as a precursor to writing. Paper with raised lines helps keep the hand aligned, and special pencil grips can ease hand strain. Children can benefit from learning the six or seven pencil strokes that combine to form roman letters.

Dyscalculia Incomprehension of simple mathematical functions. Often a child won't perceive shapes and will confuse arithmetic symbols.

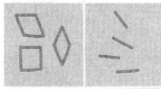

Shapes made up of four lines are seen just as four lines

Treatment: Having available in the classroom objects that a child can manipulate in order to add or subtract physically rather than on paper. Older students can perform calculations more easily by counting along a number line.

Associated problems

Dyspraxia (apraxia) Difficulty performing complex movements, including muscle motions needed for talking.

Treatment: For speech, facial exercises such as chewing gum or sucking and blowing through a straw. For other problems, kids can learn movement control through routine tasks like baking cookies.

moves or follows instruction can be an indicator of how well he processes information.

Someday, intervention may begin even earlier. Geneticists are working on procedures to identify inherited learning disorders. John DeFries, director of the Institute of Behavioral Genetics at the University of Colorado, says that researchers now believe that although as many as 20 genes may be involved in the reading process, just two or three "may account for most of the variation in reading difficulty that we see." If scientists can identify these genes, they could someday screen kids to determine which are at risk, and start working with them before they start to flounder.

At the moment, early intervention and diagnosis is the exception rather than the rule. Most children with learning disabilities don't get help until they're well along in school—usually between the ages of 9 and 14. That's because, under the law, funding follows failure. Children who are officially labeled learning disabled are eligible for special aid. But to win that, all 50 states and the federal government require proof of school problems.

Of course, that doesn't mean every child who is having trouble in school is learning disabled. Most states require a discrepancy between a child's actual achievement levels and his intellectual potential, usually determined by some type of IQ test. And that's another reason learning disabilities have become so controversial. Many critics of IQ tests believe they are culturally biased and underestimate the intellectual potential of poor and minority children. "Black kids have to be more severely disabled to be called LD," says Esther Minskoff of James Madison University. "White kids are picked up earlier."

PUBLIC AND PRIVATE SCHOOLS around the country have developed programs for learning-disabled kids; the quality varies widely. At the Lab School of Washington, a private school with 285 students in kindergarten through 12th grade, founder and director Sally Smith uses the arts—especially music, dance, painting, drama and filmmaking—to teach academic skills. She has also created clubs based on different time periods to help develop social skills as well as provide a lively history curriculum. Kids start out as cavemen and move through Egypt, the Middle Ages and the Renaissance up to modern times. "It's very experiential, very hands-on," Smith says. "We want to build on their strengths." (One of the authors of this article, Washington correspondent Pat Wingert, sends a child to the Lab School.)

Public-school programs generally have fewer resources, but teachers still try to emphasize individual attention. At Eagle Rock Elementary School in suburban Los Angeles, Joyce Jerome and two aides preside over a class of 14 learning-disabled students in grades four to six. This year's theme is the ocean, and Jerome has decorated a wall with fishing nets, colorful seashells and pictures of whales and other sea life.

One recent morning, five students—all of whom read well below their grade level—were gathered around a half-moon desk trying to read the word "enormous." Finally, one child blurted out "eee nor moose" and smiled. He won a "ticket," which can be redeemed for prizes like colored pencils and carnival-type toys in the classroom "store."

Another student, an 11-year-old girl, gets the word "nothing." She is told to break it into syllables and does so after some obvious stress. Finally, she says two words: "no thing." Jerome prompts her. "What is like no thing? What sounds like no thing?" The girl rubs her forehead with her palm. "I don't know," she says, exasperated. "Why are these words so complicated?"

Some critics of the idea of learning disabilities claim that better instruction could eliminate the problem altogether. In the last few years, much of the controversy over these problems has become entwined with the often ferocious dispute over two alternate methods of teaching reading: phonics and "whole language," which is based on children's grasping the meaning of a word from its context in a story. While a pure whole-language approach works well for some kids, others—especially those with learning disabilities—struggle to read without help in phonics.

A few researchers have even suggested that whole language is the main reason for the huge increase in the number of kids diagnosed as disabled—fueling the idea that learning disabilities is a phony diagnosis, perhaps contrived to compensate for what are really teaching disabilities. In her new book, "Why Our Children Can't Read," Diane McGuinness, a Florida psychologist, maintains that all children need direct instruction in decoding words and that the proportion of children labeled learning disabled would drop if whole-language programs were replaced with those that emphasize phonological awareness and linguistics.

Learning disabilities are hard to understand, and so is the law that attempts to

---

Sounds cannot be distinguished, changing the meaning of words

Auditory discrimination Trouble distinguishing similar sounds ("pig" and "big") or confusing the sequence of heard or spoken sounds ("ephelant").

Treatment: Speech therapists and computer programs often use strategies like repetition and exaggerating the pronunciation of each letter so that children will be better able to distinguish the sounds.

Attention deficit disorder Extreme hyperactivity and distractibility. Many children with learning disabilities suffer from ADD as well.

Treatment: Mild stimulants like Ritalin, but some kids respond poorly to medication. Behavior-modification techniques, such as motivating students to stay seated during a story reading, have been shown to help.

Dysnomia The inability to recall the names or words for common objects.

Treatment: Direct instruction by a speech or language therapist, who engages the child in word games and assigns large amounts of verbal practice.

Visual perception The inability to differentiate between foreground and background, as well as similar-looking numbers, letters, shapes, objects and symbols. Problems may include habitually skipping over lines of text.

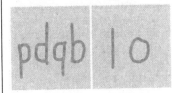

Each of the letters at left is perceived as a stick and a circle

Treatment: Direct, one-on-one instruction pointing out the child's mistakes and the visual cues they have overlooked.

SOURCE: "LEARNING DISABILITIES" BY JANET LERNER

A Parents' Guide to Learning Disabilities

Delays in normal development may be an early warning that your child has a learning disability—or a sign of a late bloomer. Here, a thumbnail guide to some common symptoms and the process of getting help:

1 Identification

The signs of learning disability vary with age. A parent or teacher of a child who consistently lags behind his or her peers and exhibits several of the following signs may consider an evaluation:

Preschool
- Starts talking later than other kids
- Has pronunciation problems
- Has slow vocabulary growth, is often unable to find the right word
- Has trouble learning numbers, the alphabet, days of the week

- Has difficulty rhyming words
- Is extremely restless and distractible
- Has trouble interacting with peers
- Displays a poor ability to follow directions or routines
- Avoids puzzles, drawing and cutting

Kindergarten through fourth grade
- Has a slow recall of facts
- Makes consistent reading and spelling errors, including letter reversals (b/d), inversions (m/w), transpositions (felt/left) and substitutions (house/home)

- Is slow to learn the connection between letters and sounds
- Transposes number sequences and confuses arithmetic signs (+,-,×,/,=)
- Is slow to learn new skills, relies heavily on memorization
- Is impulsive and lacks basic planning skills
- Has difficulty following directions or routines
- Has an unstable pencil grip
- Has trouble learning about time

2 Assessment

The parent or teacher takes the child to a school counselor or a pediatrician:

Physiological problems—like poor eyesight and hearing, as well as certain muscular diseases—can make normal children seem learning disabled. Psychological contributors, such as home life and emotional stability, should also be considered.

3 Testing

A referral is made to have the child evaluated by specialists:

Parents have the right to have their child evaluated after the age of 3, and public schools are obligated to arrange it. A psychologist, a social worker, a teacher, and a physician evaluate the student. Reading-comprehension, memory and spatial-relation tests help form a diagnosis.

4 Classification

The child is determined to be "learning disabled":

Some states require a discrepancy between a student's IQ and academic performance. Others need proof of dysfunction in things like perception and memory. Within 30 days of classification, children who qualify receive an individualized learning schedule.

5 Options/alternatives

By law, the child is entitled to an appropriate education:

A child's instruction must be continually monitored by his or her parents. If they are unsatisfied, they can lobby to change the curriculum or demand a transfer to another school—even a private one, paid at public expense.

RESEARCH BY BILL VOURVOULIAS. SOURCE: NAT'L CENTER FOR LEARNING DISABILITIES

---

help struggling kids. If a family can't work through the bureaucratic maze, a child can languish. Such was the case with Jennie Harvey. At 15, she's finally learning to read at the Cove School in suburban Chicago. Because she had severe speech problems, Jennie was enrolled in special-ed classes at the age of 3. Although she was promoted annually, by the seventh grade she still wasn't reading at a first-grade level. Her parents accepted Jennie's teachers' assessment that they were doing all they could. But three years ago they hired Rose Pech, a retired special-education teacher turned

tutor, who diagnosed a series of problems that required much more specialized instruction than Jennie had been receiving. With Pech's help, Jennie was admitted to Cove, a private school for severely learning-disabled children (the state pays the $16,000 annual tuition because the district cannot provide the same services). Jennie's story is an extreme example of lost potential; because she's learning to read so late, her teachers doubt that she can ever really catch up.

Scientists want to spare other children a similar fate. And parents like Suzanne

Mertz are learning how to make the system work for their kids. When her husband was recently transferred to Pennsylvania, she went school-shopping for Andrew before deciding which town to live in. She finally settled on Great Valley, which has an excellent learning-disabilities program. Her advice to other parents? "You can advocate for your child better than anyone," she says. "You know them best." Raising a child with learning disabilities will always be a long, hard road—but now, at least, there's reason to hope.

With TARA WEINGARTEN *in Los Angeles*

Is It Acceleration or Simply Appropriate Instruction for Precocious Youth?

John F. Feldhusen
Lanah Van Winkle
David A. Ehle

How do we arrange classroom learning experiences at a level, pace, and depth appropriate to individual students' levels of precocity and need?

How do we assess students' current levels of achievement and readiness for new material?

How do we arrange instructional conditions to place students with a teacher and curriculum material appropriate to their needs?

These questions are important to many teachers of students with special gifts and talents. Without such efforts, precocious students are often bored in school (Feldhusen & Kroll, 1991).

Robert Slavin (1990) stated the case well: "I would certainly be opposed to any plan that would `hold back' gifted children from achieving as much as they are able to accomplish" (p. 3). Yet, such is surely the school experience of many precocious youth much of the time (Westberg, Archambault, Dobyns, & Salvin, 1991). Slavin suggested that gifted programs "are most justifiable when the content of the special program represents true acceleration. Research generally does not find achievement benefits of enrichment programs" (p. 4).

We recently spoke with a junior high school student about the school reform movement. When we asked what she saw as the most serious problem with American schools today, she responded, "They won't let us learn." We thought she misunderstood the question—but as she went on, her point was clear:

> What I mean is, they seem to think they have to keep us all together all the time. That means in the subjects I'm good at I can't learn more because I'm always waiting for others to catch up. I guess if I get too far ahead I'll be doing the next year's work, but I can't understand what's wrong with that if that's what I'm ready for.

For this student it seemed so simple, and she had clearly given it much thought while she was doing all that waiting. As we reflected on her words of wisdom, two ideas emerged: She seems to be calling for "acceleration" as it is often conceptualized; and yet, the underlying philosophy that her comments reveal is not at all what we have traditionally called "acceleration."

Assessment Is Key

Effective teaching involves assessing each students' status in the curriculum sequence and posing new learning tasks slightly beyond the level already mastered (Feldhusen & Klausmeier, 1959). Good teachers have been addressing individual ability differences in this manner in their classrooms for years. In our traditional age-graded system, teachers carry a tremendous burden in planning to meet the needs of all students, one that will not lighten as long as we insist on equating "academic peer" and "age." Yet this effort becomes increasingly difficult when students vary markedly from the norm. If Julie has mastered concepts *A* and *B*, and our goal is to challenge her at a level slightly exceeding the level already mastered, does it not make sense that we should allow her to proceed to concept *C*?

What Is Acceleration?

Now comes that word—*acceleration*. Will we have to accelerate Julie before she can go on to concept *C*? Contrary to common perception, we do not have to *do* anything to Julie before she can learn advanced concepts. Julie is fine just being her own academic self, and we are here to serve her. There's nothing "accelerative" about meeting Julie's needs. If we do not meet her needs, in a sense we "decelerate" her: We hinder her learning. We agree with David Elkind (1988):

> Promotion of intellectually gifted children is simply another way of attempting to match the curriculum to the child's abilities, not to accelerate those abilities. Accordingly, the promotion of intellectually gifted children in no way contradicts the accepted view of . . . the negative effects of hurrying. Indeed, the positive effects of promoting intellectually gifted children provide additional evidence for the benefits of developmentally appropriate curricula. (p. 2)

Acceleration is a misnomer; the process is really one of bringing talented youth up to a level of instruction commensurate with their achievement levels and *readiness* so that they are properly challenged to learn the new material (Feldhusen, 1989).

Curricular Context of Acceleration

We often forget the traditional meaning of the words *acceleration* and *enrichment* when we apply them in education. Both "accelerated" and "enriched" only have meaning when used to compare two different states or situations. When we use acceleration and enrichment in the traditional educational sense, our usual reference point is the standard school curriculum. Jane is in *third* grade but is working on *fifth*-grade math; she is "accelerated" in math. Carl is planning an exploration of Mars; he is doing an "enrichment" activity in science. Adoption of a specific curriculum as a reference point, however, blurs the distinction between acceleration and enrichment. If Carl is in the second-grade enrichment program, but the space exploration activity is done by all sixth-grade students, is he doing an enrichment activity, or has he been accelerated to the sixth-grade level? Most third-grade students are learning simple single-digit multiplication; if Jane is working on three-digit multiplication, is she not doing an enrichment activity in math?

The examples of both enrichment and acceleration programs that are typically given, demonstrate the lack of a precise meaning of these concepts and the importance of relating these terms to a curriculum. The most popular subject for acceleration is math, while language arts or social studies is usually the focus of enrichment programs. It is easier to identify math instruction as being accelerated, since most students learn math concepts in a fairly structured order. On the other hand, most language arts and social studies programs are referred to as enrichment programs. They are often seen as *extended* rather than *advanced* curriculum experiences.

A Call for New Terminology

Where does this leave us? We can either change conceptions of acceleration and enrichment to reflect their commonalities and relativism, or find new terminology to better reflect the concepts involved and eliminate the confusion. Rather than talking about a program that is accelerated or enriched, why not talk about a program that focuses on *higher-level constructs*, greater appreciation of the underlying knowledge structure of a discipline, or mastery of a larger knowledge base in and associated with a field of study? These are the characteristics that differentiate an *expert* in a field from a *novice* (Johnson, Kochevar, & Zualkerman, 1992). This type of program could involve enrichment *and* acceleration; it transcends both terms to strike at the heart of the cognitive goals of gifted education. Such a program brings the content of the curriculum up to the level of the child.

If we accept the premise that gifted and talented students are precocious, doesn't it make sense to challenge them to move in the direction of more advanced learners? Coupled with strong services to meet the social and emotional needs of bright students, *a program to develop the leaders of tomorrow would result*. But what does all this mean in action in a school situation?

Providing Higher-Level Learning Opportunities

Practically, how do we go about bringing the content of the school up to the level

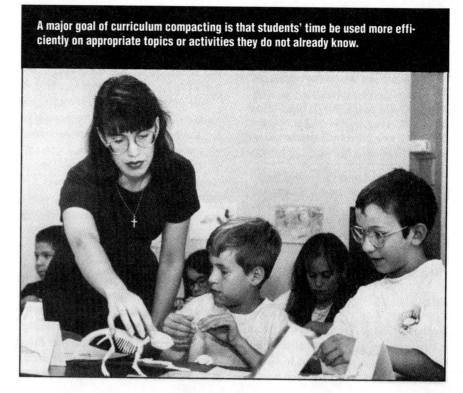

A major goal of curriculum compacting is that students' time be used more efficiently on appropriate topics or activities they do not already know.

The first step in the Diagnostic Testing followed by Prescriptive Instruction (DT-PI) model is to determine the students' current level of knowledge through appropriate tests.

of the child? First, we should not assume that a child does not know what we have not yet taught. A study by the Educational Products Information Exchange Institute (1980-81), a nonprofit educational consumer agency, revealed that 60% of the fourth graders in some of the school districts studied scored 80% or higher on a test of the content of their math texts *before* they had opened their books in September. Similar findings were reported for content tests on 4th- and 10th-grade science texts and 10th-grade social studies texts (Renzulli & Reis, 1986). Since textbooks have continued to drop in levels of difficulty over the past 10-15 years, one would not expect these percentages to be any lower today for our highly able students. We need a way to determine the exact level at which to begin appropriate instruction.

Diagnostic Testing-Prescriptive Instruction

Hoping to develop a teaching approach that would accommodate students' differing levels of knowledge as well as their rates of learning, Stanley (1978) originated the Diagnostic Testing followed by Prescriptive Instruction (DT-PI) model. Benbow (1986) developed the procedure further for use in educational programs for gifted youth. Described in simple terms, the DT-PI model has four steps:

1. Determine students' current level of knowledge through appropriate tests.

2. Identify areas of weakness by analyzing items missed on the tests.

3. Instruct the students in those areas of weakness and allow them to show mastery on a second form of the test.

4. Proceed to the next higher level and repeat Steps 1-3.

The DT-PI model of instruction has been the approach used in the Study of Mathematically Precocious Youth (SMPY) in the summer programs at The Johns Hopkins University since 1971. SMPY's longitudinal study has shown the effectiveness of such acceleration for talented youth. SMPY's most salient finding in working with 85,000 young gifted students over a 13-year period is that *school systems need far more curricular flexibility* (Benbow, 1986). Swiatek and Beubow (1991) have also conducted a 10-year follow-up of fast-paced mathematics classes and found higher achievement in classes using DT-PI methods.

Curriculum Compacting

Another technique that can be used to bring the content up to the level of the child is curriculum compacting (Reis, 1995), a system designed to adapt the regular curriculum to meet the needs of above-average students by either eliminating work that has been mastered pre-

viously or streamlining work that may be mastered at a pace commensurate with the student's ability. A major goal of curriculum compacting is that students' time be used more efficiently on appropriate topics or activities rather than completing tasks they already know. Both DP-TI and curriculum compacting strive for proficiency in the basic curriculum and then continue student learning at an appropriate level for which they are ready. The two approaches differ in that *curriculum compacting focuses on a challenging environment within the context of grade-level curriculum*, while the philosophy behind DP-TI is clearly to enable students to advance at their own pace through the scope and sequence of the curriculum.

The Bottom Line

Most teachers want their students to enjoy learning, to enjoy school, and most of all, to accomplish as much as they are capable. When their students are bored much of the school day, frustrated by repeating material they already know, and are not given the opportunity to accomplish nearly what they could, good teachers are troubled.

Each child has the right to learn new material commensurate with his or her ability and knowledge, even if other students who are ready for that material are 3 years older; age really makes no difference. If acceleration is not an accurate term, is there one? Although we are not at all convinced that we must have a word, there are some terms that appear more philosophically sound. In a recent review, Benbow (1991) made the following suggestions: "curricular flexibility," "flexible pacing," and "developmental placement."

The bottom line is that *our educational programs must respond to the abilities and readiness of individual children*. It is a sad irony that a student could say of those responsible for her education, "They won't let me learn." Let's try to loosen our dependence on the lingo of "acceleration" and "enrichment" and simply go about the business of meeting students' needs, whatever that may require. Curricular and instructional flexibility are the prerequisites. Adapting instruction to individual readiness and need is the answer.

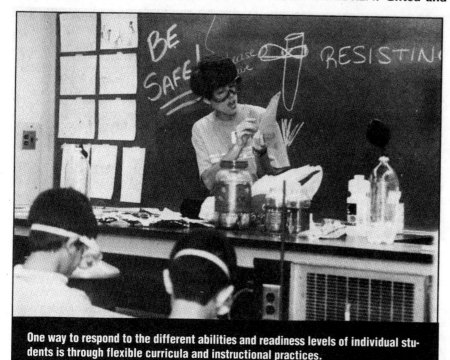

One way to respond to the different abilities and readiness levels of individual students is through flexible curricula and instructional practices.

References

Benbow, C. P. (1986). SMPY's model for teaching mathematically precocious students. In J. S. Renzulli (Ed.), *Systems and models for developing programs for the gifted and talented* (pp. 1-26). Mansfield Center, CT: Creative Learning Press, Inc.

Benbow, C. P. (1991). Meeting the needs of gifted students through use of acceleration. In M. C. Wang, M. C. Reynolds, & H. J. Walberg (Eds.), *Handbook of special education: Research and practice: Vol. 4. Emerging Programs* (pp. 23-36). New York: Pergamon Press.

Educational Products Information Exchange Institute. (1980-81). *Educational research and development report*, 3, 4.

Elkind, D. (1988). Acceleration. *Young Children, 43*(4), 2.

Feldhusen, J. F. (1989). Synthesis of research on gifted youths. *Educational Leadership, 46*(6), 6-11.

Feldhusen, J. F., & Klausmeier, H. J. (1959). Achievement in counting and addition. *The Elementary School Journal, 59*, 388-393.

Feldhusen, J. F., & Kroll, M. D. (1991). Boredom or challenge for the academically talented. *Gifted Education International, 7*(2), 80-81.

Johnson, P. E., Kochevar, L. K., & Zualkerman, I. A. (1992). Expertise and fit: Aspects of cognition. In H. L. Pick, P. Van Den Broek, & D. C. Knill (Eds.), *Cognition: Conceptual and methodological issues* (pp. 305-331).

Washington, DC: American Psychological Association.

Reis, Sally M. (1995). *Curriculum compacting communicator, 28*(2), 1, 27-32. Mansfield Center, CT: Creative Learning Press, Inc.

Renzulli, J. S., & Reis, S. M. (1986). The enrichment triad/revolving door model: A schoolwide plan for the development of creative productivity. In J. S. Renzulli (Ed.), *Systems and models for developing programs for the gifted and talented* (pp. 216-266). Mansfield Center, CT: Creative Learning Press, Inc.

Swiatek, M. A., & Beubow, C. P. (1991). A ten-year longitudinal follow-up of participants in a fast-paced mathematics course. *Journal for Research in Mathematics Education, 22*, 138-150.

Slavin, R. E. (1990). Ability grouping, cooperative learning and the gifted. *Journal for the Education of the Gifted, 14*(1), 3-9.

Stanley, J. C. (1978). SMPY's DT-PI model: Diagnostic testing followed by prescriptive instruction. *Intellectually Talented Youth Bulletin, 4*(10), 7-8.

Westberg, K. L., Archambault, F. X., Dobyns, S. M., & Salvin, T. J. (1991). *The classroom practices observation study.* (Technical Report). Storrs, CT: The National Research Center on the Gifted and Talented.

John F. Feldhusen, Director, Gifted Education Resource Institute; *Lanah Van Winkle*, Assistant Coordinator, Shared Information Services; *David A. Ehle*, Coordinator, Gifted Education Resource Institute, Summer Residential Programs, Purdue University, West Lafayette, Indiana.

Address correspondence to John F. Feldhusen, Purdue University, 1446 Liberal Arts/Education Building, West Lafayette, IN 47907-1446 (e-mail: feldhuse@vm.cc.purdue.edu).

How All Middle-Schoolers Can Be "Gifted"

By Jay A. McIntire
From *NASSP Bulletin*

AS much as we would like students not to compare themselves based on school success, grades, or other measures of achievement, they must do so to fulfill their identity formation task. They will compare themselves on any criterion that occurs to them. Instead of fighting this comparison, we should take advantage of it.

Middle-level schools, by expanding the use of certain positive aspects frequently associated with gifted education programs, can greatly increase the positive identity messages students receive. This increases the chances for students to develop identities with positive feelings and self-perceptions with respect to school and their ability to succeed in school.

Students who participate in gifted education programs receive several messages that allow them to affiliate and discriminate themselves in ways that lead to an identity based on positive traits. Perhaps the most powerful message is that the student can achieve success in school and through school. Anything educators do to provide such messages to the maximum number of students should be encouraged.

Positive influences of gifted education participation on identity formation include the following: sets students apart from peers (distinction); provides group membership (affiliation); provides positive identity message; may prove self-fulfilling; may result in an improved match between instructional level and instruction received.

Unfortunately, participation in gifted education can also result in identity messages that are confusing or might even undermine healthy identity formation. The same distinction from peers that may be positive for some can be negative for others. If the distinction is not only from most peers, but from all one's friends from various group affiliations, identification of a gift or talent can lead to identity confusion or underachievement. Some students, parents, and teachers also confuse identified high potential with increased value or even outright superiority. This is less often a problem among students than among the adults involved.

Negative influences of gifted education participation on identity formation include the following: sets students apart from peers; can be confused with increased value or worth; group membership is not equitably available; lacks connotation of effort; may set unrealistic expectations; may be seen as one-size-fits-all; high, flat profile may be identity challenge.

For many reasons, all of which must be overcome, almost all systems for identifying outstanding potential have been relatively unsuccessful in recognizing ability among members of certain minorities, individuals from economically stressed homes and communities, and students with disabilities. Thus, any positive messages (not to mention educational opportunities) are not evenly distributed.

Another equity problem is seen in some poorly designed gifted programs that treat all students the same, rather than matching differentiated learning experiences to areas of demonstrated need. Such programs not only undermine the development of talent, but deny students the opportunity to benefit from distinctions between themselves and their gifted peers based on areas of strength, interest, or other factors.

Gifted education programs also can give unintended negative identity messages to students who do not participate in them. This is especially common in schools whose gifted education programs are not sufficiently rigorous. In these cases, many students rightly say, "I could do that."

Identity Messages

If every child was gifted at something, which obviously is not the case, what identity messages would be provided by gifted education? It would be impossible for gifted programs to be one-size-fits-all, so a wide variety of individually matched programs would be provided for developing a vast range of gifts and talents. This would provide each student with a strength-based identity message while giving them group affiliation with others whose recognized potential was in a related or similar area.

Few gifted children have outstanding potential in the limited subjects covered by traditional curricula. If schools devoted time to providing in-depth learning opportunities in many more areas, we could identify and provide programs and positive identity messages for far more students with outstanding potential.

A small town once had a dance studio. Although a large number of students received positive identity messages from their experiences at this studio after school and on weekends, these achievements were rarely recognized or taken advantage of in school. Some students thought of themselves as failures in school, but successes in dance. If the school had

Reprinted from *The Education Digest*, May 1998, pp. 57-61, Ann Arbor, Michigan.

provided resources relating to dance, some of these early adolescents would have received the message that excellence in dance was appreciated by the school and that school could contribute to dance excellence.

Middle-level schools can increase the number of students for whom school seems relevant by recognizing excellence being developed outside school and fostering these developments through school. When a student is gifted and talented at home but learning-disabled or failing at school, the discrepancy may be due to a disconnect between the limited curricular options in school and the unlimited options offered by life.

Although administrators and team members already have scheduling nightmares, making space in the schedule for long-term development of individual student expertise would allow all students to receive the positive identity messages associated with students in gifted education. Such strength-based school models are becoming more common in recent school reforms. By making the development of expertise an expectation for each student, both positive group affiliation and individual distinction become possible.

Defining Broadly

It is hard to imagine an early adolescent who is recognized as the school's expert on a subject feeling incapable of learning or succeeding in high school and beyond. A feeling of expertise, when applied to any endeavor, is bound to contribute to identity development. Is expertise possible for every student (or even most)? Yes, if expertise is defined broadly.

The goal of a middle-level school should not be to develop expertise on an adult scale, but to assist each student in learning something that is unique among their school peers. By using the school's resources and expertise and the natural curiosity and interest of each student, and by providing time and support for hard work over an extended period, schools could make the production of in-house experts a central part of their missions.

Essential middle-level features such as teaming, advisory, flexible block scheduling, and curricular choices are well-suited to the development of

individual expertise. Service learning and problem-based learning determined by student choice are also well-suited to such an educational focus.

A middle school devoted to maximizing positive identity formation would be an "expert factory." With a quality staff and three years of a couple hours a week devoted to the understanding of expertise and the development of experts, there would be few students leaving for high school who did not believe they could learn and succeed.

What are requirements for the development of expertise through school? Expert performance relies on a long-term, positive interaction between a student's basic skills, abilities, interests, creativity, and prior experiences, on the one hand, and a school's context (environment, peers, culture, expectations, etc.), curriculum, teachers, teaching, leadership, and creativity.

The resulting experts from different expert factories probably would have different characteristics. Developing a definition of expertise and a set of criteria for demonstrating expertise would involve the staff, parents, and students. To demonstrate expertise before graduation, a student might need to document, via portfolio, numerous learning skills applied to their chosen area. Most portfolio standards for middle-level expertise probably would require the gathering of information using multiple sources, including demonstration of the use of reading and computer technology. Most would require communicating one's expertise through at least two modes. The possibilities are almost endless.

Would all experts have skills that seem alike in the end? Absolutely not. One student might develop expertise as a flutist; reading, listening, performing, learning the basics of how waves in air result in sound, and assisting with flute lessons for beginners might all be part of a portfolio. A second student, experiencing developmental delays, but with a favorite dog, might choose to become the school's expert on beagles.

A third student might choose to explore certain areas of mathematics, including calculus. While such study might be beyond the interest and capability of most middle-level stu-

dents, it is unlikely that the student developing calculus expertise would know as much about the flute or about beagles as the students who focused on those areas.

Positive Signs for All

By making the development of unique expertise a goal and an expectation for each student in the school, each one could gain positive identity messages and learning opportunities currently provided only to students in quality gifted education programs. Using such a focus, a middle-level school could increase the number of students receiving positive identity messages relating to school; increase the responsibility of each student for their education; increase the recognition of individual, family, and cultural values and interests; increase the level of challenge for each student; and increase learning for each student.

Gifted students would also benefit from such a system. Any differentiation of their curriculum, even outside the hours set aside for developing expertise, would be consistent with the school's overall mission. These students would continue to feel distinct based on the expertise they would be developing, but this challenging and identity-affirming experience would be shared by every student, providing for affiliation needs. The positive identity formation aspects of gifted education would be maintained without the negatives.

Implementing an expert development program would not supplant any aspect of curriculum currently provided. Such a program would not obviate the need for differentiating some curriculum for many gifted students, although it probably would for some.

To summarize, middle-level schools are uniquely able to help early adolescents develop healthy, positive identities that include an understanding that they can achieve success in at least some aspect of school and that school has something to contribute to their developing areas of personal interest. One way schools might approach this goal would be to promote the development of individual expertise.

To develop and recognize individual expertise, schools would need to vastly increase breadth of areas in which excellence is recognized, valued, and developed; become more aware of individual students' interests and goals; create a school climate in which expertise is accepted and expected; provide time and resources to the development of expertise; develop criteria students would need to document their expertise; and make developing expertise the mission, motto, and culture of the school.

Schools that develop experts would also see such positive outcomes as:

● Increased teacher appreciation and understanding of individual student strengths;

● An achievement orientation in each student;

● Diminished confusion between excellence and personal value;

● Awareness in each student that he or she can excel at something, given careful selection, quality education, and hard work over a period of time;

● Higher personal expectations and aspirations;

● Increased school understanding of personal, familial, and cultural values and interests; and

● Increased student input and responsibility.

Best of luck in developing the identities of your incoming middle-level students. You can do it. After all, you are the expert!

Jay A. McIntire is Policy Specialist, Council for Exceptional Children, 1920 Association Drive, Reston, Virginia 20191. Condensed from NASSP Bulletin, *82 (February 1998), 110-18. Published by National Association of Secondary School Principals, from which related educational materials are available by contacting NASSP, 1904 Association Drive, Reston, Virginia 20191 (phone: 703-860-0200).*

The Goals and Track Record of Multicultural Education

Paying attention to the varied learning styles of all students will do more to accomplish the goals of multicultural education than misguided programs that often divide children.

*B*ecause multicultural education is a volatile political issue— one with articulate proponents and antagonists on both sides—the research on this topic needs to be examined objectively. Many practices that schools promote make little sense in terms of how multiculturally diverse students learn. Thus, we need to examine the data concerning how poor achievement has been reversed among culturally diverse students in many schools.

What Is Multicultural Education?

Multicultural education orig- inated in the 1960s as a response to the long- standing policy of assimi- lating immigrants into the melting pot of our dominant American culture (Sobol 1990). Over the past three decades, it has expanded from an attempt to reflect the growing diversity in American classrooms to include curricular revisions that specifically address the academic needs of students. In recent years, it has been distorted by some into a movement that threatens to divide citizens along racial and cultural lines (Schlessinger 1991). Generally, multicultural education has focused on two broad goals: increasing academic achievement and promoting greater sensitivity to cultural differences in an attempt to reduce bias.

Increasing Academic Achievement

Efforts intended to increase the academic achievement of multicultural groups include programs that (1) focus on the research on culturally based learning styles as a step toward determining which teaching styles or methods to use with a particular group of students; (2)

emphasize bilingual or bicultural approaches; (3) build on the language and culture of African- or Hispanic- American students; and (4) emphasize math and science specifically for minority or female students (Banks 1994). Programs in each of these categories are problematic.

■ *Culturally based learning styles.* So long as such programs include reasonable provisions for language and cultural differences, they can help students make

Twenty percent of students in every culture are tactual learners—children who begin concentrating on new and difficult information by manipulating resources with their hands.

the transition into mainstream classes. In that sense, they may be considered similar to other compensatory programs that are not multicultural in their emphasis. As a researcher and advocate of learning styles, however, I would caution against attempting to identify or respond to so-called cultural learning styles. Researchers have clearly established that there is no

Photo courtesy of St. John's University's Center for the Study of Learning and Teaching Styles

Photo courtesy of St. John's University's Center for the Study of Learning and Teaching Styles

Photo courtesy of the Lafayette Academy

At least 20 percent of all students in every culture are kinesthetic learners who cannot sit in their seats for very long; they learn by *doing* rather than by listening or reading.

single or dual learning style for the members of any cultural, national, racial, or religious group. A single learning style does not appear even within a family of four or five (Dunn and Griggs 1995).

■ *Bilingual or bicultural approaches.* Attention to cultural and language differences can be done appropriately or inappropriately. Bi- and trilingualism in our increasingly interdependent world are valuable for, and should be required of, all students. An emphasis on bilingualism for only non-English-speaking children denies English-speaking students skills required for successful interactions internationally. Today, many adults need to speak several languages fluently and to appreciate cultural similarities and differences to succeed in their work.

Another problem arises in those classrooms in which bilingual teachers speak English ungrammatically and haltingly. Such teachers provide a poor model for non-English-speaking chil-

dren, who may remain in bilingual programs for years, unable to make the transition into English-speaking classes. Ultimately, this impairs the ability of these children to move into well-paying professions and careers—the ultimate goal of most of their parents.

■ *Selective cultural programs.* Building on the language and culture of selected groups and not of others suggests bias and bigotry. Parents should teach their children to appreciate and respect their native cultures;

schools should teach children to appreciate and respect all cultures. If the need exists to expand attention to more cultures, let us do that. But let us stop promoting one culture over another with the inevitable result of dividing our children and diminishing their sense of belonging to the dominant culture that is uniquely American—intentionally a combination of the best of all its citizens.

■ *Minority- and gender-based grouping for math and science.* Emphasizing math and science specifically for minority or female students may be based on good intentions, but it ignores the fact that minority students and female students all learn differently from one another and differently from their counterparts —whether those be high- or low-achieving classmates. Providing resources and methods that help all students learn rapidly and well should be the focus for teaching math and science—and every other subject. Are there not males and majority students who fail those subjects? The answer is to change how those subjects are taught, not to isolate certain groups and teach them as though they all have the same style of learning.

Sensitizing Ourselves to Social Agendas

Some multicultural education programs are specifically designed to increase cultural and racial tolerance and reduce bias. These are intended to restructure and desegregate schools, increase contact among the races, and encourage minorities to become teachers; and they lean heavily on cooperative learning (Banks 1994). Sleeter and Grant (1993) describe these programs as emphasizing human relations, incorporating some compensatory goals and curricular revisions to emphasize positive contributions of ethnic and cultural groups, and using learning styles to enhance students' achievement and reduce racial tensions.

Some of these programs emphasize pluralism and cultural equity in American society as a whole, seeking to apply critical thinking skills to a critique of racism and sexism. Others emphasize multilingualism or examine issues from viewpoints other than those of the dominant culture.

In my judgment, these focuses are more political than educational or social. Critical thinking is a requirement for all—not a select few. In addition, whose thinking prevails in these programs, and what are their credentials? Being a minority member or having taken a course does not automatically make a person proficient in teaching minority or female students, or in critiquing social issues. Political debate is helpful to developing young minds; one-sided, preconceived viewpoints are not.

Curriculum and Multicultural Achievement

In the debate over New York's "Children of the Rainbow" curriculum, the ideas of multicultural education captured almost daily headlines. Opponents argued that curriculum change would not increase student achievement, whereas proponents insisted that culturally diverse students performed poorly in school because they could not relate to an American curriculum.

Drew, Dunn, and colleagues (1994) tested how well 38 Cajun students and 29 Louisiana Indian students, all poor achievers, could recall story content and vocabulary immediately and after a delay. Their recall differed significantly when they were instructed with (1) traditional versus multisensory instructional resources and (2) stories in which cultural relevance matched and mismatched students' identified cultural backgrounds. Each subject was presented with four story treatments

(two culturally sensitive and two dominant American) and tested for recall immediately afterward and again one week later. The findings for Cajun subjects indicated significant differences between instructional treatments, with greater recall in each multisensory instructional condition — Cultural-Immediate, Cultural-Delayed, American-Immediate, and American-Delayed. The main effect of instructional treatment for Louisiana Indian subjects was significant as well. Recall scores were even higher when they used multisensory materials for

> What determined whether students mastered the content was how the content was taught, not the content itself.

American stories. No significant main effect emerged for test interval with either group.

This study demonstrated that what determined whether students mastered the content was *how* the content was taught, not the content itself. The culturally sensitive curriculum did not produce significantly higher achievement for these two poorly achieving cultural groups; the methods that were used did.

Teaching Methods and Multicultural Achievement

Other studies of teaching methods revealed even more dramatic results. Before being taught with methods that responded to their learning styles, only 25 percent of special education high school students in a suburban New York school district had passed the required local examinations and state competency tests to receive diplomas. In the first year of the district's learning styles program (1987–88), that number

increased to 66 percent. During the second year, 91 percent of the district's special education students were successful, and in the third year, the results remained constant at 90 percent—with a greater ratio of "handicapped" students passing state competency exams than regular education students (Brunner and Majewski 1990).

Two North Carolina elementary principals reported similarly impressive gains as a result of their learning styles programs. In an impoverished, largely minority school, Andrews (1990) brought student scores that had consistently been in the 30th percentile on the California Achievement Tests to the 83rd percentile over a three-year period by responding to students' learning styles. Shortly thereafter, Stone (1992) showed highly tactual, learning disabled (LD) elementary school students how to learn with Flip Chutes, Electroboards, Task Cards, and Pic-A-Holes while seated informally in rooms where levels of light matched their style preferences. The children were encouraged to study either alone, with a classmate or two, or with their teacher—based on their learning style strengths. Within four months, those youngsters had achieved four months' reading gains on a standardized achievement test—better than they ever had done previously and as well as would have been expected of children achieving at normal levels.

Many professional journals have reported statistically higher scores on standardized achievement and attitude tests as a result of learning style teaching with underachieving and special education students (Dunn, Bruno, Sklar, Zenhausern, and Beaudry 1990; Dunn, Griggs, Olson, Gorman, and Beasley 1995; Klavas 1993; Lemmon 1985; Perrin 1990; Quinn 1993). Indeed, a four-year investigation by the U.S. Office of Education that included on-site visits, interviews, observations, and examinations of national test data concluded that the Dunn and

Dunn Learning Styles Model was one of only a few strategies that had had a positive effect on the achievement of special education students throughout the nation (Alberg, Cook, Fiore, Friend, and Sano 1992).

What Have We Learned?

Research documents that under-achieving students —whether they are from other cultures or from the dominant U.S. culture—tend to learn differently from students who perform well in our schools (Dunn and Griggs 1995; Milgram, Dunn, and Price 1993). As indicated in the examples cited earlier, schools with diverse populations reversed academic failure when instruction was changed to complement the children's learning style strengths.

In our book, *Multiculturalism and Learning Style* (Dunn and Griggs 1995), my coauthor and I summarize research findings on each of the major cultural groups in the United States —African Americans, Asian Americans, European Americans, Hispanic Americans, and Native Americans. The research clearly shows that there is no such thing as a cultural group style. There are cross-cultural and intracultural similarities and differences among all peoples. Those differences are enriching when understood and channeled positively.

Given this information, I believe it is unwise for schools with limited budgets to support multicultural education in addition to —and apart from — regular education. Instead, schools need to make their instructional delivery systems responsive to how diverse students learn (Dunn 1995).

Educational programs should not separate young children from one another. Any separation becomes increasingly divisive over time and is likely to produce the opposite of what multicultural education is intended to accomplish. Segregated children begin to feel different from and less able than the larger groups of children they see—but are apart from. These feelings can lead to emotional insecurity and a dislike of others.

The United States was founded as a nation intended to absorb people from many nations. Monocultural education in the guise of multicultural education offends the cornerstone of those intentions. The melting pot concept does not diminish one's heritage. It unites the strengths of many cultures into a single, stronger blend of culture to reflect the best of all.

References

Alberg, J., L. Cook, T. Fiore, M. Friend, and S. Sano. (1992). *Educational Approaches and Options for Integrating Students with Disabilities: A Decision Tool.* Triangle Park, N.C.: Research Triangle Institute.

Andrews, R.H. (July–September 1990). "The Development of a Learning Styles Program in a Low Socioeconomic, Underachieving North Carolina Elementary School." *Journal of Reading, Writing, and Learning Disabilities International* 6, 3: 307–314.

Banks, J.A. (1994). *An Introduction to Multicultural Education.* Boston: Allyn and Bacon.

Brunner, C. E., and W. S. Majewski (October 1990). "Mildly Handicapped Students Can Succeed with Learning Styles." *Educational Leadership* 48, 2: 21–23.

Drew, M., R. Dunn, P. Quinn, R. Sinatra, and J. Spiridakis. (1994). "Effects of Matching and Mismatching Minority Underachievers with Culturally Similar and Dissimilar Story Content and Learning Style and Traditional Instructional Practices." *Applied Educational Research Journal* 8, 2: 3–10.

Dunn, R., J. Bruno, R.I. Sklar, R. Zenhausern, and J. Beaudry. (May–June 1990). "Effects of Matching and Mismatching Minority Developmental College Students' Hemispheric Preferences on Mathematics Scores." *Journal of Educational Research* 83, 5: 283–288.

Dunn, R., S.A. Griggs, J. Olson, B. Gorman, and M. Beasley. (1995). "A Meta-Analytic Validation of the Dunn and Dunn Research Learning Styles Model." *Journal of Educational Research* 88, 6: 353–361.

Dunn, R. (1995). *Educating Diverse Learners: Strategies for Improving Current Classroom Practices.* Bloomington, Ind.: Phi Delta Kappa.

Dunn, R., and S.A. Griggs. (1995). *Multiculturalism and Learning Styles: Teaching and Counseling Adolescents.* Westport, Conn: Praeger Publishers, Inc.

Klavas, A. (1993). "In Greensboro, North Carolina: Learning Style Program Boosts Achievement and Test Scores." *The Clearing House* 67, 3: 149–151.

Lemmon, P. (1985). "A School Where Learning Styles Make a Difference. *Principal* 64, 4: 26–29.

Milgram, R. M., R. Dunn, and G.E. Price, eds. (1993). *Teaching and Counseling Gifted and Talented Adolescents: An International Learning Style Perspective.* Westport, Conn.: Praeger Publishers, Inc.

Perrin, J. (October 1990). "The Learning Styles Project for Potential Dropouts." *Educational Leadership* 48, 2: 23–24.

Quinn, R. (1993). "The New York State Compact for Learning and Learning Styles." *Learning Styles Network Newsletter* 15, 1: 1–2.

Schlessinger, A., Jr. (1991). "Report of the Social Studies Syllabus Review Committee: A Dissenting Opinion." In *One Nation, Many Peoples: A Declaration of Cultural Independence,* edited by New York State Social Studies Review and Development Committee. New York: Author.

Sleeter, C.E., and C.A. Grant. (1993). *Making Choices for Multicultural Education: Five Approaches to Race, Class, and Gender.* 2nd ed. New York: Merrill.

Sobol, T. (1990). "Understanding Diversity." *Educational Leadership* 48, 3: 27–30.

Stone, P. (November 1992). "How We Turned Around a Problem School." *Principal* 71, 2: 34–36.

Rita Dunn is Professor, Division of Administrative and Instructional Leadership, and Director, Center for the Study of Learning and Teaching Styles, St. John's University, Grand Central and Utopia Parkways, Jamaica, NY 11439. She is the author of 17 books, including ASCD's *How to Implement and Supervise Learning Style Programs* (1996).

Multiculturalism at a Crossroads

By John Gallagher
From *Middle Ground*

LINCOLN, Nebraska, might seem an unlikely place to find a diverse population of students, but anyone who enters Charles Culler Middle School quickly forgets stereotypes about homogeneity in the American heartland. The school is 35% minority, with significant numbers of Hispanic, African-American, and Asian students. One in 10 is learning English as a second language.

All student course work reflects contributions of a multicultural society. Seventh-graders read African literature and study world history from the perspective of the different people who have shaped it. Students from other countries help teach the intricacies of mathematical equations to their U.S.-born peers, who in turn help them improve their English. And teachers and administrators make a conscious effort to practice tolerance for diversity. "You live it every day," says Culler Principal Ross Dirks. "I feel strongly that this is important."

Active involvement of teachers and students in expanding the curriculum is a hallmark of effective multicultural education, proponents claim, calling it valuable to prepare students for a changing world. In the best cases, success stems as much from the lessons adults teach outside the classroom as from the curriculum they follow inside.

Dirks tells teachers that "By the year 2010, if the demographics are correct, a white majority may no longer be a fact of life in America.

That's the world your kids will live in. They have to have knowledge about the way other people live."

Yet few issues spark as much controversy nationally as multicultural education. The term has become a regular salvo in political skirmishes, shorthand for the anxiety various groups feel about affirmative action, political correctness, and homosexuality.

Critics of multicultural education, including historian Arthur Schlesinger and former U.S. Civil Rights Commissioner Linda Chavez, say it violates basic social principles, such as the vision of America as a melting pot for generations of immigrants. Multiculturalism, they contend, stresses our differences, not common bonds, driving us apart instead of bringing us together. Other critics call it a cover for indoctrinating students in liberal political ideologies.

"Multiculturalism is still a put-off word for much of the population," says Bob Green, principal of Shea Middle School, in Phoenix, Arizona. "I think the definition of it needs to be brought out more, because it's really a basic way to address inequities and various conflicts in our nation. We're talking about equal access to education and equal opportunities."

Those who criticize multicultural education as divisive largely miss the point, writer Michael Dirda argues: By its nature, multiculturalism emphasizes links between different peoples. Thus, an integrated curriculum would expose students to the works of Homer and show them how he influenced Virgil, who influenced Dante, who influenced T.S. Eliot. Students would learn African and Asian folklore and mythology in addition to stories about the Norse Gods. Teachers might mix in the poetry of Tu Fu and Scheherazade's *The Arabian Nights* with lessons on Grimm's fairy tales or *Don Quixote*.

"In truth, most multicultural curricula are based on simple justice and common sense: Our schools are heavily Hispanic, Asian, and African American," says Dirda. "If we teach material relating to these cultures, we may capture the enthusiasm of these frequently disadvantaged students, as well as impart some useful insights to kids from other backgrounds. Ultimately, anyone should be able to sympathize with the plights of Jane Austen's heroines or the feelings of Richard Wright's Bigger Thomas. After all, the essence of being human lies in that old phrase 'our common humanity.'"

Five Features

James Banks, University of Washington professor of education and an expert on multicultural education, believes discussions of this issue will help determine the nation's future. The challenge is teaching adolescents to have a flexible, not narrow, view of the world around them. To Banks, multicultural education represents

Reprinted from *The Education Digest*, April 1998, pp. 22-28, Ann Arbor, Michigan.

much more than adding a few topics to the curriculum. He considers it an intervention strategy, not a program that can be stuffed into an existing syllabus. He believes schools with a rich multicultural focus share five characteristics:

● Content integration—expanding the curriculum to acknowledge the experiences and contributions of diverse groups.

● Knowledge construction—helping students understand how people create beliefs based on their heritage and experiences, a reflection of what Banks calls "their own cultural biographies."

● Pedagogy—using strategies that lead to higher achievement for students of color. For example, studies show Latino and African-American students learn more working in cooperative groups.

● Prejudice reduction—helping students develop more positive attitudes about people of different races and ethnicities.

● An empowering school culture—examining the impact of school policies, such as academic tracking and discipline referrals, on students from different backgrounds.

So far, Banks says, few schools embracing multicultural education meet all five goals. They tend to focus on one plank or the other, he says.

"We're stuck in the multicultural moments," agrees Howard Miller, associate professor of Middle School and Literacy Education at Lincoln University. Lots of teachers and schools "are very careful about having posters and lots of books in the library that represent different cultures, but they don't do anything with them."

Some schools are moving in the right direction by evaluating the entire educational experience to see if it fits comfortably under the large umbrella of multiculturalism. At Shea, minority students receive special math counseling because administrators found their poor skills were preventing many from attending college. Green, who conducts multicultural-education workshops around the country, says educators must ask themselves hard questions about their commitment to diversity: "What's in the curriculum? What are the teaching strategies? What do we do administratively to provide opportunities for kids? How do we conduct ourselves within our school atmosphere."

Unwanted Soul-Searching

Such soul-searching is not what everyone has in mind. Some educators still see multiculturalism as all about boosting achievement of poor, black students. Not only does this lump together black students from a wide range of backgrounds; it ignores interests of other racial and ethnic groups. Educators who view multiculturalism this narrowly deny the diversity of people within, not just among, various communities.

"What they think about is, 'How do you teach a black kid?'" says Salvario Mungo, associate professor of education at Illinois State University. "I tell them that a black kid living in Evanston, Illinois, and a black kid living in East St. Louis are going to be different."

Textbooks also can restrict multicultural emphasis. Although many experts believe textbook publishers have significantly improved their lessons to more accurately reflect the diversity of America, they acknowledge continued limitations.

"Our textbooks are certainly written from a bias," says Susan Baird, a teacher at Ashland Middle School, in Ashland, Oregon. "Even when they try to patch on a good piece on Sojourner Truth, or some other prominent person of non-Anglo culture, it's still by and large male and white."

The bigger problem may be the inclination to tack multiculturalism onto the school calendar. Advocates say it should not be limited to a "heroes and holidays" program in which teachers mention a prominent African-American scientist in passing or a short lesson about Mexico's Independence Day. For multiculturalism to work, they say, it must be infused throughout the curriculum.

"That's where multiculturalism has gotten a black eye." Green says. "We tried too many 'Tacos on Tuesday' programs, or black African weeks, and said, 'We served that well.'"

Reducing multiculturalism to such celebrations, or even displaying inclusive photos or posters around the school, may make some educators feel good. But such facile attempts rarely help students respect diversity.

These efforts also can have negative repercussions. "Members of the minority culture are offended at the one-day display," Miller says. You (also) raise the prejudice of people who say, 'Why don't we have a white history month or German-American history month?' You create a mess for yourself."

Nebraska is our only state with a mandate to teach multicultural education in all schools. Yet, even with the law behind them, Nebraska teachers have a tough job meeting goals of multicultural education. Weak administrative support can quash good intentions.

Schools can meet the letter of the law without really addressing the intent, says Bill Lopez, a middle-level instructor at the University of Nebraska's School of Education and a former middle-school teacher. When preparing his mostly white college students to lead the classrooms of tomorrow, Lopez tries to help them understand the forms racism can take and the way language relates to different cultures. He also stresses the importance of reflecting multiple perspectives when teaching significant historical events.

"The first thing I have teachers think about is what the characteristics are of a multicultural teacher," he says. "I try to do it in a constructive way, but generally, I push them toward the idea that a multicultural teacher has a vision not only of what they need to be but what they want their students to be."

Flowchart

Lopez offers a flowchart for making a multicultural middle school: Identify the players; form the multicultural committee; determine the community needs; determine the multicultural approach(es) wanted; develop a multicultural plan; determine the characteristics each player should have, based on the approach and plan; determine how to assess the characteristics each player has or should have; develop an initial inservice plan for all players, including motivational strategies; assess where the players are; develop additional inservice programs based on the assessments; provide ongoing support for players; and provide for regular review and assessment of how the plan is being implemented.

Meanwhile, the Nebraska Department of Education (NDE) offers ideas on designing and developing staff competencies, noting that effective multicultural education depends on staff who work directly with children in each school. NDE says some competencies that staff should develop in increasing their effectiveness in multicultural instruction include:

1. Recognize their personal feelings, attitudes, and perceptions as part of their cultural norms and bias.

2. Recognize the value of ethnic and cultural diversity as a basis for societal enrichment, cohesiveness, and survival.

3. Know in teachable detail about the experiences, viewpoints, and needs of various cultural groups.

4. Acquire sensitivity to words and actions insulting or hurtful to various minority groups.

5. Demonstrate through instruction and classroom or school environment how people of various groups, cultures, and backgrounds can communicate effectively and work cooperatively.

6. Use knowledge and experience of multicultural issues in selection, evaluation, and revision of instructional materials that are unbiased, factual, and complete in treating minority groups.

7. Conceptualize and describe the development of the United States as a multidimensional society of ethnic and cultural diversity where diversity has been an asset and prejudice has been a destructive force in economics, cooperation, and public policy.

Such suggestions notwithstanding, teachers and principals who have been cautious about adopting multicultural education can find some justification for moving slowly. The issue has prompted many local controversies, including the 1997 firing of Patsy and Nadine Cordova, two sisters who taught in Vaughn Junior and Senior High School in Vaughn, New Mexico. Given wide discretion and regular approval by the school administration in their choice of curricular materials, the Cordovas tried to integrate Chicano history and culture into their classes, which were more than 90% Hispanic.

Relevance

"Why didn't somebody teach me about Chicano history?" Nadine asks. "I don't want my students to walk away and say, 'No one ever tried to teach me.' At least they know I tried to teach them something relevant."

In 1996, school administrators started censoring the Cordovas' lessons. Superintendent Arthur Martinez sent Nadine a letter stating that she was teaching "racial intolerance" and "a biased political agenda." Another time, he told the teachers their classes were "preoccupied with colonizers" and taught children "that Mexicans are noble and honorable while Spanish and Anglos are greedy and hurtful people." Such lessons, he argued, acted "to place a giant chip on their fragile shoulders."

The Cordovas denied the charges, but tension between the teachers and the school district escalated until they lost their jobs. At Martinez's request, the Chief of Police escorted the sisters from the school. The Cordovas have filed a lawsuit challenging their dismissal.

Even the most carefully calibrated attempts to expand multicultural education can run into problems. Susan Baird notes that some topics she discusses in class—such as world religions—occasionally upset parents and students. She says she works hard to be sensitive to those concerns, which often reduces tension. As a result, religion has "become pretty comfortable and easy to talk about" in her class.

Students and parents have been less open-minded about homosexuality. Victoria Forrester, a sixth-grade teacher at Amelia Earhart Elementary School, in Alameda, California, almost lost her job after she spent seven minutes in class discussing the April 1997 episode of the television series, *Ellen*, in which Ellen Degeneres acknowledged that both she and her TV character were lesbians.

Forrester seized the opportunity, generated by a student's praise for the episode, to talk generally about the importance of people sticking up for themselves. But a parent complained Forrester violated his right to prevent his daughter from hearing conversations about homosexuality. The local school board cleared Forrester, but the state Commission on Teacher

Credentialing is reviewing the parent's complaint for possible action.

Parental objections don't present the only difficulties for teachers committed to multicultural education. Colleagues also can pour cold water on their ideas.

Dirks, the Lincoln principal, says he met strong resistance from teachers at the school where he previously worked, which served a largely white and middle-class population of students and staff: "It was a really closed community. When teachers asked me, 'Why are we doing this,' it really frustrated me because they didn't see the bigger part of the world. They weren't totally closed to it, but they felt it was more like one of those silly projects from the central office."

Tackling Tough Issues

Perhaps there is no way to avoid controversy in multicultural programs. Indeed, some educators believe it's wrong to try. Diluting a program to diminish debate is a disservice to students who need to grapple with tough social issues.

"If you're going to be concerned about multicultural education, you're not going to be in the business of avoiding controversy," says Lincoln University's Howard Miller. "You need to face it head on. You need to openly discuss controversial issues and let kids know they are indeed controversial. You should, in fact, design some of your program around that very fact."

Ultimately, students might be the best allies of multiculturalism. With their interest in justice and fairness, middle-schoolers in particular can learn to appreciate the need for all people to be accepted in society.

"Middle school kids think they can fix the world, and they're going to do it right now," Baird says. "It's wonderful. I would never tell them that it may take them a little longer."

John Gallagher is a freelance writer based in Brooklyn, New York. Condensed from Middle Ground, *1 (February 1998), 10-14, 42. Used with permission of National Middle School Association, from which subscriptions to* Middle Ground *are available by contacting NMSA, 2600 Corporate Exchange Dr., Ste. 370, Columbus, Ohio 43231 (phone: 800-528-NMSA).*

Multiculturalism: Practical Considerations for Curricular Change

TONY R. SANCHEZ

Tony R. Sanchez is an assistant professor of education at Indiana University Northwest, Gary, Indiana.

Many school districts today are jumping on the multicultural bandwagon by adopting, or at least encouraging, a more divisified curriculum. Proponents of multiculturalism call for an interdisciplinary approach that draws from and spans all subject areas, an approach that I believe is the most effective. I offer here a framework designed to be useful to teachers who want to change their personal or curricular perspective from one that is "mainstream" to one that is more "diverse" and are willing to incorporate that new perspective into whatever subject matter they teach.

Unfortunately, misconstruing the purposes or definition of multicultural education, many teachers either back off from it entirely or teach about different groups sequentially, resulting in a fragmented and isolated treatment. We do the latter when we assign specific groups to specific months (Black History Month, Hispanic Heritage Month, Women's History Month). During one of these periods, the attitude is that teachers will deal with that group for thirty days (maximum) and then return to the mainstream curriculum. Multiculturalism, however, belongs within the framework of the existing curriculum.

The Teacher's Role

By exposing our students to other cultures (whether the contributions of various groups or nonmainstream perspectives of an event or concept), we help them learn about other people's lifestyles and values. This awareness in turn may alter negative, stereotypic thinking, reduce intolerance, and promote cooperation (Cohen 1986). It will also expand *your* personal horizons as well as your students'.

As an educator interested in such an outcome, what might your creed be? I suspect something like this: *Within my course I will promote the recognition and understanding of diversity, and teach respect for it. By doing so, I hope not only to provide personal enrichment but also, through my teaching and actions, to help develop positive, productive interactions and attitudes.*

To put this creed into action, you most likely will do the following: teach the perspectives of the mainstream culture (don't assume students already know them); teach the perspectives of other cultures (with the message: they're equally valid to some); and examine similarities and differences between cultures (Hernandez 1989). This last point is certainly the most challenging; *both* similarities and differences should be addressed so that your students move from merely tolerating differences to viewing them as acceptable, desirable, and valuable (Noar 1989).

Implementing a multicultural curriculum requires specific components. These include (1) a teacher willing to critically evaluate his or her personal perspectives, (2) instructional materials that provide diverse but accurate perspectives, and (3) general goals and objectives.

Analyzing Your Attitude

As the teacher, you implement and guide the questioning, reasoning, analysis, and truth-seeking in your classroom. As such, you must consider your personal attitudes toward your subject area—negative and positive—and the fact that they can't be hidden from your students. What exactly is your level of commitment to the value of diverse perspectives?

Coming to grips with your values and attitudes, changing some, and developing sensitivity to diversity will require time—and courage. It will depend on your willingness to

From *The Clearing House,* January/February 1996, pp. 171-173. Reprinted with permission of the Helen Dwight Reid Educational Foundation. Published by Heldref Publications, 1319 Eighteenth St., NW, Washington, DC 20036-1802. © 1996.

work on your new perspective. Without this commitment, you may find yourself saying, "I'm not very comfortable with this diverse curriculum I'm trying out, but I think it's working out." What that really means is, "It's not working because I don't really believe in it." If that becomes the case, back off. Don't deceive yourself and your students. The payoff for this self-examination will be that the ugliness of prejudice, rejection, and exclusion—all results of ignorance and misinformation—will have no place in your classroom. You will be sensitizing your students not only to the mechanics of learning but also to their own worth and value. The rest of the process will be anticlimactic by comparison with this step.

Choosing Instructional Materials

In the next step of the process, you examine and select instructional materials that reflect accurate, quality (i.e., true) information. Choose materials that you're comfortable with, that won't require a radical change in your style (a change that many teachers needlessly fear).

Danger of Relying on Textbooks

Textbooks, as we know, account for most of the teaching/learning process (Sewall 1987). Furthermore, "Teachers tend to not only rely on, but believe in, the textbook as the source of knowledge" (Fitzgerald 1979).

Recent evaluations indicate that a diverse curriculum requires a change in this attitude. Various cultural/ethnic groups have brought attention to bear on the depiction of their respective cultures in textbooks (Garcia and Florez-Tighe 1986). The attitude shared by these groups can be summed up as follows: "The sole false perspective is that which claims to be the only one there is" (Gasset, cited in Smith and Otero 1982). The multicultural movement does *not* require abandonment of the mainstream perspective. This would only lead to isolated enclaves, fragmentation, and polarization. On the contrary, the movement promotes integrating a variety of perspectives, which must include the mainstream (Banks 1991).

Bias in textbooks appears in several forms, including stereotyping, omissions, distortions, overrepresentation in certain contexts, romanticized portrayals, token representations, and biased language. As educators, we need to examine and evaluate these materials in terms of content, language, and illustrations. Though textbook bias has been reduced in some quarters, it still remains, its manifestations sometimes blatant and other times subtle (Garcia and Florez-Tighe 1986).

How do we go about identifying such bias? We will need to explore, compare, contrast, question, and evaluate information from multiple sources (which may include students, peers, and the community). Eventually, we will strengthen our evaluative skills so that we can uncover discrepancies and contradictions. Analyzing and questioning the accuracy of the content we teach may represent a major departure for us, but it may also keep us from becoming "adults who believe everything they read—or read only what they wish to believe" (Klein 1985, 27). Passing on critical reading skills to our students may ultimately be our greatest legacy to them.

Guidelines for Multicultural Curriculum

Here are some basic guidelines to keep in mind as you purposively change your curricular perspective (Gaines 1992):

Go beyond a trivializing, "tourist" curriculum. A diversity curriculum is more than holidays, special months, food, and costumes. Rather, it means coming to know the values, viewpoints, and meaningful traditions that characterize individuals and groups (and you can still include food and costumes). These interpretations must be regular, built-in components of your subject area.

Go beyond tokenism. Do you enrich your class with African American or Hispanic perspectives simply because you have some black or Mexican students? Or, instead, do you employ multiple, unbiased perspectives because you recognize the value of alternative interpretations and want to promote acceptance and respect for different experiences and viewpoints? The former approach is characteristic of a teacher who doesn't really believe in or is uncomfortable with the notion of diversity in his or her subject area; the teacher's efforts will come off as phony. The latter approach characterizes a teacher who appreciates diversity.

Go beyond stereotyping. Give students continuous opportunities to examine images for accuracy. Too often a student's stereotypic perception goes unchallenged and therefore becomes solidified as truth. In this regard, you must expect to handle incidences of bias and ignorance that arise in the classroom. What should you do on such occasions? Here are four pieces of advice that I have found helpful:

1. *Don't ignore comments or questions that reflect misinformation.* Address the issue while a direct connection to the goals of the curriculum can still be made. Your silence on such matters can only be interpreted as confirmation.

2. *Don't excuse comments or questions that could be interpreted as culturally or racially insulting.* The students who are targets of such remarks (which can very quickly escalate into full-blown classroom incidents) will segregate themselves for protection—something that you didn't provide.

3. *Don't be afraid to step in to handle and clarify a situation.* Doing something on the spot is certainly preferable to doing nothing and allowing things to fester.

4. *Don't forget your commitment.* Your mission in establishing a diverse curriculum is to expand your students' knowledge so that they will develop more positive attitudes and behaviors that will enable them to interact effectively in our diverse society. Your responsibility in the mission is consistency.

Goals and Objectives

What learning outcomes should a multicultural curriculum promote? The following goals are frequently found in a diversified curriculum (Hernandez 1989; Kosmoski 1989):

To help students recognize and understand the values and experiences of one's own ethnic/cultural heritage

To promote sensitivity to diverse ethnicities/cultures through exposure to other cultural perspectives

To develop an awareness and respect for the similarities and differences among diverse groups

To identify, challenge, and dispel ethnic/cultural stereotyping, prejudice, and discrimination in behavior, textbooks, and other instructional materials

Goals are, of course, intended to be guidelines. A multicultural curriculum can only be effective when the teacher is given choices as to how to achieve such goals within his or her subject area or grade level. An inappropriate or too narrowly focused curriculum—a product of haste and pressure to conform—will likely result when teachers are not free to make those decisions. How to integrate a multicultural perspective into the curriculum rather than making it a blatant "add-on" is the main issue they face. Teachers usually approach this task by trial and error. Using a single, all-encompassing model to implement a diverse curriculum is not a good idea because no model can provide what is effective for all students at all times and under all circumstances. Rather, the teacher must systematically incorporate content and strategies in a comfortable balance. The process requires time, with the teacher "testing the waters" on a by-unit or by-lesson basis.

As an initial effort, many teachers employ a "cultural" unit or lesson in their standard monocentric curricula. It is usually additive instead of integral, but it serves the important purpose of "breaking the multicultural ice." Such an initial effort is almost always necessary to allow the educator to comfortably ease into a truly diverse curriculum.

Development and implementation of a multicultural curriculum must eventually be evaluated for effectiveness (California State Department of Education 1979). What must be assessed? Three chief components are (1) achievement; (2) student behavior; and (3) student attitudes (Hernandez 1989). Achievement, the primary focus of American education, can be fairly assessed through various conventional measures. Student behavior can be monitored

and evaluated formally (questionnaires, surveys, discussion groups, reduced number of disruptive incidents) and informally (teacher observations of cooperative interactions, voluntary student participation and assistance, student willingness to explore cultural similarities and differences). Student attitudes are the most difficult to assess for change. The validity of evaluation is dependent on the instrument used and should always be interpreted with caution. Research indicates that attitude change as a goal of multicultural education is indeed feasible. Studies of the use of content and strategies to change cultural/ethnic/racial attitudes and reduce prejudice show positive results, even when complex, multiple variables, such as age, socioeconomic status, and social institutions, are involved (Sanchez 1991). Establishing the foundation for such change—through diverse content and teacher modeling—cannot guarantee positive attitude changes. As educators, however, we must be willing to take the chance that this endeavor will promote understanding, acceptance, and respect.

REFERENCES

Banks, J. A. 1991. *Teaching strategies for ethnic studies.* 5th ed. Needham Heights, Mass.: Allyn and Bacon.

California State Department of Education. 1979. *Guide for multicultural education.* Sacramento, Calif.: California State Department of Education.

Cohen, C. B. 1986. Teaching about ethnic diversity. *ERIC Digest* 32: 1–2.

Fitzgerald, F. 1979. *America revisited.* Boston, Mass.: Atlantic Monthly Press/Little, Brown.

Gaines, L. 1992. What you can do. *Creative Classroom* (Sept.): 115.

Garcia, J., and V. Florez-Tighe. 1986. The portrayal of Blacks, Hispanics, and Native Americans in recent basal reading series. *Equity and Excellence* 22(4-6): 72–76.

Hernandez, H. 1989. *Multicultural education.* Columbus, Ohio: Merrill.

Klein, G. 1985. *Reading into racism.* London: Routledge and Kegan Paul.

Kosmoski, G. J. 1989. *Multicultural education.* Chicago: Third World Press.

Noar, G. 1989. *Sensitizing teachers to ethnic groups.* Needham Heights, Mass.: Allyn and Bacon.

Sanchez, T. R. 1991. *The effects of knowledge acquisition about Blacks on the racial attitudes of White high school sophomores.* Ann Arbor, Mich.: University Microfilms, Inc.

Sewall, G. T. 1987. *American history textbooks: An assessment of quality.* New York: Columbia University, Teachers College, Educational Excellence Network.

Smith, G. R., and G. Otero. 1982. *Teaching about cultural awareness.* Denver, Col.: University of Denver, Center for Teaching International Relations.

Unit 4

Unit Selections

Information Processing/Cognitive Learning

17. **Making Information Memorable: Enhanced Knowledge Retention and Recall through the Elaboration Process,** Donn Ritchie and Belinda Dunnick Karge
18. **Brain Basics: Cognitive Psychology and Its Implications for Education,** Richard L. Bucko
19. **The First Seven . . . and the Eighth,** Kathy Checkley
20. **Styles of Thinking, Abilities, and Academic Performance,** Elena L. Grigorenko and Robert J. Sternberg

Learning

21. **The Rewards of Learning,** Paul Chance
22. **Rewards versus Learning: A Response to Paul Chance,** Alfie Kohn
23. **Sticking Up for Rewards,** Paul Chance
24. **The Tyranny of Self-Oriented Self-Esteem,** James H. McMillan, Judy Singh, and Leo G. Simonetta

Instructional Strategies

25. **Improving Student Thinking,** Barry Beyer
26. **The Intelligence-Friendly Classroom: It Just Makes Sense,** Robin Fogarty

Key Points to Consider

❖ Compare and contrast the different approaches to learning. What approach do you think is best, and why? What factors are important to your answer (e.g., objectives, types of students, setting, personality of the teacher)?

❖ What teaching strategies could you use to promote greater student retention of material? What are good ways to attract and keep students' attention? Must a teacher be an "entertainer"? Why or why not?

❖ How can a teacher promote positive self-esteem, values, character, caring, and attitudes? How are they related to cognitive learning? How would you create a "caring" classroom? Discuss whether or not this would interfere with achievement of cognitive learning targets.

❖ If you wanted to create a constructivistic classroom in the subject area and/or grade in which you want to teach, what would the classroom look like? What would you emphasize, and how would your actions reflect constructivist principles and research on intelligence?

 **Links**

www.dushkin.com/online/

24. **Celebrating Our Nation's Destiny**
   http://www.census.gov/ftp/pub/edu/diversity/
25. **Education Week on the Web**
   http://www.edweek.org
26. **Online Innovation Institute**
   http://www.oii.org
27. **Teachers Helping Teachers**
   http://www.pacificnet.net/~mandel/
28. **The Teachers' Network**
   http://www.teachnet.org

These sites are annotated on pages 4 and 5.

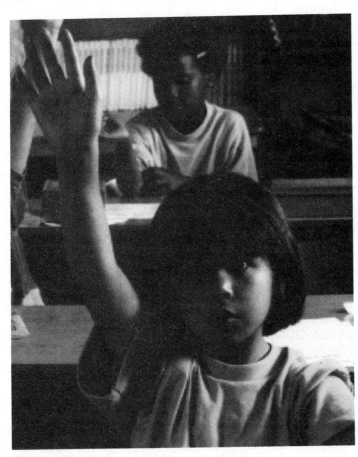

Learning and Instruction

Learning can be broadly defined as a relatively permanent change in behavior or thinking due to experience. Learning is not a result of change due to maturation. Changes in behavior and thinking of students result from complex interactions between their individual characteristics and environmental factors. A continuing challenge in education is understanding these interactions so that learning can be enhanced. This unit focuses on approaches within educational psychology that represent different ways of viewing the learning process and related instructional strategies. Each approach to learning emphasizes a different set of personal and environmental factors that influence certain behaviors. While no one approach can fully explain learning, each is a valuable contribution to our knowledge about the process.

The discussion of each learning approach includes suggestions for specific techniques and methods of teaching to guide teachers in understanding student behavior and in making decisions about how to teach. The articles in this section reflect a recent emphasis on applied research conducted in schools, research on the brain, and on constructivist theories. The relatively large number of articles on information processing/ cognitive learning and instruction, as opposed to behaviorism, also reflects a change in emphasis. Behaviorism, however, remains important in our understanding of learning and instruction.

Researchers have recently made significant advances in understanding the way our minds work.

Information processing refers to the way that the mind receives sensory information, stores it as memory, and recalls it for later use. This procedure is basic to all learning, no matter what teaching approach is taken, and we know that the method used in processing information determines to some extent how much and what we remember. The essays in the first subsection present some of the fundamental principles of brain functioning, information processing and cognition, human intelligence, and styles of thinking.

For years, behaviorism was the best-known approach to learning. Most practicing and prospective teachers are familiar with concepts such as classical conditioning, reinforcement, and punishment, and there is no question that behaviorism has made significant contributions to understanding learning. But behaviorism has also been subject to much misinterpretation, in part because it seems so simple. In fact, the effective use of behaviorist principles is complex and demanding, as debate presented in the articles in the second subsection points out.

Humanistic/social psychological learning emphasizes the affective, social, moral, and personal development of students. Humanistic learning involves acceptance of the uniqueness of each individual, stressing character, feelings, values, and self-worth. To the humanist, learning is not simply a change in behavior or thinking; learning is also the discovery of the personal meaning of information. Social psychology is the study of the nature of interpersonal relationships in social situations. In education, this approach looks at teacher-pupil relationships and group processes to derive principles of interaction that affect learning. "The Tyranny of Self-Oriented Self-Esteem" examines the application of humanistic/social psychological principles focusing on self-esteem.

Instructional strategies are the teacher behaviors and methods of conveying information that affect learning. Teaching methods or techniques can vary greatly, depending on objectives, group size, types of students, and personality of the teacher. For example, discussion classes are generally more effective for enhancing thinking skills than are individualized sessions or lectures. For the final subsection, two articles have been selected that show how teachers can use principles of cognitive psychology and intelligence in their teaching. The first article emphasizes the importance of an appropriate classroom environment that will encourage and support students' thinking, while the article by Robin Fogarty shows how constructivist classrooms can be created based on recent research on intelligence.

Making Information Memorable: Enhanced Knowledge Retention and Recall Through the Elaboration Process

DONN RITCHIE and BELINDA DUNNICK KARGE

In recent years there has been a concerted effort to reduce the amount of instructional time teachers spend on facts in lieu of increasing students' ability to comprehend a domain's higher level principles (American Association for the Advancement of Science, 1993; National Council of Teachers of Mathematics, 1991). When we consider the vast amount of information in most subject areas, this strategy seems wise, for the chance of a teacher being able to cover all the basic knowledge in any one subject area is remote. Regardless of the subject area, however, higher order processes (i.e., analysis, synthesis, and evaluation) are based on specific facts, and these facts must be understood before higher level concepts or principles can be grasped. Many students, including those with special needs, may experience difficulty when attempting to learn basic facts, retain new information, or generalize knowledge from one setting to another (e.g., from the learning disabilities resource room to the general classroom). So how can we best help these students acquire, retain, and recall knowledge?

Although teachers cannot alter students' preferred learning method, initial background knowledge, or innate intelligence, they can incorporate instructional techniques that help students to retain and recall information (Denham & Lieberman, 1980; Englert, 1983). One such technique that helps make information more memorable is a process known as elaboration.

Elaboration

Cognitive psychologists generally agree that for information to be retained in the long-term memory, it is imperative that students elaborate on the new material (Anderson, 1990; Gagné, 1985; Roehler & Duffy, 1984). Elaboration occurs when students think about a specific piece of information and construct a memory link between that piece and some related information already held in their long-term memory. However, the related information is more substantive than that used in literal comprehension. To elaborate, students must go through a thoughtful pause during which new memories are created and linked to existing mental structures (i.e., the new information is integrated with prior knowledge). This link could be anything that serves to connect the new information to that stored in long-term memory, such as inferences, continuations, examples, or details (Gagné, 1985).

With the continual expansion of knowledge, many teachers feel obligated to increase the amount of information delivered in their classes. When this occurs, information is often presented without time for students to use self-generated or teacher-generated elaborations. Even students with a strong desire to learn will suffer a reduction in their ability to recall information in these situations. In fact, Anderson (1990) found that students who elaborate on material, even without knowing of a later test, achieve higher test scores than students who are aware of an impending test but do not have time to elaborate.

Many researchers have suggested that strategy deficits relate directly to many of the educational problems that students with special needs encounter (Deshler & Schumaker, 1986; Paris & Jacobs, 1984; Simmons, Kameenui, & Darch, 1988). A strategy is an individual's approach to a task (Deshler & Lenz, 1989). Because the ability to recall information is such an important aspect of school learning, a variety of memory improvement strate-

Donn Ritchie is an associate professor in the Department of Educational Technology at San Diego State University. Belinda Dunnick Karge is a professor in the Department of Special Education at California State University, Fullerton.

From *Preventing School Failure,* Fall 1996, pp. 28-33. Reprinted with permission of the Helen Dwight Reid Educational Foundation.
Published by Heldref Publications, 1319 Eighteenth St., NW, Washington, DC 20036-1802. © 1996.

gies have been identified and researched. These strategies are taught to students either intentionally or intuitively by concerned teachers and parents. They are also offered in formal courses and sold to the public by private firms. Many of the procedures are somewhat general. They prompt students to elaborate on material simply by directing them to paraphrase, summarize, draw inferences, or generate a series of questions and answers. Other methods are more specific and prescribe methods to elaborate individual facts or lessons.

Sometimes the cognitive strategies necessary for efficient and accurate learning are unknown to the low achieving student. A grammatical rule may be learned, yet the student may not be able to generalize the rule and use it when writing a paragraph or an essay (Lucking & Manning, 1996). The students need to be taught specific elaborative methods to assure proper generalization of the knowledge they have attained.

In this article we examine 11 elaborative methods (see Table 1). Rather than provide abstract concepts, each method is illustrated with a specific example. We have taken examples from a geology class, specifically on formations generated by erosion. It is important to note, however, that the elaborative methods we suggest apply to all subject domains.

Microlevel Elaborations

Although there are numerous types, elaborations can be divided into two basic groups: microlevel and macrolevel elaborations. Whereas macrolevel elaborations help students to establish mental models that facilitate comprehension of entire lessons, microlevel elaborations help students remember specific pieces of information in the lesson. To examine microlevel elaborations, it helps to divide them into two subgroups: transformational and situational elaborations (see Table 1).

Transformational elaborations. Students sometimes lack basic knowledge structures in a content domain to which new information can be related. In these cases, elaborations can be made through a transformation of the new material (Levin, 1982, as cited in Pressley, Johnson, & Symons, 1987). This transformation is accomplished by associating the new material with a word which is acoustically similar, by using visual stimuli to iden-

tify critical attributes, or by rearranging the pieces of information into a new presentation. In other words, the new material is coded by introducing relationships that are neither naturally nor semantically inherent in it.

There are three distinct types of transformational microlevel elaborations. Probably the most common is the listing of keywords. This elaboration has its strongest practicality when two or more facts need to be tied together, such as in vocabulary definitions. In this process, the student first establishes an association between the new word and an acoustically similar word (keyword) already in the student's vocabulary. Next, the student encodes a meaningful relationship between the keyword and the information to be associated with the new word. An example of this type of elaboration, one common in geology classes, helps students remember where stalactites and stalagmites form in caves. Instead of having students memorize the points of formation by rote, the teacher can explain that stalactites have to hold on tight (tite) because they hang from the ceiling. This association provides the new vocabulary word, *stalactite*, with a link to its meaning. The keyword method is especially useful when forming associations between pieces of information that, for the student, may have no obvious or logical relationship to one another (especially important for students with learning disabilities and young children).

A second type of transformational microlevel elaboration is mathemagenic (Merrill, 1983). This elaboration requires the teacher or student to identify a critical attribute, with the help of a visual stimulus, such as arrows, boldface type, or colors, to draw attention to an important feature. An example would be for a teacher to circle the letter g in *stalagmite*, and the letter c in *stalactite*. If the visual aid is coupled with the use of a keyword mnemonic that states that g stands for *ground* and c stands for *ceiling*, students should more easily remember which formation is located on the floor and which is located on the ceiling of a cave. Providing students with a visual model has been found to improve the performance of students with learning disabilities considerably (Rivera & Smith, 1988).

TABLE 1
Elaboration Names and Implementation Procedures

Microlevel	Implementation
Transformational	Alter content to make it memorable.
Keyword	Associate to acoustically similar word.
Mathemagenic	Identify critical attribute with visual stimulus.
Representational	Reconfigure material to personal format.
Situational	Build on meaning found in context.
Precise contextual	Add additional content to strengthen link in context.
Imagery	Have students visualize the content.
Prerequisite	Introduce related material prior to content.

Macrolevel	Implementation
Generality	Compare new content to what students already know.
Advanced organizer, comparative	Compare to existing knowledge in this subject.
Experiential	Compare to students' personal experiences.
Analogy	Compare to knowledge in different subject domain.
General-to-detailed	Present global idea, then relate to specific content.
Epitome	Teach simple, concrete ideas related to lesson content
Advanced organizer, expository	Teach abstract ideas before lesson content.

The final type of transformational microlevel elaboration is representational. In this method, the student constructs a new means of representing the information, by using a chart, graph, drawing, or formula (Merrill, 1983). Representational elaborations allow students to rearrange information and then encode it in a novel or personal way, which makes it easier to recall at a later time. One form of representational elaboration, which is gaining interest in educational research, is known as concept mapping. In concept mapping, students develop "two dimensional diagrams that illustrate relationships between ideas in a content area" (Jonassen, Beissner, & Yacci, 1993, p. 155). In developing concept maps, students draw two or more concepts connected by a linking word that identifies the bridging relationship. As students reformat the concepts and relationships into the new representation, they create links among the pieces of information, thereby increasing and strengthening the relationship. For instance, after reading a text on erosional forces and their resulting deposits, students could be asked to list the three major agents of erosion (water, wind, and glaciers) and then develop a table, or draw a concept map, depicting the relationships between the agent and associated formations. Using graphics in combination with teacher-mediated mnemonic instruction is an excellent way to increase mastery of content material for students with learning disabilities (Mastropieri, Scruggs, Mc-Loone, & Levine, 1985).

Although the simpler of the two main types of microlevel elaborations, transformational elaborations can be an important means to acquiring new knowledge. These mnemonic devices, both verbal and pictorial, are widely used and can even be helpful in teaching quite young children (Foley & Wilder, 1989). The few students who appear not to benefit from instruction in keyword strategies are those who have previously developed and readily employ sophisticated elaborative strategies without external prompts (Pressley et al., 1987).

Situational elaborations. Situational elaborations are the second major type of microlevel elaborations. Instead of trans-forming material, they build on natural and meaningful associations or inferences found within the context of the lesson. For example, the construction of mental images that depict the meaning of the material, and the establishment of appropriate schema before introducing related ideas.

The first of these methods is called precise contextual elaborations (Stein et al., 1982). These elaborations provide tightly knit links between ideas in the text and the students' existing knowledge structure. They are developed as an additional thought that makes otherwise arbitrary relationships intelligible.

In a study by Stein et al. (1982), students were read incomplete phrases similar to "The extremely strong river deposited the sand . . ." and were then asked to complete the sentence with a phrase of their own to make the sentence more meaningful. Within all ability groups, it was found that students who made precise elaborations (such as adding the phrase "over the entire city," which would require a strong river) had a much better recall level of the statements than those who made imprecise elaborations (such as adding the phrase "one grain at a time," which would not require a strong river). Students who exhibited academic success were more likely to generate precise elaborations by themselves than were less successful students.

A second type of situational elaboration uses mental imagery. This method requires students to visualize the information or situation that has just been presented to them. The teacher then asks students how they perceive the situation. Accurate student-generated concepts are reinforced, and inaccurate ones are corrected. This method is beneficial because it repeats information gained through prose or lecture format and makes concepts more concrete. For example, in teaching students that geologists classify streams as youthful, mature, and old-age, teachers can reveal a few pertinent facts, then ask students to visualize and state how these streams may appear in nature. Correct assumptions (i.e., a youthful

---

Microlevel elaborations assist students in the retention of individual facts, macrolevel elaborations facilitate retention of entire lessons.

---

stream rushes straight ahead whereas an old-age stream meanders slowly from side to side) are reinforced. Classroom experience has shown that students who exhibit learning problems recall these self-generated imagery characteristics more readily than those stated by a teacher.

The third and final type of situational elaboration is called prerequisite elaboration. This type of elaboration is used to establish or reinforce a concept by bringing associated or related knowledge into the working memory before the introduction or review of a new concept. Ellis, Deshler, Lenz, Schumaker, and Clark (1993) validated the importance of prerequisite elaboration for students with mild disabilities. They found that students often exhibit less confusion and frustration when necessary skills or vocabulary are introduced early in a lesson. Similar to Ausubel's (1968) advanced organizer (a macrolevel elaboration), this method is used to impart knowledge on a specific, single concept. A geological example would be for a teacher to first remind students how the word "terminal" is used in everyday conversation to indicate the end of something. If an explanation of the glacial deposit known as a "terminal moraine" is then introduced, students will be better able to remember that a terminal moraine is found at the front end of a glacier, where advancement ceased and the glacier began to retreat.

Macrolevel Elaborations

Whereas microlevel elaborations assist students in the retention of individual

nizer would act as an "ideational scaffolding for the stable incorporation and retention of more detailed and differentiated material that follows" (p. 148). This scaffolding, or framework, is set up to establish an anchor point for forthcoming facts to attach themselves. Anchor points allow for easier integration and discrimination between new material and established, comparative knowledge. An example would be for a teacher to ask students to recall information on the deposition and composition of sand dunes. After allowing time for students to bring this knowledge to their working memory, the teacher may then describe a wind-blown soil deposit known as loess, comparing it to and contrasting it with the students' knowledge of sand dunes. The use of

on deposits found around hot springs, the information will be more readily assimilated because of their experience with the deposits formed in the beaker.

The third type of generality elaboration exists in the form of an analogy. With analogies, teachers relate new ideas to similar cognitive structures held by the students. For instance, if the concept being taught deals with the relative ages of sedimentary deposits, the teacher can make an analogy to the ages of successive layers of asphalt shingles placed on a building. As long as students understand an analogy's conceptual framework, they should be able to assimilate related concepts (Brown, 1994) and develop a level of comfort and security in connecting new ideas to their existing knowledge (Dagher, 1994).

General-to-detailed elaborations. The final type of macrolevel elaboration, which also assists in the sequencing of instruction, is the general-to-detailed elaboration. Reigeluth's (1983) elaboration theory of instruction is one such example. This elaboration begins with an "epitome" of the material to be learned, which is "a special kind of overview that teaches a few general, simple, and fundamental (but not abstract) ideas. The remainder of the instruction presents progressively more detailed ideas, which elaborate on earlier ones" (p. 338). Englert (1984) found similar evidence in working with students with disabilities. Teaching simple, concrete ideas that are related to the content of the lesson, then adding details, is a highly effective strategy to accentuate learning with this population.

Reigeluth compares his strategy to a zoom lens. When the lesson first begins, students view information through a wide-angle lens, which allows them to see the major parts and relationships between the parts. Students then have the ability to zoom in to look at individual parts in greater detail. This zooming in and out allows students to see how individual parts fit into the large picture, to see how the knowledge is structured, and to build a mental model of the information around the epitome.

If the class is studying erosional deposits, an example of an epitome would be that all erosional agents (wind, water,

---

There is little doubt that both the micro- and macrolevel elaborations increase students' ability to retain and recall information.

---

facts, macrolevel elaborations facilitate retention of entire lessons by first establishing relevant mental models to which students can associate new information. Although there are numerous types of macrolevel elaborations, they can be divided into two main groups: (a) generalities and (b) general-to-detailed. As with all elaborations, each allows for enhanced retention and recall of information by relating incoming material to existing cognitive structures (see Table 1).

Generality elaborations. There are three types of generality elaborations, each presenting a unified description of a similar topic and then relating this description to information that students are about to learn. Ausubel (1968) formally promoted this strategy, which he labeled a "comparative advanced organizer." The orga-

generalization and adaptation of learning strategies for students with disabilities (Ellis, Lenz, & Sabornie, 1987) and the importance of advance organizers for potentially low performing students in the secondary content classroom (Lenz, Alley, & Schumaker, 1987) have been well documented.

Experiential elaborations are a second type that can be included in the subgroup of generality elaborations. This elaboration uses students' personal experiences to make new information more memorable. These experiences can come from everyday life or be generated shortly before instruction by the teacher. For instance, if students set out a heated, saturated saltwater solution to evaporate over night, they will find mineral deposits in the beaker the following day. If the students' next classroom discussion focuses and glaciers) carry material until their speed decreases, at which time the materials are dropped and deposits are formed. At the next level of elaboration, the different types of erosional agents would be examined and an explanation of how these agents carry and deposit material would be presented. As students progress through the lesson, each ensuing level of instruction elaborates back to preceding levels, explaining the content in more detail.

Ausubel (1968) developed a somewhat similar technique that incorporated the general-to-detailed idea in his expository advanced organizer. Instead of presenting a few simple concepts as with an epitome, this elaboration method starts with an abstract idea that is more general and inclusive than the information presented later in the lesson. Once students become familiar with the abstract idea, they are given more detailed information that has an anchor point from which the meaning can be conceptualized. In geology, initial instruction may include the concept that erosion is an unending natural force, and if it is not counterbalanced, the resulting deposits will eventually fill in the world's ocean basins. Later instruction could detail the force that causes erosion as well as counteracting forces that push up the land.

Discussion

Implications for Educators

There is little doubt that both the micro- and macrolevel elaborations increase students' ability to retain and recall information. In addition, critical thinking may be promoted as students compare and contrast their previous knowledge to newly obtained knowledge during the process of elaboration (Stein, 1989). With these potential benefits, it is imperative that educators provide either teacher-generated elaborations or time for students to develop their own. When teachers distribute material or lecture to their classes without regard to the internal learning process of the student, those who are low performers are likely to interpret material in an arbitrary or verbatim fashion and learn through shallow processing methods, such as repetition, memorizing specific texts, or cramming for examinations.

Such methods limit students' assimilation of material or require that they spend additional time studying for comprehension.

Because individuals differ in their ability to elaborate, it is important that teachers encourage students with special needs to develop the skills of elaborating material on their own and to practice the various elaborative processes. Unfortunately, students do not gain a full understanding of the process of elaboration either by being told how to execute elaborative strategies or simply by being exposed to elaborated materials (Pressley et al., 1987). Rather, students need to be taught the techniques systematically and given the chance to implement and practice the processes over time. It is also important for teachers to instruct students in the use of multiple elaborative strategies because some are better assimilated than others, and some are better suited for specific types of problems. Exposure to different types of strategies may help students establish the general tendency to be more elaborative (Pressley et al., 1987), and individual differences in preference and prior knowledge will allow some strategies to be more easily retained and employed than others (Weinstein, Ridley, Dahl, & Weber, 1989). In addition, memory for a specific piece of information has been found to be related to the number of elaborations developed around that information (Anderson, 1990).

Conclusion

If we assume that students will always be required to master a certain amount of specific subject matter, then it is to the teacher's advantage to use strategies that help students remember information more easily. Although the learning strategies employed by a teacher and a student's prior knowledge, aptitude, and interest in subject matter all influence how well a student learns new material, comprehension is also affected by the student's ability to generate useful elaborations. We have presented 11 techniques to help establish the elaborative process for learning individual facts as well as for assimilating entire lessons (see Table 1). These techniques do more than just help students recall information for exams; they help students retain and access per-

tinent knowledge for use later in life. Because of the power of elaborative techniques, the process of teaching and using elaborations should be of paramount importance to teachers, authors, parents, and students both with and without disabilities. As both general and special educators seek best practices related to collaborative teaching environments (Karge, McClure, & Patton, 1995; Wilhite & Cessna, 1996) and inclusive settings (Cessna & Skiba, 1996; Whinnery, King, Evans, & Gable, 1995), administrators and principals seek ways to assist teachers (Lasky, Karge, Robb, & McCabe, 1995), and parents reach out to support the schools (Mostert, 1996), it is critical that all work together to use effective, efficient teaching practices. The trained use of elaborative techniques can enhance the learning potential of students with disabilities by assisting with both basic skill and higher level comprehension and retention.

REFERENCES

American Association for the Advance of Science. (1993). *Benchmarks for science literacy: Project 2061*. New York: Oxford University Press.

Anderson, J. (1990). *Cognitive psychology and its implications*. (3rd ed.). New York: W. H. Freeman.

Ausubel, D. B. (1968). *Educational psychology: A cognitive view*. New York: Holt, Rinehart, and Winston.

Brown, D. E. (1994). Facilitating conceptual change using analogies and explanatory models. *International Journal of Science Education, 16*(2), 201–214.

Cessna, K. K. & Skiba, R. J. (1996). Needs-based services: A responsible approach to inclusion. *Preventing School Failure, 40*, 117–123.

Dagher, Z. R. (1994). Does the use of analogies contribute to conceptual change? *Science Education, 78*, 601–614.

Denham, C. & Lieberman, A. (Eds.). (1980). *Time to learn*. Washington, DC: National Institute of Education.

Deshler, D. D., & Lenz, B. K. (1989). The strategies instructional approach. *International Journal of Disability, Development and Education, 36*, 203–224.

Deshler, D. D., & Schumaker, J. B., (1986). Learning strategies: An instructional alternative for low-achieving adolescents. *Exceptional Children, 52*(6), 583–590.

Ellis, E. S., Deshler, D. D., Lenz, B. K., Schumaker, J. B., & Clark, F. L. (1993). In Meyen, E. L., Vergason, G. A., Whelan, R. J. (Eds.), *Educating students with mild disabilities*. (pp. 151–155). Denver: Love.

Ellis, E. S., Lenz, B. K., & Sabornie, E. J. (1987). Generalization and adaptation of learning strategies to natural environments: Part 1. Critical agents. *Remedial and Special Education, 8*(1), 6–21.

Englert, C. S. (1983). Measuring special education

teacher effectiveness, *Exceptional Children, 50*(1), 247–254.

Englert, C. S. (1984). Effective direct instruction practices in special education settings. *Remedial and Special Education, 5,* 38–47.

Foley, M. A., & Wilder, A. (1989, April). *Developmental comparisons of the effects of type of imaginal elaboration on memory.* Paper presented at the biennial meeting of the Society for Research in Child Development. Kansas City, MO.

Gagné, E. D. (1985). *The cognitive psychology of school learning.* Boston: Little, Brown and Company.

Jonassen, D. H., Beissner, K., & Yacci, M. (1993). *Structural knowledge.* Hillsdale, NJ: Lawrence Erlbaum Associates.

Karge, B. D., McClure, M., & Patton, P. L. (1995). The success of collaboration resource programs for students with disabilities in grades 6 through 8. *Remedial and Special Education, 16*(2), 79–89.

Lasky, B., Karge, B. D., Robb, S. M., & McCabe, M. (1995). How principals can help the beginning special education teacher. *National Association of Secondary School Principals, 79*(568), 1–14.

Lenz, B. K., Alley, G. R., & Schumaker, J. B., (1987). Activating the inactive learner: Advance organizers in the secondary content classroom. *Learning Disability Quarterly, 10*(1), 53–67.

Levin, J. (1982). Pictures as prose-learning devices. In A. Flammer & W. Kintsch (Eds.), *Discourse processing.* (pp. 412–444). Amsterdam: North-Holland.

Lucking, R., & Manning, M. L. (1996). Instruction for low-achieving young adolescents: Addressing the challenge of a generation imperiled. *Preventing School Failure, 40*(2), 82–87.

Mastropieri, M. A., Scruggs, T. E., McLoone, B., & Levine, J. R., (1985). Facilitating the acquisition of science classifications in learning disabled students. *Learning Disability Quarterly, 8,* 299–309.

Merrill, M. D. (1983). Component display theory. In C. M. Reigeluth (Ed.), *Instructional theories and models: An overview of their current status* (pp. 278–333). Hillsdale, NJ: Erlbaum.

Mostert, M. P. (1996). Interprefessional collaboration in schools: Benefits and barriers in practice. *Preventing School Failure, 40*(3), 135–138.

National Council of Teachers of Mathematics. (1991). *Professional standards for teaching mathematics.* Reston, VA: Author.

Paris, S. G., & Jacobs, J. E. (1984). The benefits of informed instruction for children's reading awareness and comprehension skills. *Child Development, 55,* 2083–2093.

Pressley, M., Johnson, C. J., & Symons, S. (1987). Elaborating to learn and learning to elaborate. *Journal of Learning Disabilities, 20*(2), 76-91.

Reigeluth, C. M. (1983). Elaboration theory of instruction. In C. M. Reigeluth (Ed.) *Instructional theories and models: An overview of their current status* (pp. 335–381). Hillsdale, NJ: Erlbaum.

Roehler, L. R., & Duffy, G. G. (1984). Direct explanation of comprehension processes. In G. G. Duffy, L. R. Roehler, & J. Mason (Eds.), *Comprehension instruction: Perspectives and suggestions* (pp. 265–280). New York: Longman.

Rivera, D. & Smith, D. D. (1988). Using a demonstration strategy to teach midschool students with learning disabilities how to compute long division. *Journal of Learning Disabilities, 21*(1), 77–81.

Simmons, D. C., Kameenui, E. J., & Darch, C. (1988). Learning disabled children's metacognition of selected textual features. *Learning Disabilities Quarterly, 11*(1), 380–395.

Stein, B., Bransford, J., Franks, J., Owings, R., Vye, N., & McGraw, W. (1982). Differences in the precision of self-generated elaborations. *Journal of Experimental Psychology, 111,* 399–405.

Stein, V. (1989). Elaboration: Using what you know. (Reading-to-Write Report No. 6, Technical Report No. 25). *Office of Educational Research and Improvement,* Washington, DC (ERIC Document Reproduction Service No. ED 306 596).

Weinstein, C. E., Ridley, D. S., Dahl, T., & Weber, E. S. (1989). Helping students develop strategies for effective learning. *Educational Leadership, 46*(4), 17–19.

Whinnery, K. W., King, M., Evans, W. H. & Gable, P. A. (1995). Perceptions of students with learning disabilities: Inclusion versus pull-out services. *Preventing School Failure, 40*(1), 5–9.

Wilhite, K. & Cessna, K. K. (1996). Safeguarding the education of incarcerated juvenile offenders: The critical role of state departments of education, *Preventing School Failure, 40*(2), 56–59.

Brain Basics:
Cognitive Psychology and Its Implications for Education
Richard L. Bucko

The human brain is a unique creation composed of a hundred billion neurons connected by trillions of synapses. For millennia, people have asked how this three-pound mass of soft tissue inside the human skull performs such tasks as writing letters, solving problems, and contemplating the universe. These questions are now finding answers through recent findings about the way the human brain works. The general field of study is known as cognitive science. When applied to the study of human cognition, it is known as cognitive psychology. When applied to the field of education, it is known as brain-based learning. Brain-based learning may be the most important influence on the way we teach since the first school was founded.

Knowledge of brain-based learning will be essential to educators of the future because good teaching requires an understanding of how the brain receives, processes, and produces information. As our understanding of cognitive psychology grows, learning problems will be addressed analytically, with an understanding of the damage to connections that causes these problems. Brain-based learning can be the foundation of pragmatic future education reform based on clear evidence of how children learn.

This article will address key research findings about brain research, the thinking skills movement, popular literature on the brain, and implications for schools.

Key Findings about Brain Functions

Three technological innovations are now allowing neuroscientists to analyze and observe the connection between the various areas of the brain. First, neural imaging allows researchers to observe the inner workings of the brain. As subjects see colors or words, various areas of the brain light up on imaging screens. Different brain regions can be observed handling letters of the alphabet, numbers, tastes, and smells. In a bilingual person, one area will handle one language while another deals with the second language

Second, molecular biology is revealing the operations of genes and molecules inside brain cells. One example is from the work of Eric Kandel at Columbia University. He discovered a short string of chemical molecules, called CREB, which serves as a switch to turn certain genes in the brain on and off. CREB is needed to change short-term memory into long-term memory. As we age, CREB is less plentiful, a fact that may partially explain memory loss as we enter later years. Even the sense of smell is managed by over 1,000 genes controlling neurons that respond to various smells, connecting these odors to associated behaviors, memories, and thoughts (Flam 1996).

Third, computers have given us an exact way to think about information processing by helping us to learn how processing is localized.

The convergence of brain scans, molecular biology, and computers has opened the way for researchers to localize the regions where different concepts are stored and to observe how these regions are joined together in thought and consciousness (Hilts 1995).

The Way the Brain Works—

The wiring of the brain is far more complex than the most powerful supercomputer. We have billions of neurons and many more supporting cells within the confines of our heads. One amazing finding is that the physical structure of these cells changes as they

Richard L. Bucko is Principal of George C. Baker School in Moorestown Township Public Schools, New Jersey (enrollment 2,800). Dr. Bucko has published and presented in the area of effective instruction, and his study of the subject of brain-based learning is a continuation of his interest in this area.

respond to the environment and experience. When confronted with changes to our surroundings or new experiences, brain cells grow or shrink and new thread-like connections between neurons are established, or old ones are strengthened. If a person is blinded, for example, the other sensory portions of the brain will become stronger.

Today, brain researchers consider the brain to be organized in both a focal and diffuse manner, depending on what functions are being addressed. Basic sensory and motor functions are controlled by specific areas, while higher mental functions involve a constellation of areas across the brain.

Complex thinking requires memory applications from several locations. It may involve visual or auditory memories, concept identification, and language usage. All of this occurs while other portions of the brain are aware of sensations of feeling, temperature, visual stimuli, sounds, and possibly tangential thoughts—and all the while that thinker's brain is responsible for maintaining balance while walking and chewing gum. This is what is meant by the term *parallel processing*, the ability of the brain to perform many tasks at once.

Human speech has provided a rich area for the study of the way information travels through the brain. An incredible array of "category deficits" in human thinking arise from damage to the brain. Examples include people whose overall functioning is normal but who cannot recall the names of animals; people who can write words but not numbers; and people who can recognize faces of loved ones but cannot say their names. The range extends from unnoticeable gaps to an almost complete inability to understand language.

When studied in detail, in many patients and with the assistance of imaging equipment, the various disabilities give us a good picture of how the brain organizes and manipulates information. For example, damage to a particular part of the back of the brain can cause a person to fail to recognize categorical relationships such as a violin as a musical instrument, or robin as a bird, or any other individuals as belonging to particular categories.

After more than a century of study, cases like this have allowed researchers to tentatively identify about 20 categories that the brain uses to organize knowledge. These include plants, animals, body parts, colors, numbers, verbs, facial expressions, and sounds. There are certainly many more (Hilts 1995).

In mapping emotions, opposites such as happiness and sadness are not registered in the same place in the brain. They entail different and independent patterns of activity in different locations. Because happiness and sadness involve separate brain areas, we can have bittersweet emotions, such as when we fondly think of a deceased loved one.

In a memory, connections are made to areas of the brain that may control memory of visual images, odors, sounds, and certain words. This is a vital point for educators. Connections between the various brain areas are the foundation of thinking and knowing. Connections allow us to put two or more memory images together. These images may be of sounds, sights, ideas, or emotions. The ability to *associate* or *connect* these images stored in different areas of the brain allows us to be "smart." By connecting these images at the speed of electricity, we are able to create a simple thought, such as "I am going to take the dog out," or a more complex one, such as "It is my wife's birthday—it will make her happy if I send her flowers." We will address the implications for the classroom shortly.

Levels of Brain Function—

There is value in identifying the three levels of brain function that are addressed in a school or workplace. The nature of the organization of brain functions and their connections to one another form the *first* level of brain performance, known as neurological development. The *second* level is subskill performance. This requires the connections of several parts of the brain that are required to perform the *third*, or skill level. For example, eye-hand coordination, visual integration, and cognitive recall are subskills required to perform the skill of writing; all of these subskills contribute to writing performance.

When we think of skill performance in analytical terms, we can become more effective teachers who systematically analyze the performance of individual students. The learning difficulties or strengths of the individual are affected by developmental levels and relative strengths within a skill or subskill.

Male/Female Differences—

Yes, there are differences in the structure of male and female brains. One example is the larger size of the corpus allosum (a structure that joins the left and right hemispheres) in females. Another is the tendency of female brains to develop in a rather uniform manner, while male brains do not.

Differences in brain organization appear to result in variations in cognitive abilities. Most significantly, it is generally true that females tend to be more fluent than males in the use of language, and males tend to be better at spatial analysis. Less definite research indicates that boys excel in mathematical ability and tend to be more aggressive than females. Efforts to explain sex differences tend to focus on one or more of the following: different brain organization, hormonal effects on cerebral function, genetic sex-linkage, maturation rate, and environment (Kolb and Whishaw 1996).

The sex-based concept of left-brain dominance (highly verbal, logical thinker and basically rational) verses right brain dominance (less verbal, spatial memory strength, and intuitive processor), is receiving little support in the recent research. It is, at best, inconclusive. Each hemisphere relies heavily on the other, thereby producing a synergy that cannot be separated. According to Renate and Geoffrey Caine (1991), "schools should provide the opportunity to develop all abilities even as we continue to prefer some over others" (p. 34).

The Thinking Skills Movement

As John Dewey pointed out in the 1930s, thinking can be done well or badly, and good thinking, like good manners, can be taught. Thinking occurs in the formation of beliefs, and in making decisions and solving problems. If good thinking can be taught, it can have far-reaching applications well beyond the classroom.

Since 1956, Bloom's *Taxonomy of Educational Objectives* has provided one of the fundamental frameworks for teachers to teach thinking skills in the classroom. Writers and workshop presenters use this well-organized structure for the teaching of thinking. Bloom's Taxonomy was a notable effort—but it has not been borne out by the last few decades of research on cognitive processes (Hart 1986).

Some Bloom advocates try to adapt the taxonomy to current brain research. Adapting Bloom's model of higher and lower forms of cognition to classroom instruction may have some merit, but other approaches to developing thinking, language, and metacognitive processing seem to have more potential.

Through the 1980s, "thinking skills" was a key buzzword in teacher training. Prominent theorists included Perkins, Costa and Adler. D.N. Perkins wrote of intelligence as the combination of *Power* (natural ability/IQ), *Tactics* (thinking strategy) and *Content* combining to form *Intelligence*. Thus,

$$Intelligence = Power + Tactics + Content$$

The "unnaturalness of good thinking" required that thinking be taught in a variety of ways. Perkins described "thinking frames" or tactics/strategies that enhance intelligence.

In 1980, the Association for Supervision and Curriculum Development published a compilation of the works of various authors entitled *Developing Minds*. Edited by Arthur Costa, the book presented useful ways to enhance thinking in such content areas as writing, reading, science, and math. It included 18 articles by 18 different authors on programs for teaching thinking.

Hundreds of additional books and articles added to the vast array of materials about teaching thinking. But all of this activity took place with no clear idea of how the mind received, processed, or produced information.

It is interesting how little we have heard in recent years about "thinking skills." Is it no longer important, or was it void of valid content? Is the vacuum of knowledge about the brain being filled by meaningful and applicable cognitive research?

As early as 1986, Mortimer Adler was one of the few voices presenting an alternative view about teaching thinking. He supported content-based instruction that involved reading, writing, measuring, testing, and trying to draw conclusions. When practical thinking applications were applied to content instruction, meaningful thinking instruction took place. This approach is supported today through research that tells us that making connections within the brain is the key to long-term memory and the ability to apply classroom learning in other contexts.

For centuries, humans have recognized the importance of quality thinking. What has changed in recent years is the advance of technology that has enabled researchers to study, even to observe, what takes place when we think. It is interesting, but not surprising, that some of the foremost thinkers about thinking during the 1980s (Hart 1986) have become leaders in the application of the science of cognition and brain-based learning.

The Recent Brain Literature

Since the early 1980s, there have been a number of books on best-seller lists that have used findings about the brain as subject matter that has fascinated millions of readers. Two books by Oliver Sacks, *The Man Who Mistook His Wife for a Hat* (1987) and *An Anthropologist on Mars* (1995) depict unusual case studies of behavioral abnormalities caused by neurological damage. This seems to have a fascination for many readers.

Howard Gardner documented the concept that the brain possesses many forms of intelligence in his 1983 book *Frames of Mind*. By the 1990s, the concept of multiple intelligence had caught on in many schools. His book and its variants continued selling in the popular market. Educators are familiar with his important theory that there are at least seven intelligences: mathematical, musical, kinesthetic, linguistic, spatial, intrapersonal, and interpersonal. A strength in one does not predict a strength in another. Gardner's Harvard-based research was state-of-the-art and played a strong role in raising the consciousness of educators toward the importance of learning more about the brain. Like the popular books previously mentioned, it also raised the interest level of the general public.

The *Triarchic Mind* followed in 1988 with a description of three forms of intelligence. Robert Sternberg presented his "triarchic theory" of intelligence using three manifestations: 1) the internal world of the individual, which is the traditional view of intelligence, 2) the relationship of that intelligence to the environment around us, and 3) the relationship of intelligence to experiences we have had since the time we were born.

Emotional Intelligence (1995), by Daniel Goleman, is a serious look at the importance of those factors not measured on an IQ test. Goleman argues that our view of intelligence is far too narrow. He uses brain and behavioral research to demonstrate the factors involved when people of high IQ fail at life and those of modest IQ do extremely well. Emotional intelligence includes persistence, impulse control, enthusiasm, empathy, and social awareness.

In line with the current interest in character education, the recent book *Moral Intelligence* (1997), by Robert Coles, again uses the term intelligence in a title. Coles makes the point that during the elementary school years the child becomes a moral creature—it is the time when the conscience is, or is not, created.

These important years are the time when the malleable mind is being formed. Children are eager to absorb the world that is placed around them—the good or the bad, the moral or the immoral. The brain is a sponge during these young years when it is capable of gaining vast amounts of information. Too often our society forgets that the early years are the most important time to direct our efforts in school and at home. It is the fortunate child who is nurtured in both.

Although his work has focused on educational disabilities, Melvin Levine has been a guiding light to educators on the role of brain function. As a researcher, pediatrician, and professor at the University of North Carolina, he has been able to develop his ideas about how the developing brain functions. As a lecturer and as the author of several books, most notably, *Educational Care* (1994), he has been able to extend his influence to many schools.

Educational Care provides a guide for parents and teachers to collaborate in the management of children with school-related problems. Through the development of diagnostic instruments that integrate neurological, behavioral, and developmental findings, he has been able to better understand the workings of a child's mind and plan better ways to teach those with educational difficulties.

Applications in Education

Learning and Memory—

Cognitive psychologists have identified two separate types of memory systems. The "what" memory system holds facts such as faces, names, and dates. The "how-to" memory preserves skills such as reading or sewing. Memories of both types are stored in the short-term holding area behind the forehead where they remain for a few moments. Some of these memories are converted to long-term storage that may last for years. "What" memory tends to fade quickly, but "how-to" memory can last a lifetime (Hilts 1995).

Conversion of short-term into long-term memory involves the growth of new connections between neurons. Certain memory-enhancing strategies, such as repetition and association, are effective ways of growing connections between neurons. Actual changes to the brain occur—the size of a brain area grows or shrinks, depending on experience and practice. Memory is generally considered to be a five-step process: 1) acquisition, 2) registration, 3) storage, 4) access, 5) transfer.

Thematic instruction provides connections among storage areas of the brain, therefore reinforcing memory through dispersal. The more areas that are "touched" by the stimulus, the greater the probability of long-term retention.

Cooperative learning also provides connections to other parts of the brain through integration with other content topics or through social interaction.

Opportunities to think and speak about a topic, as well as to listen and do hands-on activities, will also enhance the probability of long term retention.

Creation of many strong connections between areas of the brain provides the key to memory enhancement. As Gardner would say, this is influenced by an individual's strength in the specific area of intelligence being addressed. The important point for educators is that the brain's *thinking* function involves retaining information and connecting the information storage locations when necessary.

John Bruer makes a strong case for the relevance of prior knowledge in his 1993 book *Schools for Learning.* A good teacher will consciously use an "anticipatory set" (capture students' attention and relate the topic to prior knowledge), because the way we understand and remember new material depends on how it relates to what we already know. Learning is an active process as well as a constructive one. Our brains make sense of what we experience by actively connecting it with prior knowledge.

The Learning Environment—

The emotional condition of one's mind can have a great influence on the brain's ability to retain information. If the learner's mind is stressed by fear and anxiety, maximum learning cannot occur. Too much of the mind's energy and attention is expended on the emotion and not on the intended learning. When divorce, peer pressure, the birth of a sibling, or other stress-causing circumstances occur, learning suffers.

Climate is a term often used to describe the character and culture of a school. A pleasant, academic orientation enhances the mind's readiness to accept and retain information. Friendly classmates, pleasant surroundings, gentle colors, cleanliness, and abundant classical music are possible ingredients of a healthy learning climate.

Far too little effort is spent in creating school environments that increase the ability to learn. The classroom is often a very unnatural environment. School typically requires long hours of attention in a sitting position—a task far more difficult for some than others.

Success for an adult in a home or work setting generally does not require being in one chair or room for an extended time. In those settings, social interaction, motivation, and energy, as well as a variety of other task-specific skills, are essential. Teaching, for example, requires energy, motivation, verbal and interpersonal skills, as well as the ability to use effective instructional strategies. Yet, the degree to which such skills are recognized and used to the greatest advantage during a typical school day is generally minimal.

The Mind/Body Connection—

Sometimes we forget that the brain benefits from care of the entire body. Good nutrition and exercise are fundamental to optimum school performance. Aerobic activity feeds the brain with oxygen and glucose—essential to increasing nerve connections. Children who exercise regularly do better in school according to many studies.

Getting more physical activity into the school day is a challenge, but it can be achieved through large-group music aerobics, class recess that involves significant activity, and gym classes that involve real movement.

Classroom learning benefits from added activity. Physical movement involving lesson content enhances brain function and learning. Studies have found that young children learn subtraction faster and retain it longer when it is presented in a variety of forms, including physical activity such as moving classmates as numbers in an equation or calculating comparable distances or times for outdoor runs.

Music and the Arts—

Like physical education classes, music and the arts can be powerful forces in the effort to create learning connections. Plato said that music "is a more potent instrument than any other for education." He was prescient in his understanding that music trains the brain for advanced forms of thinking.

In a recent University of California study, two groups of three year olds were the subject of a unique experiment. One group took piano lessons and sang daily in chorus. The other did not have music as part of their curriculum. After eight months, the musical group performed far better on a puzzle completion task (Blakeslee 1995). This skill could translate into better math and engineering skills.

Studies such as this support the belief that early music training may improve a child's ability to reason. While it may not be practical to provide students with daily classes with a music teacher, playing classical music during quiet work times in class and in the hallways can significantly increase student exposure.

The possibilities for the integration of history, math, and language into music, art, and drama are endless. Classroom dramatizations, the use of geometry in art, and other cross-curricular possibilities are only limited by the teacher's imagination.

Summary

The neurological system of each student contains a variety of skill strengths and weaknesses that influence school performance. The task is to think of the brain as an organ for learning and to match instruction and the learning environment to the way that the brain most effectively gathers and retains information.

The following practices, some of which are already used in many classrooms, can help us attune schooling to what brain-based learning research tells us:

- Use a wide variety of instruction geared toward different types of intelligence.
- Incorporate movement into instructional activities.
- Make greater use of instructional strategies that build connections among the different brain functions, such as thematic instruction and cooperative learning.
- Do more to promote students' physical fitness.
- Stress the importance of early music training to enhance children's cognitive skills, and integrate music into other subject areas.
- Create pleasant, relaxed classroom environments through pleasing colors, classical music, and cleanliness.
- Relate new topics to students' prior knowledge in order to strengthen their long-term memory of content.
- Teach critical thinking skills by applying them to content instruction through reading, writing, measuring, testing, and trying to draw conclusions.

Schools have been slow to implement instruction that reflects what we know about the brain and learning. There are many reasons—inertia, the fear of taking a chance, lack of time to reflect on and plan for change, and difficulties in communicating to educators what *does* make a difference.

Change in education is notoriously slow. Wisely, we don't want to be reckless with our children. But as more and more evidence supports the power of understanding cognitive psychology, we are on the eve of a learning revolution that could change our schools for the better.

References

Adler, Mortimer. (1986). "Why Critical Thinking Programs Won't Work." *Education Week* (September 17, 1986).

Blakeslee, Sandra. (1995). *New York Times (Science Times)*, May 16, 1995: C1.

Bloom, Benjamin et al. (1956). *Taxonomy of Educational Objectives: The Classification of Educational Goals.* New York: Longmans Green.

Bruer, John T. (1993). *Schools for Learning.* Cambridge, MA: MIT Press.

Caine, Renate and Geoffrey Caine. (1991). *Making Connections: Teaching and the Human Brain.* Alexandria, VA: Association for Supervision and Curriculum Development.

Coles, Robert. (1997). *The Moral Intelligence of Children.* New York: Random House.

Costa, Arthur L., editor. (1985). *Developing Minds* Alexandria, VA: Association for Supervision and Curriculum Development.

Flam, Faye. (1996). "Tracking Down Thoughts." *The Philadelphia Inquirer* (May 20, 1996): E-3.

Gardner, Howard (1983). *Frames of Mind.* New York): Basic Books.

Gardner, Howard. (1995). "Reflections on Multiple Intelligences." *Phi Delta Kappan* (November 1995).

Goleman, Daniel. (1995). *Emotional Intelligence.* New York: Bantam Books.

Hart, Leslie A. (1986). "A Response: All Thinking Paths Lead to the Brain." *Educational Leadership* (May 1986).

Hilts, Phillip. (1995). "Brain's Memory System Comes Into Focus." *The New York Times* (May 30, 1995): C1.

Kolb, Bryan and Ian Q. Whishaw. (1996). *Fundamentals of Human Neuropsychology.* W.H. Freeman and Co.

Levine, Melvin. (1987). *Developmental Variation and Learning Disorders.* Boston, MA: Educators Publishing Service.

Levine, Melvin. (1994). *Educational Care.* Boston, MA: Educators Publishing Service.

Perkins, D.N. (1986). "Thinking Frames." *Educational Leadership* (May, 1986).

Sacks, Oliver. (1987). *The Man Who Mistook His Wife For a Hat.* New York: Harper Perennial.

Sacks, Oliver. (1995). *An Anthropologist on Mars.* New York: Vintage Books.

Sternberg, Robert J. (1988). *The Triarchic Mind.* New York: Viking.

The First Seven . . . and the Eighth

A Conversation with Howard Gardner

Human intelligence continues to intrigue psychologists, neurologists, and educators. What is it? Can we measure it? How do we nurture it?

Kathy Checkley

Howard Gardner's theory of multiple intelligences, described in Frames of Mind *(1985), sparked a revolution of sorts in classrooms around the world, a mutiny against the notion that human beings have a single, fixed intelligence. The fervor with which educators embraced his premise that we have multiple intelligences surprised Gardner himself. "It obviously spoke to some sense that people had that kids weren't all the same and that the tests we had only skimmed the surface about the differences among kids," Gardner said.*

Here Gardner brings us up-to-date on his current thinking on intelligence, how children learn, and how they should be taught.

How do you define intelligence?

Intelligence refers to the human ability to solve problems or to make something that is valued in one or more cultures. As long as we can find a culture that values an ability to solve a problem or create a product in a particular way, then I would strongly consider whether that ability should be considered an intelligence.

First, though, that ability must meet other criteria: Is there a particular representation in the brain for the ability? Are there populations that are especially good or especially impaired in an intelligence? And, can an evolutionary history of the intelligence be seen in animals other than human beings?

I defined seven intelligences (see box) in the early 1980s because those intelligences all fit the criteria. A decade later when I revisited the task, I found at least one more ability that clearly deserved to be called an intelligence.

That would be the naturalist intelligence. What led you to consider adding this to our collection of intelligences?

Somebody asked me to explain the achievements of the great biologists, the ones who had a real mastery of taxonomy, who understood about different species, who could recognize patterns in nature and classify objects. I realized that to explain that kind of ability, I would have to manipulate the other intelligences in ways that weren't appropriate.

So I began to think about whether the capacity to classify nature might be a separate intelligence. The naturalist ability passed with flying colors. Here are a couple of reasons: First, it's an ability we need to survive as human beings. We need, for example, to know which animals to hunt and which to run away from. Second, this ability isn't restricted to human beings. Other animals need to have a naturalist intelligence to survive. Finally, the big selling point is that brain evidence supports the existence of the naturalist intelligence. There are certain parts of the brain particularly dedicated to the recognition and the naming of what are called "natural" things.

How do you describe the naturalist intelligence to those of us who aren't psychologists?

The naturalist intelligence refers to the ability to recognize and classify plants, minerals, and animals, including rocks and grass and all variety of flora and fauna. The ability to recognize cultural artifacts like cars or sneakers may also depend on the naturalist intelligence.

Now, everybody can do this to a certain extent—we can all recognize dogs, cats, trees. But, some people from an early age are extremely good at recognizing and classifying artifacts. For example, we all know kids who, at age 3 or 4, are better at recognizing dinosaurs than most adults.

Darwin is probably the most famous example of a naturalist because he saw so deeply into the nature of living things.

Are there any other abilities you're considering calling intelligences?

Well, there may be an existential intelligence that refers to the human inclination to ask very basic questions about existence. Who are we? Where do we come from? What's it all about? Why do we die? We might say that existential intelligence allows us to know the invisible, outside world. The only reason I haven't given a seal of approval to the existential intelligence is that I don't think we have good brain evidence yet on its existence in the nervous system—one of the criteria for an intelligence.

You have said that the theory of multiple intelligences may be best understood when we know what it critiques. What do you mean?

The standard view of intelligence is that intelligence is something you are born with; you have only a certain amount of it; you cannot do much about how much of that intelligence you have; and tests exist that can tell you how smart you are. The theory of multiple intelligences challenges that view. It asks, instead,

© Susie Fitzhugh

"Given what we know about the brain, evolution, and the differences in cultures, what are the sets of human abilities we all share?"

My analysis suggested that rather than one or two intelligences, all human beings have several (eight) intelligences. What makes life interesting, however, is that we don't have the same strength in each intelligence area, and we don't have the same amalgam of intelligences. Just as we look different from one another and have different kinds of personalities, we also have different kinds of minds.

This premise has very serious educational implications. If we treat everybody as if they are the same, we're catering to one profile of intelligence, the lan-

School matters, but only insofar as it yields something that can be used once students leave school.

guage-logic profile. It's great if you have that profile, but it's not great for the vast majority of human beings who do not have that particular profile of intelligence.

Can you explain more fully how the theory of multiple intelligences challenges what has become known as IQ?

The theory challenges the entire notion of IQ. The IQ test was developed about a century ago as a way to determine who would have trouble in school. The test measures linguistic ability, logical-mathematical ability, and, occasionally, spatial ability.

What the intelligence test does not do is inform us about our other intelligences; it also doesn't look at other virtues like creativity or civic mindedness, or whether a person is moral or ethical.

We don't do much IQ testing anymore, but the shadow of IQ tests is still with us because the SAT—arguably the most potent examination in the world—is basically the same kind of disembodied language-logic instrument.

The truth is, I don't believe there is such a general thing as scholastic aptitude. Even so, I don't think that the SAT will fade until colleges indicate that they'd rather have students who know how to use their minds well—students who may or may not be good test takers, but who are serious, inquisitive, and know how to probe and problem-solve. That is really what college professors want, I believe.

Can we strengthen our intelligences? If so, how?

We can all get better at each of the intelligences, although some people will improve in an intelligence area more readily than others, either because biology gave them a better brain for that intelligence or because their culture gave them a better teacher.

Teachers have to help students use their combination of intelligences to be successful in school, to help them learn whatever it is they want to learn, as well as what the teachers and society believe they have to learn.

Now, I'm not arguing that kids shouldn't learn the literacies. Of course they should learn the literacies. Nor am I arguing that kids shouldn't learn the disciplines. I'm a tremendous champion of the disciplines. What I argue against is the notion that there's only one way to learn how to read, only one way to learn how to compute, only one way to learn about biology. I think that such contentions are nonsense.

It's equally nonsensical to say that everything should be taught seven or eight ways. That's not the point of the MI theory. The point is to realize that any topic of importance, from any discipline, can be taught in more than one way. There are things people need to know, and educators have to be extraordinarily imaginative and persistent in helping students understand things better.

A popular activity among those who are first exploring multiple intelligences is to construct their own intellectual profile. It's thought that when teachers go through the process of creating such a profile, they're more likely to recognize and appreciate the intellectual strengths of their students. What is your view on this kind of activity?

My own studies have shown that people love to do this. Kids like to do it, adults like to do it. And, as an activity, I think it's perfectly harmless.

I get concerned, though, when people think that determining your intellectual profile—or that of someone else—is an end in itself.

You have to use the profile to understand the ways in which you seem to learn easily. And, from there, determine how to use those strengths to help you become more successful in other endeavors. Then, the profile becomes a way for you to understand yourself better, and you can use that understanding to catapult yourself to a better level of understanding or to a higher level of skill.

How has your understanding of the multiple intelligences influenced how you teach?

As long as you can lose one ability while others are spared, you cannot just have a single intelligence.

My own teaching has changed slowly as a result of multiple intelligences because I'm teaching graduate students psychological theory and there are only so many ways I can do that. I am more open to group work and to student projects of various sorts, but even if I wanted to be an "MI professor" of graduate students, I still have a certain moral obligation to prepare them for a world in which they will have to write scholarly articles and prepare theses.

Where I've changed much more, I believe, is at the workplace. I direct research projects and work with all kinds of people. Probably 10 to 15 years ago, I would have tried to find people who were just like me to work with me on these projects.

I've really changed my attitude a lot on that score. Now I think much more in terms of what people are good at and in putting together teams of people whose varying strengths complement one another.

How should thoughtful educators implement the theory of multiple intelligences?

Although there is no single MI route, it's very important that a teacher take individual differences among kinds very seriously. You cannot be a good MI teacher if you don't want to know each child and try to gear how you teach and how you evaluate to that particular child. The bottom line is a deep interest in children and how their minds are different from one another, and in helping them use their minds well.

Now, kids can be great informants for teachers. For example, a teacher might say, "Look, Benjamin, this obviously isn't working. Should we try using a picture?" If Benjamin gets excited about that approach, that's a pretty good clue to the teacher about what could work.

The theory of multiple intelligences, in and of itself, is not going to solve anything in our society, but linking the multiple intelligences with a curriculum focused on understanding is an extremely powerful intellectual undertaking.

When I talk about understanding, I mean that students can take ideas they learn in school, or anywhere for that matter, and apply those appropriately in new situations. We know people truly understand something when they can represent the knowledge in more than one way. We have to put understanding up front in school. Once we have that goal, multiple intelligences can be a terrific handmaiden because understandings involve a mix of mental representations, entailing different intelligences.

People often say that what they remember most about school are those learning experiences that were linked to real life. How does the theory of multiple intelligences help connect learning to the world outside the classroom?

The theory of multiple intelligences wasn't based on school work or on tests. Instead, what I did was look at the world and ask, What are the things that people do in the world? What does it mean to be a surgeon? What does it mean to be a politician? What does it mean to be an artist or a sculptor? What abilities do you need to do those things? My theory, then, came from the things that are valued in the world.

So when a school values multiple intelligences, the relationship to what's valued in the world is patent. If you cannot easily relate this activity to something that's valued in the world, the school has probably

© Susie Fitzhugh

lost the core idea of multiple intelligences, which is that these intelligences evolved to help people do things that matter in the real world.

School matters, but only insofar as it yields something that can be used once students leave school.

The Intelligences, in Gardner's Words

■ Linguistic intelligence is the capacity to use language, your native language, and perhaps other languages, to express what's on your mind and to understand other people. Poets really specialize in linguistic intelligence, but any kind of writer, orator, speaker, lawyer, or a person for whom language is an important stock in trade highlights linguistic intelligence.

■ People with a highly developed logical-mathematical intelligence understand the underlying principles of some kind of a causal system, the way a scientist or a logician does; or can manipulate numbers, quantities, and operations, the way a mathematician does.

■ Spatial intelligence refers to the ability to represent the spatial world internally in your mind—the way a sailor or airplane pilot navigates the large spatial world, or the way a chess player or sculptor represents a more circumscribed spatial world. Spatial intelligence can be used in the arts or in the sciences. If you are spatially intelligent and oriented toward the arts, you are more likely to become a painter or a sculptor or an architect than, say, a musician or a writer. Similarly, certain sciences like anatomy or topology emphasize spatial intelligence.

■ Bodily kinesthetic intelligence is the capacity to use your whole body or parts of your body—your hand, your fingers, your arms—to solve a problem, make something, or put on some kind of a production. The most evident examples are people in athletics or the performing arts, particularly dance or acting.

■ Musical intelligence is the capacity to think in music, to be able to hear patterns, recognize them, remember them, and perhaps manipulate them. People who have a strong musical intelligence don't just remember music eas-

ily—they can't get it out of their minds, it's so omnipresent. Now, some people will say, "Yes, music is important, but it's a talent, not an intelligence." And I say, "Fine, let's call it a talent." But, then we have to leave the word *intelligent* out of *all* discussions of human abilities. You know, Mozart was damned smart!

■ Interpersonal intelligence is understanding other people. It's an ability we all need, but is at a premium if you are a teacher, clinician, salesperson, or politician. Anybody who deals with other people has to be skilled in the interpersonal sphere.

■ Intrapersonal intelligence refers to having an understanding of yourself, of knowing who you are, what you can do, what you want to do, how you react to things, which things to avoid, and which things to gravitate toward. We are drawn to people who have a good understanding of themselves because those people tend not to screw up. They tend to know what they can do. They tend to know what they can't do. And they tend to know where to go if they need help.

■ Naturalist intelligence designates the human ability to discriminate among living things (plants, animals) as well as sensitivity to other features of the natural world (clouds, rock configurations). This ability was clearly of value in our evolutionary past as hunters, gatherers, and farmers; it continues to be central in such roles as botanist or chef. I also speculate that much of our consumer society exploits the naturalist intelligences, which can be mobilized in the discrimination among cars, sneakers, kinds of makeup, and the like. The kind of pattern recognition valued in certain of the sciences may also draw upon naturalist intelligence.

How can teachers be guided by multiple intelligences when creating assessment tools?

We need to develop assessments that are much more representative of what human beings are going to have to do to survive in this society. For example, I value literacy, but my measure of literacy should not be whether you can answer a multiple-choice question that asks you to select the best meaning of a paragraph. Instead, I'd rather have you read the paragraph and list four questions you have about the paragraph and figure out how you would answer those questions. Or, if I want to know how you can write, let me give you a stem and see whether you can write about that topic, or let me ask you to write an editorial in response to something you read in the newspaper or observed on the street.

The current emphasis on performance assessment is well supported by the theory of multiple intelligences. Indeed, you could not really be an advocate of multiple intelligences if you didn't have some dissatisfaction with the current testing because it's so focused on short-answer, linguistic, or logical kinds of items.

MI theory is very congenial to an approach that says: one, let's not look at things through the filter of a short-answer test. Let's look directly at the performance that we value, whether it's a linguistic, logical, aesthetic, or social performance; and, two, let's never pin our assessment of understanding on just one particular measure, but let's always allow students to show their understanding in a variety of ways.

You have identified several myths about the theory of multiple intelligences. Can you describe some of those myths?

One myth that I personally find irritating is that an intelligence is the same as a learning style. Learning styles are claims about ways in which individuals purportedly approach everything they do. If you are planful, you are supposed to be planful about everything. If you are logical-sequential, you are supposed to be logical-sequential about everything. My own research and observations suggest that that's a dubious assumption. But whether or not that's true, learning styles are very different from multiple intelligences.

Multiple intelligences claims that we respond, individually, in different ways to different kinds of content, such as language or music or other people. This is very different from the notion of learning style.

You can say that a child is a visual learner, but that's not a multiple intelligences way of talking about things. What I would say is, "Here is a child who very easily represents things spatially, and we can draw upon that strength if need be when we want to teach the child something new."

Another widely believed myth is that, because we have seven or eight intelligences, we should create seven or eight tests to measure students' strengths in each of those areas. That is a perversion of the theory. It's re-creating the sin of the single intelligence quotient and just multiplying it by a larger number. I'm personally against assessment of intelligences unless such a measurement is used for a very specific learning purpose—we want to help a child understand her history or his mathematics better and, therefore, want to see what might be good entry points for that particular child.

What experiences led you to the study of human intelligence?

It's hard for me to pick out a single moment, but I can see a couple of snapshots. When I was in high school, my uncle gave me a textbook in psychology. I'd never actually heard of psychology before. This textbook helped me understand color blindness. I'm color blind, and I became fascinated by the existence of plates that illustrated what color blindness was. I could actually explain why I couldn't see colors.

Another time when I was studying the Reformation, I read a book by Erik Erikson called *Young Man Luther* (1958).[1] I was fascinated by the psychological motivation of Luther to attack the Catholic Church. That fascination influenced my decision to go into psychology.

The most important influence was actually learning about brain damage and what could happen to people when they had strokes. When a person has a stroke, a certain part of the brain gets injured, and that injury can tell you what that part of the brain does. Individuals who lose their musical abilities can still talk. People who lose their linguistic ability still might be able to sing. That understanding not only brought me into the whole world of brain study, but it was really the seed that led ultimately to the theory of multiple intelligences. As long as you can lose one ability while others are spared, you cannot just have a single intelligence. You have to have several intelligences.

---

1. See Erik Erikson, *Young Man Luther* (New York: W. W. Norton, 1958).

Howard Gardner is Professor of Education at Harvard Graduate School of Education and author of, among other books, *The Unschooled Mind: How Children Think and How Schools Should Teach* (1991). He can be reached at Roy B. Larsen Hall, 2nd Floor, Appian Way, Harvard Graduate School of Education, Cambridge, MA 02138. **Kathy Checkley** is a staff writer for *Update* and has assisted in the development of ASCD's new CD-ROM, *Exploring Our Multiple Intelligences,* and pilot online project on multiple intelligences.

Styles of Thinking, Abilities, and Academic Performance

ELENA L. GRIGORENKO

ROBERT J. STERNBERG
Yale University

ABSTRACT: *This study was designed to investigate the role of thinking styles in academic performance. Participants were 199 gifted students enrolled in the Yale Summer School Program. Their abilities were evaluated by the Sternberg Triarchic Abilities Test; their academic performance was judged by independent raters blind to the conditions of the study; and their thinking styles were measured by two converging self-report questionnaires. The results of the study show that, after controlling for levels of abilities, styles of thinking significantly contribute to prediction of academic performance. Moreover, equally able thinkers of different styles tend to do better in different assessment settings.*

Acornerstone of modern educational psychology is that a student's level of abilities is one of the major predictors of school success. Though psychologists or educators may differ significantly on the details and on theory, there is established evidence that abilities matter (e.g., Carroll, 1993; Gardner, H., 1983; Guilford, 1967; Horn, 1994; Spearman, 1927; Sternberg, 1985, 1986, 1988b; Thurstone, 1938).

Yet abilities do not predict school performance completely. In the search for other variables that contribute to school achievement, researchers have devoted considerable attention to the so-called *stylistic aspects* of cognition. The idea of a style reflecting a person's typical or habitual mode of problem-solving, thinking, perceiving, and remembering was initially introduced by Allport (1937). Since then, researchers have developed various theories in attempts to understand the reality of styles (see Curry, 1983; Grigorenko

& Sternberg, 1995; Kagan & Kogan, 1970; Kogan, 1983; Riding & Cheema, 1991; Sternberg, 1988a; Vernon, 1973). In an examination of the literature on styles, Grigorenko and Sternberg (1995) found three general approaches to stylistic aspects of learning.

The first approach is cognition-centered, dealing with cognitive styles. Theorists and researchers in this area have sought to investigate "the characteristic, self-consistent modes of functioning which individuals show in their perceptual and intellectual activities" (Witkin, Oltman, Raskin, & Karp, 1971, p. 3). Some of the main styles studied in this literature have been leveling-sharpening (i.e., a tendency to be hypersensitive to small differences versus a tendency to maximize assimilation; Klein, 1954), equivalence range (i.e., a spontaneous differentiation of heterogeneous items into a complex of related groups; Gardner, R., 1953), field dependence-independence (i.e.,

From *Exceptional Children*, Spring 1997, pp. 295-312. © 1997 by The Council for Exceptional Children. Reprinted by permission.

an ability to differentiate an object from the context; Witkin, 1973), and impulsivity-reflectivity (i.e., a tendency to reflect/disregard alternative solutions; Kagan, 1958). There also have been attempts to integrate specific cognitive styles into a larger framework of cognitive functioning. Kagan and Kogan (1970) have matched particular cognitive styles with stages of problem-solving. Fowler (1977, 1980) and Santostefano (1986) have incorporated the notion of styles into a developmental framework, and Royce and Powell (1983) have conceptualized styles as higher-order strategies that control the deployment of lower-order abilities.

A second approach to studying styles is personality-centered. The theory of Myers and Myers (1980), based on the work of Jung (1923), follows this approach. Myers and Myers have distinguished among two attitudes, extroversion and introversion; two perceptual functions, intuition and sensing; two judgmental functions, thinking and feeling; and two ways of dealing with the outer world, judgment and perception. Gregorc (1984) has distinguished between two ways of handling each of space and time. Thus, people can be classified as abstract or concrete with respect to space, and as sequential or random with respect to time. Miller (1987, 1991) has proposed a somewhat different taxonomy, distinguishing among analytic versus holistic, objective versus subjective, and emotionally stable versus emotionally unstable individuals.

The third approach is activity-centered and tends to focus on styles of learning and teaching. These theories have probably had the most direct application in the classroom. For example, Kolb (1974) has identified four styles of learning: convergent versus divergent and assimilational versus accommodational. Dunn and Dunn (1978) have categorized styles in terms of preferred elements in a learning situation, such as various aspects of the environment (e.g., sound and light) and various aspects of interaction with the self and others (e.g., peers and adults). Renzulli and Smith (1978) have distinguished preferred styles of work in the classroom, such as projects, drill and recitation, and peer teaching. A theory of the same kind but more oriented toward the world of work is that of Holland (1973), who has distinguished among realistic, investigative, artistic, social, and enterprising styles on the job.

These three approaches differ not only in the focus of their interest, but also in the ways they address the functional aspects of styles, mentioned previously. The cognition- and the personality-centered approaches typically imply that styles are either-or constructs (a person could be either field-independent, or field-dependent, but not both). In these approaches, styles are consistent across various tasks and situations, and can be modified very little, if at all, by training during the life span. Cognitive and personality styles are most often viewed as structures, where the focus is placed on stability over time; as such, styles are "givens" in a training or educational setting (Riding & Cheema, 1991). Cognition- and personality-centered theories also usually have built-in evaluating attitudes, assuming that certain styles are better than others: It is often more beneficial in modern society to be reflective rather than impulsive, or sequential rather than random. These styles are measured primarily by specially designed laboratory tasks. In contrast, styles defined in the third, activity-centered approach are measured by methods more easily usable in educational environments. Most authors working in the activity-centered framework view styles as processes, which can be built on and used to compensate for or to remediate weaknesses. In this interpretation, styles are seen as dynamic, not as "frozen forever." There are also no "bad or good" styles—the aim is to find or develop "optimal" styles for particular situations.

THEORY OF MENTAL SELF-GOVERNMENT

Our goal was to build on this work using the theory of mental self-government (Sternberg, 1988a, 1990, 1994). The objective of the theory is to integrate various approaches to style and to provide new directions for theory applied to educational practice.

The basic idea of the theory of mental self-government (Sternberg, 1988a, 1994) is that people, like societies, have to organize or govern themselves. Thus, the theory addresses the question of how people govern and manage their everyday cognitive activities, within the school and without. In the theory of mental self-government, a style of thinking is defined as a preferred way of thinking. It is not an ability, but rather a *favored way of expressing or using one or more abilities.* Two or more people with the same levels or patterns of abilities might nevertheless have very different styles of thinking. Also, two people with similar personality characteristics might differ in their thinking styles. Thus, styles of thinking do not reside in the domain of abilities or in the domain of personality, but at the interface between the two (Sternberg, 1988a, 1988b, 1994).

The theory is organized into five major parts: functions, forms, levels, scope, and leanings of mental self-government (see Table 1). Because scope was not used in our studies, we do not describe it further. The basic idea, then, is that people can be characterized and assessed with regard to habitual functions, forms, levels, and leanings in their cognitive activities.

The theory of mental self-government is rooted in previous work on styles, and so it shares some characteristics with earlier theories. The theory of thinking styles addresses all three domains—the domain of cognition, the domain of personality, and the domain of activity: We view thinking styles as buffers between such internal characteristics as ability and personality, on the one hand, and the external situation, on the other. The theory of mental self-government provides an insight into individually preferred ways of thinking in various activities. Similar to the cognition- and the personality-centered approaches, some thinking styles imply distinct poles: A person can be either local or global, liberal or conservative, but not both (see Table 1 for definitions of these styles). On the contrary, other thinking styles (e.g., legislative, judicial, and executive), like activity-based styles, are not polarizable, because they represent distinct categories that do not lie on a continuum.

The space of thinking styles is multidimensional; the different styles are not orthogonal to each other and tend to correlate and to form profiles. Thus, for example, the executive style often correlates with the conservative style, whereas the legislative style tends to be associated with the liberal one (Martin, 1989). Moreover, although people have a general profile of the ways they choose to think, thinking styles can vary across tasks and situations. A student's preferred style in mathematics, for example, may not necessarily be his or her preferred style in a cooking class. Thus, similarly to the activity-based approach, we view styles as dynamic and adaptive, subject to change and optimization. Unlike the cognition- or the personality-based approaches to styles, we believe that the thinking styles are not fixed, but rather can vary across the life span. The styles that may lead to adaptive performance (either in learning or teaching) at the elementary-school level are not necessarily those that will work best in advanced graduate school training or at work. For example, teachers at the primary level of education tend to favor students with creative thinking styles more than do teachers at the secondary level (Sternberg & Grigorenko, 1995).

Styles are, at least in part, socialized (Sternberg, 1988a; Sternberg & Grigorenko, 1995), and may undergo developmental changes. No thinking style is, in any absolute sense, "good" or "bad." Rather, it can be more or less adaptive for a given task or situation, and what is adaptive in one setting may not be in another.

Finally, thinking styles manifest themselves in any activity, and therefore can be measured in an ecologically valid situation, as well as in a laboratory setting. In other words, thinking styles are reflected in styles of learning and teaching, styles of working and playing, and so on.

In our previous studies (Grigorenko & Sternberg, in press; Sternberg & Grigorenko, 1993, 1995), we operationalized the theory of thinking styles and applied it to various educational activities—in particular, learning and teaching. Our most relevant findings were that there was a significant variation of styles among teachers and students, and that students' thinking styles were predictive of their school success. In the present study, we have attempted to extend our research on thinking styles into the area of gifted education.

METHOD

This study was a part of a large-scale effort to validate Sternberg's *triarchic model of intelligence* (Sternberg, 1985, 1986, 1988b). The triarchic theory distinguishes among three kinds of intellectual giftedness: analytic, creative, and practical. In brief, the theory suggests that individuals gifted in these different ways excel in different activities: The analytically gifted are strong in analyzing, evaluating, and critiquing; the creatively gifted are good at discovering, creating, and inventing; and the practically gifted are strong in implementing, utilizing, and applying. A complete account of the larger study has been presented elsewhere (Sternberg & Clinkenbeard, 1995; Sternberg, Ferrari, Clinkenbeard, & Grigorenko, in press). In this article, we present only the components of the study relevant to thinking styles.

Study Questions

The general purpose of this study was to investigate relations between different types of abilities (as defined by the triarchic theory) and different thinking styles (as defined by the theory of mental self-government). We addressed four research questions, as follows:

1. *Is there a relationship between thinking styles and abilities?* In other words, did stylistic preferences differ for gifted and nongifted students? More specifically, did stylistic preferences differ

among gifted students of different abilities? For example, did creative students tend to be more legislative, and analytical students tend to be more judicial?

2. *After controlling for level of students' abilities, to what degree do thinking styles predict perfor-*

mance? In other words, when the level of abilities was accounted for, did styles contribute anything to understanding variability in academic performance?

3. *Given that four different instructional types (analytical, creative, practical, and traditional) were*

TABLE 1
Styles of Mental Self-Government

Styles	Characterization	Example Relevant to School Settings
Functions		
Legislative	is concerned with creating, formulating, imagining, and planning; likes to formulate his or her own activities	students who like to approach assignments in their own ways, who like to wander off from their textbooks, who like to explore, to do science projects, to write poetry and stories, to compose music, and to create original artworks
Executive	is concerned with implementing and doing; likes to pursue activities structured by others	students who are always ready for the class, who know the assigned material very well, who prefer solving problems over formulating them and like developing someone else's idea more than suggesting their own
Judicial	is concerned with judging, evaluating, and comparing; likes to judge the products of others' activities, or to judge the others themselves	students who like to comment and to critique, who enjoy writing critical essays and commentaries, who prefer evaluating others' ideas over formulating or implementing them
Forms		
Monarchic	tends to focus single-mindedly on one goal or need at a time; a single goal or way of doing things predominates	students who like to engage in single projects, whether in art, science, history, or business
Hierarchic	tends to allow for multiple goals, each of which may have a different priority; knows how to perform multiple tasks within the same time frame, setting priorities for getting them done	students who know how to divide homework so that more time and energy are devoted to more important and more difficult assignments
Oligarchic	tends to allow for multiple goals, all of which are equally important; likes to do multiple tasks within the same time frame but has difficulty setting priorities for getting them done	students who start many projects simultaneously, but have trouble finishing them because there is not enough time and because priorities of the projects have not been set
Anarchic	tends to eschew rules, procedures, and formal systems; often has difficulty adjusting to the school as a system	students who do not do much planning and tend to choose projects they work on in a random way; do not like to follow the established curriculum and have difficulties meeting deadlines

TABLE 1
(Continued)

Styles	Characterization	Example Relevant to School Settings
Levels		
Global	prefers to deal with the large picture and abstractions	students who like writing on the global message and meaning of a work of art, or on the significance of a particular discovery for mankind
Local	prefers dealing with details and concrete issues	students who like writing on the components of a work of art, or on the details of an experiment
Leaning		
Liberal	likes to do things in new ways, to have change in his or her life, and to defy conventions	students who like figuring out how to operate new equipment and like non-traditional challenging tasks
Conservative	likes traditions and stability; prefers doing things in tried and true ways	students who like to be shown all the steps of operating equipment and like to be given precise instructions for performing a task

used, do students with certain thinking styles who are placed in a particular instructional group that is matched or mismatched with their ability, perform any better than students with other thinking styles? For example, did creative students, scoring high on the judicial thinking style and placed in the group with analytical instruction, perform better than creative students in the same group, but with lower scores on the judicial thinking style?

4. *Given that various tools of performance evaluation (homework, written examinations, and a project) were used in this study, did students with particular thinking styles do better in one form of evaluation than another?* In other words, did specific forms of evaluation benefit students with particular thinking styles?

Participants

Participants were high school students, ranging in age from 13 to 16 years, who attended the 1993 Yale Summer Psychology Program (YSPP). The program was advertised through brochures and newsletters distributed to schools in the United States and other countries. Schools were asked to submit nominations of gifted students to the Program Committee of the YSPP. A selection procedure was based on the students' performance on the Sternberg Triarchic Abilities Test (STAT), Level H, designed for advanced high school and college students (Sternberg, 1993). The STAT was sent to schools that placed nominations. The test was administered to the nominated students in their own schools.

A total of 199 students (146 females and 53 males) were selected for participation in the summer program of 1993. (Altogether the YSPP enrolled 225 students, of whom 25 were admitted for pay, to provide tuition for eligible students. These 25 students were excluded from further analyses. Moreover, one student was expelled for discipline problems.)

Of these students, 3 (1.5%) were entering grade 9, 25 (12.6%) were entering Grade 10, 77 (38.7%) were entering Grade 11, and 94 (47.2%) were entering Grade 12. The program participants were fairly widely distributed ethnically (based on students' own reports): 60% European American, 11% African American, 6% Hispanic American, and 17% American from another ethnic minority. Further, 4% of the students were from South Africa, and 2% "other."

Materials and Procedures

Different instruments were used for identification, performance assessment, and styles evaluation. All instruments were developed prior to the study, and complete accounts of their psychometric properties can be found elsewhere. Thus, only brief technical descriptions will be provided here.

Identification. Identification and classification of students into ability groups were done using the results of the STAT multiple-choice and essay subtests. There are nine multiple-choice subtests, each including 2 sample items and 4 test items, for a total of 36 items (for details, see Sternberg et al., in press). The item types on the nine multiple-choice subtests are: (1) analytic-verbal—inferring the meanings of neologisms from natural contexts; (2) analytic-quantitative—inferring subsequent numbers on the basis of series of numbers; (3) analytic-figural—inferring the missing part of each matrix based on the matrix's overall structure; (4) practical-verbal—performing everyday reasoning; (5) practical-quantitative—performing everyday math; (6) practical-figural—performing route planning; (7) creative-verbal—solving verbal analogies preceded by counterfactual premises; (8) creative-quantitative—learning and applying novel number operations; (9) creative-figural—extracting and applying rules for figure transformations. The three essay subtests involved analytical thinking (requiring students to analyze the advantages and disadvantages of having police or security guards in a school building), creative thinking (requiring students to describe how they would reform their school system to produce an ideal one), and practical thinking (requiring students to specify a problem in their life, and to state three practical solutions for solving it). Multiple-choice subtests and essays were standardized, and then three primary STAT scores (analytical, creative, and practical) were obtained. The details of the validation of the STAT have been described in detail elsewhere (Sternberg & Clinkenbeard, 1995; Sternberg et al., in press). In brief, a varimax-rotated principal components analysis of the multiple-choice subtests of the STAT resulted in 9 specific factors (factor loadings varied from .92 to .98) with approximately equal eigenvalues, which ranged from 1.01 to 0.98. The factor structure shows that each subtest represents a unique process (analytic, creative, practical)—content (verbal, quantitative, figural) combination, suggesting that the STAT does tap into different abilities, instead of simply measuring Spearman's general ability (*g*, Spearman, 1927). The Kuder-Richardson-20 (KR-20) reliability coefficients for multiple-choice items ranged from .49 to .64. The interrater agreement on the essays ranged from .58 to .69. The multiple-choice subtests scores correlated with essay questions at $p < .01$. The correlations with the Watson-Glaser Critical Thinking Appraisal and the Concept Mastery tests used for external validation were significant, but of moderate magnitude.

Based on their STAT performance, all students enrolled in the program were classified into five different groups. The STAT subtest scores were standardized, so they could be compared across different subtests. Students were identified as "high" in an aspect of ability based on their strongest test attainment and their score in respect to the group average. Thus, we first constructed three groups: (a) a group in which students demonstrated a high level of analytical ability ($N = 39$, 19.6%); (b) a group in which students were high in creative ability ($N = 38$, 19.1%); and (c) a group in which students were high in practical ability ($N = 35$, 17.6%). For students to be classified as "high" in analytic, creative, or practical ability, their total score for a given ability was required to be at least a half-standard deviation above the group average and at least a half-standard deviation above their own scores for the other two abilities measured by the STAT (e.g., analytic higher than creative and practical). Although the half-standard deviation criterion might sound weak, recall that all students entering the program were first nominated as gifted by their schools.

For the fourth group, we defined a "balanced" gifted group ($N = 40$, 20.1%). For students to be classified as balanced, they had to score above the group average for all three abilities. Finally, the fifth group was composed of students who scored at or below the group average for all three abilities ($N = 47$, 23.6%). These students were classified as not identified as gifted.

Instruction. Students were given an intensive, 4-week, college-level psychology course. The course consisted of three main components: the *text* (Sternberg, 1995), the *lecture series*, and the *afternoon sections*. The first two components were common to all groups, whereas the last constituted the treatment and diverged across groups. There were four types of afternoon sections, in which section leaders emphasized different skills: memory (traditional educational paradigm), analytical thinking, creative thinking, or practical thinking. The students were divided among instructional groups in such a way that all groups had close to equal numbers of students of each of the five types of ability patterns. Thus, some students were placed in groups in which the type of afternoon section matched their abilities ($N = 83$, e.g., 10 of 38 creative students were placed in groups in which the section leaders taught for creative thinking), while the remaining students were mismatched ($N = 113$, e.g., 9 creative students were place in groups with the section leaders teaching for practical thinking).

Performance Assessment. In our previous studies on thinking styles, we found that thinking styles predict school success: Students were viewed by their teachers as achieving at higher levels when the students' profiles of styles matched those of their teachers (Sternberg & Grigorenko, 1995). In other words, teachers appear to value more highly students who are stylistically similar to themselves. However, the evaluation of academic performance was done through students' class grades: that is, it could have been confounded with teachers' subjective perception of a given student. Thus, we were able to show that thinking styles were relevant to school performance, but our measures of school performance were, most likely, confounded with the teacher's view of a given student. In the present study, we had a chance to eliminate the possible bias that may have resulted from the use of class grades as indicators of academic performance. In this study, students' performance was rated by independent raters, who had never met the students and thus made their judgments based only on the quality of students' writing.

All students received identical kinds of assessments: two major homework assignments, a final project, and two exams. Each of the assessments involved various tasks testing for analytical, creative, and practical skills. Some examples of assessments are (a) compare Freud's theory of dreaming to Jung's [analytical]; (b) design an experiment to test a theory of dreaming [creative]; and (c) discuss the implications of Jung's theory of dreaming for your life [practical].

Four raters scored all performance assessments, rating each task for a corresponding ability (e.g., analytic ratings for the analytic performances). All ratings were on a scale of 1 (low) to 9 (high). The effective reliabilities of quality ratings for four raters varied from .73 to .96. Principal-components analyses were used to extract the common variance in the ratings of the four judges for each of the analytic, creative, and practical ratings for the three types of assessments. The first principal-component score of these analyses was then used to assess achievement in the following analyses. Thus, there were six resulting factor scores: three abilities (analytic, creative, and practical), evaluated in three different assessment settings (two homework assignments, a final project, and two exams).

Using these scores, we created six summary measures. Three measures reflected students' performance on all homework assignments, all exams, and the final project. Three other measures reflected students' performance on analyti-

cal, creative, and practical tasks in different assessment settings. These six measures were used in the further analyses.

Evaluation of Styles. In the present study, students' thinking styles were evaluated in two different ways: (a) a self-report questionnaire and (b) a set of thinking-styles tasks. Detailed descriptions of the thinking-styles instruments can be found elsewhere (Grigorenko & Sternberg, in press; Sternberg & Grigorenko, 1995). The purpose of having different measures was to have converging operations (Garner, Hake, & Eriksen, 1956) that measured the same constructs. In this way, sources of bias and error associated with individual measures would be reduced (Campbell & Fiske, 1959). The thinking styles measures are as follows:

- *Thinking Styles Questionnaire (TSQ).* This questionnaire consisted of 104 items, 8 for each of 13 scales: legislative, executive, judicial, monarchic, hierarchic, oligarchic, anarchic, global, local, liberal, conservative, internal, and external. Items were in the form of a Likert scale with ratings ranging from 1 (low) to 7 (high). In the further analyses, we used only 11 scales: Internal and external styles were excluded, because the other thinking styles measure (see the following description) did not include the tasks measuring these styles. The scales' internal consistency coefficients, obtained from an independent sample of school students prior to the study, ranged from .55 to .83 (see Table 2), suggesting adequate reliability of the instrument.

- *Set of Thinking Styles Tasks for Students (STS).* The STS was a set of 16 different tasks and preference items for students. The tasks and preference items were assumed to map directly onto 11 thinking styles: legislative, executive, judicial, monarchic, hierarchic, oligarchic, anarchic, global, local, liberal, and conservative. Students had to solve problems and make choices, and every response was coded via a scoring map of correspondence between responses and styles. For each scale, the sum of the scores across tasks and preference items was considered to be a measure of the thinking style. When preferences and choices were reordered into dichotomous form, the KR-20 reliability coefficients ranged from .59 to .74 (Sternberg & Grigorenko, 1995).

Examples of items from the TSQ and STS, as well as internal-consistency alpha reliabilities of subscales (calculated on independent but comparable samples of students not involved in these studies), are shown in Table 2. The correlations between corresponding scales of the TSQ and STS varied between $r = .45$ ($N = 277$, $p < .0001$) for the conservative style and $r = .20$ ($N = 277$, $p < .001$) for the global style.

Principal-components analyses were used to extract the common variance in the scale scores obtained from the TSQ and STS. The first principal-component scores were then used as measures of the styles in the data analyses. The variance explained by the first principal component of each style was 64% for legislative; 69% for executive; 61% for judicial; 58% for monarchic; 50% for hierarchic; 52% for oligarchic; 50% for anarchic; 60% for global; 63% for local; 72% for liberal; and 72% for conservative. This procedure allowed us to separate out questionnaire-specific measurement error, at least to some extent, and to pre-

TABLE 2

Examples of Some of the Items and Reliability Coefficients of the Scales of the Thinking Styles Questionnaire (TSQ) and the Set of Thinking Styles Tasks for Students (STS)

Style	Sample Item	Reliability (α)
Thinking Styles Questionnaire (TSQ)		$N = 277$
Legislative	When faced with a problem, I use my own ideas and strategies to solve it.	.81
Executive	Before starting a task or project, I check to see what method or procedure should be used.	.83
Judicial	I enjoy work that involves analyzing, grading, or comparing things.	.73
Monarchic	I like to concentrate on one task at a time.	.84
Hierarchic	In talking or writing down ideas, I like to have the issues organized in order of importance.	.81
Oligarchic	I prefer to work on a project or task that is acceptable and approved by my peers.	.54
Anarchic	When there are many important things to do, I try to do as many as I can in whatever time I have.	.55
Global	I care more about the general effect than about details of a task I have to do.	.83
Local	I like to collect detailed or specific information for projects I work on.	.66
Liberal	I like to change routines in order to improve the way tasks are done.	.88
Conservative	I like situations where I can follow a set routine.	.83

Set of Thinking Styles Tasks for Students (STS)

Item Examples:

When I am studying literature, I prefer: (a) to make up my own story with my own characters and my own plot *(legislative)*; (b) to evaluate the author's style, to criticize the author's ideas, and to evaluate characters' actions *(judicial)*; (c) to follow the teacher's advice and interpretations of author's positions, and to use the teacher's way of analyzing literature *(executive)*; (d) to do something else (please describe your preferences in the space below).

An example of a task to distinguish among oligarchic, hierarchical, monarchic, and anarchic thinking styles is: You are the mayor of a large northeastern city. You have a city budget this year of $100 million. Below is a list of prob-

TABLE 2
(Continued)

lems currently facing your city. Your job is to decide how you will spend the $100 million available to improve your city. Next to each problem is the projected cost to eliminate a problem entirely. In the space on the next page, list each problem on which you will spend city money and how much money you will budget for that problem. Whether you spend money on one, some, or all problems is up to you, but be sure your plan will not exceed the $100 million available. Whether you spend all the money to solve one or a few problems or divide the money partially to solve many problems is up to you. You have one additional problem—you are up for reelection next year, so consider public opinion when making your decisions.

Problems facing your city:
(1) Drug problem ($100,000,000); (2) The roads (they are old, full of potholes, and need to be repaired) ($25,000,000); (3) You have no new land for landfill and you need to build a recycling center ($25,000,000); (4) You need shelters for the homeless ($50,000,000); (5) You must replace subway cars and city buses; you need to buy new ones for the public transportation system ($50,000,000); (6) The public school teachers are demanding a salary increase and they are going to go on strike ($30,000,000); (7) Sanitation workers are demanding a salary increase and they are going to go on strike ($30,000,000); (8) An increase in unemployment has increased the number of welfare recipients ($80,000,000); (9) The AIDS epidemic has created the need for public education on AIDS prevention and you need to build an AIDS hospital ($100,000,000); and (10) You need to build a new convention center to attract out-of-state tourists. This could generate additional revenue for the next fiscal year ($70,000,000).

serve for further analyses the styles scores reflecting only variance shared by the two instruments.

Some styles were highly correlated (e.g., local and global, $r = -.67$, $p < .001$). To reduce the factor space of styles (i.e., to decrease the number of dependent variables), we performed factor analyses with varimax rotation, using the factor scores described previously. The outcome of this analysis was a nine-factor structure, which explained 98% of the total variance. Four of the styles created two factors with different directions of factor loadings (FL). Thus, liberal and conservative styles loaded on one factor; FLs were .90 and -.89, respectively. Global and local styles also created a two-pole factor, with FLs of .93 and -.90, respectively. All other styles formed independent factors. The FLs were as follows: judicial, .99; executive, .81; legislative, .82; monarchic, .98; hierarchic, .97; oligarchic, .99; and anarchic, .99. The factor scores of these 9 factors (local-global, liberal-conservative, judicial, executive, legislative, hierarchic, oligarchic, monarchic, and anarchic) were used in the further analyses.

RESULTS

Based on the results of our previous work (Grigorenko & Sternberg, in press; Sternberg & Grigorenko, 1993, 1995) and in correspondence with the research questions of this study, we formed a set of working hypotheses:

1. *We expected to find no association of styles with abilities.* That is, we did not expect to find that students with different ability patterns would demonstrate consistent stylistic preferences.
2. *We expected that at least some thinking styles would contribute to predictions of overall academic performance,* although we did not specify which ones.
3. *We did not expect to find any difference in academic performance of matched versus mismatched students of different styles.* That is, we did not expect to find any interaction effects between types of instruction (being matched/mismatched) and thinking styles. For example, we did not expect judicial creative students to perform better in the analytical instruction group than did legislative creative students in this group.
4. *We expected that students with certain thinking styles would perform better in some forms of evaluation than in others.*

We present the results of our study with respect to the formulated research questions.

Styles, Abilities, Gender, and Grade

In the first set of analyses, we tested whether there were any group differences between styles for male versus female students, for students of differing ability patterns, and for students in different school grades. Multivariate analysis of variance was used. None of the main effects or interaction effects was significant. Thus, students' thinking styles did not differ across sex, grade, or ability patterns.

When Abilities Are Taken Into Account, Do Styles Still Predict Academic Performance?

We explored the question of whether thinking styles add anything to the explanatory power of ability measures for predicting academic performance. First, we computed correlations between academic performance measures, STAT scores, and the measures of the thinking styles (Table 3). All three STAT components correlated significantly with the assessments of performance across different abilities (the correlations ranged from $r = .34$, $p < .0001$ to $r = .15$, $p < .05$). Seven out of nine correlations between the STAT components and types of assessments were also significant, but practical and creative components of the STAT did not correlate significantly with performance on the homework assignments. It is important to note the fairly high correlations between all academic performance measures and scores on the analytical subtest of the STAT. These correlations were stronger than the diagonal correlations between subtests of the STAT and corresponding performance measures. We explain the presence of these correlations as a reflection of the fact that students' performance on all of the assignments, exams, and the final project were inevitably confounded with the general ability of each student to understand and analyze the theory with which he or she was working. This occurred despite our efforts to formulate the tasks in the manner most suitable for each of the studied abilities. The magnitude of these off-diagonal correlations, however, does not differ significantly from the magnitude of the diagonal correlations. For example, even the largest discrepancy, $r = .34$ versus $r = .17$, did not represent a significant difference: $z = 1.82$, $p > .05$. In other words, the presence of these off-diagonal correlations statistically does not undermine the discriminant validity of the STAT.

Only five styles correlated significantly with measures of performance. Indicators of the judicial style correlated significantly with performance on all tasks and in all assessment settings. In addition, students with the legislative style tended to perform better on both the final projects and the exams and on both the analytical and creative measures. On the contrary, the performance of executive students was worse on the final project and on both the creative and analytical tasks. Liberal students tended to do better on the final project, and hierarchical students did better on the creative assignments. Thus, the correlational pattern suggests that the judicial, legislative, and ex-

ecutive styles showed significant associations with academic performance. In particular, students with higher scores on the legislative and judicial thinking styles tended to do better, whereas students who scored high on the executive style tended to do worse, on average.

Among the correlations between the thinking styles measures and the STAT components, only the association between the STAT creative component and the liberal-conservative styles factor was significant ($r = .22$, $p < .005$), with liberal students being more creative. This general lack of associations between the styles and the ability measures largely supports our predictions of no differences on thinking styles in groups of students with different ability patterns. Of course, we cannot prove the null hypothesis.

Thus, the simple correlational analyses suggested that students' performance was associated not only with their levels and patterns of abilities, but also with their thinking styles. Moreover, the amount of variance explained by the STAT subtests in the measures of performance was of the same magnitude as the amount of variance explained by some of the styles (e.g., judicial). In addition, the fact that there was only one significant correlation between the STAT measures and the thinking styles suggests that associations of thinking styles with academic performance are independent of the correlations between academic performance and abilities.

To test further the predictive power of styles, we performed a series of multiple-regression analyses in which the predicted variables were the measures of achieved performance on tasks requiring use of various abilities and performance on various tasks in different assessment settings, and the predictors were the measures on the corresponding STAT component and the five thinking styles that were found to be correlated with the measures of academic performance. Thus the multiple-regression equations were both theoretically based and used the information obtained in the correlation analyses.

The independent variables predicted 16% of the variance in the summary measure of performance on the analytic tasks ($F = 5.3$, $p < .0001$). The variables that contributed significantly were the STAT analytic component ($F = 13.2$, $p < .0005$, $B = .18$), judicial style ($F = 3.6$, $p < .05$, $B = .09$), legislative style ($F = 5.0$, $p < .05$, $B = .11$), and executive style ($F = 3.4$, $p < .05$, $B = -.10$). For performance on the creative tasks, the predictors explained 15% of the variance ($F = 5.0$, $p < .0001$). Significant contributions to the explained variance were from the STAT creative component ($F = 7.3$, $p < .05$, $B = .14$), judicial style ($F = 6.8$,

TABLE 3
Correlations of Abilities, Academic Performance, and Styles

	Performance					
Item	*Analytic*	*Creative*	*Practical*	*Homework*	*Exams*	*Project*
Abilities						
STAT-Analytical	.25*	.34*	.34*	.26*	.27*	.31*
STAT-Creative	.15*	.21*	.20*	.13	.16*	.20*
STAT-Practical	.15*	.17*	.17*	.12	.18*	.15*
Thinking styles (factor scores)						
Legislative	.17*	.16*	.14	.12	.14*	.17*
Judicial	.15*	.20*	.23*	.21*	.18*	.15*
Executive	-.15*	-.16*	-.10	-.12	-.07	-.18*
Monarchic	-.06	-.06	-.08	-.05	-.04	-.10
Hierarchic	.06	.16*	.11	.13	.07	.08
Oligarchic	-.06	-.11	-.11	-.12	-.11	.03
Anarchic	-.08	-.13	-.12	-.10	-.08	-.12
Local-Global	.07	.04	.09	.05	.01	.12
Liberal-Conservative	.14	.10	.08	.03	.09	.16

Note: STAT = Sternberg Triarchic Abilities Test, Level H.
* $p < .05$.

$p < .01$, $B = .13$), and executive style ($F = 4.3$, $p < .05$, $B = -.11$). Finally, the independent variables predicted 13% of the variance in performance on the practical tasks ($F = 4.1$, $p < .001$, $B = .18$). Only two variables contributed significantly: the practical component of the STAT ($F = 6.7$, $p < .01$, $B = .14$) and judicial style ($F = 10.6$, $p < .001$, $B = .17$). Thus, performance on the analytic, creative, and practical tasks is dependent not only on the level of the corresponding ability, but also on stylistic preferences. In general, the more judicial or legislative a student was, the better his or her performance was, whereas the more executive a student was, the worse was his or her performance.

The results of the multiple-regression analyses predicting performance on various tasks in different assessment settings were homogeneous. For all three overall dependent measures

(exam, homework, and final project evaluations), the analytical component of the STAT was the best predictor ($p < .0001$ in all three models, B ranging from .24 to .27). The judicial style made a statistically significant contribution in explaining variation in performance on the exams ($F = 6.3$, $p < .01$, $B = .15$), on homework ($F = 8.0$, $p < .005$, $B = .15$), and on the final project ($F = 3.3$, $p < .05$, $B = .10$). Moreover, three other styles contributed significantly to prediction of final project performance: the legislative style ($F = 5.1$, $p < .05$, $B = .13$), the liberal style ($F = 3.8$, $p < .05$, $B = .12$), and the executive style ($F = 4.4$, $p < .05$, $B = -.13$).

Styles and Different Types of Instruction

In the previous analyses, we investigated the predictive power of styles for academic performance over and above abilities across all groups, regardless of the type of instruction. The question for the following set of analyses was whether styles make a difference in academic performance of matched versus mismatched students, that is, whether there is an interaction effect between type of instruction (matched/mismatched) and thinking styles. For example, do judicial creative students perform better in the analytical instruction group than do legislative creative students?

At the first stage of these analyses, we conducted analysis of variance to ensure that there were no accidental clusterings of thinking styles within different instructional groups or within groups of matched and mismatched students. There were not. At the second stage, we performed two series of multiple-regression analyses of academic performance, testing for (a) possible interaction effects between thinking styles and type of instruction, and (b) possible interaction effects between thinking styles and matched/mismatched placement. No main or interaction effects with type of instruction were found. There was an effect of match for the summary score on analytic tasks and homework assignments, with matched students doing better than mismatched students, but no interaction effects with thinking styles were found.

Styles and Different Types of Evaluation

Finally, a last set of analyses was based on the hypothesis that various assessment methods might favor different thinking styles (Sternberg, 1994). Specifically, we suggested that while types of assessments do not differentially benefit students of different ability patterns (e.g., creative students would do as well on the homework assignments as on the exams), various types of evaluation could be differentially beneficial for students of different styles (e.g., a judicial student would do better on the exams than on the final project).

To perform these analyses, we recoded the thinking-styles scores. We analyzed the distribution of thinking styles scores in the sample and adapted a cut-point of 1.5 standard deviations to detect the 10%-15% of the students who scored the highest on each of the 11 styles (we used raw scores on thinking styles in these analyses). (Due to the limited size of our sample, we could not adapt a traditional conservative cut-off score of 2 standard deviations above the mean.)

These students were considered to be "high" on a given style. Then we carried out analyses of variance to test whether members of the high groups performed better in particular assessment settings than in others. Table 4 shows the results of these analyses. The table shows that there is a significant difference in performance of

highly judicial, highly liberal, and highly oligarchic thinkers versus all other students on exams, judicial thinkers versus other students on homework, and executive and anarchic thinkers versus other students on the final project. Moreover, certain combinations of styles (e.g., judicial and global) tend to enhance the performance in different assessment situations.

The patterns of the means suggest that the exam format was most favorable for judicial thinkers ($\mu = .39$ in the group of highly judicial students versus $\mu = -.03$ in the group of other students) and for thinkers of other styles who were also high on the judicial style. This format of assessment was least beneficial for legislative/global thinkers ($\mu = -2.11$ in the group of legislative-global thinkers versus $\mu = -.04$ or higher in other groups), and was disadvantageous as well for oligarchic students ($\mu = -.44$ in the group of oligarchic thinkers versus $\mu = .02$ in the group of other students).

The format of the independent final project was the least beneficial for executive students ($\mu = -.44$ among executive thinkers versus $\mu = .07$ in the group of all other students) and, moreover, for students with virtually all combinations of other styles with the executive style. In addition, anarchic students tended to do worse than did all other students combined ($\mu = -.37$ versus $\mu = .08$, respectively). The independent project was the most favorable for legislative/local ($\mu = 2.30$ versus $\mu = .29$ or lower in other groups), legislative/anarchic ($\mu = .51$ versus $\mu = .05$ or lower in other groups), and legislative/liberal ($\mu = 2.28$ versus $\mu = .29$ or lower in other groups) thinkers.

Homework assignments were quite variable, and, in addition, there were few constraints on how they had to be done; for example, a student could request a consultation with a teaching fellow, or a group of students could complete the assignments together. Thus, this particular type of assessment did not appear to be consistently beneficial for students with any particular stylistic preferences, except for judicial thinkers ($\mu = .40$ versus $\mu = -.04$ in the group of all other students).

DISCUSSION

This study attempted to investigate patterns of thinking styles in a group of gifted children. We obtained the following results, in summary:

- There are no differences in thinking styles between groups of students with different ability patterns.

- Certain thinking styles contribute significantly to prediction of academic performance.
- The degree of this contribution is not affected by the type of instruction students are given.
- Students with particular thinking styles do better in some forms of evaluation than in others.

A few interesting conclusions can be drawn from the results. First, we saw no distinct patterns of particular thinking styles among the students by abilities, gender, or grade. These results are similar to those of our previous findings in a sample of unselected (nongifted) students in four different schools (Sternberg & Grigorenko, 1995). Thus, in two independent groups of students, we found no direct links between styles and abilities. A variety of styles can be associated with high levels of ability. Moreover, various types of abilities can be associated with a given style.

The finding of no difference in profiles of styles in males versus females is also not a surprising one: Previously we also found no association

between students' gender and their styles (Sternberg & Grigorenko, 1995). A lack of grade differences in styles might be explained by the fact that in both studies we worked primarily with high-school students, limiting the age range of participants to 12-17 years of age. We intentionally limited our samples to this age range due to the fact that we used self-report questionnaires requiring a certain level of metacognitive capacities to reflect stable patterns of preferences and behaviors (Schwab-Stone, Fallon, Briggs, & Crowther, 1994). However, the theory of mental self-government assumes the presence of developmental changes in stylistic preferences; future studies, implementing measures other than self-report ones, might show significant age/grade effects.

In our larger-scale study (Sternberg & Clinkenbeard, 1995; Sternberg et al., in press), we found a significant instruction-by-ability interaction and showed that performance of students with a certain ability pattern was higher on the tasks corresponding to their abilities if these students were placed in a matching instructional

TABLE 4
Styles and Types of Assessment

Styles	Exams	Homework Assignments	Final Paper
Judicial	$F(1, 186) = 3.3, p < .05$	$F(1, 186) = 5.8, p < .05$	
Executive			$F(1,186) = 4.1, p < .05$
Liberal	$F(1,186) = 3.3, p < .05$		
Oligarchic	$F(1,186) = 4.3, p < .05$		
Anarchic			$F(1,186) = 4.4, p < .05$
Legislative*Global	$F(3,186) = 3.6, p < .01$		
Legislative*Local			$F(3,186) = 3.6, p < .05$
Legislative*Liberal			$F(3,186) = 3.6, p < .05$
Legislative*Anarchic			$F(3,186) = 2.8, p < .05$
Judicial*Global	$F(3,184) = 2.3, p < .05$		
Judicial*Hierarchic	$F(3,186) = 4.5, p < .005$	$F(3,186) = 2.5, p < .05$	
Executive*Global			$F(3,186) = 4.9, p < .005$
Executive* Conservative			$F(3,186) = 4.1, p < .01$
Executive*Anarchic			$F(3,186) = 2.9, p < .05$

Note: The table shows only the styles and the combination of the styles that yielded statistically significant results. The significance values are corrected for multiple comparisons by adjusting *p* values.

group (e.g., analytical students placed in the groups with analytical instructions did better on the analytical tasks than did other students). In this study, due to the study design, we had a chance to investigate how, if at all, thinking styles modify the relationships between ability type and the mode of instruction. We discovered no significant buffering effects that could have been attributed to styles. For example, creative students, placed in instructional groups that did not match their ability, did not differ in their performance when their styles were taken into account. These findings, however, should be interpreted with caution: The whole program took only 4 weeks; and it is possible that there simply was not enough time for stylistic differences to manifest themselves.

Further, in the present study, we had a unique opportunity to evaluate the contribution various thinking styles made to students' performance in a given situation, when these evaluations were conducted by psychologists who did not meet the students in person, but judged their performance on the basis of their writing. Of course, a valid argument could be made that such a type of evaluation is biased in favor of students with a high level of writing skills. Yet, taking into account this drawback of our evaluation system, we think that these assessments were less subjective than traditional school teachers' grades, and therefore provided us with an opportunity to test whether thinking styles predict students' performance, over and above the students' abilities. This particular aspect of the design was especially interesting, due to the fact that in our previous research we showed that teachers tend to overestimate the extent to which their students share their own styles, and that students in fact receive higher grades and more favorable evaluations when their styles more closely match those of their teachers (Sternberg & Grigorenko, 1995). Thus, the opportunity to separate teacher-dependent variance in performance assessment and to study the "purer" contributions of ability and styles was explored.

We found that students' performance was associated not only with their levels and types of abilities, but also with at least three thinking styles (judicial, executive, and legislative). The highest predictive power was demonstrated by the judicial style. But, in interpreting these results, we should say that a significant portion of the YSPP academic activities was based on analytical work, which involved comparing, contrasting, and evaluating. Even though special "create-and-implement" tasks were designed to benefit creative and practical students, these tasks were based on ma-

terial that needed to be critically evaluated by a student. Thus, even the creative and practical tasks in our program involved a significant amount of analytical effort. We might have found a different "most favorable style" were the same study carried out in an art school or a boy/girl-scout program. However, the most general conclusion remains the same: Styles add to our understanding of students' performance, and therefore should be taken into consideration in school settings.

Yet one more illustration of the importance of the styles came from the last, and probably the most interesting part of the study, where we compared the performance of students in "high" and "other" groups in a particular style. In these analyses, we detected a number of interaction effects between various styles and different assessment procedures. We found that the examination format was most beneficial for judicial students, whereas the final projects favored legislative students and disadvantaged executive students. Although our sample was not large enough to study interactions between various styles in more detail, the results clearly suggest that different types of assessment benefit different types of thinkers (see also Sternberg, 1994). The take-home message of these analyses is that styles do matter, and teachers should systematically vary their assessment to meet the needs of a larger number of students.

These latter analyses are of practical value. A teacher of gifted students should try to assess the students' performance by using an array of different assessment procedures. Independent of their patterns of abilities, gifted students of different thinking styles tend to perform better when the method of assessment matches their thinking styles. Our results, obtained in this and other studies, suggest that short-answer/multiple-choice items appear to be most beneficial for executive, local, judicial, and hierarchic thinkers. Macroanalytic essays are advantageous for judicial-global students, whereas microanalytic essays will be advantageous for judicial-local thinkers. Timed assignments may be beneficial for hierarchic students and detrimental for anarchic ones. Monarchic students tend to shine when the assignment requires high commitment, whereas oligarchic students are able to divide their resources equally between a number of tasks. Open-ended assignments, projects, and portfolios will benefit legislative thinkers and may frustrate executive ones.

In summary, the diversity of styles among students implies that students need a variety of means of assessment to maximize and show to an optimal extent their talents and achievements.

REFERENCES

Allport, G. (1937). *Personality: A psychological interpretation*. New York: Holt.

Campbell, D. T., & Fiske, D. W. (1959). Convergent and discriminant validation by the multitrait multimethod matrix. *Psychological Bulletin, 56*, 81-105.

Carroll, J. B. (1993). *Human cognitive abilities: A survey of factor-analytic studies*. New York, NY: Cambridge University Press.

Curry, L. (1983). An organization of learning styles theory and constructs. *ERIC Document*. 235 185.

Dunn, R., & Dunn, K. (1978). *Teaching students through their individual learning styles*. Reston, VA: Reston Publishing.

Fowler, W. (1977). Sequence and styles in cognitive development. In F. Weizmann & I. Uzgiris (Eds.), *The structuring of experience* (pp. 265-295). New York: Plenum Press.

Fowler, W. (1980). Cognitive differentiation and developmental learning. In H. Rees & L. Lipsitt (Eds.), *Advances in child development and behavior, Vol. 15* (pp. 163-206). New York: Academic Press.

Gardner, H. (1983). *Frames of mind: The theory of multiple intelligences*. New York: Basic Books.

Gardner, R. (1953). Cognitive style in categorizing behavior. *Perceptual and Motor Skills, 22*, 214-233.

Garner, W. R., Hake, H. W., & Eriksen, C. W. (1956). Operationism and the concept of perception. *Psychological Review, 63*, 149-159.

Gregorc, A. F. (1984). Style as a symptom: A phenomenological perspective. *Theory Into Practice, 23*, 51-55.

Grigorenko, E. L., & Sternberg, R. J. (1995). Thinking styles. In D. H. Saklofske & M. Zeidner (Eds.) *International handbook of personality and intelligence* (pp. 205-229). New York: Plenum Press.

Grigorenko, E. L., & Sternberg, R. J. (in press). Styles of thinking in school settings. *Vestnik Moskovskogo Universiteta. Seria 14. Psikhologia*.

Guilford, J. P. (1967). *The nature of human intelligence*. New York: McGraw-Hill.

Holland, J. L. (1973). *Making vocational choices: A theory of careers*. Englewood Cliffs, NJ: Prentice-Hall.

Horn, J. L. (1994). Theory of fluid and crystallized intelligence. In R. J. Sternberg (Ed.), *The encyclopedia of human intelligence. Vol. 1* (pp. 443-451). New York: Macmillan.

Jung, C. (1923). *Psychological types*. New York: Harcourt Brace.

Kagan, J. (1958). The concept of identification. *Psychological Review, 65*, 296-305.

Kagan, J., & Kogan, N. (1970). Individual variation in cognitive processes. In P. A. Mussen (Ed.), *Carmichael's manual of child psychology. Vol. 1* (pp. 1273-1365). New York: Wiley.

Klein, G. S. (1954). Need and regulation. In M. R. Jones (Ed.), *Nebraska symposium on motivation* (pp. 474-505). Lincoln: University of Nebraska Press.

Kogan, N. (1983). Stylistic variation in childhood and adolescence: Creativity, metaphor, and cognitive style. In P. H. Mussen (Ed.), *Handbook of child psychology, Vol. 3* (pp. 630-706). New York: Wiley.

Kolb, D. A. (1974). On management and the learning process. In D. A. Kolb, I. M. Rubin, & J. M. McIntyre (Eds.), *Organizational psychology* (pp. 239-252). Englewood Cliffs, NJ: Prentice-Hall.

Martin, M. (1989). *Mind as mental self-government: Construct validation of a theory of intellectual styles*. Unpublished manuscript, Yale University, New Haven, Connecticut.

Miller, A. (1987). Cognitive styles: An integrated model. *Educational Psychology, 7*, 251-268.

Miller, A. (1991). Personality types, learning styles and educational goals. *Educational Psychology, 11*, 217-238.

Myers, I. B., & Myers, P. B. (1980). *Gifts differing*. Palo Alto, CA: Consulting Psychologists Press.

Renzulli, J. S., & Smith, L. H. (1978). *Learning styles inventory*. Mansfield Center, CT: Creative Learning Press.

Riding, R., & Cheema, I. (1991). Cognitive styles: An overview and integration. *Educational Psychology, 11*, 193-215.

Royce, J., & Powell, A. (1983). *Theory of personality and individual differences: Factors, systems and process*. Englewood Cliffs, NJ: Prentice-Hall.

Santostefano, S. (1986). Cognitive controls, metaphors and contexts: An approach to cognition and emotion. In D. Bearison & H. Zimiles (Eds.), *Thought and emotion: Developmental perspectives* (pp. 217-238). Hillsdale, NJ: Lawrence Erlbaum.

Schwab-Stone, M., Fallon, T., Briggs, M., & Crowther, B. (1994). Reliability of diagnostic reporting for children 6-11 years: A test-retest study of the Revised Diagnostic Schedule for Children. *The American Journal of Psychiatry, 157*, 1048-1054.

Spearman, C. (1927). *The abilities of man*. New York: Macmillan.

Sternberg, R. J. (1985). *Beyond IQ: A triarchic theory of human intelligence*. New York: Cambridge University Press.

Sternberg, R. J. (1986). *Intelligence applied: Understanding and increasing your intellectual skills*. San Diego: Harcourt Brace.

Sternberg, R. J. (1988a). Mental self-government: A theory of intellectual styles and their development. *Human Development, 31*, 197-224.

Sternberg, R. J. (1988b). *The triarchic mind: A new theory of human intelligence.* New York: Viking.

Sternberg, R. J. (1990). Thinking styles: Keys to understanding student performance. *Phi Delta Kappan, 71,* 366-371.

Sternberg, R. J. (1993). *Sternberg Triarchic Abilities Test.* Unpublished test.

Sternberg, R. J. (1994). Allowing for thinking styles. *Educational Leadership, 52*(3), 36-39.

Sternberg, R. J. (1995). *In search of the human mind.* Orlando, FL: Harcourt Brace.

Sternberg, R. J., & Clinkenbeard, P. (1995). A triarchic view of identifying, teaching, and assessing gifted children. *Roeper Review, 17,* 225-260.

Sternberg, R. J., Ferrari, M., Clinkenbeard, P., & Grigorenko, E. L. (in press). Identification, instruction, and assessment of gifted children: A construct validation of a triarchic model. *Gifted Child Quarterly.*

Sternberg, R. J., & Grigorenko, E. L. (1993). Thinking styles and the gifted. *Roeper Review, 16,* 122-130.

Sternberg, R. J., & Grigorenko, E. L. (1995). Styles of thinking in the school. *European Journal of High Ability, 6*(2), 1-19.

Thurstone, L. L. (1938). *Primary mental abilities.* Chicago: University of Chicago Press.

Vernon, P. (1973). Multivariate approaches to the study of cognitive styles. In J. R. Royce (Ed.), *Contributions of multivariate analysis to psychological theory* (pp. 139-157). London: Academic Press.

Witkin, H. A. (1973). *The role of cognitive style in academic performance and in teacher-student relations.* Unpublished report, Educational Testing Service. Princeton, New Jersey.

Witkin, H. A., Oltman, P. K., Raskin, E., & Karp, S. A. (1971). *Embedded Figures Test, Children's Embedded Figures Test, Group Embedded Figures Test.* Manual. Palo Alto: Consulting Psychologist Press.

ABOUT THE AUTHORS

ELENA L. GRIGORENKO, Associate Research Scientist, Department of Psychology and Child Study Center; and **ROBERT J. STERNBERG,** IBM Professor of Psychology and Education, Department of Psychology, Yale University, New Haven, Connecticut.

This research was supported under the Javits Act Program (Grant #R206R50001) as administered by the Office of Educational Research and Improvement of the U.S. Department of Education. Grantees undertaking such projects are encouraged to express their professional judgments freely. This article, therefore, does not necessarily represent positions or policies of the government, and no official endorsement should be inferred.

We are grateful to Pamela Clinkenbeard and Michel Ferrari for their assistance in data collection.

Copies of the instruments may be obtained at cost from the authors. Address requests for reprints to Robert J. Sternberg, Department of Psychology, Yale University, Box 208205, New Haven, CT 06520-8205 (E-mail: sterobj@yalevm.cis.yale.edu).

Manuscript received January 1996; revision accepted April 1996.

The Rewards of Learning

To teach without using extrinsic rewards is analogous to asking our students to learn to draw with their eyes closed, Mr. Chance maintains. Before we do that, we should open our own eyes.

Paul Chance

Paul Chance (Eastern Shore Maryland Chapter) is a psychologist, writer, and teacher. He is the author of Thinking in the Classroom *(Teachers College Press, 1986) and teaches at James H. Groves Adult High School in Georgetown, Del.*

A man is seated at a desk. Before him lie a pencil and a large stack of blank paper. He picks up the pencil, closes his eyes, and attempts to draw a four-inch line. He makes a second attempt, a third, a fourth, and so on, until he has made well over a hundred attempts at drawing a four-inch line, all without ever opening his eyes. He repeats the exercise for several days, until he has drawn some 3,000 lines, all with his eyes closed. On the last day, he examines his work. The question is, How much improvement has there been in his ability to draw a four-inch line? How much has he learned from his effort?

E. L. Thorndike, the founder of educational psychology and a major figure in the scientific analysis of learning, performed this experiment years ago, using himself as subject.[1] He found no evidence of learning. His ability to draw a four-inch line was no better on the last day than it had been on the first.

The outcome of this experiment may seem obvious to us today, but it was an effective way of challenging a belief widely held earlier in this century, a belief that formed the very foundation of education at the time: the idea that "practice makes perfect."

It was this blind faith in practice that justified countless hours of rote drill as a standard teaching technique. Thorndike's experiment demonstrated that practice in and of itself is not sufficient for learning. Based on this and other, more formal studies, Thorndike concluded that prac-

tice is important only insofar as it provides the opportunity for reinforcement.

To reinforce means to strengthen, and among learning researchers *reinforcement* refers to a procedure for strengthening behavior (that is, making it likely to be repeated) by providing certain kinds of consequences.[2] These consequences, called *reinforcers,* are usually events or things a person willingly seeks out. For instance, we might teach a person to draw a four-inch line with his eyes closed merely by saying "good" each time the effort is within half an inch of the goal. Most people like to succeed, so this positive feedback should be an effective way of reinforcing the appropriate behavior.

Hundreds of experimental studies have demonstrated that systematic use of reinforcement can improve both classroom conduct and the rate of learning. Yet the systematic use of reinforcement has never been widespread in American schools. In *A Place Called School*, John Goodlad reports that, in the elementary grades, an average of only 2% of class time is devoted to reinforcement; in the high schools, the figure falls to 1%.[3]

THE COSTS OF REWARD

There are probably many reasons for our failure to make the most of reinforcement. For one thing, few schools of education provide more than cursory instruction in its use. Given Thorndike's finding about the role of practice in learning, it is ironic that many teachers actually use the term *reinforcement* as a synonym for *practice.* ("We assign workbook exercises for reinforcement.") If schools of education do not teach future teachers the nature of reinforcement and how to use it effectively, teachers can hardly be blamed for not using it.

The unwanted effects of misused reinforcement have led some teachers to shy away from it. The teacher who sometimes lets a noisy class go to recess early will find the class getting noisier before recess. If high praise is reserved for long-winded essays, students will develop wordy and redundant writing styles. And it should surprise no one if students are seldom original in classrooms where only conventional work is admired or if they are uncooperative in classrooms where one can earn recognition only through competition. Reinforcement is powerful stuff, and its misuse can cause problems.

Another difficulty is that the optimal use of reinforcement would mean teaching in a new way. Some studies suggest that maximum learning in elementary and middle schools might require very high rates of reinforcement, perhaps with teachers praising someone in the class an average of once every 15 seconds.[4] Such a requirement is clearly incompatible with traditional teaching practices.

Systematic reinforcement can also mean more work for the teacher. Reinforcing behavior once every 15 seconds means 200 reinforcements in a 50-minute period — 1,000 reinforcements in a typical school day. It also implies that, in order to spot behavior to reinforce, the teacher must be moving about the room, not sitting at a desk marking papers. That may be too much to ask. Some studies have found that teachers who have been taught how to make good use of reinforcement often revert to their old style of teaching. This is so even though the teachers acknowledge that increased use of reinforcement means fewer discipline problems and a much faster rate of learning.[5]

Reinforcement also runs counter to our Puritan traditions. Most Americans have always assumed — occasional protestations to the contrary notwithstanding — that learning should be hard work and at least slightly unpleasant. Often the object of education seems to be not so much to teach academic and social skills as to "build character" through exposure to adversity. When teachers reinforce students at a high rate, the students experience a minimum of adversity and actually enjoy learning. Thus some people think that reinforcement is bad for character development.

All of these arguments against reinforcement can be countered effectively. Schools of education do not provide much instruction in the practical use of reinforcement, but there is no reason why they cannot do so. Reinforcement can be used incorrectly and with disastrous results, but the same might be said of other powerful tools. Systematic use of reinforcement means teaching in a new way, but teachers can learn to do so.[6] A great deal of reinforcement is needed for optimum learning, but not all of the reinforcement needs to come from the teacher. (Reinforcement can be provided by computers and other teaching devices, by teacher aides, by parents, and by students during peer teaching and cooperative learning.) No doubt people do sometimes benefit from adversity, but the case for the character-building properties of adversity is very weak.[7]

However, there is one argument against reinforcement that cannot be dismissed so readily. For some 20 years, the claim has been made that systematic reinforcement actually undermines student learning. Those few teachers who make extensive use of reinforcement, it is claimed, do their students a disservice because reinforcement reduces interest in the reinforced activity.

Not all forms of reinforcement are considered detrimental. A distinction is made between reinforcement involving intrinsic reinforcers — or rewards, as they are often called — and reinforcement involving extrinsic rewards.[8] Only extrinsic rewards are said to be harmful. An *intrinsic reward* is ordinarily the natural consequence of behavior, hence the name. We learn to throw darts by seeing how close the dart is to the target; learn to type by seeing the right letters appear on the computer screen; learn to cook from the pleasant sights, fragrances, and flavors that result from our culinary efforts; learn to read from the understanding we get from the printed word; and learn to solve puzzles by finding solutions. The Japanese say, "The bow teaches the archer." They are talking about intrinsic rewards, and they are right.

Extrinsic rewards come from an outside source, such as a teacher. Probably the most ubiquitous extrinsic reward (and one of the most effective) is praise. The teacher reinforces behavior by saying "good," "right," "correct," or "excellent" when the desired behavior occurs. Other extrinsic rewards involve nonverbal behavior such as smiles, winks, thumbs-up signs, hugs, congratulatory handshakes, pats on the back, or applause. Gold stars, certificates, candy, prizes, and even money have been used as rewards, but they are usually less important in teaching — and even in the maintenance of good discipline — than those mentioned earlier.

The distinction between intrinsic and extrinsic rewards is somewhat artificial. Consider the following example. You put money into a vending machine and retrieve a candy bar. The behavior of inserting money into a vending machine has been reinforced, as has the more general behavior of interacting with machines. But is the food you receive an intrinsic or an extrinsic reward? On the one hand, the food is the automatic consequence of inserting money and pressing buttons, so it would appear to be an intrinsic reward. On the other hand, the food is a consequence that was arranged by the designer of the machine, so it would seem to be an extrinsic reward.[9]

Though somewhat contrived, the distinction between intrinsic and extrinsic rewards has been maintained partly because extrinsic rewards are said to be damaging.[10] Are they? First, let us be clear about the charge. The idea is that — if teachers smile, praise, congratulate, say "thank you" or "right," shake hands, hug, give a pat on the back, applaud, provide a certificate of achievement or attendance, *or in any way provide a positive consequence (a reward) for student behavior* — the student will be less inclined to engage in that behavior when the reward is no longer available.

For example, teachers who offer prizes to students for reading books will, it is said, make the children less likely to read when prizes are no longer available. The teacher who reads a student's story aloud to the class as an example of excellent story writing actually makes the student less likely to write stories in the future, when such public approval is not forthcoming. When teachers (and students) applaud a youngster who has given an excellent talk, they make that student disinclined to give talks in the future. The teacher who comments favorably on the originality of a painting steers the young artist away from painting. And so on. This is the charge against extrinsic rewards.

No one disputes the effectiveness of extrinsic rewards in teaching or in maintaining good discipline. Some might therefore argue that extrinsic rewards should be used, even if they reduce interest in learning. Better to have students who read only when required to do so, some might say, than to have students who cannot read at all.

But if rewards do reduce interest, that fact is of tremendous importance. "The teacher may count himself successful," wrote B. F. Skinner, "when his students become engrossed in his field, study conscientiously, and do more than is required of them, but *the important thing is what they do when they are no longer being taught*" (emphasis added).[11] It is not enough for students to learn the three R's and a little science and geography; they must be prepared for a lifetime of learning. To reduce their interest in learning would be a terrible thing — even if it were done in the interest of teaching them effectively.

The question of whether rewards adversely affect motivation is not, then, of merely academic or theoretical importance. It is of great practical importance to the classroom teacher.

Extrinsic rewards are said to be damaging. Are they? First, let us be clear about the charge.

More than 100 studies have examined this question.[12] In a typical experiment, Mark Lepper and his colleagues observed 3- to 5-year-old nursery school children playing with various kinds of toys.[13] The toys available included felt tip pens of various colors and paper to draw on. The researchers noted the children's inclination to draw during this period. Next the researchers took the children aside and asked them to draw with the felt tip pens. The researchers promised some children a "Good Player Award" for drawing. Other children drew pictures without receiving an award.

Two weeks later, the researchers returned to the school, provided felt tip pens and paper, and observed the children's inclination to draw. They found that children who had been promised an award spent only half as much time drawing as they had originally. Those students who had received no award showed no such decline in interest.

Most studies in this area follow the same general outline: 1) students are given the opportunity to participate in an activity without rewards; 2) they are given extrinsic rewards for participating in the activity; and 3) they are again given the opportunity to participate in the activity without rewards.

The outcomes of the studies are also fairly consistent. Not surprisingly, there is usually a substantial increase in the activity during the second stage, when extrinsic rewards are available. And, as expected, participation in the activity declines sharply when rewards are no longer available. However, interest sometimes falls below the initial level, so that students are less interested in the activity than they had been before receiving rewards. It is this net loss of motivation that is of concern.

Researchers have studied this decline in motivation and found that it occurs only under certain circumstances. For example, the effect is most likely to occur when the initial interest in the activity is very high, when the rewards used are *not* reinforcers, and when the rewards are held out in advance as incentives.[14]

But perhaps the best predictor of negative effects is the nature of the "reward contingency" involved. (The term *reward contingency* has to do with the nature of the relationship between behavior and its reward.) Alyce Dickinson reviewed the research literature in this area and identified three kinds of reward contingency:[15]

Task-contingent rewards are available for merely participating in an activity, without regard to any standard of performance. Most studies that find a decline in interest in a rewarded activity involve task-contingent rewards. In the Lepper study described above, for instance, children received an award for drawing *regardless of how they drew*. The reward was task-contingent.

Performance-contingent rewards are available only when the student achieves a certain standard. Performance-contingent rewards sometimes produce negative results. For instance, Edward Deci offered college students money for solving puzzles, $1 for each puzzle solved. The rewarded students were later less inclined to work on the puzzles than were students who had not been paid. Unfortunately, these results are difficult to interpret because the students sometimes failed to meet the reward standard, and failure itself is known to reduce interest in an activity.[16]

Success-contingent rewards are given for good performance and might reflect either success or progress toward a goal. Success-contingent rewards do not have negative effects; in fact, they typically *increase* interest in the rewarded activity. For example, Ross Vasta and Louise Stirpe awarded gold stars to third- and fourth-graders each time they completed a kind of math exercise they enjoyed. After seven days of awards, the gold stars stopped. Not only was there no evidence of a loss in interest, but time spent on the math activity actually increased. Nor was there any decline in the quality of the work produced.[17]

Dickinson concludes that the danger of undermining student motivation stems not from extrinsic rewards, but from the use of inappropriate reward contingencies. Rewards reduce motivation when they are given without regard to performance or when the performance standard is so high that students frequently fail. When students have a high rate of success and when those successes are rewarded, the rewards *do not have negative effects*. Indeed, success-contingent rewards tend to increase interest in the activity. This finding, writes Dickinson, "is robust and consistent." She adds that "even strong opponents of contingent rewards recognize that success-based rewards do not have harmful effects."[18]

The evidence, then, shows that extrinsic rewards can either enhance or reduce interest in an activity, depending on how they are used. Still, it might be argued that, because extrinsic rewards *sometimes* cause problems, we might be wise to avoid their use altogether. The decision not to use extrinsic rewards amounts to a decision to rely on alternatives. What are those alternatives? And are they better than extrinsic rewards?

ALTERNATIVES TO REWARDS

Punishment and the threat of punishment are — and probably always have been — the most popular alternatives to extrinsic rewards. Not so long ago, lessons were "taught to the tune of a hickory stick," but the tune was not merely tapped on a desk. Students who did not learn their lessons were not only beaten; they were also humiliated: they sat on a stool (up high, so everyone could see) and wore a silly hat.

Gradually, more subtle forms of punishment were used. "The child at his desk," wrote Skinner, "filling in his workbook, is behaving primarily to escape from the threat of a series of minor aversive events — the teacher's displeasure, the criticism or ridicule of his classmates, an ignominious showing in a competition, low marks, a trip to the office 'to be talked to' by the principal, or a word to the parent who may still resort to the birch rod."[19] Skinner spent a lifetime inveighing against the use of such "aversives," but his efforts were largely ineffective. While extrinsic rewards have been condemned, punishment and the threat of punishment are widely sanctioned.

Punishment is popular because, in the short run at least, it gets results. This is illustrated by an experiment in which Deci and Wayne Cascio told students that, if they did not solve problems correctly within a time limit, they would be exposed to a loud, unpleasant sound. The threat worked: all the students solved all the problems within the time limit, so the threat never had to be fulfilled. Students who were merely rewarded for correct solutions did not do nearly as well.[20]

But there are serious drawbacks to the use of punishment. For one thing, although punishment motivates students to learn, it does not teach them. Or, rather, it teaches them only what *not* to do, not what *to* do. "We do not teach [a student] to learn quickly," Skinner observed, "by punishing him when he learns slowly, or to recall what he has learned by punishing him when he forgets, or to

119

think logically by punishing him when he is illogical."[21]

Punishment also has certain undesirable side effects.[22] To the extent that punishment works, it works by making students anxious. Students get nervous before a test because they fear a poor grade, and they are relieved or anxious when they receive their report card depending on whether or not the grades received will result in punishment from their parents.[23] Students can and do avoid the anxiety caused by such punishment by cutting classes and dropping out of school. We do the same thing when we cancel or "forget" a dental appointment.

Another response to punishment is aggression. Students who do not learn easily — and who therefore cannot readily avoid punishment — are especially apt to become aggressive. Their aggression often takes the form of lying, cheating, stealing, and refusing to cooperate. Students also act out by cursing, by being rude and insulting, by destroying property, and by hitting people. Increasingly, teachers are the objects of these aggressive acts.

Finally, it should be noted that punishment has the same negative impact on intrinsic motivation as extrinsic rewards are alleged to have. In the Deci and Cascio study just described, for example, when students were given the chance to work on puzzles with the threat of punishment removed, they were less likely to do so than were students who had never worked under the threat of punishment.[24] Punishment in the form of criticism of performance also reduces interest in an activity.[25]

Punishment is not the only alternative to the use of extrinsic rewards. Teachers can also encourage students. Encouragement consists of various forms of behavior intended to induce students to perform. We encourage students when we urge them to try, express confidence in their ability to do assignments, and recite such platitudes as "A winner never quits and a quitter never wins."[26]

In encouraging students, we are not merely urging them to perform, however; we are implicitly suggesting a relationship between continued performance and certain consequences. "Come on, Billy — you can do it" means, "If you persist at this task, you will be rewarded with success." The power of encouragement is ultimately dependent on the occurrence of the implied consequences. If the teacher tells Billy he can do it and if he tries

and fails, future urging by the teacher will be less effective.

Another problem with encouragement is that, like punishment, it motivates but does not teach. The student who is urged to perform a task is not thereby taught how to perform it. Encouragement is a safer procedure than punishment, since it is less likely to provoke anxiety or aggression. Students who are repeatedly urged to do things at which they ultimately fail do, however, come to distrust the judgment of the teacher. They also come to believe that they cannot live up to the expectations of teachers — and therefore must be hopelessly stupid.

Intrinsic rewards present the most promising alternative to extrinsic rewards. Experts on reinforcement, including defenders of extrinsic rewards, universally sing the praises of intrinsic rewards. Unlike punishment and encouragement, intrinsic rewards actually teach. Students who can see that they have solved a problem correctly know how to solve other problems of that sort. And, unlike extrinsic rewards, intrinsic rewards do not depend on the teacher or some other person.

But there are problems with intrinsic rewards, just as there are with extrinsic ones. Sometimes students lack the necessary skills to obtain intrinsic rewards. Knowledge, understanding, and the aesthetic pleasures of language are all intrinsic rewards for reading, but they are not available to those for whom reading is a difficult and painful activity.

Often, intrinsic rewards are too remote to be effective. If a student is asked to add 3 + 7, what is the intrinsic reward for answering correctly? The student who learns to add will one day experience the satisfaction of checking the accuracy of a restaurant bill, but this future reward is of no value to the youngster just learning to add. Though important in maintaining what has been learned, intrinsic rewards are often too remote to be effective reinforcers in the early stages of learning.

One problem that often goes unnoticed is that the intrinsic rewards for academic work are often weaker than the rewards available for other behavior. Students are rewarded for looking out the window, daydreaming, reading comic books, taking things from other students, passing notes, telling and listening to jokes, moving about the room, fighting, talking back to the teacher, and for all sorts of activities that are incompatible

with academic learning. Getting the right answer to a grammar question might be intrinsically rewarding, but for many students it is considerably less rewarding than the laughter of one's peers in response to a witty remark.

While intrinsic rewards are important, then, they are insufficient for efficient learning.[27] Nor will encouragement and punishment fill the gap. The teacher must supplement intrinsic rewards with extrinsic rewards. This means not only telling the student when he or she has succeeded, but also praising, complimenting, applauding, and providing other forms of recognition for good work. Some students may need even stronger reinforcers, such as special privileges, certificates, and prizes.

REWARD GUIDELINES

Yet we cannot ignore the fact that extrinsic rewards can have adverse effects on student motivation. While there seems to be little chance of serious harm, it behooves us to use care. Various experts have suggested guidelines to follow in using extrinsic rewards.[28] Here is a digest of their recommendations:

1. Use the weakest reward required to strengthen a behavior. Don't use money if a piece of candy will do; don't use candy if praise will do. The good effects of reinforcement come not so much from the reward itself as from the reward contingency: the relationship between the reward and the behavior.

2. When possible, avoid using rewards as incentives. For example, don't say, "If you do X, I'll give you Y." Instead, ask the student to perform a task and then provide a reward for having completed it. In most cases, rewards work best if they are pleasant surprises.

3. Reward at a high rate in the early stages of learning, and reduce the frequency of rewards as learning progresses. Once students have the alphabet down pat, there is no need to compliment them each time they print a letter correctly. Nor is there much need to reward behavior that is already occurring at a high rate.

4. Reward only the behavior you want repeated. If students who whine and complain get their way, expect to see a lot of whining and complaining. Similarly, if you provide gold stars only for the three best papers in the class, you are rewarding competition and should not be surprised if students do not cooperate

with one another. And if "spelling doesn't count," don't expect to see excellent spelling.

5. Remember that what is an effective reward for one student may not work well with another. Some students respond rapidly to teacher attention; others do not. Some work well for gold stars; others don't. Effective rewards are ordinarily things that students seek — positive feedback, praise, approval, recognition, toys — but ultimately a reward's value is to be judged by its effect on behavior.

6. Reward success, and set standards so that success is within the student's grasp. In today's heterogeneous classrooms, that means setting standards for each student. A good way to do this is to reward improvement or progress toward a goal. Avoid rewarding students merely for participating in an activity, without regard for the quality of their performance.

7. Bring attention to the rewards (both intrinsic and extrinsic) that are available for behavior from sources *other than the teacher*. Point out, for example, the fun to be had from the word play in poetry or from sharing a poem with another person. Show students who are learning computer programming the pleasure in "making the computer do things." Let students know that it's okay to applaud those who make good presentations so that they can enjoy the approval of their peers for a job well done. Ask parents to talk with their children about school and to praise them for learning. The goal is to shift the emphasis from rewards provided by the teacher to those that will occur even when the teacher is not present.[29]

Following these rules is harder in practice than it might seem, and most teachers will need training in their implementation. But reinforcement is probably the most powerful tool available to teachers, and extrinsic rewards are powerful reinforcers. To teach without using extrinsic rewards is analogous to asking our students to learn to draw with their eyes closed. Before we do that, we should open our own eyes.

1. The study is described in E. L. Thorndike, *Human Learning* (1931; reprint ed., Cambridge, Mass.: MIT Press, 1966).

2. There are various theories (cognitive, neurological, and psychosocial) about why certain consequences reinforce or strengthen behavior. The important thing for our purposes is that they do.

3. John I. Goodlad, *A Place Called School: Prospects for the Future* (New York: McGraw-Hill, 1984). Goodlad complains about the "paucity of praise" in schools. In doing so, he echoes B. F. Skinner, who wrote that "perhaps the most serious criticism of the current classroom is the relative infrequency of reinforcement." See B. F. Skinner, *The Technology of Teaching* (Englewood Cliffs, N.J.: Prentice-Hall, 1968), p. 17.

4. Bill L. Hopkins and R. J. Conard, "Putting It All Together: Superschool," in Norris G. Haring and Richard L. Schiefelbusch, eds., *Teaching Special Children* (New York: McGraw-Hill, 1975), pp. 342-85. Skinner suggests that mastering the first four years of arithmetic instruction efficiently would require something on the order of 25,000 reinforcements. See Skinner, op. cit.

5. See, for example, Bill L. Hopkins, "Comments on the Future of Applied Behavior Analysis," *Journal of Applied Behavior Analysis*, vol. 20, 1987, pp. 339-46. In some studies, students learned at double the normal rate, yet most teachers did not continue reinforcing behavior at high rates after the study ended.

6. See, for example, Hopkins and Conard, op. cit.

7. For example, Mihaly Csikszentmihalyi found that adults who are successful and happy tend to have had happy childhoods. See Tina Adler, "Support and Challenge: Both Key for Smart Kids," *APA Monitor*, September 1991, pp. 10-11.

8. The terms *reinforcer* and *reward* are often used interchangeably, but they are not really synonyms. A reinforcer is defined by its effects: an event that strengthens the behavior it follows is a reinforcer, regardless of what it was intended to do. A reward is defined by social convention as something desirable; it may or may not strengthen the behavior it follows. The distinction is important since some studies that show negative effects from extrinsic rewards use rewards that are *not* reinforcers. See Alyce M. Dickinson, "The Detrimental Effects of Extrinsic Reinforcement on 'Intrinsic Motivation,' " *The Behavior Analyst*, vol. 12, 1989, pp. 1-15.

9. John Dewey distrusted the distinction between extrinsic and intrinsic rewards. He wrote that "what others do to us when we act is as natural a consequence of our action as what the fire does to us when we plunge our hands in it." Quoted in Samuel M. Deitz, "What Is Unnatural About 'Extrinsic Reinforcement'?," *The Behavior Analyst*, vol. 12, 1989, p. 255.

10. Dickinson writes that "several individuals have demanded that schools abandon reinforcement procedures for fear that they may permanently destroy a child's 'love of learning.' " See Alyce M. Dickinson, "Exploring New Vistas," *Performance Management Magazine*, vol. 9, 1991, p. 28. It is interesting to note that no one worries that earning a school letter will destroy a student's interest in sports. Nor does there seem to be much fear that people who win teaching awards will suddenly become poor teachers. For the most part, only the academic work of students is said to be put at risk by extrinsic rewards.

11. Skinner, p. 162.

12. For reviews of this literature, see Edward L. Deci and Richard M. Ryan, *Intrinsic Motivation and Self-Determination in Human Behavior* (New York: Plenum, 1985); Dickinson, "The Detrimental Effects"; and Mark R. Lepper and David Greene, eds., *The Hidden Costs of Reward: New Perspectives on the Psychology of Human Motivation* (Hillsdale, N.J.: Erlbaum, 1978).

13. Mark R. Lepper, David Greene, and Richard E. Nisbett, "Undermining Children's Intrinsic Interest with Extrinsic Rewards," *Journal of Personality and Social Psychology*, vol. 28, 1973, pp. 129-37.

14. See, for example, Dickinson, "The Detrimental Effects"; and Mark Morgan, "Reward-Induced Decrements and Increments in Intrinsic Motivation," *Review of Educational Research*, vol. 54, 1984, pp. 5-30. Dickinson notes that studies producing negative effects are often hard to interpret since other variables (failure, deadlines, competition, and so on) could account for the findings. By way of example, she cites a study in which researchers offered a $5 reward to top performers. The study was thus contaminated by the effects of competition, yet the negative results were attributed to extrinsic rewards.

15. Dickinson, "The Detrimental Effects."

16. Edward L. Deci, "Effects of Externally Mediated Rewards on Intrinsic Motivation," *Journal of Personality and Social Psychology*, vol. 18, 1971, pp. 105-15.

17. Ross Vasta and Louise A. Stirpe, "Reinforcement Effects on Three Measures of Children's Interest in Math," *Behavior Modification*, vol. 3, 1979, pp. 223-44.

18. Dickinson, "The Detrimental Effects," p. 9. See also Morgan, op. cit.

19. Skinner, p. 15.

20. Edward L. Deci and Wayne F. Cascio, "Changes in Intrinsic Motivation as a Function of Negative Feedback and Threats," paper presented at the annual meeting of the Eastern Psychological Association, Boston, May 1972. This paper is summarized in Edward L. Deci and Joseph Porac, "Cognitive Evaluation Theory and the Study of Human Motivation," in Lepper and Greene, pp. 149-76.

21. Skinner, p. 149.

22. For more on the problems associated with punishment, see Murray Sidman, *Coercion and Its Fallout* (Boston: Authors Cooperative, Inc., 1989).

23. Grades are often referred to as rewards, but they are more often punishments. Students study not so much to receive high grades as to avoid receiving low ones.

24. Deci and Cascio, op. cit.

25. See, for example, Edward L. Deci, Wayne F. Cascio, and Judy Krusell, "Sex Differences, Positive Feedback, and Intrinsic Motivation," paper presented at the annual meeting of the Eastern Psychological Association, Washington, D.C., May 1973. This paper is summarized in Deci and Porac, op. cit.

26. It should be noted that encouragement often closely resembles reinforcement in form. One teacher may say, "I know you can do it, Mary," as Mary struggles to answer a question; another teacher may say, "I knew you could do it, Mary!" when Mary answers the question correctly. The first teacher is encouraging; the second is reinforcing. The difference is subtle but important.

27. Intrinsic rewards are more important to the maintenance of skills once learned. An adult's skill at addition and subtraction is not ordinarily maintained by the approval of peers but by the satisfaction that comes from balancing a checkbook.

28. See, for example, Jere Brophy, "Teacher Praise: A Functional Analysis," *Review of Educational Research*, vol. 51, 1981, pp. 5-32; Hopkins and Conard, op. cit.; and Dickinson, "The Detrimental Effects."

29. "Instructional contingencies," writes Skinner, "are usually contrived and should always be temporary. If instruction is to have any point, the behavior it generates will be taken over and maintained by contingencies in the world at large." See Skinner, p. 144.

Rewards Versus Learning:
A Response to Paul Chance

Mr. Kohn raises some questions about Paul Chance's article in the November 1992 Kappan* and suggests that an engaging curriculum — not manipulating children with artificial incentives — offers a genuine alternative to boredom in school and to diminished motivation when school lets out.

....

ALFIE KOHN

ALFIE KOHN is an independent scholar living in Cambridge, Mass., who writes and lectures widely on human behavior and education. His newest book is Punished by Rewards: The Trouble with Gold Stars, Incentive Plans, A's, Praise, and Other Bribes *(Houghton Mifflin, October 1993). ©1993, Alfie Kohn.*

I N THE COURSE of offering some suggestions for how educators can help children become more generous and empathic ("Caring Kids: The Role of the Schools," March 1991), I argued that manipulating student behavior with either punishments or rewards is not only unnecessary but counterproductive. Paul Chance, taking exception to this passage, wrote to defend the use of rewards (Backtalk, June 1991). Now, following the publication of his longer brief for behaviorism ("The Rewards of Learning," November 1992), it is my turn to raise some questions — and to continue what I hope is a constructive

[*See *Annual Editions* Article 21. Ed.]

dialogue between us (not to mention a long overdue examination of classroom practices too often taken for granted).

To begin, I should mention two points where our perspectives converge. Neither of us favors the use of punishment, and both of us think that rewards, like other strategies, must be judged by their long-term effects, including what they do for (or to) children's motivation. Chance and I disagree, however, on the nature of those effects.

Rewards, like punishments, can usually get people to do what we want for a while. In that sense, they "work." But my reading of the research, corroborated by real-world observation, is that rewards can never buy us anything more than short-term compliance. Moreover, we — or, more accurately, the people we are rewarding — pay a steep price over time for our reliance on extrinsic motivators.

REWARDS ARE INHERENTLY CONTROLLING

Applied behaviorism, which amounts to saying, "Do this and you'll get that," is essentially a technique for controlling people. In the classroom, it is a way of doing things *to* children rather than working *with* them. Chance focuses on the empirical effects of rewards, but I feel obliged to pause at least long enough to stress that moral issues are involved here regardless of whether we ultimately endorse or oppose the use of rewards.

By now it is not news that reinforcement strategies were developed and refined through experiments on laboratory animals. Many readers also realize that underlying the practice of reinforcement is a theory — specifically, the assumption that humans, like all organisms, are

basically inert beings whose behavior must be elicited by external motivation in the form of carrots or sticks. For example, Alyce Dickinson, the author Chance cites six times and from whom he borrows the gist of his defense of rewards, plainly acknowledges the central premise of the perspective she and Chance share, which is that "all behavior is ultimately initiated by the external environment."[1] Anyone who recoils from this theoretical foundation ought to take a fresh look at the real-world practices that rest on it.

I am troubled by a model of human relationship or learning that is defined by control rather than, say, persuasion or mutual problem solving. Because the reinforcements themselves are desired by their recipients, it is easy to miss the fact that using them is simply a matter of "control[ling] through seduction rather than force."[2] Rewards and punishments (bribes and threats, positive reinforcements and "consequences" — call them what you will) are not really opposites at all. They are two sides of the same coin. The good news is that our options are not limited to variations on the theme of behavioral manipulation.[3]

REWARDS ARE INEFFECTIVE

The question of how well rewards *work*, apart from what they do to children's long-term motivation, is dispatched by Chance in a single sentence: "No one disputes the effectiveness of extrinsic rewards in teaching or in maintaining good discipline" (p. 203). I found myself rereading the paragraph in which this extraordinary claim appears, searching for signs that Chance was being ironic.

In point of fact, the evidence overwhelmingly demonstrates that extrinsic rewards are ineffective at producing lasting change in attitudes or even behaviors. Moreover, they typically do not enhance — and often actually impede — performance on tasks that are any more complex than pressing a bar. This evidence, which I have been sorting through recently for a book-length treatment of these issues (*Punished by Rewards*, scheduled for publication this fall), is piled so high on my desk that I fear it will topple over. I cannot review all of it here; a few samples will have to do.

Consider first the matter of behavior change. Even behaviorists have had to concede that the token economy, a form of behavior modification once (but, mercifully, no longer) popular for controlling people in institutions, doesn't work. When the goodies stop, people go right back to acting the way they did before the program began.[4] Studies have found that rewarding people for losing weight,[5] quitting smoking,[6] or using seat belts[7] is typically less effective than using other strategies — and often proves worse than doing nothing at all.

Children whose parents make frequent use of rewards or praise are likely to be less generous than their peers.[8] On reflection, this makes perfect sense: a child promised a treat for acting responsibly has been given no reason to keep behaving that way when there is no longer a reward to be gained for doing so. The implications for behavioristic classroom management programs such as Assertive Discipline, in which children are essentially bribed or threatened to conform to rules that the teacher alone devises, are painfully clear.

Rewards (like punishments) can get people to do what we want in the short term: buckle up, share a toy, read a book. In that sense, Chance is right that their effectiveness is indisputable. But they rarely produce effects that survive the rewards themselves, which is why behaviorists are placed in the position of having to argue that we need to keep the goodies coming or replace one kind of reward with another (e.g., candy bars with grades). The fact is that extrinsic motivators do not alter the attitudes that underlie our behaviors. They do not create an enduring *commitment* to a set of values or to learning; they merely, and temporarily, change what we do. If, like Skinner, you think there is nothing to humans other than what we do, then this criticism will not trouble you. If, on the

> The good news is that our options are not limited to variations on the theme of behavioral manipulation.

other hand, you think that our actions reflect and emerge from who we *are* (what we think and feel, expect and will), then you have no reason to expect interventions that merely control actions to work in the long run.

As for the effect on performance, I know of at least two dozen studies showing that people expecting to receive a reward for completing a task (or for doing it successfully) don't perform as well as those who expect nothing. The effect is robust for young children, older children, and adults; for males and females; for rewards of all kinds (including money, grades, toys, food, and special privileges). The tasks in these studies range from memorizing facts to engaging in creative problem solving, from discriminating between similar drawings to designing collages. In general, the more cognitive sophistication and open-ended thinking required, the worse people do when they are working for a reward.[9]

At first researchers didn't know what to make of these findings. (A good sign that one has stumbled onto something important is the phrase "contrary to hypothesis" in a research report.) "The clear inferiority of the reward groups was an unexpected result, unaccountable for by theory or previous empirical evidence," a pair of experimenters confessed in 1961.[10] Rewards "have effects that interfere with performance in ways that we are only beginning to understand," said Janet Spence (later president of the American Psychological Association) in 1971.[11] Since then, most researchers — with the exception of a small cadre of un-

reconstructed behaviorists — have gotten the message that, on most tasks, a Skinnerian strategy is worse than useless: it is counterproductive.

REWARDS MAKE LEARNING LESS APPEALING

Even more research indicates that rewards also undermine *interest* — a finding with obvious and disturbing implications for the use of grades, stickers, and even praise. Here Chance concedes there may be a problem but, borrowing Dickinson's analysis, assures us that the damage is limited. Dickinson grants that motivation tends to decline when people are rewarded just for engaging in a task and also when they receive performance-contingent rewards — those "based on performance standards" (Dickinson) or "available only when the student achieves a certain standard" (Chance).

But Dickinson then proceeds to invent a new category, "success-contingent" rewards, and calls these innocuous. The term means that, when rewards are given out, "subjects are told they have received the rewards because of good performance." For Chance, though, a "success-contingent" reward is "given for good performance and might reflect either success or progress toward a goal" — a definition that appears to diverge from Dickinson's and that sounds quite similar to what is meant by "performance-contingent." As near as I can figure, the claim both Dickinson and Chance are making is that, when people come away thinking that they have done well, a reward for what they have achieved doesn't hurt. On this single claim rests the entire defense against the devastating charge that by rewarding students for their achievement we are leading them to see learning as a chore. But what does the research really say?

Someone who simply glances at the list of studies Dickinson offers to support her assertion might come away impressed. Someone who takes the time to read those studies will come away with a renewed sense of the importance of going straight to the primary source. It turns out that two of the studies don't even deal with rewards for successful performance.[12] Another one actually *disproves* the contention that success-contingent rewards are harmless: it finds that this kind of reward not only undermines intrinsic motivation but is more destructive than rewards given just for engaging in the task![13]

The rest of the studies cited by Dickinson indicate that some subjects in laboratory experiments who receive success-contingent rewards are neither more nor less interested in the task than those who get nothing at all. But Dickinson curiously omits a number of *other* studies that are also set up so that some subjects succeed (or think they succeed) at a task and are presented with a reward. These studies have found that such rewards *do* reduce interest.[14]

Such a result really shouldn't be surprising. As Edward Deci and his colleagues have been pointing out for years, adults and children alike chafe at being deprived of a sense of self-determination. Rewards usually feel controlling, and rewards contingent on performance ("If you do a good job, here's what I'll give you") are the most controlling of all. Even the good feeling produced by doing well often isn't enough to overcome that fact. To the extent that information about how well we have done *is* interest-enhancing, this is not an argument for Skinnerian tactics. In fact, when researchers have specifically compared the effects of straightforward performance feedback ("Here's how you did") and performance-contingent rewards ("Here's a goody for doing well"), the latter undermined intrinsic motivation more than the former.[15]

Finally, even if all the research really did show what Dickinson and Chance claim it does, remember that outside of the laboratory people often fail. That result is more likely to be de-motivating when it means losing out on a reward, such as an A or a bonus. This Chance implicitly concedes, although the force of the point gets lost: students do not turn off from failing per se but from failing when a reward is at stake. In learning contexts free of extrinsic motivators, students are more likely to persist at a task and to remain interested in it even when they don't do it well.

All of this means that getting children to think about learning as a way to receive a sticker, a gold star, or a grade — or, even worse, to get money or a toy *for* a grade, which amounts to an extrinsic motivator for an extrinsic motivator — is likely to turn learning from an end into a means. Learning becomes something that must be gotten through in order to receive the reward. Take the depressingly pervasive program by which children receive certificates for free pizza when they

have read a certain number of books. John Nicholls of the University of Illinois comments, only half in jest, that the likely consequence of this program is "a lot of fat kids who don't like to read."

Educational psychologists such as Nicholls, Carol Dweck, and Carole Ames keep finding that when children are led to concentrate on their performance, on how well they are doing — an inevitable consequence of the use of rewards or punishments — they become less interested in *what* they are doing. ("Do we have to know this? Will it be on the test?") I am convinced that one of the primary obligations of educators and parents who want to promote a lasting commitment to learning is to do everything in their power to help students forget that grades exist.

REWARDS IGNORE CURRICULAR QUESTIONS

One last point. Chance's defense of the Skinnerian status quo might more properly have been titled "The Rewards *for* Learning." My interest is in the rewards *of* learning, a concern that requires us to ask whether we are teaching something *worth* learning. This is a question that behaviorists do not need to ask; it is enough to devise an efficient technique to reinforce the acquisition of whatever happens to be in someone's lesson plan.

Chance addresses the matter of intrinsic motivation just long enough to dismiss it as "too remote to be effective." He sets up a false dichotomy, with an abstract math problem on one side (Why would a child be motivated to learn that $7 + 3 = 10$? he wants to know) and reinforcements (the solution to this problem) on the other. Indeed, if children are required to fill in an endless series of blanks on worksheets or to memorize meaningless, disconnected facts, they may *have* to be bribed to do so. But Chance seems oblivious to exciting developments in the field of education: the whole-language movement, the emphasis on "learner-centered" learning, and the entire constructivist tradition (in which teaching takes its cue from the way each child actively constructs meaning and makes sense of the world rather than treating students as passive responders to environmental stimuli).

I invite Chance to join the campaign for an engaging curriculum that is connected to children's lives and interests, for an approach to pedagogy in which students

are given real choices about their studies, and for classrooms in which they are allowed and helped to work with one another. Pursuing these approaches, not manipulating children with artificial incentives, offers a *real* alternative to boredom in school and to diminished motivation when school lets out.

1. Alyce M. Dickinson, "The Detrimental Effects of Extrinsic Reinforcement on 'Intrinsic Motivation,'" *The Behavior Analyst*, vol. 12, 1989, p. 12. Notice the quotation marks around "intrinsic motivation," as if to question the very existence of the phenomenon — a telltale sign of Skinnerian orthodoxy.
2. Edward L. Deci and Richard M. Ryan, *Intrinsic Motivation and Self-Determination in Human Behavior* (New York: Plenum, 1985), p. 70.
3. Behaviorists are apt to rejoin that control is an unavoidable feature of all relationships. In response I would point out that there is an enormous difference between saying that even subtle reinforcements can be controlling and asserting that all human interaction is best described as an exercise in control. The latter takes on faith that selfhood and choice are illusions and that we do only what we have been reinforced for doing. A far more defensible position, it seems to me, is that some forms of human interaction are controlling and some are not. The line might not be easy to draw in practice, but the distinction is still meaningful and important.
4. "Generally, removal of token reinforcement results in decrements in desirable responses and a return to baseline or near-baseline levels of performance," as the first major review of token economies concluded. In fact, not only does the behavior fail "to generalize to conditions in which [reinforcements] are not in effect" — such as the world outside the hospital — but reinforcement programs used each morning generally don't even have much effect on patients' behavior during the afternoon! See Alan E. Kazdin and Richard R. Bootzin, "The Token Economy: An Evaluative Review," *Journal of Applied Behavior Analysis*, vol. 5, 1972, pp. 359-60. Ten years later, one of these authors — an enthusiastic proponent of behavior modification, incidentally — checked back to see if anything had changed. "As a general rule," he wrote, with an almost audible sigh, "it is still prudent to assume that behavioral gains are likely to be lost in varying degrees once the client leaves the program." See Alan E. Kazdin, "The Token Economy: A Decade Later," *Journal of Applied Behavior Analysis*, vol. 15, 1982, pp. 435-37. Others reviewing the research on token economies have come to more or less the same conclusion.
5. The only two studies I am aware of that looked at weight loss programs to see what happened when people were paid for getting slimmer found that the incentives either had no effect or were actually counterproductive. See Richard A. Dienstbier and Gary K. Leak, "Overjustification and Weight Loss: The Effects of Monetary Reward," paper presented at the annual meeting of the American Psychological Association, Washington, D.C., September 1976; and F. Matthew Kramer et al., "Maintenance of Successful Weight Loss Over 1 Year: Effects of Financial Contracts for Weight Maintenance or Participation in Skills Training," *Behavior Therapy*, vol. 17, 1986, pp. 295-301.
6. A very large study, published in 1991, recruited subjects for a self-help program designed to help people quit smoking. Three months later, those who had been offered a prize for turning in weekly prog-

ress reports were lighting up again more often than were those who had received a no-reward treatment — and even more than those who didn't take part in any program at all. In fact, for people who received both treatments, "the financial incentive somehow diminished the positive impact of the personalized feedback." See Susan J. Curry et al., "Evaluation of Intrinsic and Extrinsic Motivation Interventions with a Self-Help Smoking Cessation Program," *Journal of Consulting and Clinical Psychology*, vol. 59, 1991, p. 323.

7. A committed behaviorist and his colleagues reviewed the effects of 28 programs used by nine different companies to get their employees to use seat belts. Nearly half a million vehicle observations were made over six years in the course of this research. The result: programs that rewarded people for wearing their seat belts were the least effective over the long haul. The author had to confess that "the greater impact of the no-reward strategies from both an immediate and [a] long-term perspective . . . [was] not predicted and [is] inconsistent with basic reinforcement theory." See E. Scott Geller et al., "Employer-Based Programs to Motivate Safety Belt Use: A Review of Short-Term and Long-Term Effects," *Journal of Safety Research*, vol. 18, 1987, pp. 1-17.

8. Richard A. Fabes et al., "Effects of Rewards on Children's Prosocial Motivation: A Socialization Study," *Developmental Psychology*, vol. 25, 1989, pp. 509-15. Praise appears to have a similar detrimental effect; see Joan E. Grusec, "Socializing Concern for Others in the Home," *Developmental Psychology*, vol. 27, l991, pp. 338-42. See also the studies reviewed in Alfie Kohn, *The Brighter Side of Human Nature: Altruism and Empathy in Everyday Life* (New York: Basic Books, 1990), pp. 201-4.

9. A complete bibliography will be available in my forthcoming book, *Punished by Rewards*. Readers unwilling to wait might wish to begin by reading Mark R. Lepper and David Greene, eds., *The Hidden Costs of Rewards* (Hillsdale, N.J.: Erlbaum, 1978), and some of Teresa Amabile's work from the 1980s documenting how rewards kill creativity.

10. Louise Brightwell Miller and Betsy Worth Estes, "Monetary Reward and Motivation in Discrimination Learning," *Journal of Experimental Psychology*, vol. 61, 1961, p. 503.

11. Janet Taylor Spence, "Do Material Rewards Enhance the Performance of Lower-Class Children?," *Child Development*, vol. 42, 1971, p. 1469.

12. In one of the studies, either money or an award was given to children just for taking part in the experiment — and both caused interest in the task to decline. See Rosemarie Anderson et al., "The Undermining and Enhancing of Intrinsic Motivation in Preschool Children," *Journal of Personality and Social Psychology*, vol. 34, 1976, pp. 915-22. In the other, a total of three children were simply praised ("good," "nice going") whenever they engaged in a task; no mention was made of how well they were performing. See Jerry A. Martin, "Effects of Positive and Negative Adult-Child Interactions on Children's Task Performance and Task Preferences," *Journal of Experimental Child Psychology*, vol. 23, 1977, pp. 493-502.

13. Michael Jay Weiner and Anthony M. Mander, "The Effects of Reward and Perception of Competency upon Intrinsic Motivation," *Motivation and Emotion*, vol. 2, 1978, pp. 67-73.

14. Chance doesn't like Deci's 1971 study, but there are plenty of others. In David Greene and Mark R. Lepper, "Effects of Extrinsic Rewards on Children's Subsequent Intrinsic Interest," *Child Development*, vol. 45, 1974, pp. 1141-45, children who were promised a reward if they drew very good pictures — and then did receive the reward, along with a reminder of the accomplishment it represented — were less interested in drawing later than were children who got nothing. See also James Garbarino, "The Impact of Anticipated Reward upon Cross-Age Tutoring," *Journal of Personality and Social Psychology*, vol. 32, 1975, pp. 421-28; Terry D. Orlick and Richard Mosher, "Extrinsic Awards and Participant Motivation in a Sport Related Task," *International Journal of Sport Psychology*, vol. 9, 1978, pp. 27-39; Judith M. Harackiewicz, "The Effects of Reward Contingency and Performance Feedback on Intrinsic Motivation," *Journal of Personality and Social Psychology*, vol. 37, 1979, pp. 1352-63; and Richard A. Fabes, "Effects of Reward Contexts on Young Children's Task Interest," *Journal of Psychology*, vol. 121, 1987, pp. 5-19. See too the studies cited in, and conclusions offered by, Kenneth O. McGraw, "The Detrimental Effects of Reward on Performance: A Literature Review and a Prediction Model," in Lepper and Greene, eds., p. 40; Mark R. Lepper, "Extrinsic Reward and Intrinsic Motivation," in John M. Levine and Margaret C. Wang, eds., *Teacher and Student Perceptions: Implications for Learning* (Hillsdale, N.J.: Erlbaum, 1983), pp. 304-5; and Deci and Ryan, p. 78.

15. Richard M. Ryan et al., "Relation of Reward Contingency and Interpersonal Context to Intrinsic Motivation: A Review and Test Using Cognitive Evaluation Theory," *Journal of Personality and Social Psychology*, vol. 45, 1983, pp. 736-50. "Rewards in general appear to have a controlling significance to some extent and thus in general run the risk of undermining intrinsic motivation," the authors wrote (p. 748).

Sticking Up for Rewards

It is ironic that honest feedback or a straightforward contingency between work and rewards should be called manipulative, while "persuasion" and "mutual problem solving" should not, Mr. Chance retorts.

....

PAUL CHANCE

PAUL CHANCE (Eastern Shore Maryland Chapter) is a psychologist, writer, and former teacher. He is the author of Thinking in the Classroom *(Teachers College Press, 1986).*

IT IS DIFFICULT to know how to respond to Alfie Kohn's critique.* It is so disjointed and so full of misrepresentations of fact and theory that it is like a greased pig: one can scarcely get a grip on it, let alone wrestle it to the ground. I will illustrate what I mean with a few examples and then reply to what I believe to be Kohn's major objections.

Item: To reward, Kohn says, is to say to a student, "Do this and you'll get that." But this is only one kind of reward — and one that I specifically advised readers to avoid when possible. It is these "contractual rewards" (or incentives) that are apt to be problematic.[1] My article focused on rewards that provide feedback about performance. Such "informational rewards" reflect effort or the quality of performance (e.g., "Good try, Janet"; "Great job, Billy"). As we shall see, even researchers who criticize contractual rewards do not normally object to informational rewards.

[*See Annual Editions Article 22. Ed.]

Item: Kohn says that I ask, Why would a child be motivated to learn that 7 + 3 = 10? But my question was, *How* can a child learn that 7 + 3 = 10 without some sort of response from the environment? A teacher, a peer tutor, or a computer program may provide the necessary feedback, but the natural environment rarely does. This was the point of E. L. Thorndike's line experiment, described in my article.

Item: Kohn suggests that the use of rewards is manipulative and controlling. It is ironic that honest feedback or a straightforward contingency between work and rewards should be called manipulative, while "persuasion" and "mutual problem solving" should not. Students, I suspect, know the truth of the matter. As for control: a parent rewards a baby's crying when he or she offers a bottle, and the baby rewards the parent's action by ceasing to cry. Each controls the other. Students and teachers exert the same sort of reciprocal control in the classroom.[2]

Item: Nowhere do I suggest that students must "fill in an endless series of blanks on worksheets or memorize meaningless, disconnected facts," nor is there any reason to assume that the use of rewards implies such practices. The truth is that rewards are useful whether the student is memorizing dates, mastering algebra word problems, or learning to think.[3] Some sort of extrinsic reinforcement (informational reward) is usually necessary, in the early stages at least, for learning to occur efficiently.

Item: Kohn refers to "practices too often taken for granted." Evidently he believes the mythology that rewards are widely used in our schools. Yet I noted in my article that John Goodlad found that only 2% of class time is devoted to reinforcement in elementary school — and only 1% in high school.[4] Other research consistently shows that reinforcement is notable by its absence. Harold

Stevenson, for example, compared elementary classrooms in America and Asia. He found pronounced differences in the activities of teachers when students were engaged in seatwork. In half of the classes observed in the Chicago area, the teachers provided no feedback about student performance; this seldom happened in Taiwan and almost never happened in Japan.[5]

Item: I do not assume, as suggested, that "humans, like all organisms, are basically inert beings." Nor do I know any psychologist who would embrace this view. Behavioral psychologists in particular emphasize that we learn by *acting on* our environment. As B. F. Skinner put it: "[People] act on the world, and change it, and are changed in turn by the consequences of their actions."[6] Skinner, unlike Kohn, understood that people learn best in a responsive environment. Teachers who praise or otherwise reward student performance provide such an environment.

Item: Kohn implies that I consider grades a reward. In fact, I noted (as Skinner and others had before me) that grades are more often a form of punishment. Incidentally, F. S. Keller, a behaviorist, proposed a system of education that could eliminate grades. In the Keller plan, students are required to demonstrate mastery of each skill before moving to the next. Mastery of each unit in the curriculum is recorded, so grades become superfluous.[7]

Item: Kohn says that "moral issues are involved." The implication is that I and other teachers who use rewards are immoral. If it is immoral to let students know they have answered questions correctly, to pat a student on the back for a good effort, to show joy at a student's understanding of a concept, or to recognize the achievement of a goal by providing a gold star or a certificate — if this is immoral, then count me a sinner.

From *Phi Delta Kappan*, June 1993, pp. 787-790. © 1993 by Phi Delta Kappa, Inc. Reprinted by permission.

The above points illustrate, I think, the slippery nature of Kohn's critique and may lead the reader to question his scholarship and his motives for writing. I now turn to what seem to be his major criticisms of rewards.

✍ Kohn insists that rewards undermine interest in rewarded activities.[8] Notice that Kohn does not argue that *some* rewards — or *some uses of* rewards — undermine interest. There is, in his view, no such thing as a good reward. Simple feedback, praise, smiles, hugs, pats on the back, gold stars, applause, certificates of completion, public and private commendations, prizes, special privileges, money, informational rewards, and contractual rewards — they are all one to Kohn, and they are all bad.

The best-known researchers who have found rewards sometimes troublesome are Edward Deci, Richard Ryan, Mark Lepper, and David Greene. Kohn cites all four in making his case. What he does not tell us (though he must surely know it) is that all of these researchers reject his view.[9]

Deci and Ryan believe that rewards can undermine motivation if used in a controlling way. But they add, "When used to convey to people a sense of appreciation for work well done, [rewards] will tend to be experienced informationally and will *maintain or enhance intrinsic motivation*" (emphasis added).[10]

Lepper and Greene take a similar stand. They note, "If rewards provide [a student] with new information about his ability at a particular task, this may *bolster his feelings of competence and his desire to engage in that task for its own sake*" (emphasis added).[11] They add, "If a child does not possess the basic skills to discover the intrinsic satisfaction of complex activities such as reading, the use of extrinsic rewards may be required to equip him with these skills."[12]

The position taken by Deci, Ryan, Lepper, and Greene reflects the consensus among researchers who are concerned about the possible negative effects of rewards. Mark Morgan, for example, reviewed the research and wrote that "the central finding emerging from the present review is that rewards can have either undermining or enhancing effects depending on circumstances."[13] He concludes that "the evidence seems to support strongly the hypothesis that rewards that emphasize success or competence on a task enhance intrinsic motivation."[14]

✍ Kohn claims that rewards do not work. It is true that not all rewards are

> Certain rewards (e.g., attention, positive feedback, praise) are almost always effective reinforcers when used properly.

reinforcing. Teachers must not assume that a reward will strengthen behavior merely because that is the teacher's intention. What is reinforcing for one student may not be for another. But there is overwhelming evidence that certain rewards (e.g., attention, positive feedback, praise) are almost always effective reinforcers when used properly.

In a study by Bill Hopkins and R. J. Conard, cited in my article, teachers who provided frequent feedback, praise, and other rewards saw much faster learning.[15] Students in these classes advanced at the normal rate in spelling, at nearly twice the normal rate in mathematics, and at more than double the usual rate in reading.[16] Studies showing similar gains, due at least partly to frequent use of rewards (especially feedback and praise), are easily found by those who seek them.[17]

Even contractual rewards may be useful in some circumstances. In one program, high-risk, low-income adolescents and young adults in Lafayette Parish, Louisiana, were paid $3.40 an hour to participate in a summer program of academic instruction and job training. Students gained an average of 1.2 grade levels in reading and 1.5 grade levels in math in just eight weeks.[18]

It may be the case that the Lafayette Parish students stopped reading when money was no longer available. It probably cannot be said, however, that they read less than they did before participating in the program. If students show little or no interest in an activity, it is silly to refuse to provide rewards for fear of undermining their interest in the activity — a point made by Greene and Lepper.[19]

Kohn ignores such evidence and instead cites studies on the use of contractual rewards in weight control, smoking, and seat belt programs.[20] I am (understandably, I think) reluctant to take Kohn's assessment of these programs at face value.[21] But let us assume for the sake of argument that he is right. Note that none of these programs has anything to do with the value of rewards in classroom learning. Kohn's logic is, "If rewards do not help people stop smoking, they cannot help students learn to write." By the same logic, we would have to conclude that since aspirin is of no use in treating cancer, it must not be effective in treating headache. It is a bizarre logic.

✍ The benefits of rewards, says Kohn, are only temporary. Obviously this is not true if we are speaking of academic learning: the child who learns the Pythagorean theorem at the hands of a teacher who provides frequent feedback and praise does not suddenly forget Pythagoras because his next teacher no longer pays attention to his efforts. Nor is there any reason to think that students who are paid to read become illiterate when the money runs out.

But perhaps Kohn has other kinds of learning in mind. Teachers who praise and attend to students when they are on-task will find those students spending less time staring out the window or doodling in their notebooks.[22] If the teacher abruptly stops rewarding on-task behavior, the rate of window staring and doodling will return to its previous level.[23] To conclude from this that teachers should not reward behavior is ridiculous. It is like saying that regular exercise is pointless because your muscles get flabby again when you stop exercising. The point is not to stop.

It should be noted, moreover, that one of the things we can strengthen with rewards is persistence. Once our students are on-task for short periods, we can then begin rewarding longer periods of on-task behavior. We must be careful not to raise the standard too quickly, but we can *gradually* require more from our students. Persistence at other kinds of activities can also be built up by systematically providing rewards (especially praise) for meeting successively higher standards. Many teachers do this over the course of a school year, often without realizing it.

When behavior is rewarded intermittently in this way, it tends to become stronger. That is, it becomes *less* likely to fall off when rewards are no longer available. This is a well-established phenomenon called the partial reinforcement effect (PRE). The PRE reflects the fact that, in an uncertain world, persistence often pays off.

ONE FINAL comment: I realize that this reply to Kohn's remarks will have little impact on most readers. Kohn is selling what educators want to buy — and what many of them have been buying for several decades. It is the philosophy of education that says that students must teach themselves, that the teacher's job is to let students explore and discover on their own, and that teachers can, at most, "facilitate learning."[24]

This philosophy renders the teacher essentially impotent and leads ultimately to the conclusion that, when students fail, it is their own fault.[25] If students do not learn, it is because of some deficiency in them: lack of ability, lack of motivation, hyperactivity, attention deficit disorder — we have lots of choices. The failure is never due to inadequate teaching. Learning depends, after all, on things inside the student, well out of the teacher's reach.

I reject this view. I believe that a fair reading of the research on classroom learning points to a better way. That better way includes a teacher who is actively engaged in the educational process. Such a teacher recognizes the importance of, among other things, providing students with opportunities to perform and providing consequences for that performance. Those consequences include feedback, praise, smiles, and other forms of informational reward. In certain circumstances, they may include contractual rewards. This view of education places responsibility for learning squarely on the teacher's shoulders. Perhaps that is why there is so much opposition to it.

1. B. F. Skinner was not fond of contractual rewards himself, but he agreed that they may sometimes be necessary. See B. F. Skinner, "The Contrived Reinforcer," *The Behavior Analyst*, Spring 1982, pp. 3-8.

2. In an *Industry Week* survey, about one in three employees complained about a lack of praise for their work, a fact reported in Randall Poe and Carol L. Courter, "Fast Forward," *Across the Board*, September 1991, p. 5. Would workers want more praise if they considered it manipulative and controlling?

3. For instance. students can learn to find logical errors in a text by reading texts containing such errors and receiving feedback and praise for their efforts. See Kent R. Johnson and T. V. Joe Layng, "Breaking the Structuralist Barrier: Literacy and Numeracy with Fluency," *American Psychologist*, vol. 47, 1992, pp. 1475-90. For more on the use of rewards to teach thinking, see Paul Chance, *Thinking in the Classroom* (New York: Teachers College Press, 1986), Ch. 9.

4. John I. Goodlad, *A Place Called School: Prospects for the Future* (New York: McGraw-Hill, 1984), p. 112. Goodlad argues that teachers should be taught the skills of "providing students with knowledge of their performance, and giving praise for good work" (p. 127). For the most part they are not taught these skills. Ernest Vargas notes that, "with the exception of a stray course here or there," the 1,200 colleges of education in this country offer little instruction in reinforcement and related techniques. See Ernest A. Vargas, "Teachers in the Classroom: Behaviorological Science and an Effective Instructional Technology," *Youth Policy*, July/August 1988, p. 35.

5. Harold W. Stevenson, "Learning from Asian Schools," *Scientific American*, December 1992, pp. 70-76. Stevenson suggests that the American preference for seatwork and the failure to provide feedback may be due partly to the fact that Americans teach longer hours than their Asian counterparts.

6. Quoted in James G. Holland, "B. F. Skinner (1904-1990)," *American Psychologist*, vol. 47, 1992, p. 667.

7. F. S. Keller, "Goodbye, Teacher . . . ," *Journal of Applied Behavior Analysis*, Spring 1968, pp. 79-89. See also Paul Chance, "The Revolutionary Gentleman," *Psychology Today*, September 1984, pp. 42-48.

8. Studies reporting a loss of interest following rewards typically involve 1) contractual rewards and 2) behavior that is already occurring at a high rate. This is, of course, a misuse of contractual rewards, since the purpose of such rewards is to boost the rate of behavior that occurs *infrequently*.

9. In my article, I provided guidelines for the effective use of rewards. These guidelines were drawn, in part, from the recommendations of Deci, Ryan, Lepper, and Greene.

10. Edward L. Deci and Richard M. Ryan, *Intrinsic Motivation and Self-Determination in Human Behavior* (New York: Plenum, 1985), p. 300.

11. David Greene and Mark R. Lepper, "Intrinsic Motivation: How to Turn Play into Work," *Psychology Today*, September 1974, p. 54. Elsewhere they write that "the effects of rewards depend upon the manner and context in which they are delivered." See Mark R. Lepper and David Greene, "Divergent Approaches," in idem, eds., *The Hidden Costs of Reward* (New York: Erlbaum, 1978), p. 208.

12. Greene and Lepper, p. 54.

13. Mark Morgan, "Reward-Induced Decrements and Increments in Intrinsic Motivation," *Review of Educational Research*, Spring 1984, p. 13.

14. Ibid., p. 9. Another of Kohn's sources, Teresa Amabile, also specifically defends the use of informational rewards. See Teresa Amabile, "Cashing in on Good Grades," *Psychology Today*, October 1989, p. 80. See also idem, *The Social Psychology of Creativity* (New York: Springer-Verlag, 1983).

15. Bill L. Hopkins and R. J. Conard, "Putting It All Together: Superschool," in Norris G. Haring and Richard L. Schiefelbusch, eds., *Teaching Special Children* (New York: McGraw-Hill, 1975), pp. 342-85.

16. The students also enjoyed school more and were better behaved.

17. See, for example, Charles R. Greenwood et al., "Out of the Laboratory and into the Community," *American Psychologist*, vol. 47, 1992, pp. 1464-74; R. Douglas Greer, "L'Enfant Terrible Meets the Educational Crisis," *Journal of Applied Behavior Analysis*, Spring 1992, pp. 65-69; and Johnson and Layng, op. cit.

18. Steven Hotard and Marion J. Cortez, "Evaluation of Lafayette Parish Job Training Summer Remedial Program: Report Presented to the Lafayette Parish School Board and Lafayette Parish Job Training Department of Lafayette Parish Government," August 1987. Note that this research may not represent the best use of contractual rewards, since payment was only loosely contingent on performance.

19. "Clearly," they write, "if a child begins with no intrinsic interest in an activity, there will be no intrinsic motivation to lose." See Greene and Lepper, p. 54.

20. Note that Kohn cites no evidence that his own preferred techniques — persuasion and mutual problem solving — are effective in helping people lose weight, quit smoking, or use seat belts. Indeed, reward programs have been used to treat these problems precisely because persuasion and education have proved ineffective.

21. For instance, in the study on smoking that Kohn cites, the researchers note that "the incentive was not linked directly to smoking cessation." See Susan J. Curry et al., "Evaluation of Intrinsic and Extrinsic Motivation Interventions with a Self-Help Smoking Cessation Program," *Journal of Consulting and Clinical Psychology*, vol. 59, 1991, p. 309. The researchers rewarded participants for completing progress reports, *not* for refraining from smoking.

22. Teacher attention can be an effective reward for on-task behavior. See R. Vance Hall, Diane Lund, and Deloris Jackson, "Effects of Teacher Attention on Study Behavior," *Journal of Applied Behavior Analysis*, Spring 1968, pp. 1-12.

23. Some might argue that we should merely provide students with more interesting (i.e., intrinsically rewarding) material. While interesting learning materials are certainly desirable, it is probably unrealistic to expect that students will always have interesting material with which to work. It may therefore be desirable for them to learn to concentrate on work even when it is not particularly agreeable.

24. The roots of today's constructivist "revolution" are described in Lawrence A. Cremin, "The Free School Movement," *Today's Education*, September/October 1974, pp. 71-74; and in B. F. Skinner, "The Free and Happy Student," *New York University Education Quarterly*, Winter 1973, pp. 2-6.

25. This is apparently the prevailing view. Galen Alessi has found that school psychologists, for instance, rarely consider poor instruction the source of a student's difficulties. Instead, the student and, in a few cases, the student's parents are said to be at fault. Galen Alessi, "Diagnosis Diagnosed: A Systematic Reaction," *Professional School Psychology*, vol. 3, 1988, pp. 145-51.

The Tyranny of Self-Oriented Self-Esteem

Many modern self-esteem programs emphasize a self-focus, although a focus directed on external-to-self goals may be more productive.

James H. McMillan, Judy Singh, and Leo G. Simonetta

JAMES H. McMILLAN, Ph.D., is a professor of educational studies at Virginia Commonwealth University in Richmond, Virginia. JUDY SINGH is a doctoral student in education at Virginia Commonwealth University. LEO G. SIMONETTA is an assistant professor and social psychologist at the Center for Urban Policy Research at Georgia State University in Atlanta.

I n Ryann's second-grade classroom there was a poster on one wall to celebrate each individual student. For one week during the year each student was the "special child" of the class, and the space on the poster indicated unique and valued things about the child, such as a favorite color, hobbies, or family. Students put up pictures and other items to announce publicly what they thought was good about themselves. (Ryann, daughter of one of the authors, liked being a "special child" for a week, but the parent was not as enthusiastic.)

Activities of this type are common in elementary schools, all seeking to boost the self-esteem of the students. They assume that self-esteem is the key to achievement, and in fact much evidence, both anecdotal and research-based, shows that students achieve more with self-esteem. Teachers also seem to accept self-esteem as critical for intellectual development and necessary for students to excel or even achieve needed competence in academic tasks. According to Barbara Lerner, "Teachers generally seem to accept the modern dogma that self-esteem is the critical variable for intellectual development—the master key to learning. Children . . . cannot achieve excellence, or even competence, until their self-esteem is raised."[1]

Linking self-esteem to success and overall well-being is so well accepted that there are many institutes, foundations, task forces, and centers dedicated to promoting self-esteem programs. For example, there is the California Task Force to Promote Self-Esteem and Personal and Social Responsibility, the Center for Self-Esteem, the National Council for Self-Esteem, and the Foundation for Self-Esteem.[2] In addition, an increasing number of books, monographs, audio- and videocassettes stress developing self-esteem, as well as "how to" programs for teachers at all levels. The fundamental idea is that once educators focus on improving students' self-esteem, not only will behavior and achievement improve, but students also will be more satisfied, better adjusted, and happier. The assumption is that concentrating on enhancing self-esteem will produce these positive outcomes.

But is it possible, with the best of intentions, to overemphasize self-esteem with self-oriented activities? What are we teaching our children by encouraging and reinforcing a self-focus, and what are its long-term consequences? Since the mid-'60s, psychology has transformed our way of thinking about explanations for people's behaviors, shifting from out-

What are we teaching our children by encouraging and reinforcing a self-focus, and what are its long-term consequences?

side the self (behaviorism) to within the self. The psychologist Martin Seligman terms our current culture one of "maximal selfs," in which the individual should be gratified, fulfilled, self-actualized, and in control.[3] Seligman argues that this revolutionary change has caused increased depression, hopelessness, and other personal difficulties because of the dual burden of high expectations and self-control. Since the focus is on ourselves as being responsible, and on an expectation that we will be most content and happy if we concentrate on what is best for us, coping with failure to reach our expectations becomes difficult. If Seligman is correct, many facets of current self-esteem programs may be based on fundamentally flawed and misdirected theory. In this article the theory of self-oriented self-esteem programs will be reviewed, with illustrations of suggested practices based on this theory and the results that can be expected from this approach. An alternative theory will be recommended, with suggested practices.

Self-oriented Self-esteem

Many self-esteem programs fundamentally encourage students to think more about themselves, to be more introspective and self-oriented. The idea is that the self can be enhanced by focusing on it positively. Barbara Lerner refers to this as "feel-good-now self-esteem."[4] Jack Canfield, a well-known advocate of self-esteem

enhancement, has suggested several strategies for the classroom that emphasize introspection: 1) assume an attitude of 100 percent responsibility by getting students to think about what they are saying to themselves; 2) focus on the positive—"I spend a lot of my time having students recall, write about, draw, and share their past experiences"; 3) learn to monitor your self-talk by replacing negative thoughts with positive—"I can learn to do anything I want, I am smart, I love and accept myself the way I am"; and 4) identify your strengths and weaknesses.[5]

A popular self-esteem book for educators suggests enhancing self-esteem with one or more of the following: improving self-evaluation skills; developing a sense of personal worth; reflecting on self-esteem; thinking of oneself in positive terms; discovering reasons the individual is unhappy; or examining sources of and influences on self-esteem. Their emphasis is on enhancing students' positive self-perceptions.[6] Such ideas are often implemented in classroom activities that teach students introspective thinking: for example, keeping a journal about themselves and indicating "what I like best about myself";[7] teaching a unit entitled "I Am Great" that emphasizes their individuality through self-portraits, silhouettes of themselves, "who am I," and "coat of arms" exercises;[8] and programs such as Developing Understanding of Self and Others (DUSO), Toward Affective Development, and Dimensions of Personality. Some less-complex programs simply encourage student self-talk with phrases such as "I'm terrific" or "I'm great." All these activities or programs are designed to promote self-acceptance and self-awareness, to help students become aware of their unique characteristics, and to "put children in touch with themselves."[9]

Although these are well-intentioned programs, their encouragement of self-introspection may distort a normal, healthy perspective about oneself into self-importance, self-gratification, and ultimately selfishness. If

the message is that "me" is most important, will selfishness be viewed as normal and expected? Are we making a virtue of self-preoccupation? If so, such "selfism" may have negative consequences. As William Damon points out, "A young mind might too readily interpret a blanket incantation toward self-esteem as a lure toward self-centeredness."[10] Damon believes that placing the child at the center of the universe is psychologically dangerous because "…it draws the child's attention away from the social realities to which the child must adapt for proper character development."[11] Children taught to place themselves first care most for their own personal experiences, and in doing so they do not learn how to develop respect for others. According to Lerner, the feel-good-now variety of self-esteem eventually leads to unhappiness, restlessness, and dissatisfaction.[12] Finally, Seligman argues that our obsession with self is responsible for an alarming increase in depression and other mental difficulties,[13] and it is well-documented that such problems result from rumination and obsessive thinking about oneself.[14]

There are other negative consequences of overemphasizing self-oriented self-esteem. For most students, and surely young children, the idea of self-esteem is abstract and hard to understand. Generalized statements such as "you're valued," or "you're great," or "you're special" have no objective reality. They are simply holistic messages that, untied to something tangible and real, have little meaning.[15] Teachers making such statements will lose credibility because children are adept at discerning valid feedback from such vague generalizations. Students may develop a skepticism toward and distrust of adults, or even worse may learn to tune them out entirely, as the teacher "shades the truth … [with] … empty rhetoric, transparent flattery, bland distortions of reality."[16] By trying to bolster self-esteem with messages that are not "entirely" true, teachers inadvertently undermine the trust of the child. For students who already have a low self-esteem, such statements reinforce a noncaring attitude from adults. From the perspective of children, caring adults "tell it like it is" and don't hide the truth—they don't cover up or make things up that aren't true.

In contrast, there is ample evidence that our mental health improves as we forget ourselves and focus on activities that are not self-oriented. Often we are most happy when we are so involved in outside pursuits that we don't think about ourselves. This leads us to an alternative theoretical foundation for self-esteem: the notion that healthy self-esteem results not from self-preoccupation and analysis but just the opposite—from **not** being self-oriented but being occupied by interests and pursuits external to self. Indeed, many self-esteem enhancement programs appear to be based on this idea.

Accomplishment and External-to-Self-oriented Self-esteem

As an alternative to the self-orientation approach, we suggest that a healthy esteem results not from self-preoccupation and analysis but from activities that result in meaningful accomplishment or have an external-to-self orientation. Accomplishment means that self-esteem is enhanced as children work hard to meet externally set, reasonable standards of achievement. Lerner calls this "earned" self-esteem: "Earned self-esteem is based on success in meeting the tests of reality—measuring up to standards—at home and in school. It is necessarily hard-won, and develops slowly, but is stable and long-lasting, and provides a secure foundation for further growth and development. It is not a precondition for learning but a product of it."[17]

Achieving meaningful success in schoolwork enhances self-esteem after many years of meeting standards and demands. A foundation for self-esteem based on tangible evidence is internalized by students because it makes sense to them in their social environment. Internally meaningful

Accomplishment means that self-esteem is enhanced as children work hard to meet externally set, reasonable standards of achievement.

performance and accomplishment can be attributed to ability and effort. Such internal attributions underlie a sense of self-efficacy so that the child becomes confident in being a capable learner. Striving for achievement also directs children's thinking off themselves and on something external to themselves. This change in thinking orientation determines self-esteem programs that theoretically are diametrically opposed to self-oriented programs.

Recently there have been signs that psychologists may be changing their views about the emphasis on selfism to enhance self-esteem. Seligman maintains that many have lost a sense of commitment to larger entities outside themselves—country, church, community, family, God, or a purpose that transcends themselves. Without these connections people are left to find meaning and fulfillment in themselves.[18] The negative consequences of de-emphasizing other people, groups, community, and the larger society include vandalism, violence, racial tensions, high divorce rates, and drug abuse. Some psychologists attribute the growth of the "me" generation and selfish behavior to the emphasis on individuality and related themes.[19] Others argue that schools should promote selflessness by emphasizing group welfare over individuals, involvement rather than iso-

lation, and self-denial rather than self-centeredness.

These authors suggest that student well-being is best enhanced by pursuits that take attention away from self, in which one gets "lost." Such pursuits could include a hobby; a concern for helping others; having a purpose or cause bigger than oneself; submitting to duty or to a role in community; or academic success following meaningful effort. The hypothesis is that self-esteem is a by-product of successful external-to-self experiences. The more success a student has in such activities, the stronger his or her own self-esteem will be.

From a social-psychological perspective, participating constructively with others is necessary for positive self-esteem. As stated by Damon:

> Growing up in large part means learning to participate constructively in the social world. This in turn means developing real skills, getting along with others, acquiring respect for social rules and legitimate authority, caring about those in need, and assuming social responsibility in a host of ways. All of these efforts necessarily bring children out of themselves. They require children to orient themselves toward other people and other people's standards.[21]

By focusing outside themselves children learn respect for others and an objective reference for acquiring a stable and meaningful sense of themselves. It is the outward focus that forms the foundation for self-esteem.

Some examples of self-esteem programs appear to be based on this external-to-self hypothesis. One is a successful program in which students are involved in an art project structured to enhance a feeling of belonging and accomplishment. Self-esteem is improved by involving students in meaningful group activity, not by self-introspection.[22] Another program reports that children acquire self-esteem from successful experiences and appropriate feedback in motor skill development.[23] Several other programs also stress successful achievement in affecting self-esteem.[24] In each case the program involves students in some meaningful activity, rather than focusing on themselves.

Conclusion

Clearly, educators need to concentrate their efforts on improving students' self-esteem. The important question is: How should this be done? We have suggested that approaches emphasizing meaningful achievement and external-to-self pursuits will result in more healthy self-esteem than programs that are self-oriented. Teachers and administrators need to design programs directing student attention away from the self, not toward it. Paradoxically, positive self-esteem develops as students forget about self-esteem, focus on external pursuits, and obtain positive feedback following meaningful involvement and effort

Teachers and administrators need to design programs directing student attention away from the self, not toward it.

1. Barbara Lerner, "Self-esteem and Excellence: The Choice and the Paradox," *American Educator* 9 (1985): 10-16.

2. Jack Canfield, "Improving Students' Self-esteem," *Educational Leadership* 48 (1990): 48-50.

3. Martin E. P. Seligman, "Boomer Blues: With Too Great Expectations, the Baby-Boomers Are Sliding into Individualistic Melancholy," *Psychology Today* 22 (1988): 50-55.

4. Lerner, "Self-esteem and Excellence."

5. Canfield, "Improving Students' Self-esteem."

6. James A. Beane and Richard P. Lipka, *Self-concept, Self-esteem, and the Curriculum* (Boston: Allyn and Bacon, 1984).

7. Anne E. Gottsdanker-Willenkens and Patricia Y. Leonard, "All about Me: Language Arts Strategies to Enhance Self-Concept," *Reading Teacher* 37 (1984): 801-802.

8. Richard L. Papenfuss, John D. Curtis, Barbara J. Beier, and Joseph D. Menze, "Teaching Positive Self-concepts in the Classroom," *Journal of School Health* 53 (1983): 618-620.

9. Frederic J. Medway and Robert C. Smith, Jr., "An Examination of Contemporary Elementary School Affective Education Programs," *Psychology in the Schools* 15 (1978): 266.

10. William Damon, "Putting Substance into Self-Esteem: A Focus on Academic and Moral Values," *educational HORIZONS* (fall 1991):13.

11. Ibid., 17.

12. Lerner, "Self-esteem and Excellence."

13. Seligman, "Boomer Blues."

14. Thomas J. Lasley and John Bregenzer, "Toward Selflessness," *Journal of Human Behavior and Learning* 3 (1986): 20-27.

15. Damon, "Putting Substance into Self-esteem."

16. Ibid., 15.

17. Lerner, "Self-esteem and Excellence," 13.

18. Martin E. P. Seligman, *Learned Optimism: The Skill to Conquer Life's Obstacles, Large & Small* (New York: Random House, 1990).

19. Sami I. Boulos, "The Anatomy of the 'Me' Generation," *Education* 102 (1982): 238-242.

20. Lasley and Bregenzer, "Toward Selflessness."

21. William Damon, "Putting Substance into Self-esteem," 16-17.

22. Marilee M. Cowan and Faith M. Clover, "Enhancement of Self-concept through Disciplined-based Art Education," *Art Education* 44 (1991): 38-45.

23. Linda K. Bunker, "The Role of Play and Motor Skill Development in Building Children's Self-confidence and Self-esteem," *Elementary School Journal* 91 (1991): 467-471.

24. David L. Silvernail, *Developing Positive Student Self-concept* (Washington, D.C.: National Education Association, 1987).

Improving Student Thinking

BARRY BEYER

Believe it or not, our students—regardless of age or grade level—not only *can* think but they *do*. They make decisions, attack problems, pose hypotheses, evaluate information, and even make inferences. Unfortunately, of course, many don't carry out these operations very skillfully or consistently, or at all the appropriate times or places, at least in our classes. Consequently, they often fail to develop the kinds of subject matter understandings, insights, and knowledge that we try so hard to help them develop. Isn't there something we can do in our classrooms to help our students improve the quality of their thinking, so they can think better and learn the subjects they study as well as they really could and as well as we would like them to?

The answer, happily, is a resounding y*es!*

Research, exemplary classroom practice, and accumulated teaching experience indicate that there are at least four things you and I can do right now in our classrooms that will improve the abilities and inclinations of our students to think better than they do when left on their own. And, we can do these *at the same time* that we engage our students in achieving the various subject matter learning objectives called for by our curricula. Specifically, we can

- provide a classroom learning environment that makes thinking possible and students willing to engage in it;
- make the invisible substance of thinking visible and explicit;
- guide and support student execution of newly encountered, difficult, or complex thinking operations during their initial efforts to apply them; and
- integrate instruction in thinking with instruction in subject matter.

Barry Beyer is professor emeritus in the Graduate School of Education at George Mason University in Fairfax, Virginia. He is the author of Improving Student Thinking: A Comprehensive Approach *(Boston: Allyn and Bacon, 1998).*

Before we consider some of the many ways to incorporate these approaches into our daily teaching, however, it is important to note that *improving* thinking differs considerably from *facilitating* thinking. The latter consists of making thinking easier. It is commonly a one-time intervention to help students overcome a temporary obstacle or to ease them through a difficult thinking task. Improving thinking, on the other hand, means making thinking work better—more rapidly, accurately, "expertly"—in the long run than it does now. This requires a continuing, systematic, long-term effort to move students toward achieving and maintaining the highest levels possible of skilled, self-directed, self-correcting thinking. The four approaches described here are especially useful for achieving that goal.

Providing Thoughtful Learning Environments

Unless the learning environments of our classrooms nurture and support student thinking, especially higher-order thinking, our students are unlikely to be very receptive to serious efforts on our part to help them improve their thinking. Among the features of such learning environments two stand out as especially crucial: (1) repeated opportunities to engage in meaningful thinking beyond the level of recall and (2) encouragement to engage and remain engaged in such thinking. By ensuring that our classrooms consistently exhibit these features, we make them "thinker-friendly" as well as "thinking-friendly." Specialists call such classrooms thoughtful classrooms (Wiggins 1987).

Providing Thinking Opportunities

The secret to providing repeated classroom opportunities to engage in thinking is to engage students in productive learning tasks. These are tasks that require students to produce knowledge new to them, rather than simply to reproduce information or knowledge claims already presented to them in texts, lectures, or media. One powerful way to do this is to frame learning assignments or lessons around thoughtful questions.

A thoughtful question is a question that—to produce an

acceptable response—requires students to go substantially beyond where they are and, like the crew of the Enterprise, "to boldly go where no man has gone before." To answer these questions, students must locate and use information they may not yet possess as well as restructure familiar information to produce something they do not already know. "What did Columbus discover?" is not a very thoughtful question. "Who discovered Columbus—and why?" is much more thoughtful.

Thoughtful questions stimulate thinking and trigger additional related questions. They engage students in defining terms; posing hypotheses; identifying, finding, assessing, and manipulating data; making and testing inferences; generating and evaluating conclusions and arguments; and applying concepts, principles, and other kinds of knowledge. They are not yes/no questions. They cannot be answered simply by recall. They do not have a single preferred "right" answer (Newmann 1990; Wiggins 1987). Organizing lessons, units, or topics around such questions provides students continued opportunities to engage in all kinds of thinking to generate worthwhile and meaningful subject matter learning.

Productive learning activities also provide considerable opportunities for sustained thinking. Activities like judging the accuracy of a given claim or body of information or generating a strong argument in support of a conclusion may require as few as only one or two classroom periods (Beyer 1997). Longer tasks such as the following provide even more opportunities for continued student thinking:

> *Create and justify the "good citizenship merit badge" requirements for a specific kind of person in a given culture or place at a particular time in history, such as for a Nez Perce youth in the 1870s, an enslaved or free African American in the 1850s, or a king's vassal in the Middle Ages.*

Organizing our lessons around thoughtful questions and productive learning tasks helps make thinking a central part of student learning in our classrooms.

Encouraging Student Thinking

Providing opportunities to think, however, is fruitless unless students take advantage of them. And, as we all know, too many students frequently do not! It is thus also essential that we encourage students to seize and sustain engagement in thinking opportunities if we are to create and maintain a thoughtful learning environment.

The kind of encouragement required here is not the redouble-your-effort kind derived from simple cheerleading or from exhortations like, "Think! Think again! Now think harder!" On the contrary, it is the kind of encouragement that *emboldens* students to engage in thinking. This means providing them some tangible aid, prompt, or other support that gives them reason to feel that they will or can succeed at the task at hand.

We can provide such encouragement by arranging students so they face each other as well as by surrounding them with bulletin board displays of quotations, cartoons,

puzzles, and copies of their own work that illustrate the importance and value of good thinking. Providing wait time for them to think before we accept their responses to our questions or claims and before we respond to their assertions or answers also serves that purpose (Rowe 1974). So, too, does our modeling the behaviors and dispositions of skillful thinking and helping our students exhibit these behaviors and dispositions. Rather than cutting thinking off with remarks such as, "Good answer!", we can build on their responses to sustain continued thinking by, for instance, asking for evidence to support the accuracy of a response or for examples or more details or assumptions underlying it.

We can also encourage student thinking by minimizing or eliminating the negative risks of thinking (Lipman 1991; Nickerson 1988-89). We can consistently emphasize the positive value of rejected hypotheses and "wrong answers" in leading us to valid hypotheses and "answers." We can constantly employ the language of thinking by using precise thinking terms to denote the specific cognitive actions, skills, conditions, or products in which we wish to engage students. For instance, instead of asking, "What do you think will happen next?" we should ask, "What do you *predict* will happen next?" (Olson and Astington 1990; Perkins 1992). And we can keep classroom discourse focused on truth and proof rather than on who says what, welcome and explore divergent or unusual views, and reward the validated products of high-risk thinking (Newmann 1990).

When engaging in new or difficult thinking tasks is a normal and expected part of our classrooms and "emboldening boosts" are consistently given, students have reason to believe that they can engage successfully in such thinking. It is this kind of support—combined with the topics we ask them to think about—that encourages them to take advantage of the thinking opportunities we provide.

Making Thinking Visible

Before we can repair or strengthen something that is broken or is not working as well as it should be, we need to be aware of exactly how it presently functions. We also need to be aware of how it works or might work when functioning as it could or should function. This is as true of student thinking as it is of any other procedure or process. The first step in improving student thinking thus consists of making students conscious of how they presently think and how others more skilled than they carry out the same thinking operations. This means we need to make the seemingly invisible thinking processes visible and explicit, especially when our students are focusing on new or complex thinking operations.

The Invisible Substance of Thinking

What is there we can make visible and explicit about any act of thinking? Cognitive scientists assert that every thinking skill (operation, strategy, or act) consists of three elements: one or more *procedures* (series of steps and/or rules) by which it is or can be executed skillfully and efficiently; the *conditions* under which it is appropriately employed; and any *declarative knowledge* associated with it, such as the criteria employed in making judgments or evaluations or the heuristics (rules of thumb) that guide expert application of a procedure (Anderson 1983; Nickerson 1988-89). Students benefit immensely from becoming conscious of and articulating exactly how they presently execute a given thinking operation or skill as well as how experts do it, of where and when it is appropriate to employ the operation, and of anything they know—or should know—that would make its application more efficient, effective, and "expert" (Papert 1980; Vygotsky 1962).

Making the Invisible Visible

We help students make visible and explicit these normally unarticulated elements of any thinking skill in several ways. One is by engaging students in reflecting on what they did to carry out a thinking operation they have just completed. This is known as *metacognitive reflection*. Once students have completed a thinking task, we have them think back on exactly what they did mentally, step by step, to complete it, and why they took those steps. In doing this, students articulate what they recall doing, listen to how some of their peers believe they did the same thing, and then analyze these accounts to identify apparently useful, and even additional unarticulated, steps and rules. By continuously articulating and then comparing these procedural descriptions with each other and with explicit procedures employed by individuals more skilled than they in carrying out the same operation, students can spot weaknesses or omissions in the way they do it, identify steps or rules that appear to be especially useful in carrying out the thinking operation, and adapt or incorporate these into how they execute it in the future (Beyer 1997; Nickerson, Perkins, and Smith 1985; Sternberg 1984).

Another way to make the invisible of thinking visible and explicit is to model a thinking operation to be developed (Pressley and Harris 1990; Rosenshine and Meister 1992). *Modeling* consists of demonstrating step-by-step how a skill is executed, with accompanying explanation noting the key steps in the procedure and why these steps are important. If we are proficient at executing the thinking skill in question and can verbalize clearly how we do it, we ourselves can model it for our students. We may also use written protocols or videos or essays that model this procedure, if any are available. Occasionally, a student who has demonstrated skill in carrying out the thinking operation can model the procedure. Then, if we provide an immediate opportunity to apply the modeled procedure while it is still visible to them, students can attempt to replicate it. With continued practice and reflection they can adopt or adapt it to develop a skilled routine of their own for executing the skill.

The key here is making students conscious of exactly how they presently carry out a thinking act or skill (imper-

fect as their awareness or execution may be), of how their peers do it, and of how more skilled thinkers do it. Metacognitive reflection and modeling serve these ends well. Improving the quality of student thinking requires repeated use of both of these techniques with each thinking skill we teach.

Guiding and Supporting Student Thinking

Providing continuing guidance and support to students who are trying to apply newly encountered thinking skills proves indispensable to moving them toward skillful, autonomous use of these skills (Rosenshine and Meister 1992). Two kinds of such guidance and support prove especially effective to this end: scaffolding and cueing. Once students have become conscious of a procedure or routine for executing a new thinking operation, scaffolding and cueing can be used to guide their continuing follow-up practice and application of the procedure in a variety of contexts.

Scaffolding Thinking

A scaffold is a skeletal framework of a thinking procedure—such as a checklist—that makes the steps in that thinking procedure explicit. Students use the scaffold to steer themselves through these steps as they try to carry them out. Such devices allow students to concentrate on applying the rules and steps of an unfamiliar or complex thinking procedure to a given body of information without having also to try to recall what steps to employ. Use of thinking scaffolds minimizes procedural errors in trying to apply a newly encountered thinking skill and enables students to internalize a more effective skill-using routine sooner than they otherwise might if they had to carry out the skill, from memory, exclusively on their own (McTighe and Lyman 1988).

There are three kinds of devices that prove especially effective as scaffolds for thinking. *Procedural checklists*, such as that for decision making shown in figure 1, are the most explicit. They provide a list, in order, of the mental steps by which a specific thinking procedure can be effectively carried out. *Process-structured questions* are less explicit. Like the example in figure 1, these devices walk students through the steps in a thinking procedure not by telling them the steps directly but by asking a series of questions that require students to execute in sequence each of the steps that constitutes the given thinking procedure. *Graphic organizers*, like that in figure 1, are charts or diagrams that present visually—and occasionally with written prompts— the steps in a thinking procedure (McTighe and Lyman 1988). As students fill in the various sections of the thinking skill organizer, they move through these steps. Graphic organizers provide less explicit support and guidance than either checklists or process-structured questions but can still effectively scaffold or structure student thinking.

Not all checklists, lists of questions, or graphic organizers scaffold thinking, however. Many checklists and ques-

FIGURE 1
Scaffolds for Student Thinking

A Procedural Checklist
for Decision Making

- Identify a choosing opportunity.
- State the problem/goal.
- State the criteria of the "best" choice/decision.
- List the possible alternative choices.
- List the possible consequences of selecting each alternative.
- Evaluate each consequence in terms of the criteria identified above.
- Select the alternative that best meets the identified criteria.

Process-Structured Questions
for Decision Making

1. What do you want to make a decision about?
2. What do you want to accomplish by making this decision?
3. How will you know when you have made the "best" choice?
4. What are all the alternatives you have to choose from?
5. What are the possible consequences of each alternative—long range as well as short range?
6. What are the pluses and minuses of each consequence?
7. Which alternative is "best"? Why?

A Graphic Organizer
for Decision Making

Situation/opportunity:						
Problem:			Goal/criteria:			
Alternatives:	Consequences/costs/etc.:				Evaluation:	
Decision:			Reasons:			

tions trigger thinking but do not, by the way they are arranged or worded, effectively move students through the steps in a cognitive procedure. Furthermore, as commonly used, many webs, matrices, charts, and diagrams tend to represent the products of thinking—products such as concepts, generalizations, and so on—rather than a procedure by which a thinking product is generated. To be effective in scaffolding thinking, checklists, question sets, and graphic organizers must activate and present a cognitive procedure in a clear, step-by-step fashion.

Cueing Thinking

A *cue* is a prompt that reminds us of what to do or say next without telling us all that we are to do or say. Cueing thinking consists of prompting students to employ a specif-

ic thinking operation. Cues are usually much less explicit than scaffolds. They also depend much more for their effectiveness on the degree to which students have already internalized—stored in memory—under that cue label or signal the procedures and the rules that constitute the action or skill they seek to call forth. Cueing thinking proves helpful to improving student thinking only after students have become consciously aware (through metacognitive reflection and/or modeling) of an effective skill-using procedure and have had enough scaffolded practice in applying it to have stored that specific knowledge in memory.

Thinking cues take many forms (Rosenshine and Meister 1992). They range from the more explicit, such as previewing and rehearsing a skill about to be applied, to simply naming that operation, to even less explicit devices such as mnemonics and symbols. We can *preview* a thinking operation that students are about to employ by having volunteers provide its various names, report any special rules or heuristics that they know might guide its use (including the criteria it applies, if it is a critical thinking operation), tell why it is appropriate to use at this point, and define it. Asking for the definition last allows students to use the preceding volunteered information as cues for searching their memories for this definition or as information from which to construct an appropriate working definition.

We can help students *rehearse* a thinking skill they are about to practice by having volunteers report one or more routines or procedures by which it can be effectively employed and/or any rules, criteria, and heuristics that direct or inform its use. When students have been applying a skill for some time, however, merely *stating the technical label* of the skill—or words associated with it—customarily serves as a sufficient cue. *Mnemonics*, if devised or learned earlier by the students when they were first articulating or devising skilled procedures for executing a skill, also can serve as useful thinking cues. For example, consider the acronym **DECIDE** as a cue for the process of decision making:

> **D**efine goal
> **E**numerate alternatives
> **C**onsider consequences
> **I**nvestigate effects
> **D**etermine best alternative
> **E**xecute

Acronyms like this one not only aid students in recalling the skill to employ but can actually cue the steps in a procedure for executing it (Beyer 1997).

Integrating Instruction in Thinking with Subject Matter

Thinking is affected and shaped as much by the subject matter to which it is applied as that subject matter is shaped by the kind of thinking that is employed to process it and the skill with which that thinking is applied. Efforts to improve student thinking, therefore, need to be carefully integrated into instruction in subject matter (Resnick and Klopfer 1989). *We can and should teach thinking and subject matter at the same time.*

To accomplish this, we must do at least two things. First, we must ensure that our students have repeated opportunities throughout our courses to apply the thinking skills in which they need to improve. This can be done, in part, by focusing on topics and themes within our subjects that are relevant to our students and to life today and in the future. It can also be accomplished by building student study around productive thinking activities and questions, as described above.

In addition, we must provide explicit instruction and then guided practice—as appropriate—in each thinking operation to be improved the first dozen or so times students are called upon to apply it. One way to plan for this

instruction is to identify prior to beginning a course the specific thinking skills we believe our students will need to improve. Next, we can plan specific opportunities for the students, once they have first encountered the need to use these skills, to apply each at first frequently and then intermittently thereafter. Then we can design in advance the appropriate skill instruction for each point in this skill-using sequence using the subject matter our students are to be studying along the way.

Another way to provide such instruction is to be always alert while teaching to any thinking skills with which our students seem to be having difficulty. The first time we notice such difficulty we then can switch our instructional focus from subject matter to how to carry out the skill by introducing that skill. John Bransford (1993) calls this "just-in-time teaching." Appropriate guided practice can follow, over a sequence of subsequent lessons, as described above.

Both of these teaching approaches capitalize on what research tells us about student motivation to learn. And that is that students are more willing to attempt and to attend to learning a new skill when they are introduced to it and provided guidance in applying it at a time they have a perceived need to use it but realize they cannot do it effectively (Sigel 1984). Such skill lessons do not ignore the topic or subject being studied at the time. Indeed, they should use this subject matter as a vehicle for articulating the skill so students learn about this content while they also improve their proficiency in executing the skill.

Once a thinking skill has been introduced—made visible and explicit—we need to provide guided practice in it each time the students must apply it to develop further subject matter learning. Such practice not only helps students move toward skilled, autonomous use of the skill but also helps them develop the kinds of complex subject matter learning we usually wish them to develop. In guided practice of a skill, students first attend to how they executed the skill and then to the subject matter knowledge developed by its application. In time, little attention at all need be given to the skill. Upon our cue, students will soon be able to execute it effectively and eventually can do so on their own initiative. By combining instruction in thinking and subject matter in this way we capitalize on the symbiotic relationship between content and thinking: content serves as a vehicle for applying thinking and thinking serves as a tool for understanding content and producing knowledge.

Combining These Approaches to Improve Student Thinking

Many of us have long been aware of these four teaching approaches. However, we have too often elected to employ only one of them, the one that we or someone deems is "best" for us or our students. This is most unfortunate because, in order to improve the quality of student thinking and subject matter learning, we need to use all—rather than just one—of these approaches in our classrooms.

Each of the four approaches described here addresses a different element of what is required to improve thinking. Thoughtful classrooms provide the kind of nurturing thinking environment so essential for all the other approaches to "take." Making the invisible substance of thinking visible and explicit requires such an environment and establishes the baseline from which improvement can proceed. Scaffolding and cueing student thinking provide the guidance and support students need to apply with increasing efficiency, ease, and what math instructors call "elegance" the thinking procedures that they are developing. And employing all of these approaches in the subject matter being studied gives purpose to and motivates continued student skill development.

Is This Worth Doing?

Is the effort to do this worth it? Of course it is. All our students think. But most of them can think better—more often—and with greater success than they now do. And many, if not most, of them certainly can learn more or better in our courses than they do now. Interestingly, research demonstrates that in classes where teachers attend continuously and explicitly to the cognitive skills needed to understand subject matter, students not only improve their proficiency in these thinking skills but they also attain higher achievement in subject matter (Estes 1972). Use of the teaching approaches described here will help us accomplish precisely these goals.

REFERENCES

Anderson, J. R. 1983. *The architecture of cognition.* Cambridge, Mass.: Harvard University Press.

Beyer, B. K. 1997. *Improving student thinking: A comprehensive approach. Boston:* Allyn and Bacon.

Bransford, J. 1993. Teaching thinking. Presentation at the ASCD National Conference on Thinking and Learning, San Antonio, Tex. (26 Feb.).

Estes, T. H.. 1972. Reading in the social studies: A review of research since 1950. In *Reading in the content areas,* edited by J. Laffery. Newark, Del.: International Reading Association.

Lipman, M. 1991. *Thinking in education.* Cambridge: Cambridge University Press.

McTighe, J., and F. T. Lyman, Jr. 1988. Cueing thinking in the classroom: The promise of theory embedded tools. *Educational Leadership* 45 (April): 18–24.

Newmann, F. M. 1990. Higher order thinking in teaching social studies. *Journal of Curriculum Studies* 22 (Jan.-Feb.): 41–56.

Nickerson, R. 1988-1989. On improving thinking through instruction. In *Review of research in education* (vol. 15), edited by E. Z. Rothkopf. Washington, D.C.: American Educational Research Association.

Nickerson, R. S., D. N. Perkins, and E. E. Smith. 1985. *The teaching of thinking.* Hillsdale, N.J.: Lawrence Erlbaum Associates.

Olson, D. R., and J. W. Astington. 1990. Talking about text: How literacy contributes to thought. *Journal of Pragmatics* 14:705–21.

Papert, S. 1980. *Mindstorms: Children, computers and powerful ideas.* New York: Basic Books.

Perkins, D. 1992. *Smart schools.* New York: The Free Press.

Pressley, M., and K. R. Harris. 1990. What we really know about strategy instruction. *Educational Leadership* 48 (Sept.): 31–34.

Resnick, L., and L. E. Klopfer, eds. 1989. *Toward the thinking curriculum.* Alexandria, Va.: Association for Supervision and Curriculum Development.

Rosenshine, B. V., and C. Meister. 1992. The use of scaffolds for teaching higher level cognitive strategies. *Educational Leadership* 49 (April): 26–33.

Rowe, M. B. 1974. Wait time and rewards as instructional variables. *Journal of Research in Science Teaching* 11:8–94.

Sigel, I. E. 1984. A constructivist perspective for teaching thinking. *Educational Leadership* 42 (Nov.): 18–22.

Sternberg, R. J. 1984. How can we teach intelligence? *Educational Leadership* 42 (Sept.): 38–50.

Vygotsky, L. S. 1962. *Thought and language.* Cambridge, Mass.: MIT Press.

Wiggins, G. 1987. Creating a thought-provoking curriculum. *American Educator* 11 (winter): 12–13.

The Intelligence-Friendly Classroom

It Just Makes Sense

By Robin Fogarty

Ms. Fogarty provides guidelines that serve as a bridge between theory and practice in the intelligence-friendly classroom.

Illustration by Mario Noche

IF WE KNOW that intelligence is emotional, then it just makes sense to use visceral hooks. If we know that intelligence is nurturable, then it just makes sense to create rich environments. If we know that intelligence is constructed, then it just makes sense to provide tools for the mind. If we know that intelligence is experiential, then it just makes sense to challenge through doing. If we know that intelligence is multiple, then it just makes sense to target many dimensions. If we know that intelligence is modifiable, then it just makes sense to mediate learning. If we know that intelligence is elusive, then it just makes sense to vary the ways we measure it.

If we know all these things and believe what we know to be true, then the "intelligence-friendly classroom" should be a given. It is as simple and logical as an "if . . . then" syllogism.

Defining Intelligence-Friendly Classrooms

Let's look more closely at the term "intelligence-friendly classroom" and see just what it means. An intelligence-friendly classroom is a classroom in which the teaching/learning process is governed by what is known about developing the intellectual potential of human beings. Literally, intelligence-friendly means "friendly to intelligence," which can be translated into friendly to the growth patterns of human intellect and friendly to the learner in foster-

ROBIN FOGARTY has taught at all levels, from kindergarten through college. She lives in Chicago and trains teachers around the world in cognitive strategies and cooperative interaction. Her most recent book is Brain-Compatible Classrooms *(SkyLight Training and Publishing, Inc., 1998).*

ing intelligent behavior for problem solving, decision making, and creative thinking. Figuratively, the intelligence-friendly classroom serves as a caring companion and mindful guide to the intellect of each and every child in it. Just as a friend in the real world furnishes certain kinds of support that are reliable, time-tested, and tried and true, so intelligence-friendly classrooms provide similar systems of support that foster the ongoing development of human intelligence potential.

In brief, intelligence-friendly classrooms are classrooms that celebrate the joy of the learner's emotional and intellectual world, not through rhetoric and repetition, but through richness and relationships. In this article, I'll take a closer look at these intelligence-friendly classrooms and investigate their theoretical underpinnings briefly and their practical implications in more depth.

Theoretical Underpinnings

Guidelines for the intelligence-friendly classroom are grounded in the works of the leading voices in the field. First, I offer a cursory examination of the various theories of intelligence and then suggest what each of them implies for the intelligence-friendly classroom.

• *Traditional theory of general intelligence.* Intelligence is inherited and unchanging.

• *Piaget's theory of developmental psychology.* Intelligence is developmentally constructed in the mind by the learner and moves from concrete to abstract stages of understanding.

• *Vygotsky's theory of social mediation.* Intelligence is a function of activity mediated through material tools, psychological tools, and other human beings.

• *Feuerstein's theory of structural cognitive modifiability.* Intelligence is a function of experience and can be changed through guided mediation.

• *Gardner's theory of multiple intelligences.* Intelligence is made up of eight realms of knowing (verbal, visual, mathematical, musical, bodily, interpersonal, intrapersonal, naturalistic) for solving problems and creating products valued in a culture.

• *Sternberg's successful intelligence.* Intelligence is triarchic, with analytic, creative, and practical components that need to be balanced.

• *Perkins' theory of learnable intelli-*

gence. Intelligence is made up of neural, experiential, and reflective components that help us know our way around the good use of our minds.

• *Costa's theory of intelligence behaviors.* Intelligence is composed of acquired habits or states of mind that are evident in such behaviors as persistence, flexibility, decreased impulsiveness, enjoyment of thinking, and reflectiveness.

• *Goleman's theory of emotional intelligence.* Intelligence is both cognitive and emotional, with the emotional (self-awareness, self-regulation, motivation, empathy, and social skill) ruling over the cognitive.

• *Coles' theory of moral intelligence.* Intelligence is composed of cognitive, psychological or emotional, and moral realms.

Implications for Application

The intelligence-friendly classroom is an intricate and complex microcosm of nuance and activity that propels the teaching/learning process. The following eight guidelines, derived from the various theories of intelligence, have compelling implications for today's classroom. I explain each guideline briefly and offer a sampling of useful strategies. While some readers may find the suggestions familiar and already part of their current teaching repertoire, others may discover new ideas or, perhaps, novel ways to revisit an old idea with a fresh approach. Whatever the case, the guidelines serve as a bridge between theory and practice in the intelligence-friendly classroom.

1. *Set a safe emotional climate.* The intelligence-friendly classroom is a safe and caring place for all learners, regardless of race, color, creed, age, aptitude, or ability to go about the business of learning. In setting a climate for thinking, risk-taking becomes the norm, and learners understand that to learn is to make mistakes as well as to experience successes.

Specific strategies to use include the following: establishing classroom rules, being aware of verbal and nonverbal teaching behaviors (e.g., wait time), organizing diverse small-group work that feels "safe," tapping into the emotional and moral intelligences, setting up the room to facilitate student-to-student interactions as well as student-to-teacher interactions, and incorporating learner-centered structures (e.g., multi-age groupings) that foster the creation of intelligence-friendly learning communities.

2. *Create a rich learning environment.* An enriched environment requires attention to the physical aspects of the intelligence-friendly classroom. The ideal classroom resembles a children's museum, in which students are repeatedly and implicitly invited to interact with the learning environment. In such a stimulus-rich setting, explorations, investigations, and inquiries are irresistible.

This enriched environment presents science equipment, art supplies, tools and workbenches, toys and building blocks, optical illusion posters, and an electronic circus of computers, telephones, and fax machines. The intelligence-friendly classroom has different mini-environments for quiet reflection, noisy projects, learning centers, and one-on-one tutorials. The sensory input — ranging from print-rich materials, music, and recordings to visually appealing bulletin boards and to signs, games, puzzles, and lab setups — provides an intriguing and engaging place for teaching for intelligence.

3. *Teach the mind-tools and skills of life.* Teaching the skills of life involves both mind and body "tools" that range from communication and social skills to the microskills of thinking and reflecting, to the technological skills needed for the Information Age, to the skills needed for solving algebraic equations or programming computers, and even to the skills needed to learn a craft or participate in athletics.

More specifically, these skills might include critical thinking skills (e.g., prioritizing, comparing, and judging), creative thinking skills (e.g., inferring, predicting, and generalizing), social skills (e.g., communicating, team building, leading, and resolving conflicts), technological skills (e.g., keyboarding, surfing the Net, and taking virtual field trips), visual skills (e.g., painting, sculpting, and drawing), skills in the performing arts (e.g., dancing, acting, and playing a musical instrument), and skills of the elite athlete (e.g., diving, skiing, and swimming).

4. *Develop the skillfulness of the learner.* The developmental path of skill training moves through fairly predictable stages: novice, advanced beginner, competent user, proficient user, expert. Inherent in this developmental arc is the understanding that skillfulness is achieved through mediation, practice, coaching, and rehearsal.

Skill development often occurs through formal teaching/learning structures, such as direct instruction models, that demonstrate the skill for students. Skills are also developed through independent readings and research and through the dialogue, discussion, and articulation of peer coaching, mentoring, or internships. Skill development can even happen with experiences in which the skill is embedded in application and in poised moments for achieving peak performances.

5. *Challenge through the experience of doing.* Learning is a function of experience and is shaped by internal processes that actually construct ideas in the mind, as well as by the external processes of social interaction. In the intelligence-friendly classroom, a constructivist philosophy of education reigns. Active, experiential learning is the norm, as the learner is invited to become an integral part of the teaching/learning process.

Specific strategies that abound in the constructivist classroom include hands-on learning with lots of manipulatives and lab-like situations; small-group, cooperative tasks; the frequent use and unique application of graphic organizers (e.g., concept maps, attribute webs, flow charts, and Venn diagrams); and authentic experiential curriculum models (e.g., problem-based learning, case studies, project and service learning, performance tasks, and the use of relevant overarching themes).

6. *Target multiple dimensions of intelligence.* The multiple intelligences (MI) approach taps into the unique profile of intelligences of each learner. The education community embraces MI theory because it provides a natural framework for inspired practice. MI approaches to curriculum, instruction, and assessment target a full spectrum of teaching/learning strategies that encompass the many ways of knowing and of expressing what we know. The MI classroom is abuzz with activity as all eight of the intelligences are given fair time in the curriculum for authentic, relevant opportunities for development.

This does not mean that every lesson shows evidence of all eight intelligences, but rather that the learning is structured in naturally integrated ways that call upon various intelligences. For example, while creating a school newspaper, students interview (interpersonal), write (verbal), design and lay out (visual), and critique (logical) as natural parts of the process.

7. *Transfer learning through reflection.* The reflective use of learning is the cornerstone of the intelligence-friendly classroom. It drives personal application and transfer of learning. It makes learning personal, purposeful, meaningful, and relevant and gives the brain reason to pay attention, understand, and remember. Reflection is sometimes the missing piece in today's classroom puzzle, as the pacing of the school day often precludes time for reflection. Yet reflection, introspection, and mindfulness must accompany collaborations and discussions because the time for reflection is the time for internalizing the learning.

Specific strategies that enhance reflection include the use of reading-response journals in which the reader writes a personal, immediate response to what has been read; learning logs that record the learner's thoughts, comments, and questions prior to or following a learning experience; lab reports; personal diaries; sketch books; writer's notebooks; portfolios; partner dialogues and conversations with a mentor; mediation interventions; and metacognitive strategies of planning, monitoring, and evaluating through self-regulation.

8. *Balance assessment measures.* Human nature demands feedback. Whether that feedback is internally motivated or externally given, all of us who are intent on learning anxiously await the critique, the judgment. In the intelligence-friendly classroom, this critical phase of the learning process is integral to all other interactions. The feedback, analysis, and evaluation are ongoing as well as summative.

Assessment occurs by the traditional means of grades and rankings for required classwork, homework assignments, quizzes, criterion-referenced tests, and standardized tests. In addition, to provide the proper balance to the assessment process, both portfolio assessments (e.g., project portfolios, best-work portfolios, electronic portfolios, and videotape analysis) and performance assessments (speeches, presentations, plays, concerts, athletic performances, and lab experiments) occur.

A Final Note

In closing, let's circle back for a moment and revisit the title of this article: "The Intelligence-Friendly Classroom: It Just Makes Sense." Think about how I've described the intelligence-friendly classroom and about how it matches or fails to match any preconceived notions you might have had as you began to read. Intelligence-friendly? What does that mean? What does that look like? Sound like? Did you learn in an intelligence-friendly classroom? Do you teach in one? Would you know one if you saw one?

Of course you would. The intelligence-friendly classroom is no enigma. It makes perfect sense. It draws on the many powers of intelligence of both the teacher and the learner. It is the teaching/learning process in all its glorious colors. It is the science of good, sound pedagogy coupled with the art of uniquely creative minds.

The intelligence-friendly classroom is part of the noble vision of schooling that led many of us into the field. It is the reason that we do what we do. It's about children, and it's about helping those children be as smart as they can be in every way they can be. The intelligence-friendly classroom just makes sense.

Unit 5

Unit Selections

Motivation 27. **A New Look at School Failure and School Success,** William Glasser
28. **I Think I Can, I Think I Can: Understanding and Encouraging Mastery Motivation in Young Children,** Penny Hauser-Cram
29. **Using Motivational Theory with At-Risk Children,** Rachel Buck Collopy and Theresa Green

Classroom Management and Discipline 30. **Moving beyond Management as Sheer Compliance: Helping Students to Develop Goal Coordination Strategies,** Mary McCaslin and Thomas L. Good
31. **Connecting Instruction and Management in a Student-Centered Classroom,** Nancy K. Martin
32. **How to Manage Disruptive Behavior in Inclusive Classrooms,** Vera I. Daniels
33. **How to Defuse Defiance, Threats, Challenges, Confrontations . . . ,** Geoff Colvin, David Ainge, and Ron Nelson
34. **Why Violence Prevention Programs Don't Work— and What Does,** David W. Johnson and Roger T. Johnson

Key Points to Consider

❖ Discuss several ways to motivate both at-risk and typical students. What difference is there?

❖ Why should motivational style be consistent with instructional techniques?

❖ How are motivation and classroom management related?

❖ Discuss several ways to discipline both typical students and those with exceptionalities.

❖ How are classroom management and discipline different? Discuss whether discipline can be developed within students or whether it must be imposed by teachers, supporting your argument with data derived from your reading.

 **Links**   **www.dushkin.com/online/**

29. **Canada's Schoolnet Staff Room**
   http://www.schoolnet.ca/home/e/

30. **Early Intervention Solutions**
   http://www.earlyintervention.com

31. **National Institute on the Education of At-Risk Students**
   http://www.ed.gov/offices/OERI/At-Risk/

These sites are annotated on pages 4 and 5.

The term *motivation* is used by educators to describe the processes of initiating, directing, and sustaining goal-oriented behavior. Motivation is a complex phenomenon, involving many factors that affect an individual's choice of action and perseverance in completing tasks. Furthermore, the reasons why people engage in particular behaviors can only be inferred; motivation cannot be directly measured.

Several theories of motivation, each highlighting different reasons for sustained goal-oriented behavior, have been proposed. We will discuss three of them: behavioral, humanistic, and cognitive. The behavioral theory of motivation suggests that an important reason for engaging in behavior is that reinforcement follows the action. If the reinforcement is controlled by someone else and is arbitrarily related to the behavior (such as money, a token, or a smile), then the motivation is extrinsic. In contrast, behavior may also be initiated and sustained for intrinsic reasons such as curiosity or mastery.

Humanistic approaches to motivation are concerned with the social and psychological needs of individuals. Humans are motivated to engage in behavior to meet these needs. Abraham Maslow, a founder of humanistic psychology, proposes that there is a hierarchy of needs that directs behavior, beginning with physiological and safety needs and progressing to self-actualization. Some other important needs that influence motivation are affiliation and belonging with others, love, self-esteem, influence with others, recognition, status, competence, achievement, and autonomy.

The dominant view of motivation in the educational psychology literature is the cognitive approach. This set of theories proposes that our beliefs about our successes and failures affect our expectations and goals concerning future performance. Students who believe that their success is due to their abilities and efforts are motivated toward mastery of skills. Students who blame their failures on inadequate abilities have low self-efficacy and tend to set ability and performance goals that protect their self-image.

William Glasser, in the unit's first selection, contends that when teachers use coercive management techniques, students feel that teachers do not care about them and they become unmotivated. When choice theory is implemented, however, the student-teacher relationship is nurtured, and students want to learn. The next two selections address achievement motivation. Penny Hauser-Cram introduces the concept of mastery motivation. She describes how parents and caregivers can negatively affect mastery motivation by being too directive, and she offers suggestions for encouraging mastery

motivation. The goal is for all children to learn to persist in the face of difficulty and to seek challenges. Then, Rachel Collopy and Theresa Green describe how one elementary school has adopted achievement goal theory and its emphasis on mastery motivation. The article describes many of the changes made at the school to create an emphasis on learning rather than the relative ability of students.

No matter how effectively students are motivated, teachers always need to exercise management of behavior in the classroom. Classroom management is more than controlling the behavior of students or disciplining them following misbehavior. Instead, teachers need to initiate and maintain a classroom environment that supports successful teaching and learning. The skills that effective teachers use include preplanning, deliberate introduction of rules and procedures, immediate assertiveness, continual monitoring, consistent feedback to students, and specific consequences.

The first two articles in this subsection describe the most current thinking about classroom management techniques that best meet the needs of learner-centered classrooms. Mary McCaslin and Thomas Good believe that teachers who value teaching for understanding need to help students internalize a commitment to certain standards of behavior, rather than settle for compliance. They suggest that this can be accomplished by teaching students to coordinate their multiple academic and social goals. Next Nancy Martin argues that student-teacher relationships need to be nurtured in student-centered classrooms. Teacher-centered classroom management techniques conflict with the philosophy of student-centered instruction and can undermine its effectiveness.

The next three articles address specific disciplinary issues facing teachers today: disciplining students in inclusive classrooms, confrontational students, and violence in the schools. Vera Daniels addresses a concern of many teachers: how to discipline students with disabilities and still preserve their rights. Colvin, Ainge, and Nelson observe that even effective classroom managers are sometimes faced with confrontational students. The authors discuss diffusing tactics that can minimize the likelihood of escalating conflict. Finally, Johnson and Johnson argue that violence prevention needs to focus on helping students resolve conflicts in appropriate ways, such as using peer mediation. The adults in schools, too, need to model constructive ways to resolve conflicts by eliminating corporal punishment.

Motivation and Classroom Management

A New Look at School Failure and School Success

BY WILLIAM GLASSER, M.D.

The cause of both school failure and marriage failure is that almost all people believe in and practice stimulus/response psychology, Dr. Glasser contends. He suggests a better alternative—CHOICE THEORY^SM—to nurture the warm, supportive human relationships that students need to succeed in school and that couples need to succeed in marriage.

JOHN IS 14 years old. He is capable of doing good work in school. Yet he reads and writes poorly, has not learned to do more than simple calculations, hates any work having to do with school, and shows up more to be with his friends than anything else. He failed the seventh grade last year and is well on his way to failing it again. Essentially, John chooses to do nothing in school that anyone would call educational. If any standards must be met, his chances of graduation are nonexistent.

We know from our experience at the Schwab Middle School, which I will describe shortly, that John also knows that giving up on school is a serious mistake. The problem is he doesn't believe that the school he attends will give him a chance to correct this mistake. And he is far from alone. There may be five million students between the ages of 6 and 16 who come regularly to school but are much the same as John. If they won't make the effort to become competent readers, writers, and problem solvers, their chances of leading even

minimally satisfying lives are over before they reach age 17.

Janet is 43 years old. She has been teaching math for 20 years and is one of the teachers who is struggling unsuccessfully with John. She considers herself a good teacher but admits that she does not know how to reach John. She blames him, his home, his past teachers, and herself for this failure. All who know her consider her a warm, competent person. But for all her warmth, five years ago, after 15 years of marriage, Janet divorced. She is doing an excellent job of caring for her three children, but, with only sporadic help from their father, her life is no picnic. If she and her husband had been able to stay together happily, it is almost certain that they and their children would be much better off than they are now.

Like many who divorce, Janet was aware that the marriage was in trouble long before the separation. But in the context of marriage as she knew it, she didn't know what to do. "I tried, but nothing I did seemed to help," she says. She is lonely and would like another marriage but, so far, hasn't been able to find anyone she would consider marrying. There may be more than a million men and women teaching school who, like Janet, seem capable of relationships but are either divorced or unhappily married. No one doubts that marriage failure is a huge problem. It leads to even more human misery than school failure.

William Glasser, M.D., is the founder and president of the William Glasser Institute in Chatsworth, Calif. In 1996 he changed the name of the theory he has been teaching since 1979 from "control theory" to CHOICE THEORY^SM. He is currently writing a new book on the subject. All his books are published by HarperCollins.

From *Phi Delta Kappan*, April 1997, pp. 596-602. © 1997 by Phi Delta Kappa, Inc. Reprinted by permission.

I bring up divorce in an article on reducing school failure because there is a much closer connection between these two problems than almost anyone realizes. So close, in fact, that I believe the cause of both these problems may be the same. As soon as I wrote those words, I began to fear that my readers would jump to the conclusion that I am blaming Janet for the failure of her marriage or for her inability to reach John. Nothing could be further from the truth. The fact that she doesn't know something that is almost universally unknown cannot be her fault.

If you doubt that the problems of John and Janet are similar, listen to what each of them has to say. John says, "I do so little in school because no one cares for me, no one listens to me, it's no fun, they try to make me do things I don't want to do, and they never try to find out what I want to do." Janet says, "My marriage failed because he didn't care enough for me, he never listened to me, each year it was less fun, he never wanted to do what I wanted, and he was always trying to make me do what he wanted." These almost identical complaints have led John to "divorce" school, and Janet, her husband.

Are these Greek tragedies? Are all these students and all these marriages doomed to failure no matter what we do? I contend they are not. *The cause of both school failure and marriage failure is that almost no one, including Janet, knows how he or she functions psychologically.* Almost all people believe in and practice an ancient, commonsense psychology called stimulus/response (SR) psychology. I am one of the leaders of a small group of people who believe that SR is completely wrongheaded and, when put into practice, is totally destructive to the warm, supportive human relationships that students need to succeed in school and that couples need to succeed in marriage. The solution is to give up SR theory and replace it with a new psychology: *choice theory.*

To persuade a teacher like Janet to give up what she implicitly believes to be correct is a monumental task. For this reason I have hit upon the idea of approaching her through her marriage failure as much as through her failure to reach students like John. I think she will be more open to learning something that is so difficult to learn if she can use it in both her personal and her professional lives. From 20 years of experience teaching choice theory, I can also assure her that learning this theory can do absolutely no harm.

If John could go to a school where choice theory was practiced, he would start to work. That was conclusively proved at the Schwab Middle School. To explain such a change in behavior, John would say, "The teachers care about me, listen to what I have to say, don't try to make me do things I don't want to do, and ask me what I'd like to do once in a while. Besides, they make learning fun." If Janet and her husband had practiced choice theory while they still cared for each other, it is likely that they would still be married. They would have said, "We get along well because every day we make it a point to show each other we care. We listen to each other, and when we have differences we talk them out without blaming the other. We never let a week go by without having fun together, and we never try to make the other do what he or she doesn't want to do."

Where school improvement is concerned, I can cite hard data to back up this contention. I also have written two books that explain in detail all that my staff and I try to do to implement choice theory in schools. The books are *The Quality School* and *The Quality School Teacher.*[1] Where marriage failure is concerned, I have no hard data yet. But I have many positive responses from readers of my most recent book, *Staying Together,*[2] in which I apply choice theory to marriage.

The most difficult problems are human relationship problems. Technical problems, such as landing a man on the moon, are child's play compared to persuading all students like John to start working hard in school or helping all unhappily married couples to improve their marriages. Difficult as they may be to solve, however, relationship problems are surprisingly easy to understand. They are all some variation of "I don't like the way you treat me, and even though it may destroy my life, your life, or both our lives, this is what I am going to do about it."

> To persuade a teacher like Janet to give up what she implicitly believes to be correct is a monumental task.

READERS familiar with my work will have figured out by now that choice theory used to be called control theory because it teaches that the only person whose behavior we can control is our own. I find choice theory to be a better and more positive-sounding name. Accepting that you can control only your own behavior is the most difficult lesson that choice theory has to teach. It is so difficult that almost all people, even when they are given the opportunity, refuse to learn it. This is because the whole thrust of SR theory is that we do not control our own behavior, rather, our behavior is a response to a stimulus from outside ourselves. Thus we answer a phone in response to a ring.

Choice theory states that we never answer a phone because it rings, and we never will. We answer a phone—and do anything else—because it is the most satisfying choice for us at the time. If we have something better to do, we let it ring. Choice theory states that the ring of the phone is not a stimulus to do anything; it is merely *information*. In fact, all we can ever get from the outside world, which means all we can give one another, is information. But information, by itself, does not make us do anything. Janet can't make her husband do anything. Nor can she make John do anything. All she can give them is information, but she, like all SR believers, doesn't know this.

What she "knows" is that, if she is dissatisfied with someone, she should try to "stimulate" that person to change. And she wastes a great deal of time and energy trying to do this. When she discovers, as she almost always does, how hard it is to change another person, she begins to blame the person, herself, or someone else for the failure. And from blaming, it is a very short step to punishing. No one takes this short step more frequently and more thoroughly than husbands, wives, and teachers. As they attempt to change their mates, couples develop a whole repertoire of coercive behaviors aimed at punishing the other for being so obstinate. When teachers attempt to deal with students such as John, punishment—masquerading as "logical consequences"—rules the day in school.

Coercion in either of its two forms, reward or punishment, is the core of SR theory. Punishments are by far the more common, but both are destructive to relationships. The difference is that rewards are more subtly destructive and generally less offensive. Coercion ranges from the passive behaviors of sulking and withdrawing to the active behaviors of abuse and violence. The most common and, because it is so common, the most destructive of coercive behaviors is criticizing—and nagging and complaining are not far behind.

Choice theory teaches that we are all driven by four psychological needs that are embedded in our genes: the need to belong, the need for power, the need for freedom, and the need for fun. We can no more ignore these psychological needs than we can ignore the food and shelter we must have if we are to satisfy the most obvious genetic need, the need for survival.

Whenever we are able to satisfy one or more of these needs, it feels very good. In fact, the biological purpose of pleasure is to tell us that a need is being satisfied. Pain, on the other hand, tells us that what we are doing is not satisfying a need that we very much want to satisfy. John suffers in school, and Janet suffers in marriage because neither is able to figure out how to satisfy these needs. If the pain of this failure continues, it is almost certain that in two years John will leave school, and of course Janet has already left her marriage.

If we are to help Janet help John, she needs to learn and to use the most important of all the concepts from choice theory, the idea of the *quality world*. This small, very specific, personal world is the core of our lives because in it are the people, things, and beliefs that we have discovered are most satisfying to our needs. Beginning at birth, as we find out what best satisfies our needs, we build this knowledge into the part of our memory that is our quality world and continue to build and adjust it throughout our lives. This world is best thought of as a group of pictures, stored in our brain, depicting with extreme precision the way we would like things to be—especially the way we want to be treated. The most important pictures are of people, including ourselves, because it is almost impossible to satisfy our needs without getting involved with other people.

Good examples of people who are almost always in our quality worlds are our parents and our children—and, if our marriages are happy, our husbands or wives. These pictures are very specific. Wives and husbands want to hear certain words, to be touched in certain ways, to go to certain places, and to do specific activities together. We also have special things in our quality world. For example, the new computer I am typing this article on is very much the computer I wanted. I also have a strong picture of myself teaching choice theory, something I believe in so strongly that I spend most of my life doing it.

When we put people into our quality worlds, it is because we care for them, and they care for us. We see them as people with whom we can satisfy our needs. John has long since taken pictures of Janet and of most other teachers—as well as a picture of himself doing competent schoolwork—out of his quality world. As soon as he did this, neither Janet nor any other SR teacher could reach him. As much as they coerce, they cannot make him learn. This way of teaching is called "bossing." Bosses use coercion freely to try to make the people they boss do what they want.

To be effective with John, Janet must give up bossing and turn to "leading." Leaders never coerce. We follow them because we believe that they have our best interests at heart. In school, if he senses that Janet is now caring, listening, encouraging, and laughing, John will begin to consider putting her into his quality world. Of course, John knows nothing about choice theory or about the notion of a quality world. But he can be taught and, in a Quality School, this is what we do. We have evidence to show that the more students know about why they are behaving as they do, the more effectively they will behave.

Sometime before her divorce, Janet, her ex, or both of them took the other out of their quality worlds. When this happened, the marriage was over. If they had known choice theory and known how important it is to try to preserve the picture of a spouse in one's quality world, they could have made a greater effort than they did to care, listen, encourage, and laugh with each other. They certainly would have been aware of how destructive bossing is and would have tried their best to avoid this destructive behavior.

As I stated at the outset, I am not assigning blame for the failure of Janet's marriage. I am saying that, as soon as one or the other or both partners became dissatisfied, the only hope was to care, listen, encourage, and laugh and to completely stop criticizing, nagging, and complaining. Obviously, Janet and her ex-

husband would have been much more likely to have done this if they had known that the only behavior you can control is your own.

When Janet, as an SR teacher, teaches successfully, she succeeds with students because her students have put her or the math she teaches (or both) into their quality worlds. If both she and the math are in their quality worlds, the students will be a joy to teach. She may also succeed with a student who does not particularly want to learn math, but who, like many students, is open to learning math if she gives him a little attention.

John, however, is hard core. He is more than uninterested; he is disdainful, even disruptive at times. To get him interested will require a real show of interest on her part. But Janet resents any suggestion that she should give John what he needs. Why should she? He's 14 years old. It's his job to show interest. She has a whole classroom full of students, and she hasn't got the time to give him special attention. Because of this resentment, all she can think of is punishment.

> **When Janet punishes John, she gives him more reasons to keep her and math out of his quality world.**

When Janet punishes John, she gives him more reasons to keep her and math out of his quality world. Now he can blame her; from his standpoint, his failure is no longer his fault. Thus the low grades and threats of failure have exactly the opposite effect from the one she intends. That is why she has been so puzzled by students like John for so many years. She did the "right thing," and, even though she can see John getting more and more turned off, she doesn't know what else to do. She no more knows why she can't reach John than she knows why she and her husband found it harder and harder to reach each other when their marriage started to fail.

FROM THE beginning to the end of the 1994–95 school year, my wife Carleen and I worked to introduce Quality School concepts into the Schwab Middle School, a seventh- and eighth-grade school that is part of the Cincinnati Public School System. (Carleen actually began training many staff members in choice theory during the second semester of the 1993–94 school year.) This school of 600 regularly attending students (750 enrolled) has at least 300 students like John, who come to school almost every day. With the help of the principal, who was named best principal in Ohio in 1996, and a very good staff, we turned this school around.

By the end of the year, most of the regularly attending students who were capable of doing passable schoolwork were doing it.[3] Indeed, some of the work was much better than passable. None of the students like John were doing it when we arrived. Discipline problems that had led to 1,500 suspensions in the previous year slowly came under control and ceased to be a significant concern by the end of the school year.

By mid-February, after four months of preparation, we were able to start a special program in which we enrolled all the students (170) who had failed at least one grade and who also regularly attended school. Most had failed more than one grade, and some, now close to 17 years of age, had failed four times. Teachers from the regular school staff volunteered for this program. Our special program continued through summer school, by the end of which 147 of these 170 students were promoted to high school. The predicted number of students who would go to high school from this group had been near zero. Getting these students out of the "on-age" classes where they had been disruptive freed the regular teachers to teach more effectively, and almost all the "on-age" students began to learn. The "on-age" seventh-graders at Schwab had a 20% increase in their math test scores, another positive outcome of the program.

We were able to achieve these results because we taught almost all the teachers in the school enough choice theory to understand how students need to be treated if they are to put us into their quality worlds. Using these concepts, the teachers stopped almost all coercion—an approach that was radically different from the way most of these students had been treated since kindergarten. When we asked the students why they were no longer disruptive and why they were beginning to work in school, over and over they said, "You care about us." And sometimes they added, "And now you give us choices and work that we like to do."

What did we do that they liked so much? With the district's permission, we threw out the regular curriculum and allowed the students to work at their own pace. We assigned lessons that, when successfully completed, proved that the students were ready for high school. The seven teachers in the special program (called the Cambridge Program)—spurred on by the challenge that this was their school and that they could do anything they believed necessary—worked day and night for almost two months to devise these lessons, in which the students had to demonstrate that they could read, write, solve problems, and learn the basics of social studies and science.

We told the students that they could not fail but that it was up to them to do the work. We said that we would help them learn as much as we could, and teachers from the "on-age" classes volunteered their free periods to help. Some of the students began to help one another. The fear began to dissipate as the staff saw the students begin to work. What we did was not so difficult that any school staff, with the leadership of its principal, could not do it as well. Because we had so little time, Carleen and I were co-leaders with the principal. A little extra money (about $20,000) from a state grant was also spent to equip the room for the Cambridge Program with furniture, carpeting, and computers, but it was not more than any school could raise if it could promise the results we achieved.

THESE Quality School ideas have also been put to work for several years in Huntington Woods Elementary School in Wyoming, Michigan. This nearly 300-student K–5 school is located in a small middle-class town and is the first school to be designated a Quality School. There were very few Johns in this school to begin with, so the task was much easier than at Schwab. Nonetheless, the outcomes at Huntington Woods have been impressive.

- All students are doing competent schoolwork, as measured by the Michigan Education Assessment Program (MEAP). The percentages of Huntington Woods students who score satisfactorily as measured against a state standard are 88% in reading and 85% in math (compared to state averages of 49% in reading and 60% in math).
- As measured by both themselves and their teachers, all students are doing some quality work, and many are doing a great deal of quality work.

- While there are occasional discipline incidents, there are no longer any discipline problems.
- The regular staff works very successfully with all students without labeling them learning disabled or emotionally impaired.
- Even more important than these measurable outcomes, the school is a source of joy for students, teachers, and parents.

I emphasize that no extra money was spent by the district to achieve these results. The school, however, did some fund raising to pay for staff training.

I CITE Schwab and Huntington Woods because I have worked in one of these schools myself and have had a great deal of contact with the other. They are both using the ideas in my books. Huntington Woods has changed from an SR-driven system, and Schwab has made a strong start toward doing so. Moreover, Schwab's start has produced the results described above. And more than 200 other schools are now working with me in an effort to become Quality Schools.

So far only Huntington Woods has evaluated itself and declared itself a Quality School. Even Schwab, as improved as it is, is far from being a Quality School. But, in terms of actual progress made from where we found it, what Schwab has achieved is proportionally greater than what Huntington Woods has achieved.

While many schools have shown interest in what has been achieved at Huntington Woods and at Schwab, very few of them have accepted the core idea: change the system from SR theory to choice theory. Indeed, there are many successful SR schools around the country that are not trying to change the fundamental system in which they operate, and I believe their success is based on two things.

First, for a school to be successful, the principal is the key. When an SR school succeeds, as many do, it is led by a principal whose charisma has inspired the staff and students to work harder than they would ordinarily work. This kind of success will last only as long as the principal remains. I am not saying that some charismatic principals do not embrace many of the ideas of the Quality School, or that the principal doesn't have to lead the systemic change that choice theory makes possible. However, once the system has been changed, it can sustain itself (with the principal's support, of course, but without a charismatic leader).

Second, the SR schools that are working well have strong parental support for good education and few Johns among their students. Where such support is already present or can be created by hard-working teachers and principals, schools have a very good chance of being successful without changing their core system. After all, it is these schools that have traditionally made the SR system seem to work. In such schools, Janet would be a very successful teacher.

While Huntington Woods had the kind of support that would have made it a good school without changing the system, the staff wanted it to become a Quality School and set about changing the system from the outset. With the backing of the superintendent, the staff members were given an empty building and the opportunity to recruit new staff members, all of whom were anxious to learn the choice theory needed to change the system. The fact that Huntington Woods has a charismatic leader is certainly a plus, but it is her dedication to the ideas of choice theory that has led to the school's great success. With very high test scores, no discipline problems, and no need for special programs, Huntington Woods has gone far beyond what I believe the typical SR school could achieve. Many educators who have visited the school have said that it is "a very different kind of school."[4]

Schwab today is also very different from the school it was. And what has been accomplished at Schwab has been done with almost no active parental support. The largest number of parents we could get to attend any meeting—even when we served food and told them to bring the whole family—was 20, and some of them were parents of the few students who live in the middle-class neighborhood where the school is located. Almost all the Schwab students who are like John are bused in from low-income communities far from the school, a fact that makes parents' participation more difficult.

At Schwab an effort was made to teach all the teachers choice theory. Then Carleen and I reminded them continually to use the theory as they worked to improve the school. At Huntington Woods, not only were the teachers and principal taught choice theory in much more depth than at Schwab and over much more time than we had at Schwab, but all the students and many parents were also involved in learning this theory and beginning to use it in their lives.

Unfortunately, Janet has never taught in a school that uses choice theory. When she brings up her problems with John in the teachers' lounge, she is the beneficiary of a lot of SR advice: "Get tough!" "Show him right away who's boss." "Don't let him get away with anything." "Call his mother, and demand she do something about his behavior." "Send him to the principal." Similarly, like almost everyone whose marriage is in trouble, Janet has been the beneficiary of a lot of well-intended SR advice from family and friends—some of which, unfortunately, she took.

Her other serious problem is that she works in an SR system that is perfectly willing to settle for educating only those students who want to learn. The system's credo says, "It's a tough world out there. If they don't make an effort, they have to suffer the consequences." Since Janet is herself a successful product of such a system, she supports it. In doing so, she believes it is right to give students low grades for failing to do what she asks them to do. She further believes it is right to refuse to let them make up a low grade if they don't have a very good attitude—and sometimes even if they do.

In her personal life, she and her husband had seen so much marriage failure that, when they started to have trouble, it was easy for them to think of divorce as almost inevitable. This is bad information. It discourages both partners from doing the hard work necessary to learn what is needed to put their marriage back together. Life is hard enough without the continuing harangues of the doomsayers. In a world that uses choice theory, people would be more optimistic.

There has been no punishment in the Huntington Woods School for years. There is no such thing as a low grade that cannot be improved. Every student has access to a teacher or another student if he or she needs personal attention. Some students will always do better than others, but, as the MEAP scores show, all can do well. This is a Quality system, with an emphasis on continual improvement, and there is no settling for good enough.

Unfortunately for them, many Schwab students who experience success in school for the first time will fail in high school. The SR system in use there will kill them off educationally, just as certainly as if we shot them with a gun. They didn't have enough time with us and were too fragile when we sent them on. However, if by some miracle the high school pays attention to what we did at Schwab, many will succeed. There was some central office support for our efforts, and there is some indication that this support will continue.

The Huntington Woods students are less fragile. They will have had a good enough start with choice theory so that, given the much stronger psychological and financial support of their parents, they will probably do well in middle school. Indeed, data from the first semester of 1995–96 confirm that they are doing very well.

It is my hope that educators, none of whom are immune to marriage failure, will see the value of choice theory in their personal lives. If this happens, there is no doubt in my mind that they will begin to use it with their students.

1. William Glasser, *The Quality School* (New York: HarperCollins, 1990); and idem, *The Quality School Teacher* (New York: HarperCollins, 1994).
2. William Glasser, *Staying Together* (New York: HarperCollins, 1995).
3. The school also had about four classes of special education students who were in a special program led by capable teachers and were learning as much as they were capable of learning.
4. See Dave Winans, "This School Has Everything," *NEA Today*, December 1995, pp. 4–5.

Research in Review

I Think I Can, I Think I Can: Understanding and Encouraging Mastery Motivation in Young Children

Penny Hauser-Cram

"**S**he works very hard when she's trying to build a block construction." "He is so curious about how gadgets work." These are comments often made by parents and teachers in their conversations about young children. Children's motivation to solve problems, figure out how objects work, and complete tasks they set out to do is a central part of the way teachers and parents view children. Is such motivation intrinsic? Are children with developmental disabilities as motivated as other children? How is motivation influenced by caregivers? Does motivation vary in different contexts, such as the classroom and the home? What do we know about motivation, and how can preschool teachers encourage it?

Perspectives on motivation

Based largely on Piaget's (1952) writings, developmental theorists (White 1959; Hunt 1965) have proposed that children's motivation to explore the world around them is the foundation upon which learning occurs. Such motivation is considered to be intrinsic, universal, and an integral part of de-

© BmPorter/Don Franklin

Based largely on Piaget's writings, developmental theorists have proposed that children's motivation to explore the world around them is the foundation upon which learning occurs. Such motivation is considered to be intrinsic, universal, and an integral part of development. All children are born with curiosity and a desire to learn about the world.

© BmPorter/Don Franklin

Penny Hauser-Cram, Ed.D., is an associate professor of developmental and educational psychology at the School of Education at Boston College. Penny's research focuses on the development of children with disabilities.

*This is one of a regular series of Research in Review columns. The column in this issue was invited by Research in Review Editor **Martha B. Bronson**, Ph.D., professor at Boston College, Chestnut Hill, Massachusetts.*

velopment. All children are born with curiosity and a desire to learn about the world.

White (1959) contended that children have a need to produce an effect on their environment and that they achieve this through exploration and play. He proposed that children have "an urge toward competence," and he defined this urge as effectance or competence motivation. Harter (1975) further defined effectance motivation as a "desire to solve cognitively challenging problems for gratification inherent in discovering the solution" (p. 370). She highlighted several key components: curiosity, preference for challenge, internal criteria of success, and working for one's own satisfaction.

In studying motivation in school-age children, Dweck (1986) described some children as "mastery-oriented" (i.e., challenge seeking and persistent in attempting to solve difficult problems) and others as "helpless" (i.e., challenge avoidant and low in persistence). She maintained that some children exhibit "learned helplessness" because they believe, based on past experiences, that they have little control over the events that affect them. Children who exhibit patterns of learned helplessness attribute their successes to external factors, such as luck, and their failures to internal factors, such as ability (Dweck & Elliott 1983). Researchers suggest that teachers can promote mastery-oriented, rather than helpless, behavior by providing tasks in which the goal is learning (i.e., developing different strategies) rather than performance (i.e., focusing on correct or incorrect responses) (Stipek 1996).

Studies on toddlers and preschool-age children have focused on mastery motivation, which is assumed to be a precursor to later development of motivation to achieve academically. *Mastery motivation* is defined as a "psychological force that stimulates an individual to attempt independently, in a focused and persistent manner, to solve a problem or master a skill or task which is at least moderately challenging for him or her" (Morgan, Harmon, & Maslin-Cole 1990, 319). Key components of this definition include (1) attempts to master a task independent of adult direction; (2) persistence in mastering a task even when difficulties arise; and (3) selection of a task that is neither extremely easy nor extremely difficult. Researchers have stressed the importance of individually determined moderate challenge as children persist less with tasks that they find too easy or too difficult (Redding, Morgan, & Harmon 1988). Thus, by identifying the kinds of tasks individual children engage in and persist with, teachers can provide opportunities that will offer optimal challenges.

Based largely on Dewey's and Dewey students' writings and teachings, proponents of Progressive Education and its descendent, developmentally appropriate practice, have for a century been refining ways of capturing this natural motivation to learn by involving children in project planning, "learning through doing" personally meaningful yet worthwhile concepts and skills, participating in classroom management, and the language-experience approach to teaching reading, which helps each child convert interesting experiences into conversation, writing, and reading.

Regardless of their theoretical background, intelligent, sensitive adults who closely observe children discover the same things—because that's the way children are—there are a number of "universals."

How does mastery motivation change during early childhood?

Most developmental psychologists contend that children begin life as motivated beings. Children strive to understand the world and to affect it. Developmentally, children progress through several shifts in motivation, so the motivated child behaves differently at different phases of life. The motivated infant, younger than six

months of age, explores objects through reaching, mouthing, and visual exploration. Around nine months infants begin to understand simple notions of cause-and-effect, and the motivated infant of this age begins to engage in goal-directed activity with unfamiliar tasks (Jennings 1993). Another transition occurs around 18 months of age when children begin to be able to compare their behavior with that of a standard (Jennings 1993). The motivated toddler attempts to approximate the standard. During the preschool years motivated children begin to self-select challenging tasks and prefer tasks that "make them think" to those that are easy for them to accomplish (Stipek 1996).

How does motivation relate to cognition?

Motivation and cognition are conceptually different, but researchers have found that the two constructs are intertwined during infancy (Yarrow et al. 1982; Yarrow et al. 1983). Infant mastery motivation measures have been found to be better predictors of preschool measures of cognition than are standardized infant developmental quotients (Messer et al. 1986). Measures of mastery motivation may be good indicators of the way in which children approach learning about objects. Infants and toddlers who appear more motivated may take full advantage of a range of spontaneous learning opportunities and ultimately demonstrate more advanced cognitive performance.

During the preschool period, correlations between measures of motivation and those of intelligence are only modestly related (Morgan, MacTurk, & Hrncir 1995). While the motivated preschooler is one who persists at difficult tasks, and thus creates and engages in cognition enriching activities, cognitively advanced preschoolers are not necessarily highly motivated. The low correlation between intelligence and motivation indicates that aspects of children's lives other than cognition, such as the actions of important adults, may explain differences in mastery motivation.

How do caregivers affect mastery motivation?

Motivation is often assumed to be intrinsic, but it also appears to be affected by the transactions between children and their parents and other caregivers. The role played by caregivers, however, varies with the age of the child (Busch-Rossnagel, Knauf-Jensen, & DesRosiers 1995). For example, Yarrow and his colleagues (Yarrow et al. 1984) reported that parents who provided more sensory stimulation for their young infants had infants who were more persistent in their exploration of objects. After children begin engaging in cause-and-effect actions with objects, during the latter part of the first year of life, caregivers' role in providing stimulation becomes more complex. Parents who interfere in children's attempts to engage in autonomous activity diminish children's motivated behavior (Frodi, Bridges, & Grolnick 1985; Wachs 1987; Hauser-Cram 1993). Researchers (e.g., Morgan et al. 1991) contend that parents who are highly directive may encourage children to be efficient responders but not effective initiators. In contrast, parents who provide a range of challenges and support children's autonomy have children who display high levels of mastery motivation.

Eriksonians emphasize the industriousness of children in this age range. They have a strong, innate urge to become competent. During the preschool years, motivated children begin to self-select challenging tasks and prefer tasks that "make them think" to those that are easy for them to accomplish. Motivation is intrinsic, but it also is affected by transactions between children and the important adults in their lives.

What do we know about motivation in children with developmental or physical disabilities?

Although less research has been conducted on motivation in children with disabilities, a picture of motivated behavior has begun to emerge. Researchers studying children with physical disabilities and mental retardation (MacTurk et al. 1985; Hauser-Cram 1996) have reported that levels of persistence on challenging tasks are similar for children with and without disabilities during the infant and toddler years. Discrepancies in mastery motivation of children with and without disabilities begin to emerge during the preschool and early school-age years (Harter & Zigler 1974; Jennings, Connors, & Stegman 1988).

Although the cause of the decline in motivated behavior of children with disabilities has not been determined, home and classroom factors may provide a clue. Studies of parent-child interaction in the home indicate that many parents of children with developmental disabilities and delays are highly directive in their play (Mahoney, Fors, & Wood 1990). Preschool classroom observation studies indicate that teachers, too, often highly direct children with disabilities (Hauser-Cram, Bronson, & Upshur 1993; Bronson, Hauser-Cram, & Warfield 1997). In both settings children with disabilities may have little opportunity for executing autonomy and independence in attempts to master tasks.

Can parents and teachers accurately assess mastery motivation?

Although the preponderance of studies on mastery motivation have been based on behavioral assessments, an increasing number are incorporating parents' or teachers' ratings of children's motivated behavior. Ratings are quicker and easier to gather, and they have been found to correlate significantly with behavioral assessments (Morgan et al. 1993). Furthermore, ratings can take advantage of parents' and teachers' knowledge of children in multiple settings and with a wide range of tasks.

The Dimensions of Mastery Questionnaire (DMQ) has been found to be a reliable and valid source of ratings of children's persistence on object-oriented tasks, social-symbolic activities, and gross-motor play (Morgan et al. 1993). In studies in which parents and teachers have been asked to use the DMQ to rate the same child's mastery motivation, parents usually provide more positive ratings.

This trend was reported in a recent study of three-year-old children with developmental disabilities (Hauser-Cram et al. 1997). Results of this study also indicated that parents' ratings of mastery motivation were more predictive of children's later performance than were teachers' ratings. Therefore, parents' perceptions of children's motivated behavior offer unique and valuable information to teachers.

© Elisabeth Nichols

© BmPorter/Don Franklin

Parents and teachers who interfere in children's attempts to engage in autonomous activity diminish children's motivated behavior. Researchers contend that parents and teachers who are highly directive may encourage children to be efficient responders but not effective initiators. In contrast, parents and teachers who provide a range of challenges and support children's autonomy have children who display high levels of mastery motivation.

What can teachers do to encourage mastery motivation?

Research on mastery motivation does not have a long history, but much of the research has been undertaken with a view toward application and intervention. Several important suggestions emerge from the studies conducted so far.

1. Provide a moderate choice of activities. Choosing activities promotes autonomy and offers children some control over their own learning. Research indicates that a modest number of choices, rather than no choice or a large number of choices, is optimal in enhancing intrinsic motivation (Stipek 1996).

2. Provide children with activities that offer opportunities to learn rather than opportunities only to be correct or incorrect. For example, provide problem-posing tasks, games, or other activities in which there are several possible ways to solve the problems posed.

3. Support children's activities in ways that do not interfere with autonomy. Sometimes this requires adults to wait rather than anticipate a child's needs when she encounters difficulty with a task. If the child is getting very frustrated, a well-timed suggestion (e.g., "Maybe if you turn that piece around . . .") rather than a direct command (e.g., "That piece fits here") may support her attempts to persist.

4. Ask parents about their perspectives on their child's motivation. Parents know what children enjoy doing and what challenges provide them with pride in accomplishment.

What future research is needed on children's mastery motivation?

Current work on mastery motivation is somewhat limited by a focus on the individual child's independent activities, yet preschool classrooms are social organizations where children play and learn together. Future work on mastery motivation will benefit by considering the influence of the social context in which children learn. To what extent do peers challenge each other as they persist together on a joint enterprise? To what extent do the social dynamics of a classroom offer a range of challenges appropriate for each child? To what extent do children develop a sense of shared agency in making a difference in their preschool classroom? Many questions will undoubtedly emerge as we extend the construct of mastery motivation to include the collective intricacies of the social settings in which children engage in learning. Adults, siblings, and peers are all potential partners in children's motivation, and future research can help us understand these partnerships and the ways in which all can contribute to optimizing mastery-oriented behavior in young children.

References

Bronson, M.B., P. Hauser-Cram, & M.E. Warfield. 1997. Classrooms matter: Relations between the classroom environment and the social and mastery behavior of five-year-old children with disabilities. *Applied Developmental Psychology* 18: 331–48.

Busch-Rossnagel, N.A., D.E. Knauf-Jensen, & F.S. DesRosiers. 1995. Mothers and others: The role of the socializing environment in the development of mastery motivation. In *Mastery motivation: Origins, conceptualizations, and applications,* eds. R.H. MacTurk & G.A. Morgan, 117–45. Norwood, NJ: Ablex.

Dweck, C., & E.S. Elliott. 1983. Achievement motivation. In *Handbook of child psychology, Vol. 4: Socialization, personality, and social development.* 4th ed., series ed. P.H. Mussen, vol. ed. E.M. Hetherington, 643–91. New York: Wiley.

Dweck, C.S. 1986. Motivational processes affecting learning. *American Psychologist* 41: 1040–48.

Frodi, A., L. Bridges, & W. Grolnick. 1985. Correlates of mastery-related behavior: A short-term longitudinal study of infants in their second year. *Child Development* 56: 1291–98.

Harter, S. 1975. Developmental differences in the manifestations of mastery motivation on problem-solving tasks. *Child Development* 46: 370–78.

Harter, S., & E. Zigler. 1974. The assessment of effectance motivation in normal and retarded children. *Developmental Psychology* 45: 661–69.

Hauser-Cram, P. 1993. Mastery motivation in three-year-old children with Down syndrome. In *Mastery motivation in early childhood: Development, measurement, and social processes,* ed. D.J. Messer, 230–50. London: Routledge.

Hauser-Cram, P. 1996. Mastery motivation in toddlers with developmental disabilities. *Child Development* 67: 236–48.

Hauser-Cram, P., M.B. Bronson, & C.C. Upshur. 1993. The effects of the classroom environment on classroom behaviors of young children with disabilities. *Early Childhood Research Quarterly* 8: 479–97.

Hauser-Cram, P., M.W. Krauss, M.E. Warfield, & A. Steele. 1997. Congruence and predictive power of mothers' and teachers' ratings of mastery motivation in children with mental retardation. *Mental Retardation* 35: 355–63.

Hunt, J. McV. 1965. Intrinsic motivation and its role in psychological development. In *Nebraska symposium on motivation,* ed. D. Levine, 189–282. Lincoln: University of Nebraska Press.

Jennings, K.D. 1993. Mastery motivation and the formation of self-concept from infancy through early childhood. In *Mastery motivation in early childhood: Development, measurement, and social processes,* ed. D.J. Messer, 36–54. London: Routledge.

Jennings, K.D., R.E. Connors, & C.E. Stegman. 1988. Does a physical handicap alter the development of mastery motivation during the preschool years? *Journal of the American Academy of Child and Adolescent Psychiatry* 27: 312–17.

MacTurk, R., P.M. Vietze, M.E. McCarthy, S. McQuiston, & L.J. Yarrow. 1985. The organization of exploratory behavior in Down syndrome and nondelayed infants. *Child Development* 56: 573–81.

Mahoney, G., S. Fors, & S. Wood. 1990. Maternal directive behavior revisited. *American Journal on Mental Retardation* 94: 398–406.

Messer, D.J., M.E. McCarthy, S. McQuiston, R.H. MacTurk, L.J. Yarrow, & P.M. Vietze. 1986. Relations between mastery motivation in infancy and competence in early childhood. *Developmental Psychology* 22: 336–72.

Morgan, G.A., R.J. Harmon, & C.A. Maslin-Cole. 1990. Mastery motivation: Definition and measurement. *Early Education and Development* 1: 318–39.

Morgan, G.A., R.H. MacTurk, & E.J. Hrncir. 1995. Mastery motivation: Overview, definitions, and conceptual issues. In *Mastery motivation: Origins, conceptualizations, and applications,* eds. R.H. MacTurk & G.A. Morgan. Norwood, NJ: Ablex.

Morgan, G.A., C.A. Maslin-Cole, Z. Biringer, & R.J. Harmon. 1991. Play assessment of mastery motivation in infants and young children. In *Play diagnosis and assessment,* eds. C.E. Schaefer, K. Gitlin, & A. Sandgrund, 65–86. New York: Wiley.

Morgan, G.A., C. Maslin-Cole, R.J. Harmon, N.A. Busch-Rossnagel, K. Jennings, P. Hauser-Cram, & L. Brockman. 1993. Parent and teacher perceptions of young children's mastery motivation: Assessment and review of research. In *Mastery motivation in early childhood: Development, measurement, and social processes,* ed. D. Messer, 109–31. London: Routledge.

Piaget, J. 1952. *The origins of intelligence in children.* New York: International Universities Press.

Redding, R.E., G.A. Morgan, & R.J. Harmon. 1988. Mastery motivation in infants and toddlers: Is it greatest when tasks are moderately challenging? *Infant Behavior and Development* 11: 419–30.

Stipek, D.J. 1996. Motivation and instruction. In *Handbook of educational psychology,* eds. D. Berliner & R. Calfee, 85–113. New York: Macmillan.

Wachs, T.D. 1987. Specificity of environmental action as manifest in environmental correlates of infant's mastery motivation. *Developmental Psychology* 23: 782–90.

White, R.W. 1959. Motivation reconsidered: The concept of competence. *Psychological Review* 66: 297–333.

Yarrow, L., R.H. MacTurk, P.M. Vietze, M.E. McCarthy, R.P. Klein, & S. McQuiston. 1984. Developmental course of parental stimulation and its relationship to mastery motivation during infancy. *Developmental Psychology* 20: 492–503.

Yarrow, L., S. McQuiston, R. MacTurk, M. McCarthy, R. Klein, & P. Vietze. 1983. Assessment of mastery motivation during the first year of life: Contemporaneous and cross-age relationships. *Developmental Psychology* 19: 159–71.

Yarrow, L., G. Morgan, K. Jennings, & R. Harmon. 1982. Infants' persistence at tasks: Relationships to cognitive functioning and early experience. *Infant Behavior and Development* 5: 131–41.

Editor's note: As Penny Hauser-Cram tells us, developmental psychologists have focused mainly on mastery motivation in individual children and are now beginning to consider the influence of the social context in which children learn.

The latter is one of the areas of expertise of excellent early childhood educators. They have learned much through their work, which is with groups, about the group dynamics, interpersonal relations, cooperative behaviors, and peer example that power or impede children as they strive to create a project, conquer a difficulty, or solve a problem they've encountered.

We will all benefit when specialists in these two related areas—developmental psychology and early childhood education—pool their knowledge and move on to learn more.

Using Motivational Theory with At-Risk Children

Rawsonville Elementary used achievement goal theory to create a learner-centered school, where success is measured not by relative ability but by individual accomplishment.

Rachel Buck Collopy
and Theresa Green

Rachel Buck Collopy is a doctoral student, Combined Program in Education and Psychology, 1400 School of Education, University of Michigan, Ann Arbor, MI 48109. **Theresa Green** is Principal, Rawsonville Elementary School, 3110 Grove Rd., Ypsilanti, MI 48198.

Rawsonville Elementary is a neighborhood school near Detroit, where the automotive industry is the major employer. Recent layoffs have affected many families in the area, and more than half of the school's 480 students receive reduced or free lunch. Of the district's six elementary schools, Rawsonville has been identified as most in need of Chapter 1 services. For years, the school improvement team had worked hard to improve student motivation and learning. Yet, something was still missing. The number of at-risk and underachieving students entering the school continued to increase.

At the same time, a group of researchers at the University of Michigan had been testing a theory of student motivation known as achievement goal theory (see Maehr and Midgley 1991, Maehr and Pintrich 1991). Their work confirmed what other studies had indicated: The goals that students pursue have a powerful influence on the quality of their learning. Schools, through their policies and practices, give strong messages to students about how success is defined within their walls. As collaborative partners, the faculty at Rawsonville Elementary and the researchers at the University of Michigan aimed to create a school where the emphasis was on learning rather than on relative ability.

Emphasizing Achievement, Not Ability

Often in schools where students adopt ability goals, students come to believe that success is defined in terms of how they do in comparison to others. Implicit in the comparative definition of success is the belief that some students are smart, some are average, and some are dumb. The goal becomes trying to look smart—or at least not to look dumb. Mistakes and failure, because they indicate lack of ability, are threats to a child's self-esteem (Covington 1984). Students who adopt ability goals are more likely to avoid challenging tasks and to give up in the face of difficulty (Elliott and Dweck 1988).

In contrast, learning goals define success in terms of developing skills, expanding knowledge, and gaining understanding. Success means being able to do something you could not do before. When students adopt learning goals, they take on more challenging tasks, persist longer, are less debilitated by mistakes and failure, and use higher-level thinking skills than when they focus on ability goals (See Ames 1992 for a review of research).

As partners in a three-year collaboration, we aimed to make Rawsonville a school where the emphasis was on learning rather than on relative ability. Achievement goal theory does not mandate policies and practices. Rather, practitioners use it as a framework to develop consistent, integrated policies and practices that are appropriate to the needs and strengths of their students, staffs, and communities. The issues of most urgent concern to teachers were our starting point.

Creating Learning-Focused Classrooms

Having heard a lot about the long-term negative effects of retaining students, Rawsonville's teachers were eager to find alternatives to retention. Their early discussions focused on add-ons of financial, human, and material resources. Then, two teachers suggested fundamentally changing the structure of the classroom. If several grades were taught together, they proposed, children would focus on their own improvement and progress at their own developmental pace.

A flood of questions followed.

From *Educational Leadership*, September 1995, pp. 37-40. © 1995 by Rachel Buck Collopy and Theresa Green. Reprinted by permission.

FIGURE 1
Rawsonville Elementary School's Principles of Recognition

1. Recognize individual student effort, accomplishment, and improvement.

2. Give all students opportunities to be recognized.

3. Give recognition privately whenever possible.

4. Avoid using "most" or "best" for recognizing or rewarding, as in "best project" or "most improved." These words usually convey comparisons with others.

5. Avoid recognizing on the basis of absence of mistakes. For example, avoid giving awards for students who get "fewer than five words wrong on a spelling test."

6. Avoid using the same criteria for all students. For example, avoid giving an award to "all students who get an *A* on the science test, or all students who do four out of five projects."

7. Recognize students for taking on challenging work or for stretching their own abilities (even if they make mistakes).

8. Recognize students for coming up with different and unusual ways to solve a problem or approach a task.

9. Try to involve students in the recognition process. What is of value to them? How much effort do they feel they put in? Where do they feel they need improvement? How do they know when they have reached their goals?

10. It's OK to recognize students in various domains (behavior, athletics, attendance), but every student should have the opportunity to be recognized *academically*.

11. Try to recognize the quality of students' work rather than the quantity. For example, recognizing students for reading a lot of books could encourage them to read easy books.

12. Avoid recognizing grades and test scores. This takes the emphasis away from learning and problem solving.

13. Recognition must be real. Do not recognize students for accomplishing something they have not really accomplished, for improving if they have not improved, or for trying hard if that is not the case.

■ Report cards would reflect progress and mastery rather than emphasizing comparative performance with letter grades.

Four teachers decided to pilot the classrooms during 1990–91. At the beginning, they were understandably anxious about possible student failures. By the end of the first year, however, they reported that students were more willing to participate in learning activities, more enthusiastic about learning, and showed greater concern for the learning of classmates. Now, half of Rawsonville's classrooms contain children of two or three grade levels.

Developing a learning-focused environment for children did not stop at the doorway of multi-age classrooms. The theoretical framework of achievement goal theory can be used to redesign single-age classrooms, too. Since Rawsonville's self-renewal began five years ago, the teachers of single-age classrooms have also moved toward an emphasis on improvement, understanding, and effort. Teachers now share methods and techniques that encourage students to adopt learning goals across all classrooms.

School change, of course, is about more than just changing classrooms. Classrooms exist within schools and are affected by the policies and practices of the wider school culture. The efforts of an individual teacher to emphasize learning goals can be undermined by school policies that emphasize relative ability and comparative performance.

Abandoning the Honor Roll
As her understanding of achievement goal theory increased, Rawsonville's principal realized that the traditional honor roll defined the goal of learning as outperforming others, not improving regardless of relative performance. Each term, only a small group of students received honor roll certificates. In addition to serving as a disincentive for the children who never received the certificates, the honor roll also discouraged high-achieving children from trying challenging tasks.

More than just the ages of students would be different in these classrooms. All areas of schooling—from curriculum, materials, and scheduling to teaching methods, classroom management, and evaluation—needed to be reconsidered. Together, we gathered information from experts in other schools and universities. We discussed the obstacles to change. Most important, we confronted our assumptions about the way learning and schooling had to be conducted and began to dream about how it could be.

As the learning-focused, multi-age classrooms began to take shape, it became clear that high- as well as low-achieving students would benefit from the proposed changes:

■ Students would stay with the same teacher for at least two years.

■ The approach to instruction would be interdisciplinary and thematic.

■ Students would progress at their own speed—focusing on meeting learning objectives, not following a lockstep curriculum.

■ The learning-focused classrooms would take advantage of the variety of skill levels through peer tutoring, cooperative learning, and inter-age cooperation.

The principal's decision to eliminate the honor roll started a firestorm of controversy. Many teachers felt that they had lost a carrot to urge students to try hard; they also pointed out that many parents took pride in the honor roll certificates. As they searched for ways to recognize children in a learning-focused manner, teachers came up with Rawsonville's Principles of Recognition. Instead of dictating uniform recognition policies and practices, these principles serve as guidelines that respect the professionalism, creativity, and personal style of teachers.

Other schoolwide recognition policies were also guided by the new principles. As an alternative to making the honor roll, every upper elementary student now receives a certificate recognizing him or her for an area of improvement, accomplishment, and effort. Similarly, at the 5th grade awards ceremony, every graduate is applauded for an accomplishment. In the past, only a handful of students were recognized for their achievements—and often these students received several awards. By the fifth or sixth time a student went up to collect an award, other students would groan instead of applaud.

The faculty at Rawsonville Elementary have also redesigned other schoolwide policies and practices in line with a more learning-focused environment. Rather than emphasizing rewards and punishments, discipline procedures now focus on teaching children to become problem solvers. The use of mini-lessons on conflict resolution and peer mediation, for example, has lessened discipline problems more than rewarding the "good" and punishing the "bad" ever did.

After the three-year collaboration with the University of Michigan formally ended, Rawsonville sought out a second collaborative relationship with another nearby university with the goal of increasing students' computer literacy. Staff have implemented classroom computer use within the framework of achievement goal theory. Teachers now view computers as a way to help all children—not just slow learners or gifted students—learn problem-solving and reasoning skills.

Continuing the Effort

Rawsonville Elementary's approach is but one example of how to put achievement goal theory into practice. Other schools may decide to focus on other pressing issues or design solutions that are theoretically consistent with, but superficially different from, Rawsonville's. What is important is the theoretical perspective, the philosophical underpinnings, that these changes in practice exemplify.

Today, because a large proportion of children entering Rawsonsville is still considered at risk, the faculty's commitment to the course they have set has become more important than ever. At the beginning of each school year, the principal and teachers review the changes they made and discuss the rationale behind them. Teachers have taken over the researchers' role of questioning: Will every child benefit from this experience? What message will this give about the goal of learning? What does this say about what is valued at this school?

Now that we know that achievement goal theory can be put into practice, what difference has it made? Teachers have reported improved attendance, increased enthusiasm for learning, and decreased discipline problems. As one teacher said, "I could never go back to teaching the way I did before." Referring to students' improved attitude toward learning, a 20-year veteran wrote:

Some students became so interested in some aspect of classwork that they did correlating activities on their own at home. Children brought in books, magazines, newspapers, and artifacts that pertained to areas of study. They wrote plays, drew pictures, and made dioramas.... During our study of Japan, one little boy got so interested in haiku that he borrowed my books on it and began writing it—in school and at home. His mom reported that he was driving them "cuckoo" with his "haiku."

Parents are very supportive of these efforts to change. Through formal and informal feedback, they report that their children have become more confident, more willing to take on challenges, more excited about school, and better at working independently and with others. About her son, one parent wrote on a survey that she saw "great improvement in all areas—from a student who was failing and had low self-esteem to an interested, highly motivated *learner*!"

One clear example stands out of the extent to which the school community has embraced the changes brought about by achievement goal theory. At a recent PTO meeting, two parents suggested adding competitive rewards to an annual school event. Other parents told them that Rawsonville is not about winning and losing. It is about every child having access to the same enriching and educational experiences. It is about *learning*.

References

Ames, C. (1992). "Classrooms: Goals, Structures, and Student Motivation." *Journal of Educational Psychology* 84, 3: 261–271.

Covington, M. V. (1984). "The Self-Worth Theory of Achievement Motivation: Findings and Implications." *Elementary School Journal* 85: 5–20.

Elliott, E. S., and C. S. Dweck. (1988). "Goals: An Approach to Motivation and Achievement." *Journal of Personality and Social Psychology* 54: 5–12.

Maehr, M. L., and C. Midgley. (1991). "Enhancing Student Motivation: A Schoolwide Approach." *Educational Psychologist* 26, 3 & 4: 399–427.

Maehr, M. L., and P. R. Pintrich. (1991). *Advances in Motivation and Achievement, Vol. 7.* Greenwich, Conn.: JAI Press.

Authors' note: An earlier version of this paper was presented at the annual meeting of the American Educational Research Association, Atlanta, 1993. This work was supported in part by grants from the Office of Educational Research and Improvement. The opinions expressed, however, are those of the authors and do not represent OERI policy.

This collaboration would not have been possible without Carol Midgley and Martin Maehr of the University of Michigan and the teachers of Rawsonville Elementary School.

Moving beyond Management as Sheer Compliance:
Helping Students to Develop Goal Coordination Strategies

by Mary McCaslin and Thomas L. Good

Specific classroom situations require individualized management techniques, not a "rubber-stamp" approach. A cohesive relationship between teaching style and behavior management style is essential.

Mary McCaslin and Thomas L. Good are associate professor and professor, respectively, of educational psychology in the College of Education at the University of Arizona, Tucson.

Historically classroom management has been seen largely as controlling students—getting them to respond quickly to teacher demands, needs, and goals. Although for some educators this conception is beginning to change, much emphasis remains on behavioral control.[1] This is especially the case in "packaged" prescriptive management programs.[2] When control strategies fail, students' noncompliance is met with an arsenal of punishment and removal strategies.[3]

We begin by noting that there are distinctly different ways to conceptualize management goals and, within a particular management goal, there are many competing views of how to think about management. We will argue that teachers can and should promote the goal for students to develop their capacity for self-regulation. Although there are no foolproof prescriptions for successful management, teachers can help students to achieve more capacity for self-direction by encouraging them to conceptualize problem-solving behaviors vis-à-vis their own academic and social goals (much as one teaches curriculum content in a problem-solving fashion). Helping students to develop strategies for coordinating their goals is one important aspect of facilitating student capacity for adaptive self-regulation of their learning, motivation, and behavior.

Discipline Goals

It is possible to distinguish among three discipline goals: compliance, identification, and internalization.[4] Compliance is achieved when an individual behaves simply to get a reward or to avoid a punishment. Identification occurs when an individual acts "appropriately" when a valued model is salient (especially when they are present in a situation). Internalization is inferred when an individual's behavior is stable across a variety of settings in the absence of external inducements. In our opinion, these three discipline goals differ in terms of students' commitment to a standard of action (compliance = I'll stop or start when you tell (consequate) me to do it; identification = I'll start because I know you would want me to; internalization

When control strategies fail, students' noncompliance is met with an arsenal of punishment and removal strategies.

= I act this way because I have accepted your value as my own). Sheer compliance is a sufficient goal for many classroom tasks (e.g., raise your hand for recognition in school whether or not you value hand raising or sanctioned recognition). For other tasks, however, compliance is at best a starting point.

We write this paper for educators who want to achieve more than sheer compliance. However, make no bones about it, compliance is a major goal of classroom management (students must be safe, bullies cannot harass, students must be on time, individuals cannot continuously monopolize classroom discussion). Whether or not a student prefers or values aggression, it cannot be tolerated. Similarly, a student who complies by accepting peer conflict resolution rather than fighting after school represents a favorable discipline outcome (whether or not the student values conflict resolution).

We prefer goals that include internalization rather than only sheer compliance for three basic reasons. First, the success of a compliance model depends upon constant monitoring (if the teacher turns her or his back, students misbehave; if the electricity in the fence goes off, the cattle flee). Second, if compliance obtained through the judicious use of rewards (and to a lesser extent punishment) is the only controlling mechanism, appropriate behavior and dispositions will not transfer from one setting to another (students may not steal in school, but may do so in the mall; students may try to do their best when the popcorn party is this week, but not take their work seriously the week after the party). In short, compliance with rules and acceptable standards of behavior is, of course, always one goal, but sheer compliance is less durable and transferable than compliance that occurs because of identification (with sports

stars who don't smoke or fight—i.e., the "squash it" campaign) or internalization (fighting and smoking are detrimental and things I will not do). A third reason to promote more than compliance is that some complex forms of instruction simply cannot occur if students operate at only a sheer compliance level. For example, if small-group instruction is to work effectively, it is necessary that students value and support cooperative and divergent exchanges. Additionally, students' behavior in small groups often is unsupervised; thus, group management will vary widely as a function of students' commitment to a standard of action and valuing of diversity.

Representations of Management

There are multiple ways to conceptualize management issues in school settings. Indeed, how a teacher or administrator frames a management problem is a critical determinant of how he or she responds to a specific classroom issue. For example, different beliefs about why a student misbehaves influences specific strategies that teachers use in attending to particular classroom events. As can be seen in Table 1, students may misbehave for different reasons and, of course, some of these reasons occur simultaneously.

Table 1: Reasons Why Students Misbehave

1. Lonely or scared
2. Out of control or hostile
3. Face-saving or don't know what to do
4. Have failed to learn, bored or frustrated
5. Physiological need (pain, sleep deprivation, withdrawal) or satiation
6. Distracted by peers, events, or memories

A student who is bored because the work is inappropriately difficult is different from the student who is bored because he or she is satiated and needs a change of activity. Similarly, students who misbehave because they do not know what to do require a different response than students who misbehave because they are distracted by peers. The possible reasons for misbehavior are countless but Table 1 helps to make the point—students misbehave because of cognitive, emotional, and physiological reasons. This analysis also helps to explain why prescriptive programs with regimented responses for student misbehavior often miss the mark. If teachers have management goals other than sheer compliance, then it is important to determine *why* students misbehave. And, even if sheer compliance is the goal, knowing why students misbehave prevents inefficient and potentially counterproductive use of discipline strategies (offering help to a student bored with unchallenging work).

It also is possible to discuss management in terms of *when* students misbehave as somewhat independent from *why* they misbehave (see Table 2).

Table 2: When Misbehavior Occurs

1. Before the lesson starts
2. In the initial stages of a lesson
3. Transition from one lesson activity to another
4. Transition from teacher-directed to student-directed control of the lesson
5. Conclusion of a lesson

Data illustrate that the times listed in Table 2 are when misbehavior most often occurs—especially when whole-class instructional models are being used. The literature on classroom management provides strategies for how to proactively circumvent these "time-based" problems.[5] Further, it's important to understand that these timing problems typically occur because of teachers' instructional or managerial errors. Informed teachers recognize that sometimes students misbehave

for reasons that are primarily due to teacher behavior.

Another conceptualization of management is problem ownership. Table 3 defines five types of problem ownership: teacher-owned, student-owned, shared between teacher and student, class-owned, and school-owned problems.[6] If a teacher is angry (as in teacher-owned problem situations) the teacher must recognize the anger to deal capably with student misbehavior (i.e., do more than punish).

Educators who conceptualize management from the perspective of problem ownership have provided

rich strategies for dealing with different types of problem students (e.g., shy, hostile, hyperactive) as a function of problem ownership.[7] Most classification systems for dealing with problem ownership have dealt only with the first three types of problems that are caused by other persons. However, it is also possible to conceptualize problems that are classroom-based or school-based due to official *policies*, not only the individuals who enforce them. Some schools, for example, have allowed businesses (McDonald's, Pizza Hut) to advertise in schools and sponsor school programs. Channel One monitors the news that students watch and advertises products along with news broadcasts.[8] One critic of such practices illustrates how a school-level function (allowing tennis shoes to be advertised) may cre-

ate classroom-level problems (fighting over tennis shoes). Alex Molnar puts it this way, "At a time when poor children have been killed for their shoes, they are forced to watch advertising messages for high-priced sneakers. At a time when American children are increasingly overweight and at risk of coronary disease, they have been taught how the heart functions from a poster advertising junk food and then served high-fat meals by the fast food concessionaires that run their school cafeterias. At a time when too many children abuse alcohol, they are taught history by a brewery."[9]

Table 3: Problem Ownership Definitions	
Ownership	**Problem**
Teacher-owned	Student behavior prevents teacher need satisfaction (makes teacher angry)
Student-owned	Student need satisfaction is stymied by someone other than teacher
Shared	Teacher and student partially prevent one another's need satisfaction
Class-owned	Classroom structure prevents students' and teachers' need satisfaction
School-owned	School policies keep students and teachers from achieving needs

---

Yet another way to conceptualize management is the possible interaction between the roles that teachers and students may adopt. Here, the number of comparisons is almost infinite; however, for discussion purposes, some examples are provided in Table 4. As is the case in most representations, this conception interacts with others. For example, an authoritarian teacher typically has a lower threshold for "seeing" a management problem in the first place (especially defiance) than does a laissez-faire teacher.

Table 4 has been organized to show how a particular teacher role may exacerbate certain types of problems students have and how certain student roles may highlight vulnerabilities in certain types of teachers. For example, teachers differ in the amount of control they exert in the classroom. Laissez-faire teachers tend to be relatively tolerant of a range of student behavior (e.g., noise, movement), choosing not to intervene unless required to do so. These teachers' management "plan" is more about reaction and remediation than proactive prevention. In these classrooms students who do not provoke teacher attention do not receive teacher attention. Thus, in such classrooms, the shy or passive student is likely to receive too little structure, demands, or guidance to become more actively engaged and self-regulating. In contrast, the authoritarian teacher who runs a "tight ship" is apt to be over-controlling and thereby triggers the defiant student who likes to test boundaries. Similarly, teachers differ in their relative emphasis of academic or social goal orientation in their classroom. Teachers who value academic goals relatively more than social ones may well find themselves "locking horns" with the underachiever who has grown comfortable with the "gentleman's C." Teachers who attend to social development as a primary goal will likely confront the "I'm the best, I'm the king/queen of the world" student as a major challenge to their instructional goals. Table 4 presents two anchors of teacher behavior on each of two dimensions. Consider the likely management issues that arise when, for example, a laissez-faire teacher with an academic focus implements project-based science. What types of behavior would you predict from each of the student roles listed? What if they were members of the same group?

Researchers who have examined the extensive literature on individual differences have noted that five major personality factors describing dispositions teachers and students bring to the classroom can be de-

---

Table 4: Management as a Function of Teacher Role and Student Role

Teacher Role	Student Role
1. Laissez-faire Control	Passive student
2. Authoritarian Control	Defiant student
3. Academic Focus	Underachieving student
4. Social Focus	Self-aggrandizing student

Table 5: Five Personality Factors

1. Agreeableness, Altruism, Affection vs. Hostility
2. Extroversion, Energy, Enthusiasm vs. Introversion
3. Conscientiousness, Control, Constraint vs. Impulsiveness
4. Neuroticism, Negativism, Nervousness vs. Emotional Stability
5. Intellectual Openness, Originality, Flexibility vs. Narrowness, Simplicity, Shallowness

This table has been condensed from Richard Snow, Lyn Corno, and Doug Jackson, III, "Individual Differences in Affective and Conative Functions," in D. Berliner and R. Calfee, eds., Handbook of Educational Psychology *(New York: Macmillan, 1996), 243-310.*

---

rived from the research (see Table 5).[10] As suggested by Table 5, a teacher with one personality orientation necessarily must deal with many students whose personalities may differ in major ways from one another and from the teacher. An introverted teacher who prefers to be low-key in the classroom, for example, can (and sometimes must) project enthusiasm, firmness, or assertiveness as the educational context affords or demands.

Table 5 indicates the complexity of potential interactions. For example, each factor (e.g., agreeable vs. hostile) is associated with multiple characteristics (affectionate, unselfish, trusting, etc.); however, even the most agreeable person will be cold and unfriendly in some situations. Basic personality dispositions (e.g., honesty) are more likely to be exhibited in some situations but not others (e.g., Joan would never cheat on an exam but would copy off another student's homework). Given such complexity it simply is not possible to understand student disposition,

behavior, and needs without *listening* to them.[11]

As seen through the representations we have introduced, classroom management is complex: what constitutes a good management strategy depends (at least) upon the teacher's role, personality, goals, and strategies; characteristics of the management "problem"; and the role, personality, developmental level, and goals of the students. Again, we emphasize a key premise of this article—if teachers want to influence students and want them to respond for reasons other than sheer compliance, teachers cannot let packaged, prescriptive programs do their thinking for them.

Teach for Understanding; Manage for Compliance: Any Questions?

Ironically, and unfortunately, many who write about classroom management answer "no" to the above question. We contend that to teach for understanding while managing for compliance is self-defeating. Too many classroom-management writers ignore the important link between the need for more advanced management approaches (i.e., moving beyond sheer compliance) if certain types of instructional processes and goals are to be achieved. It is not uncommon to find educational writers who strongly advocate a thinking or problem-solving curriculum while directly, or indirectly, arguing for behavioral control of students. For example, Carolyn Evertson and her colleagues note that Walter Doyle incorrectly ". . . suggests that classrooms with complex organization will require more direct management and control than simpler settings."[12] In marked contrast to Doyle's position, Evertson and colleagues note that classroom researchers contend that "instead of more teacher control, these settings will need a different *kind* of teacher control."[13] They argue that when complex instructional goals are required, it is more efficacious for the teacher to delegate authority to students or groups of students, rather than attempting to supervise directly the multitude of overlapping activities, claiming that "direct supervision is more appropriate to [and, we would add, theoretically consistent with] simpler routine tasks."[14] Simply put, if the teacher is trying to create a trusting, cooperative learning environment for students, then the management system must also promote these same dispositions, behaviors, and skills—in part through opportunities for thinking and problem solving in the academic *and* social spheres.

Goal Coordination: Moving beyond Compliance

We have presented several representations of management and each one provides a legitimate lens for thinking about how to conceptualize and implement classroom management goals and strategies. Now we want to introduce another representation; one that we feel is especially relevant for contemporary classrooms. Elsewhere, we have suggested that in many classrooms there is a fundamental mismatch in the promotion of a problem-solving curriculum while using a behavioral control approach to management.[15] It seems highly unlikely that students will profit from the incongruous messages we send when we manage for obedience and teach for exploration and risk taking. We put our argument this way:

Educators have created an oxymoron: a curriculum that urges problem solving and critical thinking and a management system that requires compliance and narrow obedience. The management system at least dilutes, if not obstructs, the potential power of the curriculum for many of our students. Students are asked to think and understand, but in too many classrooms they are asked to think noiselessly, without peer communication or social exchange. And the problems they are asked to think about must be solved, neatly, within (at most) forty-five-minute intervals. In the problem-solving curriculum, in too many cases, the teacher sets the performance goals, identifies relevant resources, establishes criteria for evaluation, and eventually announces winners and losers. Students generally gain recognition and approval by paying close attention to recommended procedures and by taking few academic risks (e.g., reading and extensively footnoting fifteen secondary sources rather than venturing their own informed opinions).[16]

If we want students to develop thoughtful work habits it seems necessary to help them think about how they acquire, elaborate, and integrate academic knowledge; consider the relations among their knowledge, beliefs, and identity; and locate those processes and persons who support them in complicated learning. Simply put, if we want students to understand (i.e., not memorize) academic content, value the process of academic learning, and internalize their education, then we need to help students understand their own behavior in school settings and develop a capacity for managing and regulating themselves and others in a way that supports their learning goals.

Multiple Goals

Teachers can help students become more adept at self-manage-

It seems highly unlikely that students will profit from the incongruous messages we send when we manage for obedience and teach for exploration and risk taking.

Teachers can help students become more adept at self-management, or "self-regulation," by helping them learn to coordinate their social and academic lives.

ment, or "self-regulation," by helping them learn to coordinate their social and academic lives. This involves identifying goals and their interrelationships and strategically coordinating among them. Students (like teachers) pursue multiple goals simultaneously (with more and less success). Often students must choose between competing goals (asking the teacher a question about the trig assignment at the end of class or catching up with a friend who won't be seen the rest of the school day to ask about substituting that afternoon at McDonald's). Further, as we note in *Listening in Classrooms*, students often pursue a goal for multiple reasons (e.g., strategic use of study time as a way both to learn and ensure weekend privileges), and strategies and goals can be *multifunctional* (e.g., "obvious" effort may promote achievement and it is also an effective impression-management strategy).[17] Also, relations among goals are multidimensional. When multiple goals are pursued at the same time and do not overlap, time pressure can make it difficult to establish priorities and then pursue goals sequentially. In addition, goal coordination becomes more complex when multiple goals are difficult (i.e., they take time, attention, and energy to achieve). Third, personal goals often clash with others' needs and interests. Conflict with others makes goal pursuit and coordination more difficult and costly. Teachers sometimes inadvertently create goal conflict and thwart learning goal coordination. For example, teachers typically give deadline extensions when performance events occur midweek. Students who receive extensions do not learn how to prioritize and follow through; instead, they learn that the teacher devalues school work. Peers without extensions may learn to prioritize; however, they also may learn that their multiple goals and time constraints are not noteworthy. Both groups of students have had another piece added to their friendship task.

Dealing with multiple goals is a part of life and people who can do so successfully are apt to be more productive and satisfied than those who cannot. Single-mindedness—all the eggs in one basket—is not a healthy life strategy. Students must learn to identify individual goals, assess their relative importance, and their relationship. Teachers also need to understand the goal coordination task that they impose on students when they assign multiple, simultaneous, and difficult requirements. Teachers who are mindful of students' goal coordination tasks can co-regulate students' learning how to strategically organize and achieve them. Teachers can help students accomplish personal goals by teaching (a) goal-compatibility features and (b) goal-coordination strategies.

Goal Compatibility

Educational researchers have argued that goals can be *compatible* in three ways.[18] First, they may be compensatory as effort (to some extent) can compensate for ability. Second, compatible goals can be complementary as, for example, cooperative behavior complements cooperative learning. Third, compatible goals can be instrumental—studying now makes it easier to be admitted to college later. Goals (like many classroom goals) can be largely *independent* of each other. For example, wanting to be on time to sit with friends at lunch is usually independent of wanting to do well on a chemistry test. Finally, goals can be *incompatible* by interfering or negating one another. Goal interference can occur when teachers inadvertently place students, especially preadolescents, in a conflict between the

Students should be allowed, taught, and expected to assume more responsibility for their own goals and behavior as they progress through school.

goal of being a good student and the goal of being a good friend. For example, often teachers ask one student to explain to another (who has been unable to answer) how a process works or why an answer is incorrect. Students may solve the goal-conflict by feigning ignorance—friendship matters more than being right and a "good" student. Incompatible goals also might negate one another. A student who strives to improve her game, meet the no-pass-no-play academic criterion, and "party hearty" risks failure of academic and athletic goals. And, if "caught," she neither plays, nor remains in school, nor is allowed to go out with friends. Prioritizing and choosing among independent and incompatible goals is essential if students are to meet any of them. Think of how much energy, time, and emotion is spent futilely because an individual does not realize that he cannot have his cake and eat it too, and as a result, achieves neither experience.

Goal-Coordination Strategies

In addition to helping students recognize the degree of compatibility (or lack thereof) among goals, teachers can also help students develop strategies to coordinate among them. In Table 6 we describe four strategies that Dodge and colleagues argue promote goal coordination.[19] We add two strategies (points 5, 6) to their list and place the strategies on a continuum of inclusiveness from greater inclusiveness to less.

School-Wide Co-regulation

If teachers are to be notably effective in helping students to develop goal-coordination strategies and, more broadly, to increase their capacity for self-regulation, teachers will need to work with colleagues at earlier and later grade levels. Elsewhere it has been argued that often first- and second-grade students have more opportunity for self-di-

---

Table 6: Goal-coordination Strategies

1. *A single, integrative strategy:* Although this is the most efficient and inclusive strategy, the goals obviously need to be compatible. One example is the high-ability, highly focused student who is involved in the school yearbook and student government, has a part-time job at the local Quick Print, and hopes to attend college to study journalism. This student's achievement, belongingness, power, independence, and present and future career needs are met with a single broad, integrative strategy.

2. *Multiple, simultaneous strategies:* Simultaneous strategies require goals to be compatible with or independent of each other and for some to be less difficult so that the student can do more than one thing at a time. Academically more-capable students are often able to meet the demands of the task, follow procedures, and catch up on the "chit-chat" with their group members. Thus, they follow the routines like "good" students, successfully complete the task like "smart" students, and maintain friendly banter like "popular" students.

3. *Deferment strategies:* Deferment strategies result when the student realizes that she or he can't "have it all" and prioritizes. Nonpriority goals are put on the back burner, not abandoned. As compared with the integrative and simultaneous strategies, deferment means less gets done because less can get done. We suspect this is the initial reasoning as students begin to restrict their hobbies: piano is deferred for now to allow more time for flute and the school band; soccer takes priority over track, etc.

4. *Modification strategies:* Goals or the criteria for their successful attainment are modified to make goals more compatible. Students may decide that each and every paper in English does not have to be their best; it is important that some of their time be spent on science class, too. Learning to modify goals is a particularly important skill that teachers can help students to develop. Adolescents as well as first-graders can easily lose a sense of proportion in the goals they set and their abilities to meet them.

5. *Goal substitution:* One goal replaces the original goal. Although goal substitution need not have a negative connotation, it is often offered as an explanation for student gang membership and general theories of "negative identity." That is, students who are unable to achieve belongingness in family or sense of place and recognition in school substitute membership and status in gangs to fulfill unmet needs. All of us have had "goal-substitution" experiences, however, and they typically are positive, involving more realistic aspirations. Consider the student who wants to be part of the school play; although stage fright and basic lack of talent may prohibit being cast in an acting role, scenery always needs painting.

6. *Goal abandonment:* By goal abandonment we mean to simply give up on a goal without deferring, modifying, or substituting another. In the specific instance, goal abandonment may be appropriate. For example, simply giving up and going home to regroup may help a student cope with temporary embarrassment. Giving up the goal to always be the best at whatever one does is probably a good idea—as long as it does not translate into giving up trying or giving up altogether.

This table has been adopted (slightly condensed) from McCaslin and Good, Listening in Classrooms.

---

rection, self-evaluation, and choice than do sixth-grade or twelfth-grade students.[20] Unfortunately, the progress that one teacher makes in helping students to develop their capacity for self-regulation in a given year can be dissipated the following year when the next teacher imposes a more controlling (and therefore regressive) system.[21] As we have noted previously, it is time to examine the connectedness of classroom management systems. Educators need to become more sensitive to building better bridges between grades.[22] Students should be allowed, taught, and expected to assume more responsibility for their own goals and behavior as they progress through school.

In this article, we have argued that there are many ways to conceptualize classroom management and we have recommended that teachers can benefit from using multiple perspectives. We argue that successful management has to be conceptualized as fluid and transitional: that is, teachers must continue to adjust their management system to changes in context, including students' expanding needs and abilities.

1. See Mary McCaslin and Thomas L. Good, *Listening in Classrooms* (New York: Harper Collins, 1996); Mary McCaslin and Tom Good, "Compliant Cognition: the Misalliance of Management and Instructional Goals in Current School Reform," *Educational Researcher* 21 (1992): 4-17; Carolyn Evertson and Catherine Randolph, "Perspectives on Classroom Management for Learner-centered Classrooms," in H. Waxman and H. Walberg, eds., *New Directions for Research on Teaching* (Berkeley, Calif.: McCutchan, in press); and Alfie Kohn, *Beyond Discipline: From Compliance to Community* (Alexandria, Va.: Association for Supervision and Curriculum Development, 1996).

2. For an example of one type of the packaged management programs that we find self-defeating, see Lee Canter and Marlene Canter, *Assertive Discipline: Positive Behavior Management for Today's Classroom* (Santa Monica, Calif.: Lee Canter and Associations, 1992).

3. Some of the school-level control strategies in popular use are blatantly contradictory. For example, some schools that have zero-tolerance programs for drugs (i.e., students are kicked out of school for any violation and placed on the street where they can acquire drugs among other things) have tough policies on student truancy that are imposed by state law (e.g., prosecute parents of heavy-truancy students). Apparently it is okay for the school to allow students not to go to school, but the same option does not exist for parents!

4. Herbert C. Kelman, "Compliance, Identification, and Internalization: Three Processes of Attitude Change," *Journal of Conflict Resolution*, vol. 2 (1958): 51-60; and Herbert C. Kelman, "Processes of Opinion Change," *Public Opinion Quarterly* 25 (1961): 57-78.

5. See Thomas L. Good and Jere Brophy, *Looking in Classrooms*, 7th ed. (New York: Harper Collins, 1997).

6. Thomas Gordon, *Teacher Effectiveness Training* (New York: Wyden, 1974); and Jere Brophy and Mary McCaslin, "Teachers' Reports of How They Perceive and Cope with Problem Students," *Elementary School Journal* 93, no. 1 (1992): 3-68.

7. Ibid, Brophy and McCaslin, "Teachers' Reports."

8. Bradley Greenberg and Jeffrey Brand, "Channel 1: But What about the Advertising?" *Educational Leadership* 51 (1994): 56-58.

9. See Alex Molnar, *Giving Kids the Business: The Commercialization of American Schools* (New York: Westview Press, 1996), 49.

10. See Richard Snow, Lyn Corno, and Doug Jackson III, "Individual Differences in Affective and Conative Functions," in D. Berliner and R. Calfee, eds., *Handbook of Educational Psychology* (New York: Macmillan, 1996), 243-310.

11. Mary McCaslin and Thomas L. Good, *Listening in Classrooms* (New York: Harper Collins, 1996).

12. See Carolyn Evertson, K. Weeks, and C. Randolph, *Creating Learning-centered Classrooms: Implications for Classroom Management* (Nashville, Tenn.: Vanderbilt University, March 1997, mimeo); Walter Doyle, "Classroom Organization and Management," in M. Wittrock, ed., *Handbook of Research on Teaching*, 3rd ed. (New York: MacMillan, 1986), 392-431.

13. See Hermine Marshall, "Beyond the Workplace Metaphor: Toward Conceptualizing the Classroom as a Learning Setting," *Theory into Practice* 29 (1990): 94-101; and Alfie Kohn and Lotan, "Teachers as Supervisors of Core Technology," *Theory into Practice* 29 (1990): 78-84.

14. Ibid, Marshall, "Beyond the Workplace."

15. See Mary McCaslin and Thomas L. Good, "Compliant Cognition: the Misalliance of Management and Instructional Goals in Current School Reform," *Educational Researcher* 21 (1992): 4-17.

16. Ibid.

17. See McCaslin and Good, *Listening in Classrooms*, 65, 66.

18. See Kenneth Dodge, Steven Asher, and Jennifer Parkhust, "Social Life as a Goal-Coordination Task," in C. Ames and R. Ames, eds., *Research on Motivation and Education: Volume 3: Goals and Cognition* (New York: Academic Press, 1989), 107-135.

19. Ibid.

20. Thomas L. Good, "What Is Learned in Elementary Schools," in Tommy Tomlinson and Herbert Walberg, eds., *Academic Work and Educational Excellence* (Berkeley, Calif.: McCutchan, 1986), 87-114.

21. Nedra Fetterman, *The Meaning of Success and Failure: A Look at Social Instructional Environments of Four Elementary School Classrooms*, unpublished doctoral dissertations, Bryn Mawr College, Bryn Mawr, Pa.

22. Mary McCaslin and Thomas L. Good, "Classroom Management and Motivated Student Learning," in Tommy Tomlinson, ed., *Motivating Students to Learn: Overcoming Barriers to High Achievement* (Berkeley, Calif.: McCutchan, 1993), 245-261.

Connecting Instruction and Management in a Student-Centered Classroom

Nancy K. Martin

M s. Thompson's seventh grade students have been studying the solar system and are busily working in cooperative learning groups. Each group has been assigned one planet and their objective is to create a description of a being that could live on "their" planet. Because Ms. Thompson has done a good job of orchestrating positive interdependence, students are relying on their groups to achieve their objective while the teacher serves as a facilitator (Johnson, Johnson, Holubec, & Roy, 1988). The noise level here is slightly higher than in the typical classroom as students interact with each other and fulfill their assigned roles. The teacher explained the rules for behavior to the students prior to beginning the project: "Keep hands, feet, and objects to yourself," "Let others have a chance to speak," and "Contribute to your group." She has predetermined consequences for both appropriate and inappropriate behavior and shared those with the class.

Ray and Bill have been having trouble getting along together and today does not seem to be an exception as they continue to "pick on" each other. Even though a warning has been issued to both students, there is yet another altercation between them. Ms. Thompson explains, "Boys, this means detention for both of you." Ray turns pale and looks upset. Bill continues poking Ray with his pencil and says, "Detention's no big deal. I don't care." Ms. Thompson explains to Bill that a call to his parents will be made.

The classroom environment promoted by this teacher is typical of many middle school teachers. The instruction was creative and student centered, but the classroom management techniques were expedient and teacher centered. There can be little doubt that an interesting, well-organized lesson is the single best means to prevent off-task behavior. Still, when coupled with teacher-centered behavior management methods, the subtle but unmistakably clear message students receive is: "It's 'us' against 'them.'"

Classroom atmosphere is an important consideration for educators at all levels. However, it is especially important for teachers at the middle level because of the many developmental changes their students experience simultaneously. In addition to physical, social, and cognitive changes, young adolescents also encounter new academic demands and are required to make the adjustment from a small self-contained classroom with one teacher to a larger, possibly less personal school structure (Santrock, 1987). The purpose of this article is to consider the elements of a student-centered learning environment and the connection between the teacher's instructional methods and his or her approach to classroom management.

Historically classrooms have been teacher-centered. Instructors were accepted as experts conveying the subject matter. The focus in this type of classroom was on the teacher's needs (e.g. the content to be covered and student obedience). Student activity was limited and students were, at best, passive learners. They spoke when recognized by the teacher and were typically not allowed to interact with each other during lessons. Although rote learning may have flourished in the teacher-centered classroom, active learning (problem-solving and critical thinking) was unlikely to emerge. As we prepare to enter the 21st century, this type of learning environment is no longer favorable. If the classroom is to be the center of "intellectual inquiry, students and teachers must feel free

Nancy K. Martin teaches at the University of Texas at San Antonio.

From *Middle School Journal,* March 1997, pp. 3-9. © 1997 by the National Middle School Association (NMSA). Reprinted by permission.

to pursue ideas and make mistakes" (Prawat, 1992, p. 10). Recently, student-centered instruction has gained new advocacy (Aaronsohn, 1993).

Unlike classrooms of the past, student-centered classrooms focus on student "interaction with meaningful content, with each other, and with the teacher as facilitator of that independence" (Aaronsohn, 1993, p. 3).

Today quality instruction is characterized by developmentally appropriate methods that consider the intrinsic needs of students. Students' decision-making skills are fostered and opinions are validated by focusing on creativity and critical thinking rather than rote learning.

Although often considered separately, classroom management and instruction cannot be isolated from each other because they work together to create a classroom atmosphere (Martin & Baldwin, 1994). Yet many schools across the country encourage and use student-focused instructional methods while simultaneously adopting packaged approaches to classroom management, even though these approaches may not be designed to support student-centered instruction. Without student-centered instruction and classroom management, a truly learner-focused environment cannot exist. Still, when I try to convey this connection to teachers, I am frequently met with skepticism: "Can't I be student centered in my instruction and teacher centered in my classroom management?" The answer is no; you are trying to mix oil with water.

The student-centered classroom is an outgrowth of a philosophy sensitive to the whole child. Therefore, by definition it must focus on the psychological and emotional aspects of the child as well as on the cognitive and intellectual domains. As Wilson (1994) explains, "teachers who view their students simply as academic learners fail to consider the impact of each student's affective state on achievement in the middle school. ... Teachers

who appear too busy to respond to significant social/affective related needs of young adolescents assure an incomplete learning ethos in their classrooms, counter-productive to excellence in scholarship" (p. 53).

The Goal of Classroom Management

This brings to light important questions. First, what is the overall goal of classroom management? In the teacher-centered classroom, control is key to being able to "cover" the material. Keeping pupils still and quiet in the most expedient fashion possible is the primary objective. Traditional, teacher-centered classroom management techniques usually require appropriate behavior in response to some type of reward. Therefore, the teacher must be present to view the behavior and dispense the reinforcer. By utilizing systems such as these, we run the risk of creating a situation in which students behave only for what they "get" and the teacher's absence implies permission to misbehave.

One of the most widely used teacher-centered paradigms is Canter's (1992) *Assertive Discipline*. More than 750,000 teachers have been trained in the use of this model which advocates the use of incentive systems and punishment and focuses on teacher control and student obedience (Hill, 1990). Canter (1992) defines the assertive teacher as, "One who clearly and firmly communicates her expectations to her students, and is prepared to reinforce her words with appropriate actions. She responds in a manner which maximizes her potential to get her needs to teach met, but in no way violates the best interest of the students" (p. 14). This model consists of a set of rules and a hierarchy of predetermined rewards and consequences. When the child misbehaves, he or she is allowed one warning before the predetermined consequence is automatically doled out without consideration of the individual child or the motivation of the misbehavior.

Consider the following scenario typical of the assertive discipline classroom. As Mr. Martinez is presenting his lesson, he sees Emily turn and whisper to Jason. "Emily, that's a warning."

"But, Mr. Martinez, I . . ."

"No 'buts', Emily. You know the rules. Next time, you go to detention. " The classroom belongs only to Mr. Martinez; there is no sense of community here. Emily is likely to become resentful and other students may be upset or angry by observing similar interactions.

In the student-centered classroom, however, Mr. Martinez's response would be very different. Here, the teacher might simply ask, "Emily, is there something I can help you with?"

"What page are we on, Mr. Martinez? I didn't hear you say."

"Page 53, Emily, but remember that the assignment is always written on the board so your can look there in the future." In this simple exchange, the teacher has first tried to be pro-active by putting information on the board. But when Emily did not remember or notice, she was still given the benefit of the doubt. She was listened to and respected. In this scenario, we see reciprocal interaction; not a one-way or topdown exchange.

Assertive Discipline, on the other hand, treats all students the same. But being fair means not treating all children the same. When a physician has a waiting room full of patients with different illnesses, he or she does not come out and say: "Today is aspirin day; all patients will be treated equally and given aspirin to solve their ailments" (Mendler, 1993, p. 5). In the student-centered classroom, misbehavior is considered a golden opportunity to foster self-discipline and responsibility. To that end, consequences are tailored to individual students and their needs. The consequences for appropriate and inappropriate behavior should not be predetermined but, instead, considered on an individual basis. Unlike the physician who gives all patients aspirin or the teacher who doles out the same consequences to all students, one should consider the specific situation and tailor the response to fit the needs and motives of the "patient."

Student-centered classrooms are characterized by the teacher's consideration of the student's developmental tasks, needs, motives, and feelings. As middle school students struggle with the development of a personal identity and greater social independence, the student-centered environment fosters the development of an internalized moral code (Alexander, 1965/1995). Student input, discussion, and compromise are important parts of this teacher's classroom management plan so self-discipline and responsibility are encouraged. Therefore, classroom rules and policies could be the objective for a cooperative learning assignment at the beginning of the year. To foster a student-centered environment, students could brainstorm ideas, discuss, and possibly vote on how the classroom community should function within the broader school context.

Student-Centered Classroom Management Sounds Good, But...

Another important questions is this: Why are teachers reluctant to implement student-centered theories of classroom management that encourage self-discipline and responsibility? In my work with teachers, I have found six frequently expressed reasons.

1. What will others think if . . . ? Teachers often feel pressured to create a quiet and orderly classroom environment so material can be "covered" and/or because of concern about the opinions of others (e.g., administrators, colleagues, or parents). Aaronsohn (1993) quotes a student teacher who said, " [My cooperating teacher] evaluated me on how I controlled the class—on who was off task.... How am I going to make the school people happy?" (p. 26). Indeed, the piece of advice probably most often given to new teachers is, "Go in there, take control and don't smile until Christmas."

"Can't I be student centered in my instruction and teacher centered in my classroom management?" The answer is no; you are trying to mix oil with water.

On the other hand, student-centered, intrinsic classroom management strategies focus on the whole child, his or her needs and motives. A consequence for inappropriate behavior is only successful if it results in students realizing the repercussions of their actions, envisioning other behavioral choices, and making a sincere plan to use those choices in the future. The student-centered classroom may be lively with active learners but intrinsic classroom management techniques are also needed for students to become self-disciplined, independent learners.

The importance of administrative and collegial encouragement is paramount in overcoming the "what will people think" obstacle. Without such support, it is unlikely that a student-focused atmosphere will materialize. School administrators and fellow teachers must provide the moral support and professional development opportunities necessary if student-centered classroom management practices are to predonimate.

2. Forget classroom management theory. If it works, use it. This is the "fly-by-the-seat-of-the-pants" approach to classroom management. Teachers have been using it for decades. Aaronsohn (1993) explains, "'the way it is' is a powerful model ... since 'it's always been that way'" (p. 7). Traditionally educators have learned how to manage classrooms from each other where the focus is on practice rather than theory. When classroom management is taught and learned in this manner we run the risk of making the same mistakes year after year without realizing why.

When a physician has a waiting room full of patients with different illnesses, he or she does not come out and say: "Today is aspirin day; all patients will be treated equally and given aspirin to solve their ailments."

Theory is important because it provides us with an explanation of observations. We may all see and experience the same things but our explanation for the underlying causes of these events can be very different. A consistent theoretical perspective lends the teacher a coherent base from which to draw. Without it, we are left with a mere "bag of tricks" and are often at a loss for alternatives when a particular discipline method inevitably fails. Dismissing theory as unimportant is analogous to walking a tightrope without a net.

The teacher's transition to a student-centered classroom environment is a gradual process that involves a great deal of introspection and cannot be accomplished overnight. It is not unusual to see practicing teachers who want to hang on to the old, comfortable classroom management techniques because they "work," even though they may not be appropriate. Many things work; this does not mean they are necessarily appropriate. Extra work given as punishment, writing "lines," and teacher sarcasm are all examples of interventions that may "work" in that they temporarily stop the behavior but are never appropriate.

No one wants to develop a pool of techniques that does not work; that would be silly. At the same time, educators have a responsibility to critically evaluate classroom management techniques. Are these techniques accomplishing what we think they are and, if so, how well? When a student misbehaves, we typically use a discipline technique, see its immediate impact, and think it is effective. Claiming it "works," we prepeatedly use it. If it really worked, we would not need it again. Even worse, at times educators embarrass and humiliate students into compliance. Strategies such as these can leave deep emotional scars and have long-term negative effects. Both teacher-centered and student-centered models of classroom management can be used effectively for short-term control of children's classroom behavior. However, it is dangerous to value discipline for its own sake "without regard for the effects of these programs on the overall learning and development of children" (Benshoff, Poidevant, & Cashwell, 1994, p. 166). It is imperative that we consider what happens later. What happens to the student's self-esteem, motivation for learning, or dignity (Mendler, 1993)? Any interaction that diminishes these is inappropriate, even though it may stop the misbehavior.

3. My philosophy is "eclectic." I use a combination of models and classroom management techniques. Without student-centered classroom management techniques, there can be no student-centered classroom. Altering curriculum and instruction is of little use if the overall classroom atmosphere is still teacher-centered. This is a difficult change to make as it usually requires letting go of some of the teacher implemented rules and requirements. As a result, teachers have a tendency to combine conflicting models that sound good with ones that "feel" right to them as traditional teachers (e.g., Canter's (1992) *Assertive Discipline* with Glasser's (1986) *Control Theory* or Ginott's (1972) ideas with behavior modification). In theory as well as in practice, this is impossible. It cannot be done. When the teacher "combines" a teacher-centered model of classroom management with a student-centered model, at least one of them is bastardized—usually the student-centered one.

The teacher-student relationship is at the heart of student-centered classroom management. Mutual respect and trust are prerequisite to success. When teachers try to combine conflicting models, students learn that they are only listened to when they agree with the teacher. One experienced teacher explained his professional transition as follows:

> In the past, I have combined many different ideas. Many of those ideas send conflicting signals to students. I want trust in a classroom but I also want students to do what I say when I say. I want to meet the needs of students but I also want students to sit down and shut up. I want to talk to students when I want to talk to students. When I look at all that is happening in my classroom, I realize that what I do is a major part of behavior problems. I have to let go. I have to free myself from past experiences and provide an environment that meets the needs of my students instead of meeting only my needs.

Traditionally, classroom management techniques were likely drawn from no particular theoretical base at all or from theories such as behaviorism where the focus is on extrinsic control via reinforcements. Classic behavior modification does not recognize students as active participants in the learning process but instead views them as passive learners who simply respond to the environment. Behaviorally based models of classroom management such as Canter's (1992) *Assertive Discipline* or

Jones's (1987) model cannot co-exist with a student-centered curriculum.

Others present very different theories and models for classroom management that focus on the individual and advocate free will rather than determinism (e.g., Dreikurs, Grunwald, & Pepper, 1982; Glasser, 1986; Ginott, 1972; Gordon, 1974). Glasser (1986) described all behavior as a choice and believes that, "None of what we do is caused by any situation outside of ourselves" (p. 17). A good teacher is one who considers his or her role as one of a modern manager who shares power, rather than the traditional, teacher-centered manager who does not (Glasser, 1986).

Similarly, Dreikurs, Grunwald, and Pepper (1982) maintained that humans are social beings and all behavior is enacted with some purpose in mind. Specifically, humans attempt to find their place in the group in which they function such as the family or class. Again, the focus is on the individual and the origin of behaviors. In other words, both Glasser and Dreikurs addressed the underlying cause for the behaviors of both the teacher and the student. Control—and therefore, responsibility—lies within each individual. Likewise, Ginott (1972) and Gordon (1974) encouraged teachers to invite students' cooperation and encouraged the use of "I-messages," realizing that students make their own decisions and choices regarding behavior.

4. How can we teach students respect for authority if we give them too much control? I answer this question with another question. How can we teach students respect for anyone if we do not show them the respect all people deserve? Teaching respect begins by giving respect. Teacher-centered models of classroom management are focused on the teacher and, therefore, by definition disregard students' needs.

In addition, the idea that control is ours to give is an illusion. Any "control" one has over another exists only because the recipient allows it. As an individual, I can influence others, but I cannot actually control anyone except myself—and sometimes even that is difficult. Because students may be used to teacher-centered classrooms, they may not be aware that they are the ones who control their behavior. As a result, they may be giving others more power over their lives than they should. Student-centered classroom management models teach students that they—not others—are responsible for their behavior.

If students are out of control today, it is partly because their sense of personal control has been taken away from them. They have felt disregarded and disempowered by traditional, teacher-centered—sometimes

authoritarian—school systems. A sense of validation can go a long way to facilitate some of the developmental struggles associated with young adolescence.

Unfortunately, not all authority figures have children's best interests in mind. Because we have seen an increase in drug use, gang activity, reported cases of child abuse and molestation, students today should be encouraged to differentiate between those who do and do not deserve their trust and respect. It is a dangerous proposition to teach our children otherwise.

5. Some classroom management theories are not appropriate for the type of student I teach. Younger (older, "typical," exceptional) students need more teacher control. Simultaneously, other teachers say, "I should use a less controlling (student-centered) classroom management model because my students are younger (older, typical, exceptional)." Neither age nor exceptionality is the issue. If the classroom management theory is appropriate for one group, it is appropriate for another. Although this may seem to conflict with the previous "aspirin" analogy, it does not. A theory is an umbrella that encompasses a collection of techniques. In the student-focused classroom, interventions are designed with the particular students and specific situations in mind. Although the manner in which the theory is implemented in specific instances may differ, the theoretical base does not.

As an individual, I can influence others, but I cannot actually control anyone except myself—and sometimes even that is difficult.

6. I like the sound of this theory but I do not see how to actually use it. It looks good on paper but may be too idealistic. Teachers often see the merit of a student-centered classroom management theory or model and want to put it into practice but do not see how to bridge the all-important gap between theory and application. Attending workshops or university classes pertaining to classroom management and instruction is an important first step. Exposure to ideas must occur before change can happen. However, an equally important issue surrounds what happens after teachers return to their classrooms. After educators have been exposed to new theories and techniques, do they actually translate them into practice? There is a temptation to try the new techniques learned and, if they do not work the way the teacher thinks they should or do not show "results" in a short time period, discard them as not practical for the real classroom.

Old habits are hard to break. Fortunately, there are several student-centered "packages" of classroom management that provide clear guidelines for implementation and can serve as "training wheels" for the teacher until student-centered classroom management comes naturally. Based on student-focused, intrinsic theories, Albert (1989), Gathercoal (1990), and Dinkmeyer, McKay, and Dinkmeyer (1980) present student-focused models of classroom management.

To illustrate how a student-centered model might look in practice, return to the classroom scenario with Ms. Thompson, Ray, and Bill. Using a teacher-centered classroom management model, Ms. Thompson assigned the predetermined consequence to both boys. However, a more student-centered Ms. Thompson would take a holistic perspective and consider all she knows about both students before she acts. As Ray and Bill "pick on" each other, Ms. Thompson notes, "You two seem to have a problem. In a little while, I would like to discuss what I can do to help you solve it but in the meantime, I want you two to move away from each other." Bill says, "I ain't going anywhere 'cause I wasn't doing anything!" Ray moves a few seats away from Bill, seems to calm down, and is on task the rest of the class period.

Bill, on the other hand, is a much tougher customer to deal with because of the emotion his defiance is likely to evoke. Automatic detention may only serve to make him more angry—not a lasting solution to the problem. He is lashing out at the teacher and, although tempted to respond in a similar manner, Ms. Thompson explains, "Bill, solving this problem is more important than punishing you for your misbehavior. I'd like to help you do that. Fill out this card and we will visit in a few minutes." Bill is given a card with the following four questions on it (Charles, 1992, p. 121):

1. What were you doing when the problem started?
2. Was it against the rules?
3. Can we work things out so it won't happen again?
4. What could you and I do to keep it from happening?

When Ms. Thompson finds a few spare minutes, the answers are used to structure a conversation between her and Bill.

Based on Glasser's intrinsic theory of motivation, the objectives of the conference are three fold: to point out the connection between Bill's behavior and its results, to obtain a sincere commitment from Bill to do better, and to plan a strategy more likely to be successful for Bill in the future (Charles, 1992). Ms. Thompson also

explains to Bill that he is the only one who can truly control his behavior. His behavior is his choice and under his control. In pointing this out to Bill, she is not losing control; she is only acknowledging something he already has. Such acknowledgment will only lead to validation of his self-worth and decrease the likelihood that the misbehavior will re-occur.

Since Ray and Bill control their own behavior but can be influenced by others, their parents may be involved to work as partners with the teacher and their child—but this would be a last resort. This is a very different perspective than the teacher-centered approach of calling the parent and charging them with "fixing" their child. No one can be "fixed" without their cooperation and input.

Summary & Conclusion

If learning is fostered by a student-centered environment, then quality instruction requires the creation of a "learning community" within the classroom. In such a community, students feel psychologically and intellectually safe to explore, to try, to make mistakes, and explore again. Their needs are acknowledged and validated. In order for such an environment to exist, all components of it must be addressed and in place.

As knowledge is dynamic and changing, so is society. If our schools are to be effective in the next century, we must respond to this evolution. "Simple" changes in curriculum and instruction techniques are not enough to create a student-centered environment; classroom management theory and models must also follow suit in order for a truly student-focused learning environment to exist. This is especially important when dealing with young adolescents who are in the midst of myriad developmental changes. As they seek to develop a clear sense of self, they may try on a number of personas. Student-focused classroom environments facilitate the development of a healthy identity and an internalized moral structure.

Both student- and teacher-centered approaches to classroom management can create orderly environments, provide structure, and set limits. Still, no matter how expedient, teacher-centered models do not address students' emotional needs or long-term concerns regarding self-discipline, responsibility, or critical reasoning. They do not touch the students' humanness. Teacher-centered, obedience models of classroom management many appear to allow us the opportunity to cover more material and teach more facts, but at what cost? The irony is that the more control we take the more control we loose. When the focus is on controlling others, there is little freedom left for us. Comprehensive student-focused classroom communities are necessary to develop independent, self-disciplined, life-long learners. Communities such as these only come about when both the instruction and the classroom management center on the students.

References

Aaronsohn, E. (1993, April). *Supporting student-centered teaching: Reconceptualizing the roles of teacher and teacher educator.* Paper presented at the annual meeting of the American Educational Research Association, Atlanta, GA.

Albert, L. (1989). *A teacher's guide to cooperative discipline: How to manage your classroom and promote self-esteem.* Circle Pines, MN: AGS.

Alexander, W. M. (1995). The junior high school: A changing view. *Middle School Journal, 26*(3), 21-24. (Reprinted from *Readings in Curriculum*, pp. 418-425, by G. Hass & K. Wiles, Eds., 1965, Boston: Allyn and Bacon)

Benshoff, J. M., Poidevant, J. M., & Cashwell, C. S. (1994). School discipline programs: Issues and implications for school counselors. *Elementary School Guidance and Counseling, 17*, 163-169.

Canter, L. (1992). *Assertive discipline: Positive behavior management for today's classroom.* Santa Monica, CA: Lee Canter & Associates.

Charles, C.M. (1992). *Building classroom discipline* (4th ed.). White Plains, NY: Longman.

Dinkmeyer, D., McKay, G. D., & Dinkmeyer, D. (1980). *STET: Systematic training for effective teaching.* Circle Pines, MN: AGS.

Dreikurs, R., Grunwald, B. B., & Pepper, F. C. (1982). *Maintaining sanity in the classroom* (2nd ed.). New York: Harper & Row.

Gathercoal, F. (1990). *Judicious discipline.* Davis, CA: Caddo Gap Press.

Ginott, H. (1972). *Teacher and child.* New York: Avon Books.

Glasser, W. (1986). *Control theory in the classroom.* New York: Harper & Row.

Gordon, T. (1974). *Teacher effectiveness training.* New York: Wyden.

Hill, D. (1990). Order in the classroom. *Teacher, 1*(7), 70-77.

Johnson, D.W., Johnson, R.T., Holubec, E.J., Roy, P. (1988). *Circles of learning: Cooperation in the classroom.* Reston, VA: Association for Supervision and Curriculum Development.

Jones, F. (1987). *Positive classroom discipline.* New York: McGraw-Hill.

Martin, N. K., & Baldwin, B. (1994, January). *Beliefs regarding classroom management style: Differences between novice and experienced teachers.* Paper presented at the annual meeting of the Southwest Educational Research Association, San Antonio, TX.

Mendler, A. N. (1993). Discipline with dignity in the classroom: Seven principles. In F. Schultz (Ed.), *Education 94/95.* (pp. 110-112). Guilford, CT: The Dushkin Publishing Group.

Prawat, R. S. (1992). From individual differences to learning communities: Our changing focus. *Educational Leadership, 49*(7), 9-13.

Santrock, J. W. (1987). *Adolescence* (4th ed.). Dubuque, IA: Wm. C. Brown Publishers.

Wilson, J. H. (1994). An open letter to middle level educators: A parent's concern. *Middle School Journal, 26*(1), 53.

How to Manage Disruptive Behavior in Inclusive Classrooms

Vera I. Daniels

Maintaining appropriate classroom behavior can be a complex and difficult task. This task becomes more stressful when it involves students with disabilities. When students with disabilities display disruptive behavior, classroom teachers must carefully and methodically think about the discipline strategies they might employ. Although the disruptive behavior some of these students exhibit is similar to that of students without disabilities, the discipline strategies used to correct or redirect disruptive behavior can vary considerably (see box, "Due Process").

This article provides classroom teachers in inclusion settings with suggestions for addressing behavioral infractions of students with disabilities. In using these strategies, teachers and other practitioners should develop skills in diagnostic, reflective thinking and in making choices among strategies.

The Same or Different Disciplinary Strategies?

Generally, classroom teachers can use the same disciplinary practices to manage the disruptive behavior of students with disabilities that they use to manage the behavior of students without disabilities. Much of the undesirable behavior exhibited by both groups is similar in nature. The differences, however, may originate in the teacher's selection of the particular behavioral intervention.

When selecting behavior interventions for students with disabilities, teachers should ensure that the strategies are developmentally appropriate and take into consideration the student's disability and due process rights. Here are 10 questions that may help you diagnostically analyze situations that foster disruptive behavior in students with disabilities. These discussions may provide guidance as you select behavior-reduction strategies.

Question 1. Could this misbehavior be a result of inappropriate curriculum or teaching strategies?

Inappropriate curriculum and teaching strategies can contribute to student misbehavior—but not all misbehavior is attributable to these factors. Some

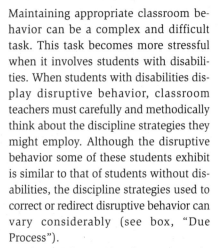

When you identify the instructional needs of students within the context of the classroom and make curricular adaptations both in content and instructional delivery, you can greatly reduce the occurrence of student misbehavior.

misbehavior may arise as a function of the teacher's inability to meet the diverse needs of all students. Consider these factors:

- Group size.
- Group composition.
- Limited planning time.
- Cultural and linguistic barriers.
- Lack of access to equipment, materials, and resources.

If the misbehavior evolves as a result of inappropriate curriculum or teaching strategies, redress the content and skill level components of your curriculum, its futuristic benefit for the student, and the formats you use in instructional delivery. When you identify the instructional needs of students within the context of the classroom, using a diagnostic prescriptive approach, and make curricular adaptations both in content and instructional delivery, you can greatly reduce the occurrence of student misbehavior.

Question 2. Could this misbehavior be a result of the student's inability to understand the concepts being taught?

When there is a mismatch between teaching style and the learning styles of students, misbehavior inevitably results. Incidents of misbehavior may also result when students refuse to learn concepts because they are unable to see the relationship between the skills being taught

Due Process in Discipline

In the movement toward inclusive classrooms (and inclusion schools), general education classrooms have included an increasing number of students with mild disabilities (e.g., emotional/behavioral disorders, learning disabilities, mild mental disabilities) (U.S. Department of Education, 1996). The guiding principle of this movement is the provision of equitable educational opportunities for all students, including those with severe disabilities, with needed supplementary aids and support services, in age-appropriate general education classes in their neighborhood schools (National Center on Educational Restructuring and Inclusion, 1994).

Educators, researchers, and policymakers are beginning to examine educational practices and outcomes for students both with and without disabilities in inclusion classrooms. Researchers and others are looking at four factors:

- The ability of classroom teachers to provide instruction to students with disabilities in general classroom settings.
- The academic, behavioral, and social outcomes for students with and without disabilities.
- Legal ramifications that may result from inappropriate instructional and management practices.
- Litigation and case law resulting from the use of disciplinary practices such as suspension, expulsion, and time-out.

The Individuals with Disabilities Education Act Amendments (IDEA, 1997, formerly known as the Education for All Handicapped Children Act, Public Law 94-142) encourages the inclusion of children with disabilities in the least restrictive environment (LRE) to the maximum extent appropriate with children who are not disabled. Specifically, this act states:

> Special classes, separate schooling or other removal of children with disabilities from the regular educational environment occurs only when the nature or severity of the disability of a child is such that education in regular classes with the use of supplementary aids and services cannot be achieved satisfactorily.

Although the procedural safeguards in IDEA historically provided the foundation for ensuring access to a free and appropriate public education for all children with disabilities in the LRE, these safeguards have not always been clear when it comes to the discipline of students with disabilities.

Much of the past controversy concerning the discipline of students with disabilities has focused on the use of *corporal punishment, suspension, expulsion, time out,* and case law resulting from the use of these procedures (Katsiyannis, 1995; Sorenson, 1990; Yell, 1990). The passage of the IDEA Amendments of 1997, however, should significantly lessen much of the future controversy and court litigation on disciplinary practices of students with disabilities. The due process procedures in the IDEA

- Retain the "stay-put" provision.
- Add clarification to the procedural safeguard provisions to facilitate conflict resolution.
- Describe how schools may discipline children with disabilities, including those who affect the school safety of peers, teachers, and themselves.
- Provide comprehensive guidelines on the matter of disciplining children with disabilities so that both educators and administrators will have a better understanding of their areas of discretion in disciplining student with disabilities.

Finally, in cases where the child's behavior is not a manifestation of the disability, IDEA permits a public agency to apply the same disciplinary procedures that would ordinarily apply to children without disabilities.

and how these skills transcend to the context of the larger environment.

In these situations, you should employ strategies and tactics that show students how component skills have meaning in the classroom and in the community. If you find that the cause of the inappropriate behavior is related to the student's lack of prerequisite skills or abilities to acquire concepts, you can use a simple procedure known as *task analysis.* By using this procedure, you can pinpoint specific functional levels of students on targeted skills and provide sequential instructional programs that will move the student with disabilities toward mastery of a targeted goal at a pace appropriate for the student (Moyer & Dardig, 1978).

Question 3. Could this misbehavior be an underlying result of the student's disability?

Some disruptive behavior may be a result of the student's disability (e.g., emotional/behavioral disorders). Meanwhile, other behavior may result from deliberate actions taken by the student to cause classroom disruption. Determining the underlying cause of a student's disruptive behavior involves a careful analysis of the behavior, as follows:

- Try to clarify what kinds of behavior are causing concern.
- Specify what is wrong with that behavior.
- Decide what action should be taken to address the behavior.
- Specify what behavior you desire from the student.
- Implement a plan to correct conditions, variables, or circumstances that contribute to the problem behavior (Charles, 1996).

You should analyze the disruptive behavior and render a professional judg-

---

*F*eedback (verbal and nonverbal) is an important factor in the learning paradigm that is too often neglected, overlooked, or haphazardly orated.

Teachers can pinpoint students' functional levels on targeted skills and provide sequential instructional programs that will move the student with disabilities toward mastery of a targeted goal at a pace appropriate for the student.

ment as to its cause. Redl and Wattenberg (cited in Charles, 1996) suggested that teachers employ a procedure of "diagnostic thinking" when faced with incidents of student misbehavior. These procedures include forming a first hunch, gathering facts, exploring hidden factors, taking action, and remaining flexible. While such a task is not easy, having a knowledge base of the general characteristics (e.g., academic, behavioral, social/emotional, learning, physical) of students with disabilities and the associated etiologies (causes) can be helpful.

Question 4. Could this misbehavior be a result of other factors?

Many aspects of classroom life may contribute to students' misbehavior: the physical arrangement of the classroom, boredom or frustration, transitional periods, lack of awareness of what is going on in every area of the classroom.

Remember, however, that classroom climate and physical arrangements can also *encourage* desirable behavior. You should regularly assess your teaching and learning environment for conditions or procedures that perpetuate or encourage misbehavior. Because inappropriate behavioral manifestations of students can also stem from certain types of teaching behavior, teachers need to become more cognizant of the kinds of behavior they emit and the relationship between their teaching behavior and the resultant behavior of students. Examine your instruction and interactions with students in ongoing classroom life, as follows:

- The development of relevant, interesting, and appropriate curriculums.
- The manner in which you give recognition and understanding of each student as an individual with his or her unique set of characteristics and needs.
- Your own behavior as a teacher, and characteristics such as those identified by Kounin (1970)—"withitness, overlapping"—that reduce misbehavior, increase instructional time, and maintain group focus and movement management of students.

Question 5. Are there causes of misbehavior that I can control?

As a teacher, you can control many variables to thwart undesirable behavior. You may modify or change your curriculum; make adaptations in instruction to address multiple intelligences; and make changes in your communication style, attitude toward students with disabilities, and expectations of these students.

Analyze how much positive feedback you give students. If you find that you use limited feedback (encouragement or praise), which accentuates positive behavior of students (and also communicates respect and promotes self-esteem and self-confidence), you may be contributing to behavior problems. Feedback (both verbal and nonverbal) is an important factor in the learning paradigm that is too often neglected, overlooked, or haphazardly orated.

Question 6. How do I determine if the misbehavior is classroom based?

This is a difficult question. Conducting a self-evaluation of teaching style and instructional practices—as in the previous questions—may provide some insight into whether the behavior is related to the disability or is classroom based.

You may find a classroom ecological inventory (Fuchs, Fernstrom, Scott, Fuchs, & Vandermeer, 1994) helpful in determining cause-effect relationships of student misbehavior. The classroom ecological inventory could help you assess salient features of the learning environment of your school or classroom. In such analysis, you can gather specific information about the student, the behavior, and the environmental conditions and

settings associated with the behavior (Evans, Evans, & Gable, 1989).

By taking into account the learning ecology, you can be more decisive and selective in your use of resources for managing student behavior and, at the same time, obtain a more accurate and complete picture of a particular student for developing a more appropriate and comprehensive behavior-change program. Classroom ecological inventories can be useful for collecting information about a wide range of events, variables, and conditions that can influence and affect a student's behavior.

Conducting a *functional analysis* or functional assessment can also be useful in examining cause-effect relationships of students' behavior. Functional assessments can also help you address serious problem behavior displayed by "target" students. These analyses examine the circumstances or functional relationships between, or surrounding, the occurrence or nonoccurrence of the challenging behavior. The assessments can help you identify variables and events that are consistently present in those situations (Dunlap et al., 1993; Foster-Johnson & Dunlap, 1993). You may identify events, variables, and circumstances that contribute to the problem. In addition, you may devise a comprehensive, individualized approach to designing interventions logically related to the target behavior—and, in the process, better meet the student's specific needs.

Question 7. How do I teach students to self-regulate or self-manage behavior?

You *can* teach students to self-regulate or self-manage their behavior by teaching them to use the skills of self-management:

- Self-instruction, self-recording, or self-monitoring.
- Self-reinforcement, self-evaluation, and self-punishment.
- Multiple-component treatment packages (Carter, 1993; Hughes, Ruhl, & Peterson, 1988; Rosenbaum & Drabman, 1979).

Many studies (e.g., McCarl, Svobodny, & Beare, 1991; Nelson, Smith, Young, & Dodd, 1991; Prater, Joy, Chilman, Temple, & Miller, 1991) focusing on self-management techniques have shown the effectiveness of self-management procedures in behavior change and academic productivity. These studies included students from many different populations, ranging from average achievers to students with mild, moderate, and severe disabilities.

Teachers have found many advantages in using self-monitoring procedures: These procedures improve target behavior, stress the student's role in behavior change, allow generalization to non-school environments, free teachers for other tasks, and teach students responsibility and self-determination (Frith & Armstrong, 1986). Furthermore, these procedures are relatively simple to implement; they quickly reach a point in which little supervision is required; and, they help students become more successful and independent in their classroom and in everyday life (Dunlap, Dunlap, Koegel, & Koegel, 1991). Of course, teaching students self-management skills should not be regarded as a substitute for a high-quality curriculum of instruction (Dunlap et al., 1991) that emphasizes academic and social learning skills. Here are some steps for teaching self-management skills:

- Defining the target behavior.
- Defining the desired behavior.
- Developing the data-collection system.
- Teaching the students how to use the self-management system.
- Implementing the system.
- Evaluating the effectiveness of the system (Carter, 1993).

Additional steps may include identifying functional reinforcers and fading

---

Before you discipline any student with disabilities, you should talk to administrative officials about the rules, policies, regulations, and procedural safeguards outlined in the IDEA Amendments of 1997.

---

use of the self-monitoring procedure (Dunlap et al., 1991).

Question 8. How do I determine what methods of control are appropriate without violating the rights of students with disabilities mandated under P.L. 105-17?

Determining which behavior-reduction methods to use with students with disabilities is not as difficult as you may think. As mentioned previously, the behavioral interventions typically used with students without disabilities can also be used with students with disabilities—with a few exceptions.

Yell and Shriner (1997) provided a comprehensive account of major issues effecting the discipline of students with disabilities addressed in Section 615 K of P.L. 105-17 (the IDEA Amendments of 1997):

- Disciplinary procedures.
- Behavior-intervention plans.
- Manifestation determination. "Manifestation determination" refers to a review process (conducted by the student's IEP team and other qualified personnel) to determine the relationship between a student's disability and misconduct. This review process is conducted when school officials seek a change of placement, suspension, or expulsion for more than 10 school days.
- Interim, alternative educational settings.
- The "stay put" provision.
- IDEA protection for students not yet eligible for special education.
- Referral to law enforcement and judicial authorities.

When applying behavior-reduction techniques, use a common sense approach and be reasonable in your application. Regardless of the behavioral infraction, before you discipline any student with disabilities, you should talk to administrative officials (e.g., principal, special education supervisors, school attorney) about the rules, policies, regulations, and procedural safeguards outlined in the IDEA Amendments of 1997 that govern the discipline of students with disabilities.

Positive Feedback

Madsen and Madsen (1983) emphasized the following ways that teachers can give positive feedback to students to encourage desirable behavior in the classroom:

- Words (spoken-written: *wonderful, excellent, absolutely right, fantastic, terrific, marvelous, splendid, all right, clever, thank you, that's good work, well thought out, that shows a great deal of work, I agree, keep working hard, you've improved*).
- Physical expressions (facial-bodily: smiling, nodding, signaling OK, thumbs up, shaking head).
- Closeness (nearness-touching: interacting with class at recess, sitting on desk near students, walking among students, patting shoulder, touching hand).
- Activities (individual-social: leading student groups, running errands, putting away materials, choosing activities, leading discussions, movies, playing records, visiting another class, making a game of subject matter, presenting skits).
- Things (materials, food, playthings, awards, e.g., games, book markers, stapler, bulletin board, puzzles, popcorn, ice cream, cookies, candy bars, medals, plaques, citations).

Question 9. How do I use reinforcement strategies to reduce disruptive behavior?

Teachers can use many types of reinforcers to teach desirable behavior. Madsen and Madsen (1983) identified five categories of responses available for teaching desired behavior: the use of words, physical expressions, physical closeness, activities, and things used as rewards or positive feedback (see box, "Positive Feedback").

Remember that the effectiveness of such reinforcers is contingent on continuous, systematic use across time. Also, consider the appropriateness of each response for your individual students.

Other reinforcement-based intervention strategies may also be effective: differential reinforcement of low rates of responding (DRL); differential reinforcement of other behavior(s) (DRO), also referred to as *differential reinforcement of zero responding;* differential reinforcement of incompatible behavior (DRI); and differential reinforcement of alternative behavior(s) (DRA). Many teachers have found such strategies effective in developing alternative response behavior to inappropriate, disruptive, or undesirable behavior.

Even though these procedural alternatives use a positive (reinforcement) approach to behavior reduction, teachers have found both advantages and disadvantages in the use of such procedures. In deciding whether to use differential reinforcement procedures, you should review the works of Alberto and Troutman (1995) and Schloss and Smith (1994).

Question 10. Is it appropriate for me to use punishment?

Punishment, the most controversial aversive behavior management procedure, has been used and abused with students with disabilities (Braaten, Simpson, Rosell, & Reilly, 1988). Because of its abuse, the use of punishment as a behavioral change procedure continues to raise a number of concerns regarding legal and ethical ramifications. Although punishment is effective in suppressing unacceptable behavior, it does have some limitations:

- The reduction in disruptive behavior may not be pervasive across all settings.
- The effect may not be persistent over an extended period of time.
- The learner may not acquire skills that replace the disruptive behavior (Schloss, 1987).

A decision regarding the use of punishment as a behavior reduction technique is an individual one. Some professionals suggest that punishment-based interventions should be eliminated, whereas others favor a variety of behavior-control procedures, including punishers (Braaten et al., 1988; Cuenin & Harris, 1986). Inasmuch as the use of

Classroom ecological inventories can be useful for collecting information about a wide range of events, variables, and conditions that can influence and affect a student's behavior.

punishers inhibit, reduce, or control the future occurrence of an unacceptable behavior, the effects of punishers are limited. By itself, punishment will not teach desirable behavior or reduce the desire of misbehavior (Larrivee, 1992).

Whereas the use of punishment remains a matter of individual choice, currently used punishers by classroom teachers include the following:

- Response cost.
- Time out.
- Overcorrection.
- Contingent exercise.
- Aversive conditioning (Braaten et al., 1988; Cuenin & Harris, 1986).

Questions such as whether, when, or if you might use punishment will always be tainted with controversy. Whatever decision you make, keep the following cautions in mind:

- Punishment should be used discriminately, rather than routinely.
- It should be combined with positive procedures.
- Punishment should be used only in response to repeated misbehavior for students who persist in the same kinds of misbehavior.
- It should be employed consciously and deliberately as a part of a planned response to repeated misbehavior.
- Punishment should be used only when students are not responsive to reward-based interventions or praise/ignore strategies (Larrivee, 1992).
- Punishment should be used only as a "treatment of last resort" (Larrivee), and only after you have taken appropriate steps to ensure that the due process rights of students will not be violated and that the procedures will

not cause psychological or emotional harm to the student.

Final Thoughts

There is no "one plan fits all" for determining how teachers should respond to the disruptive behavior of students with disabilities in inclusion settings. An initial starting point would include establishing classroom rules, defining classroom limits, setting expectations, clarifying responsibilities, and developing a meaningful and functional curriculum in which all students can receive learning experiences that can be differentiated, individualized, and integrated.

Many publications describe effective classroom-based disciplinary strategies (Carter, 1993; Schloss, 1987), but few (Ayres & Meyer, 1992; Carpenter & McKee-Higgins, 1996; Meyer & Henry, 1993; Murdick & Petch-Hogan, 1996) address effective classroom-based disciplinary strategies for students with disabilities in inclusion settings. Classroom teachers can use a variety of strategies to discipline students with disabilities in inclusion settings. The approaches most likely to be successful combine humanistic and cognitive behavioral attributes and take into consideration the teacher's diagnostic-reflective thinking and choice-making skills regarding the following:

- Student's behavior.
- Student's disability.
- Curriculum.
- Instructional program.
- Classroom environment.
- Due process rights.

In formulating a discipline plan, teachers must first clarify personal values in terms of acceptable and unacceptable classroom behavior. By setting classroom rules, defining limits, clarifying responsibilities, and developing a meaningful and functional curriculum, teachers can begin to build a system of discipline that will accentuate the positive behavior of all students.

Finally, classroom teachers should contact appropriate administrators and seek information on administrative policies, rules, and regulations governing disciplinary practices for students with disabilities.

*B*y setting classroom rules, defining limits, clarifying responsibilities, and developing a meaningful and functional curriculum, teachers can build a system of discipline that will accentuate the positive behavior of all students.

References

Alberto, P. A., & Troutman, A. C. (1995). *Applied behavior analysis for teachers*. (4th ed.). Englewood Cliffs, NJ: Prentice-Hall.*

Ayers, B., & Meyer, L. H. (1992). Helping teachers manage the inclusive classroom: Staff development and teaming star among management strategies. *The School Administrator, 49*(2), 30-37.

Braaten, S., Simpson, R., Rosell, J., & Reilly, T. (1988). Using punishment with exceptional children: A dilemma for educators. *TEACHING Exceptional Children, 20*(2), 79-81.

Carpenter, S. L., & McKee-Higgins, E. (1996). Behavior management in inclusive classrooms. *Remedial and Special Education, 17*(4), 195-203.

Carter, J. F. (1993). Self-management: Education's ultimate goal. *Teaching Exceptional Children, 25*(3), 28-32.

Charles, C. M. (1996). *Building classroom discipline* (5th ed.). New York: Longman.*

Cuenin, L. H., & Harris, K. R. (1986). Planning, implementing, and evaluating time-out interventions with exceptional students. *TEACHING Exceptional Children, 18*(4), 272-276.

Dunlap, L. K., Dunlap, G., Koegel, L. K., & Koegel, R. L. (1991). Using self-monitoring to increase independence. *TEACHING Exceptional Children, 23*(3), 17-22.

Dunlap, G., Kern, L., dePerczel, M., Clarke, S., Wilson, D., Childs, K. E., White, R., & Falk, G. D. (1993). Functional analysis of classroom variables for students with emotional and behavioral disorders. *Behavioral Disorders, 18*(4), 275-291.

Evans, S. S., Evans, W. H., & Gable, R. A. (1989). An ecological survey of student behavior. *TEACHING Exceptional Children, 21*(4), 12-15.

Frith, G. H., & Armstrong, S. W. (1986). Self-monitoring for behavior disordered students. *TEACHING Exceptional Children, 18*(2), 144-148.

Foster-Johnson, L., & Dunlap, G. (1993). Using functional assessment to develop effective individualized interventions for challenging behaviors. *TEACHING Exceptional Children, 25*(3), 44-50.

Fuchs, D., Fernstrom, P., Scott, S., Fuchs, L., & Vandermeer, L. (1994). Classroom ecological inventory: A process for mainstreaming. *TEACHING Exceptional Children, 26*(3), 11-15.

Hughes, C. A., Ruhl, K. L., & Peterson, S. K. (1988). Teaching self-management skills. *TEACHING Exceptional Children, 20*(2), 70-72.

Katsiyannis, A. (1995). Disciplining students with disabilities: What principals should know. *NASSP Bulletin, 79*(575), 92-96.

Kounin, J. S. (1970). *Discipline and group management in classrooms*. New York: Holt, Rinehart & Winston.*

Larrivee, B. (1992). *Strategies for effective classroom management: Creating a collaborative climate* (Leader's Guide to Facilitate Learning Experiences). Boston: Allyn & Bacon.*

Madsen, C. H., Jr., & Madsen C. K. (1983). *Teaching/discipline: A positive approach for educational development* (3rd ed.). Raleigh, NC: Contemporary Publishing Company.*

McCarl, J. J., Svobodny, L., & Beare, P. L. (1991). Self-recording in a classroom for students with mild to moderate mental handicaps: Effects on productivity and on-task behavior. *Education and Training in Mental Retardation, 26*(1), 79-88.

Meyer, L. H., & Henry, L. A. (1993). Cooperative classroom management: Student needs and fairness in the regular classroom. In J. Putnam (Ed.), *Cooperative learning and strategies for inclusion: Celebrating diversity in the classroom* (pp. 93-121). Baltimore: Paul H. Brookes.*

Moyer, J. R., & Dardig, J. C. (1978). Practical task analysis for special educators. *Teaching Exceptional Children, 11*(1), 16-18.

Murdick, N. L., & Petch-Hogan, B. (1996). Inclusive classroom management: Using preintervention strategies, *Intervention in School and Clinic, 13*(3), 172-196.

National Center on Educational Restructuring and Inclusion. (1994). *National study of inclusive education*. New York: Author. (ERIC Document Reproduction Service No. ED 375 606)

Nelson, J. R., Smith, D. J., Young, R. K., & Dodd, J. M. (1991). A review of self-management outcome research conducted with students who exhibit behavioral disorders. *Behavioral Disorders, 16*(13), 169-179.

Prater, M. E., Joy, R., Chilman, B., Temple, J., & Miller, S. R. (1991). Self-monitoring of on-task behavior by adolescents with learning disabilities. *Learning Disability Quarterly, 14*(13), 164-177.

Rosenbaum, M. S., & Drabman, R. S. (1979). Self-control training in the classroom: A review and critique. *Journal of Applied Behavior Analysis, 12*(3), 467-485.

Schloss, P. J. (1987). Self-management strategies for adolescents entering the work force. *TEACHING Exceptional Children, 19*(4), 39-43.*

Schloss, P. J., & Smith, M. A. (1994). *Applied behavior analysis in the classroom*. Boston: Allyn & Bacon.

Sorenson, G. P. (1990). Special education discipline in the 1990s. *West's Educational Law Reporter, 62*(2), 387-398.

U.S. Department of Education. (1996). *18th annual report to Congress on the implementation of the Individuals with Disabilities Education Act*. Washington, DC: Office of Special Education. (ERIC Document Reproduction Service No. ED 400 673)

Yell, M. L. (1990). The use of corporal punishment, suspension, expulsion, and time-out with behaviorally disordered students in public schools: Legal considerations. *Behavioral Disorders, 15*(2), 100-109.

Yell, M. L., & Shriner, J. G. (1997). The IDEA Amendments of 1997: Implications for special and general education teachers, administrators, and teacher trainers. *Focus on Exceptional Children, 30*(1), 1-19.

*Books*Now

To order books marked by an asterisk (*), please call 24 hrs/365 days: 1-800-BOOKS-NOW (266-5766) or (702) 258-3338; ask for ext. 1212 or visit them on the web at http://www.BooksNow.com/TeachingExceptional.htm. Use Visa, M/C, or AMEX or send check or money order + $4.95 S&H ($2.50 each add'l item) to: Books Now, 660 W. Charleston Blvd., Las Vegas, NV 89102.

Vera I. Daniels *(CEC Chapter #386), Professor, Institute for the Study and Rehabilitation of Exceptional Children and Youth, and Department of Special Education, Southern University and A & M College, Baton Rouge, Louisiana.*

Address correspondence to the author at P.O. Box 9523, Baton Rouge, LA 70813 (e-mail: vdaniels@premier.net).

Special thanks is extended to the teacher and students appearing in the photographs and to the school principal.

How to Defuse

CONFRONTATIONS

DEFIANCE THREATS CHALLENGES

The T-shirt attention getter...
Prohibited cookies on the bus...
Profanity in class...
Outright refusal to do classwork...
Chair-throwing...

A comprehensive system of behavior management has three critical components: prevention, defusion, and follow-up.

Geoff Colvin
David Ainge
Ron Nelson
■

Do some of your students engage in confrontational behavior like this? Here's a litany of such behavior: attention-getting, defiance, challenges, disrespect, limit testing, verbal abuse, blatant rule violations, threats, and intimidation. Some students test the patience of teachers who have what they thought was an effective behavior-management system. This article presents teacher-tested ways to *defuse* such behavior and allow the students to learn and participate in positive ways.

Special education teachers have always had the task of managing students who display seriously disturbing behavior. More recently, these teachers are expected to provide support and consultation to general education teachers who need assistance on managing the behavior of all students in inclusive classrooms. Special education teachers can assist other educators in a comprehensive system of behavior management composed of three critical components: prevention, defusion, and follow-up (see box, "Three Approaches to Behavior Management").

We focus here particularly on *defusion*, an approach that is helpful with students who are continually confrontational. Such behavior not only leads to class disruption, but also can readily escalate to more serious behavior—and threats to the safety of both staff and stu-dents. Let's look at some examples of confrontational behavior and then explore how we can deal with it.

Three Confrontational Students

● Joe steps onto the school bus holding a monster cookie in his hand. Above his head is a large sign that reads, "No food on the bus." Joe looks at the driver, takes a huge bite of the cookie, and takes another step on the bus. The bus driver points to the sign and says quite emphatically, "Look, no food on the bus. You'll have to give me that cookie." Joe says equally emphatically, "No," and takes another bite. The driver looks him right in the eye and says, "If you don't give me the cookie, you will not ride the bus." Joe says, "So," takes another bite of the cookie, and begins to move toward his seat. The driver calls transportation to have the student removed from the bus.

● Sarah walks into the classroom wearing a T-shirt displaying a toilet bowl with an arrow coming up out of the bowl and a written statement underneath, "Up your AZ." Some students giggle, and another asks, "Where did you get that?" The teacher comes over and says, "Sarah, that shirt is not acceptable in a public school. You had better go to the restroom and turn it inside out." Sarah looks at the teacher and says, "I'm not gonna do that. My dad gave it to me and you can't make me turn it inside out." The teacher says that if she does not cooperate, she will be sent to the office. Sarah throws her book down and heads to the back of the room.

- Jamie is sitting at his desk, arms folded, shoulders rounded, feet firmly planted on the floor, and staring at the floor with a scowl on his face, while the rest of the class is working on an independent math assignment. The teacher eventually approaches Jamie and prompts him to start on his math. He scowls and says in a harsh tone that he can't do it. So the teacher offers to help him. He says he still can't do it. The teacher provides more detail with the explanation and directs him to make a start. He says he hates math. The teacher tells him that he needs to start or he will have to do his math during the break. He utters a profanity and storms out of the room.

What Happened?

In each case, the supervising staff person reacts to a problem behavior in a direct manner. There is a high likelihood that the student *expects* a response. In fact, the student not only expects a response, but he or she expects a *particular* response.

For all practical purposes, the staff person is *already set up for confrontation*. In other words, the student displays engaging behavior that is highly likely to elicit a predictable response from staff that includes a clear direction. The student refuses to follow the direction, which engages staff further, leading to ultimatums and additional problem behavior.

Moreover, if the staff person becomes confrontational at this point, there is a strong likelihood that the student will react with more serious behavior. In effect, we can see a pattern—a cycle—of successive interactions beginning with problem behavior leading to more serious behavior, such as throwing a book (Sarah), continuing to disregard requests (Joe), or profanity (Jamie). These vignettes have five common features:

1. The student displays defiant, challenging, or inappropriate behavior.

2. The supervising staff person reacts to the problem behavior and provides a direction in opposition to the student's behavior.

3. The student challenges the direction by not complying and by displaying other inappropriate behavior.

4. The staff person reacts to the noncompliance and presents an ultimatum.

5. The student takes up the challenge of the ultimatum with further defiance and exhibits hostile and explosive behavior.

What Strategies Can Help?

When students exhibit confrontational behavior, you need approaches that are likely to defuse the problem behavior, rather than lead to more serious behavior. Defusing strategies minimize the likelihood that interactions between you and the student will escalate the confrontation. We have found five defusing strategies that work—in order of least intrusive student behavior to more serious confrontational behavior. These strategies range from ignoring the behavior to delaying a response and allowing the student to calm down.

Focus on the Task to Defuse Minor Attention-Getting Behavior

Students often display minor problem behavior to secure attention: talking out in class, moving out of their seats, starting work slowly, and pencil tapping. Once you respond to such behavior, the student may exhibit more attention-getting behavior. The basic approach for managing this level of problem behavior is to use a *continuum* of steps based on the level of attention you provide:

- Attend to the students exhibiting expected behavior, and ignore the students displaying the problem behavior.

- Redirect the student to the task at hand. Do not respond to or draw attention to the problem behavior.

- Present a choice between the expected behavior and a small negative consequence (such as a loss of privilege).

For example, Michael is out of his seat wandering around the room while other students are seated and engaged in a class activity. The teacher moves among the students who are on task, acknowledges their good work and ignores Michael. Michael continues to move around the class. The teacher approaches him and says privately, "Michael, listen, it's math time. Let's go." and points to his seat. Michael still does not return to his seat. The teacher secures his attention and says calmly and firmly, "Michael, you have been asked to sit down and start work or you will have to do the work in recess. You decide." The teacher follows through on whatever Michael chooses to do.

Present Options Privately in the Context of a Rule Violation

Sometimes students will break a rule to challenge you. They know you will react and give a direction. The student will then refuse to follow the direction. In this way, a confrontation scene is established. For example, in the cases of Joe and Sarah, the staff member gave the students a direction that the students refused to follow—the cookie was not turned in to the driver, the T-shirt was not turned inside out. Here are steps to follow in such cases:

- State the rule or expectation.

- Request explicitly for the student to "take care of the problem."

- Present options for the student on how to take care of the problem.

In this way, you lessen the chance of confrontation when you present options and focus how the student might decide to take care of the problem, rather than whether the student follows a specific direction.

For example, the bus driver might have quietly said something like this to Joe: "Look, there is no food on the bus, thank you. You had better take care of that. You can eat it before you get on or leave it here and collect it later." Note the options the bus driver might have provided.

Or, to deal with Sarah's offensive T-shirt, the teacher might take Sarah aside and say, "Sarah, that shirt is not OK in a public school. It has a rude message. You can turn it inside out, get a shirt from the gym, or wear a jacket."

Reduce Agitation in a Demand Situation

Sometimes students are already agitated when they enter a situation. When you or other people place demands on them, their behavior will likely escalate.

For example, Jamie's body posture and tone of voice suggest he is upset.

First, communicate concern to the student. Then allow the student time and space. Give the student some choices or options.

When the teacher tries to prompt him to work, even in a very reasonable manner, his behavior escalates to storming out of the room. Here, the teacher might have used agitation-reduction techniques.

Signs of Agitation. Students show agitation by either increasing distracting behavior or decreasing active, engaged behavior (Colvin, 1992). Here are common signs of increases in *distracting behavior*:

- Darting eyes
- Nonconversational language
- Busy hands
- Moving in and out of groups
- Frequent off-task and on-task behavior
- Starting and stopping activities
- Moving around the room

Paradoxically, sometimes agitation doesn't seem to live up to its name. Some students can be agitated and not show it. Watch for the following *decreases in behavior* and a lack of engagement in class activities:

- Staring into space
- Subdued language
- Contained hands
- Lack of interaction and involvement in activities
- Withdrawal from groups and activities
- Lack of responding in general
- Avoidance of eye contact

Techniques for Reducing Agitation. Once you recognize that the student's behavior is agitated, your primary goal is to use strategies to calm the student down and assist him or her to become engaged

in the present classroom activity. Because these strategies are supportive in nature, you need to use them *before* the behavior becomes serious; otherwise, you risk reinforcing the seemingly endless chain of inappropriate behavior. The critical issue is *timing*. Use the following techniques at the *earliest* indications of agitation:

Teacher support: Communicate concern to the student.

Space: Provide the student with an opportunity to have some isolation from the rest of the class.

Choices: Give the student some choices or options.

Preferred activities: Allow the student to engage in a preferred activity for a short period of time to help regain focus.

Teacher proximity: Move near or stand near the student.

Independent activities: Engage the student in independent activities to provide isolation.

Movement activities: Use activities and tasks that require movement, such as errands, cleaning the chalkboard, and distributing papers.

Involvement of the student: Where possible, involve the student in the plan. In this way, there is more chance of ownership and generalization to other settings.

Relaxation activities: Use audiotapes, drawing activities, breathing and relaxation techniques.

Now let's replay Jamie's situation. This time, the teacher determines that Jamie seems to be agitated—he shows a *decrease* in behavior. The teacher says, as privately as possible, "Jamie, it's time for math. Are you doing OK? Do you need some time before you start?" In this way, the teacher is recognizing the agitation, communicating concern to Jamie, and giving him time to regain his focus.

Preteach and Present Choices to Establish Limits and Defuse Noncompliance

Use this strategy to establish limits and to defuse sustained noncompliance. Essentially, the student is refusing to follow the teacher's directions.

For example, suppose that Scott has been off task and distracting other students for several minutes. The teacher has tried to provide assistance, redirect

Three Approaches to Behavior Management

Prevention. The teacher places a strong focus on teaching desirable behavior and orchestrating effective learning activities. These proactive strategies are designed to establish a positive classroom structure and climate for students to engage in productive, prosocial behavior.

Defusion. Teachers use strategies designed to address problem behavior after the behavior has commenced. The goal here is to arrest the behavior before it escalates to more serious behavior and to assist the student to resume class activities in an appropriate manner.

Follow-up. A teacher or an administrator may provide consequences for the problem behavior and endeavors to assist the student to terminate the problem behavior and to engage in appropriate behavior in the future.

The goal of these approaches is to provide information to the student on the limits of behavior and to use problem-solving strategies to enable the student to exhibit alternative appropriate behavior in subsequent events (Biggs & Moore, 1993; Colvin & Lazar, 1997; Kameenui & Darch, 1995; Myers & Myers, 1993; Sprick, Sprick & Garrison, 1993; Sugai & Tindal, 1993; Walker, Colvin, & Ramsey, 1995).

him, and give a formal direction to begin work. Scott refuses to cooperate. At this point, the teacher wants to communicate to him that "enough is enough," and to establish some classroom limits. When the teacher tries to establish limits, however, Scott may become more hostile and aggressive.

The following steps in the preteaching strategy can establish limits without escalating the behavior. Role-playing

*T*he most important thing to remember is that your responses can change things.

these steps can help students learn how to use self-control.

Preteach the procedures: Carefully rehearse the procedures with the student, give explanations, model the steps, and describe the consequences. Do preteaching at a neutral time when the student is relatively calm and cooperative.

Deliver the information to the students without being confrontational:

1. Present the expected behavior and the negative consequence as a decision; place responsibility on the student.

2. Allow a few seconds for the student to decide. This small amount of time helps the student calm down, enables face saving in front of peers, enables you to pull away from the conflict, and leaves the student with the decision.

3. Withdraw from the student and attend to other students. You thus help the student focus on the decision, not attend to you.

Follow through: If the student chooses the expected behavior, briefly acknowledge the choice and continue with the lesson or activity. If the student has not chosen the expected behavior, deliver the negative consequence. Debrief with the student and problem solve.

For example, if Sarah refused to take care of the T-shirt problem, the teacher could say. "Sarah, you have been asked to take care of the shirt (expected behavior), or I will have to make an office referral (negative consequence). You have a few seconds to decide." The teacher moves away from Sarah and addresses some other students or tasks. The teacher follows through on the choice made by the student.

Disengage and Delay Responding in the Presence of Serious Threatening Behavior

Students may escalate to a point of serious confrontational behavior involving threats or intimidation. For example, the teacher may have presented options, given the student time, and provided a consequence: "Eric, you are asked to start work or you will have to stay after school. You have a few seconds to decide." Eric walks over to the teacher and says, "I know where you live."

Suppose a more serious situation occurs, such as this real incident: An administrator told a student to go to the in-school suspension area or he would call his probation officer. The student picked up a cup of coffee from the secretary's desk, moved to the administrator, held the coffee in his face, and said, "You call my P.O. and I will throw this in your f_____ face."

In each of these cases, there is a direct threat to a staff member and the danger that the student's behavior may escalate. Whether the student's behavior becomes more serious *depends on the staff member's initial response to the threat*. The primary intent of this strategy is to avoid responding directly to the student's behavior and to disengage momentarily and then to redirect the student.

We are *not* suggesting that this strategy is all you need to do. Rather, the primary purpose of this strategy is to defuse a crisis situation. Once the crisis has been avoided, you should follow up and address the previous threatening behavior so that such behavior does not arise again. Here are steps to use in disengaging and delaying:

Break the cycle of successive interactions by delaying responding: This pattern consists of successive hostile or inflammatory interactions between you and the student—the student challenges you to respond. The first step is to *delay responding*, because the student is expecting an immediate response. To delay responding, very briefly look at the student, look at the floor, look detached, and pause.

Prevent explosive behavior by making a disengaging response: Do not leave the student waiting too long; otherwise, an "extinction burst" may occur. That is, if events do not go the way the student expects them to, he or she may exhibit explosive behavior, such as throwing a chair at the wall (or staff, or another student), or throwing the coffee cup. To prevent this burst, disengage swiftly and engage in something neutral or unrelated (Lerman & Iwata, 1995). For example, say to the student, "Just a minute," and move and pick up something on your desk.

Return to the student, redirect, and withdraw: If the student has not exhibited further problem behavior and is waiting, simply return to the student and present the original choice.

For example, approach the student and say, "You still have a moment or two to decide what you wish to do," and withdraw. If the student engages in more serious behavior, implement emergency procedures and policies established by the school or district.

Follow through: If the student chooses the expected behavior, acknowledge the choice briefly and debrief later. If the student does not choose the expected behavior, deliver consequences and debrief later.

Debrief: The debriefing activity is designed to help the student problem solve by reviewing the incident and events leading up to the incident, identifying the triggers, and examining alternatives. The debriefing finishes with a focus or agreement on what the student will try to do next time that would be an appropriate response to the situation (Sugai & Colvin, in press).

Now Let's Debrief

How many Sarahs and Jamies and Erics do you know? Are you tired of throwing up your hands and sending these stu-

*D*efusing strategies minimizes the likelihood that interactions between you and the student will escalate the confrontation.

Sometimes students will break a rule to challenge you; others are already agitated when you try to correct them.

dents to the office, or facing hostility and muttered challenges—or even threats to your own safety? Are you equally concerned that these students (and other students in your class) may be missing out on learning opportunities?

The most important thing to remember is that *your responses can change things*. Go back to the section on "Disengage and Delay Responding" and memorize it. Then follow the steps in "Preteaching," and you are on your way to helping students control their own be-

havior and create a better environment for learning.

References

Biggs, J. B., & Moore, P. J. (1993). *The process of learning.* New York: Prentice Hall.

Colvin, G. (1992). *Video program: Managing acting-out behavior.* Eugene, OR: Behavior Associates.

Colvin, G., & Lazar, M. (1997). *The effective elementary classroom: Managing for success.* Longmont, CO: Sopris West.

Kameenui, E. J., & Darch, C. B. (1995). *Instructional classroom management: A proactive approach to behavior management.* White Plains, NY: Longman.

Lerman, D., & Iwata, B. (1995). Prevalence of the extinction burst and its attenuation during treatment. *Journal of Applied Behavior Analysis, 28*, 93-94.

Myers, C. B., & Myers, L. K. (1993). *An introduction to teaching and schools.* Fort Worth, TX: Rinehart and Winston.

Sprick, R., Sprick, M., & Garrison, M. (1993). *Interventions: Collaborative planning for students at risk.* Longmont, CO: Sopris West.

Sugai, G., & Colvin, G. (in press). Debriefing: A proactive addition to negative consequences for problem behavior. *Education and Treatment of Children.*

Sugai, G., & Tindal, G. (1993). *Effective school consultation: An interactive approach.* Pacific Grove, CA: Brooks/Cole.

Walker, H., Colvin, G., & Ramsey, E. (1995). *Antisocial behavior in school: Strategies and best practices.* Pacific Grove, CA: Brooks/Cole.

Geoff Colvin (Oregon Federation), *Research Associate, Special Education and Community Resources, University of Oregon, Eugene.* **David Ainge,** *Senior Lecturer, Special Education Department, James Cook University, Queensland, Australia.* **Ron Nelson** (CEC Chapter #374), *Associate Professor, Applied Psychology Department, Eastern Washington University, Spokane.*

Address correspondence to Geoff Colvin, Special Education and Community Resources, University of Oregon, Eugene, OR 97405 (e-mail: geoff_colvin@ccmail.uoregon.edu).

Why Violence Prevention Programs Don't Work—and What Does

David W. Johnson and Roger T. Johnson

David W. Johnson is Professor of Educational Psychology, and **Roger T. Johnson** is Professor of Curriculum and Instruction, University of Minnesota, Cooperative Learning Center, 202 Pattee Hall, 150 Pillsbury Drive, S.E., Minneapolis, MN 55455-0298.

The best school programs in conflict resolution tend to follow six key principles.

"Joshua was chasing Octavia. He pushed her down, and she kicked him."

"Danielle is going to beat up Amber after school. They were spitting in each other's faces and calling each other names."

"Tom shoved Cameron up against the lockers and threatened him. Cameron said he's going to bring a knife to school tomorrow to get even."

Schools are filled with conflicts. The frequency of clashes among students and the increasing severity of the ensuing violence make managing such incidents very costly in terms of time lost to instructional, administrative, and learning efforts.

If schools are to be orderly and peaceful places in which high-quality education can take place, students must learn to manage conflicts constructively without physical or verbal violence. The following six principles may be helpful to schools that are trying to accomplish this goal.

1. Go beyond violence prevention to conflict resolution training.

To curb violence among students, many schools have implemented violence prevention programs. Some schools focus on anger management and general social skills. Others invite guest speakers (for example, police officers) to school, employ metal detectors, or ask police to patrol the school. Still others show videotapes of violent encounters and structure discussions around how fights start and alternative ways to manage aggression.

The proliferation of such programs raises the question: Do they work? In a review of three popular violence prevention curriculums—Violence Prevention Curriculum for Adolescents, Washington [D.C.] Community Violence Prevention Program, and Positive Adolescent Choices Training—Webster (1993) found no evidence that they produce long-term changes in violent behavior or decrease the risk of victimization. The main function of such programs, Webster argues, is to provide political cover for school officials and politicians.

In their survey of 51 violence prevention programs, Wilson-Brewer and colleagues (1991) found that fewer than half of the programs even claimed to have reduced levels of violence, and few had any data to back up their claims. Tolan and Guerra (in press), after reviewing the existing research on violence prevention, concluded that (1) many schools are engaged in well-intentioned efforts without any evidence that the programs will work, and (2) some programs actually influence relatively nonviolent students to be more violence-prone.

Why don't violence prevention programs work? Here are a few possible reasons.

1. Many programs are poorly targeted. First, they lump together a broad range of violent behaviors and people, ignoring the fact that different people turn to violence for different reasons. Second, few programs focus on the relatively small group of children and adolescents who commit most of the acts of serious violence. In our studies of a peer mediation program in inner-city schools, for example, we found that less than 5 percent of students accounted for more than one-third of the violent incidents in the school (Johnson and Johnson 1994a).

2. The programs provide materials

Few violence prevention programs focus on the relatively small group of children and adolescents who commit most of the acts of serious violence.

but don't focus on program implementation. Many programs assume that (a) a few hours of an educational intervention can "fix" students who engage in violent behavior, (b) a few hours of training can prepare teachers to conduct the program, and (c) no follow-up is needed to maintain the quality of the program. In other words, the programs ignore the literature on successful innovation within schools (Johnson and Johnson, in press) and, therefore, are often poorly implemented.

3. Proponents of violence prevention programs confuse methods that work in neighborhoods with those that work in schools. Conflicts on the street often involve macho posturing, competition for status, access to drugs, significant amounts of money, and individuals who have short-term interactions with one another. The school, on the other hand, is a cooperative setting in which conflicts involve working together, sharing resources, making decisions, and solving problems among students who are in long-term relationships. Different conflict resolution procedures are required in each setting. Street tactics should not be brought into the school, and it is naive and dangerous to assume that school tactics should be used on the street.

4. Many programs are unrealistic about the strength of the social forces that impel children toward violence. To change the social norms controlling street behavior requires a broad-based effort that involves families, neighbors, the mass media, employers, health care officials, schools, and government. Schools do not have the resources to guarantee health care, housing, food, parental love, and hope for the future for each child. Educators cannot eliminate the availability of guns (especially semi-automatic handguns), change the economics of the

drug trade (and other types of crime), or even reduce the dangers of walking to and from school. Because there is a limit to what schools can do in reducing violence among children and adolescents outside of school, violence prevention programs should be realistic and not promise too much.

Initiating a violence prevention program will not reduce the frequency of violence in schools and in society as a whole. While violence does need to be prevented, programs that focus exclusively on violence prevention may generally be ineffective. Schools must go beyond violence prevention to conflict resolution training.

2. Don't attempt to eliminate all conflicts.

The elimination of violence does not mean the elimination of conflict. Some conflicts can have positive outcomes (Johnson and Johnson 1991, 1992). They can increase achievement, motivation to learn, higher-level reasoning, long-term retention, healthy social and cognitive development, and the fun students have in school. Conflicts can also enrich relationships, clarify personal identity, increase ego strength, promote resilience in the face of adversity, and clarify how one needs to change.

It is not the presence of conflict that is to be feared but, rather, its destructive management. Attempts to deny, suppress, repress, and ignore conflicts may, in fact, be a major contributor to the occurrence of violence in schools. Given the many positive outcomes of conflict, schools need to teach students how to manage conflicts constructively.

3. Create a cooperative context.

The best conflict resolution programs seek to do more than change individual students. Instead, they try to transform

the total school environment into a learning community in which students live by a credo of nonviolence.

Two contexts for conflict are possible: cooperative and competitive (Deutsch 1973, Johnson and Johnson 1989). In a competitive context, individuals strive to win while ensuring their opponents lose. Those few who perform the best receive the rewards. In this context, competitors often misperceive one another's positions and motivations, avoid communicating with one another, are suspicious of one another, and see the situation from only their own perspective.

In a cooperative context, conflicts tend to be resolved constructively. Students have clear perceptions of one another's positions and motivation, communicate accurately and completely, trust one another, and define conflicts as mutual problems to be solved. Cooperators typically have a long-term time orientation and focus their energies both on achieving mutual goals and on maintaining good working relationships with others.

Students cannot learn to manage conflicts constructively when their school experience is competitive and individualistic. In such a context, constructive conflict resolution procedures are often ineffective and, in fact, may make the students who use them vulnerable to exploitation. Instead, schools should seek to create a cooperative context for conflict management, which is easier to do when the majority of learning situations are cooperative (Johnson and Johnson 1989, Johnson et al. 1993).

4. Decrease in-school risk factors.

Three factors place children and adolescents at risk for violent behavior. The first is academic failure. One way that schools can promote higher achievement and greater competence in using higher-level reasoning by students is to emphasize cooperative learning more than competitive or individualistic learning (Johnson and Johnson 1989). The more students know and the greater their ability to analyze situations and think through decisions, the better able

Conflict resolution programs present in school are either cadre, where a small number of students are trained to serve as peer mediators, or total school body programs, where every student learns how to manage conflicts.

they will be to envision the consequences of their actions, respect differing viewpoints, conceive of a variety of strategies for dealing with conflict, and engage in creative problem solving.

A second factor that puts children and adolescents at risk for violent and destructive behavior is alienation from schoolmates. In order to create an infrastructure of personal and academic support, schools need to encourage long-term caring and committed relationships. Two procedures for doing so are (1) using cooperative base groups that last for a number of years (Johnson et al. 1992, 1993); and (2) assigning teams of teachers to follow cohorts of students through several grades, instead of changing teachers every year (Johnson and Johnson 1994a).

Third, children and adolescents who have high levels of psychological pathology are more at risk for violent and destructive behavior than students who are psychologically well adjusted. David Hamburg, the president of Carnegie Corporation, states that reversing the trend of violence among the young depends on teaching children how to share, work cooperatively with others, and help others. The more children and adolescents work in cooperative learning groups, the greater will be their psychological health, self-esteem, social competencies, and resilience in the face of adversity and stress (Johnson and Johnson 1989).

In summary, schools must not overlook the in-school factors that place students at risk for engaging in violence and other destructive ways of managing conflicts. Anything that allows students to fail, remain apart from classmates, and be socially inept and have low self-esteem, increases the probability that students will use destructive conflict strategies.

5. Use academic controversy to increase learning.

To show students that conflicts can have positive results, schools should make academic controversies an inherent and daily part of learning situations. It is unclear whether cognitive, social, and moral development can take place in the absence of conflict. Academic *controversy* exists when one student's ideas, information, conclusions, theories, and opinions are incompatible with those of another, and the two seek to reach an agreement (Johnson and Johnson 1992).

For example, teachers can assign students to cooperative learning groups of four, divided into two pairs. One pair is assigned a pro position on an issue and the other pair, the con position. Each pair prepares a persuasive presentation (consisting of a thesis statement, rationale, and conclusion) to convince the other side of the position's validity. The two pairs then meet, and each side presents the best case possible for its position. Afterward, during an open discussion,

students refute the opposing position (by discrediting the information and/or the inductive and deductive logic used) while rebutting criticisms of their position. At the same time, they try to persuade the other pair to change their minds. Next, a perspective reversal occurs in which each pair presents the best case possible for the opposing position. Finally, after trying to view the issue from both perspectives simultaneously, the students drop all advocacy and come to a consensus about their "best reasoned judgment" based on a synthesis of the two positions.

Over the past 25 years, we have conducted numerous studies on academic controversy. Similar to cooperative learning, academic controversy results in increased student achievement, critical thinking, higher-level reasoning, intrinsic motivation to learn, perspective-taking, and a number of other important educational outcomes (Johnson and Johnson 1979, 1992).

6. Teach all students how to resolve conflicts constructively.

Most of the diverse conflict resolution programs present in schools are either cadre or total student body programs. In the *cadre approach,* a small number of students are trained to serve as peer mediators for the entire school. While this approach is relatively easy and inexpensive to implement, having a few peer mediators with limited training is not likely to decrease the severity and frequency of conflicts in a school.

In the *total student body approach,* every student learns how to manage conflicts constructively by negotiating agreements and mediating their schoolmates' conflicts. The responsibility for peer mediation is rotated throughout the entire student body (or class) so that every student gains experience as a mediator. A disadvantage of this approach is the time and commitment required by the faculty. The more students who are trained how to negotiate and mediate, however, the greater the number of conflicts that will be managed constructively in the school.

An example of the total student body approach is the *Teaching Students to Be Peacemakers Program,* which we have implemented in several countries (Johnson and Johnson 1991). We conceive the training as a 12-year spiral curriculum in which each year students learn increasingly sophisticated negotiation and mediation procedures.

Until recently, very little research validating the effectiveness of conflict resolution training programs in schools has existed. Over the past five years, we have conducted seven studies in six different schools in both suburban and urban settings and in two different countries (Johnson and Johnson 1994b). Students in 1st through 9th grades were involved in

represents a model of how to integrate conflict resolution training into an academic class.

After their training, students generally managed their conflicts without involving adults. The frequency of student-student conflicts teachers had to manage dropped 80 percent, and the number of conflicts referred to the principal was reduced by 95 percent. Such a dramatic reduction of referrals of conflicts to adults changed the school discipline program from arbitrating conflicts to maintaining and supporting the peer mediation process.

Knowing how to negotiate agreements and mediate schoolmates' conflicts empowers students to regulate their own behavior. Self-regulation is a central and significant hallmark of cognitive and social development. Using competencies in resolving conflicts constructively also increases a child's ability to build and maintain high-quality relationships with peers and to cope with stress and adversity.

In short, training only a small cadre of students to manage conflicts constructively and to be peer mediators will not change the way other students manage their conflicts. For this reason, schools must teach all students skills in negotiation and mediation.

Teaching every student how to negotiate and mediate will ensure that future generations are prepared to manage conflicts constructively in career, family, community, national, and international settings.

The negotiation procedure consists of six steps. Students in conflict: (1) define what they want, (2) describe their feelings, and (3) explain the reasons underlying those wants and feelings. Then the students: (4) reverse perspectives in order to view the conflict from both sides, (5) generate at least three optional agreements with maximum benefits for both parties, and (6) agree on the wisest course of action.

The mediation procedure consists of four steps: (1) stop the hostilities, (2) ensure that the disputants are committed to the mediation process, (3) facilitate negotiations between the disputants, and (4) formalize the agreement.

Once the students complete negotiation and mediation training, the school (or teacher) implements the Peacemakers Program by selecting two students as mediators each day. It is the actual experience of being a mediator that best teaches students how to negotiate and resolve conflicts. In addition to using the procedures, students receive additional training twice a week for the rest of the school year to expand and refine their skills.

the studies. We found that before training, most students had daily conflicts, used destructive strategies that tended to escalate the conflict, referred the majority of their conflicts to the teacher, and did not know how to negotiate. After training, students could apply the negotiation and mediation procedures to actual conflict situations, as well as transfer them to nonclassroom and nonschool settings, such as the playground, the lunchroom, and at home. Further, they maintained their knowledge and skills throughout the school year.

Given the choice of using a "win-lose" or a "problem-solving" negotiation strategy, virtually all untrained students used the former, while trained students primarily chose the problem-solving approach. In addition, students who were taught the negotiation procedure while studying a novel during an English literature unit not only learned how to negotiate, but performed higher on an achievement test on the novel than did students in a control group, who spent their entire time studying the novel. This study

Making the Future a Better Place

Every student needs to learn how to manage conflicts constructively. Without training, many students may never learn how to do so. Teaching every student how to negotiate and mediate will ensure that future generations are prepared to manage conflicts constructively in career, family, community, national, and international settings.

There is no reason to expect, however, that the process will be easy or quick. It took 30 years to reduce smoking in America. It took 20 years to reduce drunk driving. It may take even longer to ensure that children and adolescents can manage conflicts constructively. The more years that students spend learning and practicing the skills of peer mediation and conflict resolution, the more likely they will be to actually use those skills both in the classroom and beyond the school door.

References

Deutsch, M. (1973). *The Resolution of Conflict.* New Haven, Conn.: Yale University Press.

Johnson, D. W., and R. Johnson. (1979). "Conflict in the Classroom: Controversy and Learning." *Review of Educational Research* 49, 1: 51–61.

Johnson, D. W., and R. Johnson. (1989). *Cooperation and Competition: Theory and Research.* Edina, Minn.: Interaction Book Company.

Johnson, D. W., and R. Johnson. (1991). *Teaching Students to Be Peacemakers.* Edina, Minn.: Interaction Book Company.

Johnson, D. W., and R. Johnson. (1992). *Creative Controversy: Intellectual Challenge in the Classroom.* Edina, Minn.: Interaction Book Company.

Johnson, D. W., and R. Johnson. (1994a). *Leading the Cooperative School.* 2nd ed. Edina, Minn.: Interaction Book Company.

Johnson, D. W., and R. Johnson. (1994b). *Teaching Students to Be Peacemakers: Results of Five Years of Research.* Minneapolis: University of Minnesota, Cooperative Learning Center.

Johnson, D. W., and R. Johnson. (In press). "Implementing Cooperative Learning: Training Sessions, Transfer to the Classroom, and Maintaining Long-Term Use." In *Staff Development for Cooperative Learning: Issues and Approaches,* edited by N. Davidson, C. Brody, and C. Cooper. New York: Teachers College Press.

Johnson, D. W., R. Johnson, and E. Holubec. (1992). *Advanced Cooperative Learning.* 2nd ed. Edina, Minn.: Interaction Book Company.

Johnson, D. W., R. Johnson, and E. Holubec. (1993). *Cooperation in the Classroom.* 6th ed. Edina, Minn.: Interaction Book Company.

Tolan, P., and N. Guerra. (In press). *What Works in Reducing Adolescent Violence: An Empirical Review of the Field.* Denver: Center for the Study of Prevention of Violence, University of Colorado.

Webster, D. (1993). "The Unconvincing Case for School-Based Conflict Resolution Programs for Adolescents." *Health Affairs* 12, 4: 126–140.

Wilson-Brewer, R., S. Cohen, L. O'Donnell, and I. Goodman. (1991). "Violence Prevention for Young Adolescents: A Survey of the State of the Art." Eric Clearinghouse, ED356442, 800-443-3742.

Unit Selections

35. **The Challenges of Assessing Young Children Appropriately,** Lorrie A. Shepard
36. **Transforming Student Assessment,** D. Monty Neill
37. **Practicing What We Preach in Designing Authentic Assessments,** Grant Wiggins
38. **What Happens between Assessments?** Jay McTighe
39. **Lessons Learned about Student Portfolios,** Elizabeth A. Hebert
40. **Grades: The Final Frontier in Assessment Reform,** Gregory J. Cizek

Key Points to Consider

❖ What are some important principles for assessing young children? How is the purpose of the assessment related to these principles?

❖ How can assessment be integrated with instruction? Does this change the traditional way teachers assess students?

❖ What are some examples of alternative assessment? What are the strengths and limitations of these assessments?

❖ Many educators believe that schools should identify the brightest, most capable students. What are the assessment implications of this philosophy? How would low-achieving students be affected?

❖ What principles of assessment should teachers adopt for their own classroom testing? Is it necessary or feasible to develop a table of specifications for each test? How do we know if the tests that teachers make are reliable and if valid inferences are drawn from the results?

❖ How can teachers grade thinking skills such as analysis, application, and reasoning? How should objectives for student learning and grading be integrated? What are some grading practices to avoid? Why?

 **Links** www.dushkin.com/online/

32. **Awesome Library for Teachers**
   http://www.neat-schoolhouse.org/teacher.html
33. **Carfax**
   http://www.carfax.co.uk/subjeduc.htm
34. **Phi Delta Kappa International**
   http://www.pdkintl.org
35. **Washington (State) Commission on Student Learning**
   http://csl.wednet.edu/

These sites are annotated on pages 4 and 5.

In which reading group does Jon belong? How do I construct tests? How do I know when my students have mastered the course objectives? How can I explain test results to Mary's parents? Teachers answer these questions, and many more, by applying principles of assessment. Assessment refers to procedures for measuring and recording student performance and constructing grades that communicate to other levels of proficiency or relative standing. Assessment principles constitute a set of concepts that are integral to the teaching-learning process. Indeed, a significant amount of teacher time is spent in assessment activities, and with more accountability has come a greater emphasis on assessment.

Assessment provides a foundation for making sound evaluative judgments about students' learning and achievement. Teachers need to use fair and unbiased criteria in order to assess student learning objectively and accurately and to make appropriate decisions about student placement. For example, in assigning Jon to a reading group, the teacher will use his test scores as an indication of his skill level. Are the inferences from the test results valid for the school's reading program? Are his test scores consistent over several months or years? Are they consistent with his performance in class? The teacher should ask and then answer these questions so that he or she can make intelligent decisions about Jon. On the other hand, will knowledge of the test scores affect the teacher's perception of classroom performance and create a self-fulfilling prophecy? Teachers also evaluate students in order to assign grades, and the challenge is to balance "objective" test scores with more subjective, informally gathered information. Both kinds of evaluative information are necessary, but both can be inaccurate and are frequently misused.

The first article in this unit examines assessment principles in the context of large-scale and classroom assessment of young children, emphasizing the importance of matching assessment methods with the purpose of assessment. In "Transforming Student Assessment," principles for integrating assessment with instruction are delineated. This kind of integration is consistent with recent theories of learning. The next two authors discuss performance-based, "authentic" assessment. This form of assessment has great potential to integrate measurement procedures with instructional methods more effectively and to focus student learning on the application of thinking and problem-solving skills in real-life contexts. A related form of assessment, using portfolios, is described in "Lessons Learned about Student Portfolios."

In the last article, Gregory Cizek examines grading practices and makes suggestions on how to assign grades so that the results provide accurate and helpful information as well as motivate students.

The Challenges of Assessing Young Children Appropriately

In the past decade, testing of 4-, 5-, and 6-year-olds has been excessive and inappropriate. Given this history of misuse, Ms. Shepard maintains, the burden of proof must rest with assessment advocates to demonstrate the usefulness of assessment and to ensure that abuses will not recur.

Lorrie A. Shepard

`LORRIE A. SHEPARD is a professor of education at the University of Colorado, Boulder. She is past president of the National Council on Measurement in Education, past vice president of the American Educational Research Association, and a member of the National Academy of Education. She wishes to thank Sharon Lynn Kagan, M. Elizabeth Graue, and Scott F. Marion for their thoughtful suggestions on drafts of this article.*

PROPOSALS to "assess" young children are likely to be met with outrage or enthusiasm, depending on one's prior experience and one's image of the testing involved. Will an inappropriate paper-and-pencil test be used to keep some 5-year-olds out of school? Or will the assessment, implemented as an ordinary part of good instruction, help children learn? A governor advocating a test for every preschooler in the nation may have in mind the charts depicting normal growth in the pediatrician's office. Why shouldn't parents have access to similar measures to monitor their child's cognitive and academic progress? Middle-class parents, sanguine about the use of test scores to make college-selection decisions, may be eager to have similar tests determine their child's entrance into preschool or kindergarten. Early childhood experts, however, are more likely to respond with alarm because they are more familiar with the complexities of defining and measuring development and learning in young children and because they are more aware of the widespread abuses of readiness testing that occurred in the 1980s.

Given a history of misuse, it is impossible to make positive recommendations about how assessments could be used to monitor the progress of individual children or to evaluate the quality of educational programs without offering assurances that the abuses will not recur. In what follows, I summarize the negative history of standardized testing of young children in order to highlight the transformation needed in both the substance and purposes of early childhood assessment. Then I explain from a measurement perspective how the features of an assessment must be tailored to match the purpose of the assessment. Finally, I describe differences in what assessments might look like when they are used for purposes of screening for handicapping conditions, supporting instruction, or monitoring state and national trends.

Note that I use the term *test* when referring to traditional, standardized developmental and pre-academic measures and the term *assessment* when referring to more developmentally appropriate procedures for observing and evaluating young children. This is a semantic trick that plays on the different connotations of the two terms. Technically, they mean the same thing. Tests, as defined by the *Standards for Educational and Psychological Testing*, have always included systematic observations of behavior, but our experience is with tests as more formal, one-right-answer instruments used to rank and sort individuals. As we shall see, assessments might be standardized, involve paper-and-pencil responses, and so on, but in contrast to traditional testing, "assessment" implies a substantive focus on student learning for the purpose of effective intervention. While *test* and *assessment* cannot be reliably distinguished technically, the difference between these two terms as they have grown up in common parlance is of symbolic importance. Using the term *assessment* presents an opportunity to step away from past practices and ask why we should try to measure what young children know and can do. If there are legitimate purposes for gathering such data, then we can seek the appropriate content and form of assessment to align with those purposes.

Negative History of Testing Young Children

In order to understand the negative history of the standardized testing of young children in the past decade, we need to understand some larger shifts in curriculum and teaching practices. The distortion of the curriculum of the early grades dur-

From *Phi Delta Kappan*, November 1994, pp. 206-212. © 1994 by Phi Delta Kappa, Inc. Reprinted by permission.

ing the 1980s is now a familiar and well-documented story. Indeed, negative effects persist in many school districts today.

Although rarely the result of conscious policy decisions, a variety of indirect pressures — such as older kindergartners, extensive preschooling for children from affluent families, parental demands for the teaching of reading in kindergarten, and accountability testing in higher grades — produced a skill-driven kindergarten curriculum. Because what once were first-grade expectations were shoved down to kindergarten, these shifts in practice were referred to as the "escalation of curriculum" or "academic trickle-down." The result of these changes was an aversive learning environment inconsistent with the learning needs of young children. Developmentally inappropriate instructional practices, characterized by long periods of seatwork, high levels of stress, and a plethora of fill-in-the-blank worksheets, placed many children at risk by setting standards for attention span, social maturity, and academic productivity that could not be met by many normal 5-year-olds.

Teachers and school administrators responded to the problem of a kindergarten environment that was increasingly hostile to young children with several ill-considered policies: raising the entrance age for school, instituting readiness screening to hold some children out of school for a year, increasing retentions in kindergarten, and creating two-year programs with an extra grade either before or after kindergarten. These policies and practices had a benign intent: to protect children from stress and school failure. However, they were ill-considered because they were implemented without contemplating the possibility of negative side effects and without awareness that retaining some children and excluding others only exacerbated the problems by creating an older and older population of kindergartners.[1] The more reasonable corrective for a skill-driven curriculum at earlier and earlier ages would have been curriculum reform of the kind exemplified by the recommendations for developmentally appropriate practices issued by the National Association for the Education of Young Children (NAEYC), the nation's largest professional association of early childhood educators.[2]

The first response of many schools, however, was not to fix the problem of inappropriate curriculum but to exclude those children who could not keep up or who might be harmed. Readiness testing was the chief means of implementing policies aimed at removing young children from inappropriate instructional programs. Thus the use of readiness testing increased dramatically during the 1980s and continues today in many school districts.[3]

Two different kinds of tests are used: developmental screening measures, originally intended as the first step in the evaluation of children for potential handicaps; and pre-academic skills tests, intended for use in planning classroom instruction.[4] The technical and conceptual problems with these tests are numerous.[5] Tests are being used for purposes for which they were never designed or validated. Waiting a year or being placed in a two-year program represents a dramatic disruption in a child's life, yet not one of the existing readiness measures has sufficient reliability or predictive validity to warrant making such decisions.

Developmental and pre-academic skills tests are based on outmoded theories of aptitude and learning that originated in the 1930s. The excessive use of these tests and the negative consequences of being judged unready focused a spotlight on the tests' substantive inadequacies. The widely used Gesell Test is made up of items from old I.Q. tests and is indistinguishable statistically from a measure of I.Q.; the same is true for developmental measures that are really short-form I.Q. tests. Assigning children to different instructional opportunities on the basis of such tests carries forward nativist assumptions popular in the 1930s and

Illustration by Kay Salem

1940s. At that time, it was believed that I.Q. tests could accurately measure innate ability, unconfounded by prior learning experiences. Because these measured "capacities" were thought to be fixed and unalterable, those who scored poorly were given low-level training consistent with their supposedly limited potential. Tests of academic content might have the promise of being more instructionally relevant than disguised I.Q. tests, but, as Anne Stallman and David Pearson have shown, the decomposed and decontextualized prereading skills measured by traditional readiness tests are not compatible with current research on early literacy.[6]

Readiness testing also raises serious equity concerns. Because all the readiness measures in use are influenced by past opportunity to learn, a disproportionate number of poor and minority children are identified as unready and are excluded from school when they most need it. Thus children without preschool experience and without extensive literacy experiences at home are sent back to the very environments that caused them to score poorly on readiness measures in the first place. Or, if poor and minority children who do not pass the readiness tests are admitted to the school but made to spend an extra year in kindergarten, they suffer disproportionately the stigma and negative effects of retention.

The last straw in this negative account of testing young children is the evidence that fallible tests are often followed by ineffective programs. A review of controlled studies has shown no academic benefits from retention in kindergarten or from extra-year programs, whether developmental kindergartens or transitional first grades. When extra-year children finally get to first grade, they do not do better on average than equally "unready" children who go directly on to first grade.[7] However, a majority of children placed in these extra-year programs do experience some short- or long-term trauma, as reported by their parents.[8] Contrary to popular belief that kindergarten children are "too young to notice" retention, most of them know that they are not making "normal" progress, and many continue to make reference to the decision years later. "If I hadn't spent an extra year in kindergarten, I would be in __ grade now." In the face of such evidence, there is little wonder that many early childhood educators ask why we test young children at all.

Principles for Assessment And Testing

The NAEYC and the National Association of Early Childhood Specialists in State Departments of Education have played key roles in informing educators about the harm of developmentally inappropriate instructional practices and the misuse of tests. In 1991 NAEYC published "Guidelines for Appropriate Curriculum Content and Assessment in Programs Serving Children Ages 3 Through 8."[9] Although the detailed recommendations are too numerous to be repeated here, a guiding principle is that *assessments should bring about benefits for children, or data should not be collected at all.* Specifically, assessments "should not be used to recommend that children stay out of a program, be retained in grade, or be assigned to a segregated group based on ability or developmental maturity."[10] Instead, NAEYC acknowledges three legitimate purposes for assessment: 1) to plan instruction and communicate with parents, 2) to identify children with special needs, and 3) to evaluate programs.

Although NAEYC used *assessment* in its "Guidelines," as I do, to avoid associations with inappropriate uses of tests, both the general principle and the specific guidelines are equally applicable to formal testing. In other words, tests should not be used if they do not bring about benefits for children. In what follows I summarize some additional principles that can ensure that assessments (and tests) are beneficial and not harmful. Then, in later sections, I consider each of NAEYC's recommended uses for assessment, including national, state, and local needs for program evaluation and accountability data.

I propose a second guiding principle for assessment that is consistent with the NAEYC perspective. *The content of assessments should reflect and model progress toward important learning goals.* Conceptions of what is important to learn should take into account both physical and social/emotional development as well as cognitive learning. For most assessment purposes in the cognitive domain, content should be congruent with subject matter in emergent literacy and numeracy. In the past, developmental measures were made as "curriculum free" or "culture free" as possible in an effort to tap biology and avoid the confounding effects of past opportunity to learn. Of course, this was an impossible task because a child's ability to "draw a triangle"

or "point to the ball on top of the table" depends on prior experiences as well as on biological readiness. However, if the purpose of assessment is no longer to sort students into programs on the basis of a one-time measure of ability, then it is possible to have assessment content mirror what we want children to learn.

A third guiding principle can be inferred from several of the NAEYC guidelines. *The methods of assessment must be appropriate to the development and experiences of young children.* This means that — along with written products — observation, oral readings, and interviews should be used for purposes of assessment. Even for large-scale purposes, assessment should not be an artificial and decontextualized event; instead, the demands of data collection should be consistent with children's prior experiences in classrooms and at home. Assessment practices should recognize the diversity of learners and must be in accord with children's language development — both in English and in the native languages of those whose home language is not English.

A fourth guiding principle can be drawn from the psychometric literature on test validity. *Assessments should be tailored to a specific purpose.* Although not stated explicitly in the NAEYC document, this principle is implied by the recommendation of three sets of guidelines for three separate assessment purposes.

Matching the Why and How Of Assessment

The reason for any assessment — i.e., how the assessment information will be used — affects the substance and form of

> *The intended use of an assessment will determine the need for normative information or other means to support the interpretation of results.*

the assessment in several ways. First, the degree of technical accuracy required depends on use. For example, the identification of children for special education has critical implications for individuals. Failure to be identified could mean the denial of needed services, but being identified as in need of special services may also mean removal from normal classrooms (at least part of the time) and a potentially stigmatizing label. A great deal is at stake in such assessment, so the multifaceted evaluation employed must have a high degree of reliability and validity. Ordinary classroom assessments also affect individual children, but the consequences of these decisions are not nearly so great. An inaccurate assessment on a given day may lead a teacher to make a poor grouping or instructional decision, but such an error can be corrected as more information becomes available about what an individual child "really knows."

Group assessment refers to uses, such as program evaluation or school accountability, in which the focus is on group performance rather than on individual scores. Although group assessments may need to meet very high standards for technical accuracy, because of the high stakes associated with the results, the individual scores that contribute to the group information do not have to be so reliable and do not have to be directly comparable, so long as individual results are not reported. When only group results are desired, it is possible to use the technical advantages of matrix sampling — a technique in which each participant takes only a small portion of the assessment — to provide a rich, in-depth assessment of the intended content domain without overburdening any of the children sampled. When the "group" is very large, such as all the fourth-graders in a state or in the nation, then assessing a representative sample will produce essentially the same results for the group average as if every student had been assessed.

Purpose must also determine the content of assessment. When trying to diagnose potential learning handicaps, we still rely on aptitude-like measures designed to be as content-free as possible. We do so in order to avoid confusing lack of opportunity to learn with inability to learn. When the purpose of assessment is to measure actual learning, then content must naturally be tied to learning outcomes. However, even among achievement tests, there is considerable variability in the degree of alignment to a specif-

ic curriculum. Although to the lay person "math is math" and "reading is reading," measurement specialists are aware that tiny changes in test format can make a large difference in student performance. For example, a high proportion of students may be able to add numbers when they are presented in vertical format, but many will be unable to do the same problems presented horizontally. If manipulatives are used in some elementary classrooms but not in all, including the use of manipulatives in a mathematics assessment will disadvantage some children, while excluding their use will disadvantage others.

Assessments that are used to guide instruction in a given classroom should be integrally tied to the curriculum of that classroom. However, for large-scale assessments at the state and national level, the issues of curriculum match and the effect of assessment content on future instruction become much more problematic. For example, in a state with an agreed-upon curriculum, including geometry assessment in the early grades may be appropriate, but it would be problematic in states with strong local control of curriculum and so with much more curricular diversity.

Large-scale assessments, such as the National Assessment of Educational Progress, must include instructionally relevant content, but they must do so without conforming too closely to any single curriculum. In the past, this requirement has led to the problem of achievement tests that are limited to the "lowest common denominator." Should the instrument used for program evaluation include only the content that is common to all curricula? Or should it include everything that is in any program's goals? Although the common core approach can lead to a narrowing of curriculum when assessment results are associated with high stakes, including everything can be equally troublesome if it leads to superficial teaching in pursuit of too many different goals.

Finally, the intended use of an assessment will determine the need for normative information or other means to support the interpretation of assessment results. Identifying children with special needs requires normative data to distinguish serious physical, emotional, or learning problems from the wide range of normal development. When reporting to parents, teachers also need some idea of what constitutes grade-level performance, but such "norms" can be in the form

of benchmark performances — evidence that children are working at grade level — rather than statistical percentiles.

To prevent the abuses of the past, the purposes and substance of early childhood assessments must be transformed. Assessments should be conducted only if they serve a beneficial purpose: to gain services for children with special needs, to inform instruction by building on what students already know, to improve programs, or to provide evidence nationally or in the states about programmatic needs. The form, substance, and technical features of assessment should be appropriate for the use intended for assessment data. Moreover, the methods of assessment must be compatible with the developmental level and experiences of young children. Below, I consider the implications of these principles for three different categories of assessment purposes.

Identifying Children with Special Needs

I discuss identification for special education first because this is the type of assessment that most resembles past uses of developmental screening measures. However, there is no need for wholesale administration of such tests to all incoming kindergartners. If we take the precepts of developmentally appropriate practices seriously, then at each age level a very broad range of abilities and performance levels is to be expected and tolerated. If potential handicaps are understood to be relatively rare and extreme, then it is not necessary to screen all children for "hidden" disabilities. By definition, serious learning problems should be apparent. Although it is possible to miss hearing or vision problems (at least mild ones) without systematic screening, referral for evaluation of a possible learning handicap should occur only when parents or teachers notice that a child is not progressing normally in comparison to age-appropriate expectations. In-depth assessments should then be conducted to verify the severity of the problem and to rule out a variety of other explanations for poor performance.

For this type of assessment, developmental measures, including I.Q. tests, continue to be useful. Clinicians attempt to make normative evaluations using relatively curriculum-free tasks, but today they are more likely to acknowledge the fallibility of such efforts. For such difficult assessments, clinicians must have specialized training in both diagnostic assessment and child development.

When identifying children with special needs, evaluators should use two general strategies in order to avoid confounding the ability to learn with past opportunity to learn. First, as recommended by the National Academy Panel on Selection and Placement of Students in Programs for the Mentally Retarded,[11] a child's learning environment should be evaluated to rule out poor instruction as the possible cause of a child's lack of learning. Although seldom carried out in practice, this evaluation should include trying out other methods to support learning and possibly trying a different teacher before concluding that a child can't learn from ordinary classroom instruction. A second important strategy is to observe a child's functioning in multiple contexts. Often children who appear to be impaired in school function well at home or with peers. Observation outside of school is critical for children from diverse cultural backgrounds and for those whose home language is not English. The NAEYC stresses that "screening should never be used to identify second language learners as 'handicapped,' solely on the basis of their limited abilities in English."[12]

In-depth developmental assessments are needed to ensure that children with disabilities receive appropriate services. However, the diagnostic model of special education should not be generalized to a larger population of below-average learners, or the result will be the reinstitution of tracking. Elizabeth Graue and I analyzed recent efforts to create "at-risk" kindergartens and found that these practices are especially likely to occur when resources for extended-day programs are available only for the children most in need.[13] The result of such programs is often to segregate children from low socioeconomic backgrounds into classrooms where time is spent drilling on low-level prereading skills like those found on readiness tests. The consequences of dumbed-down instruction in kindergarten are just as pernicious as the effects of tracking at higher grade levels, especially when the at-risk kindergarten group is kept together for first grade. If resources for extended-day kindergarten are scarce, one alternative would be to group children heterogeneously for half the day and then, for the other half, to provide extra enrichment activities for children with limited literacy experiences.

Classroom Assessments

Unlike traditional readiness tests that are intended to predict learning, classroom assessments should support instruction by modeling the dimensions of learning. Although we must allow considerable latitude for children to construct their own understandings, teachers must nonetheless have knowledge of normal development if they are to support children's extensions and next steps. Ordinary classroom tasks can then be used to assess a child's progress in relation to a developmental continuum. An example of a developmental continuum would be that of emergent writing, beginning with scribbles, then moving on to pictures and random letters, and then proceeding to some letter/word correspondences. These continua are not rigid, however, and several dimensions running in parallel may be necessary to describe growth in a single content area. For example, a second dimension of early writing — a child's ability to invent increasingly elaborated stories when dictating to an adult — is not dependent on mastery of writing letters, just as listening comprehension, making predictions about books, and story retellings should be developed in parallel to, not after, mastery of letter sounds.

Although there is a rich research literature documenting patterns of emergent literacy and numeracy, corresponding assessment materials are not so readily available. In the next few years, national interest in developing alternative, performance-based measures should generate more materials and resources. Specifically, new Chapter 1 legislation is likely to support the development of reading assessments that are more authentic and instructionally relevant.

For example, classroom-embedded reading assessments were created from ordinary instructional materials by a group of third-grade teachers in conjunction with researchers at the Center for Research on Evaluation, Standards, and Student Testing.[14] The teachers elected to focus on fluency and making meaning as reading goals; running records and story summaries were selected as the methods of assessment.

But how should student progress be evaluated? In keeping with the idea of representing a continuum of proficiency, third-grade teachers took all the chapter books in their classrooms and sorted them into grade-level stacks, 1-1 (first grade, first semester), 1-2, 2-1, and so on up to fifth grade. Then they identified representative or marker books in each category to use for assessment. Once the books had been sorted by difficulty, it became possible to document that children were reading increasingly difficult texts with understanding. Photocopied pages from the marker books also helped parents see what teachers considered to be grade-level materials and provided them with concrete evidence of their child's progress. Given mandates for student-level reporting under Chapter 1, state departments of education or test publishers could help develop similar systems of this type with sufficient standardization to ensure comparability across districts.

In the meantime, classroom teachers — or preferably teams of teachers — are left to invent their own assessments for classroom use. In many schools, teachers are already working with portfolios and developing scoring criteria. The best procedure appears to be having grade-level teams and then cross-grade teams meet to discuss expectations and evaluation criteria. These conversations will be more productive if, for each dimension to be assessed, teachers collect student work and use marker papers to illustrate continua of performance. Several papers might be used at each stage to reflect the tremendous variety in children's responses, even when following the same general progression.

Benchmark papers can also be an effective means of communicating with parents. For example, imagine using sample papers from grades K-3 to illustrate expectations regarding "invented spelling." Invented spelling or "temporary spelling" is the source of a great deal of parental dissatisfaction with reform curricula. Yet most parents who attack invented spelling have never been given a rationale for its use. That is, no one has explained it in such a way that the explanation builds on the parents' own willingness to allow successive approximations in their child's early language development. They have never been shown a connection between writing expectations and grade-level spelling lists or been informed about differences in rules for first drafts and final drafts. Sample papers could be selected to illustrate the increasing mastery of grade-appropriate words, while allowing for misspellings of advanced words on first drafts. Communicating criteria is helpful to parents, and, as we have seen in the literature on performance assessment, it also helps children to understand what is expected and to become better at assessing their own work.

Monitoring National and State Trends

In 1989, when the President and the nation's governors announced "readiness for school" as the first education goal, many early childhood experts feared the creation of a national test for school entry. Indeed, given the negative history of readiness testing, the first thing the Goal 1 Technical Planning Subgroup did was to issue caveats about what an early childhood assessment must *not* be. It should not be a one-dimensional, reductionist measure of a child's knowledge and abilities; it should not be called a measure of "readiness" as if some children were not ready to learn; and it should not be used to "label, stigmatize, or classify any individual child or group of children."[15]

However, with this fearsome idea set aside, the Technical Planning Subgroup endorsed the idea of an early childhood assessment system that would periodically gather data on the condition of young children as they enter school. The purpose of the assessment would be to inform public policy and especially to help "in charting progress toward achievement of the National Education Goals,

> *Beginning in 1998-99, a representative sample of 23,000 kindergarten students will be assessed and then followed through grade 5.*

and for informing the development, expansion, and/or modification of policies and programs that affect young children and their families."[16] Assuming that certain safeguards are built in, such data could be a powerful force in focusing national attention and resources on the needs of young children.

Unlike past testing practices aimed at evaluating individual children in comparison with normative expectations, a large-scale, nationally representative assessment would be used to monitor national trends. The purpose of such an assessment would be analogous to the use of the National Assessment of Educational Progress (NAEP) to measure major shifts in achievement patterns. For example, NAEP results have demonstrated gains in the achievement of black students in the South as a result of desegregation, and NAEP achievement measures showed gains during the 1980s in basic skills and declines in higher-order thinking skills and problem solving. Similar data are not now available for preschoolers or for children in the primary grades. If an early childhood assessment were conducted periodically, it would be possible to demonstrate the relationship between health services and early learning and to evaluate the impact of such programs as Head Start.

In keeping with the precept that methods of assessment should follow from the purpose of assessment, the Technical Planning Subgroup recommended that sampling of both children and assessment items be used to collect national data. Sampling would allow a broad assessment of a more multifaceted content domain and would preclude the misuse of individual scores to place or stigmatize individual children. A national early childhood assessment should also serve as a model of important content. As a means to shape public understanding of the full range of abilities and experiences that influence early learning and development, the Technical Planning Subgroup identified five dimensions to be assessed: 1) physical well-being and motor development, 2) social and emotional development, 3) approaches toward learning, 4) language usage, and 5) cognition and general knowledge.

Responding to the need for national data to document the condition of children as they enter school and to measure progress on Goal 1, the U.S. Department of Education has commissioned the Early Childhood Longitudinal Study: Kindergarten Cohort. Beginning in the 1998-99 school year, a representative sample of 23,000 kindergarten students will be assessed and then followed through grade 5. The content of the assessments used will correspond closely to the dimensions recommended by the Technical Planning Subgroup. In addition, data will be collected on each child's family, communi-

ty, and school/program. Large-scale studies of this type serve both program evaluation purposes (How effective are preschool services for children?) and research purposes (What is the relationship between children's kindergarten experiences and their academic success throughout elementary school?).

National needs for early childhood data and local needs for program evaluation information are similar in some respects and dissimilar in others. Both uses require group data. However, a critical distinction that affects the methods of evaluation is whether or not local programs share a

> *Fearing that "assessment" is just a euphemism for more bad testing, many early childhood professionals have asked, Why test at all?*

common curriculum. If local programs, such as all the kindergartens in a school district, have agreed on the same curriculum, it is possible to build program evaluation assessments from an aggregation of the measures used for classroom purposes. Note that the entire state of Kentucky is attempting to develop such a system by scoring classroom portfolios for state reporting.

If programs being evaluated do not have the same specific curricula, as is the case with a national assessment and with some state assessments, then the assessment measures must reflect broad, agreed-upon goals without privileging any specific curriculum. This is a tall order, more easily said than done. For this reason, the Technical Planning Subgroup recommended that validity studies be built into the procedures for data collection. For example, pilot studies should verify that what children can do in one-on-one assessment settings is consistent with what they can do in their classrooms, and assessment methods should always allow children more than one way to show what they know.

Conclusion

In the past decade, testing of 4-, 5-, and 6-year-olds has been excessive and inappropriate. Under a variety of different names, leftover I.Q. tests have been used to track children into ineffective programs or to deny them school entry. Prereading tests held over from the 1930s have encouraged the teaching of decontextualized skills. In response, fearing that "assessment" is just a euphemism for more bad testing, many early childhood professionals have asked, Why test at all? Indeed, given a history of misuse, the burden of proof must rest with assessment advocates to demonstrate the usefulness of assessment and to ensure that abuses will not recur. Key principles that support responsible use of assessment information follow.

• No testing of young children should occur unless it can be shown to lead to beneficial results.

• Methods of assessment, especially the language used, must be appropriate to the development and experiences of young children.

• Features of assessment — content, form, evidence of validity, and standards for interpretation — must be tailored to the specific purpose of an assessment.

• Identifying children for special education is a legitimate purpose for assessment and still requires the use of curriculum-free, aptitude-like measures and normative comparisons. However, handicapping conditions are rare; the diagnostic model used by special education should not be generalized to a larger population of below-average learners.

• For both classroom instructional purposes and purposes of public policy making, the content of assessments should embody the important dimensions of early learning and development. The tasks and skills children are asked to perform should reflect and model progress toward important learning goals.

In the past, local newspapers have published readiness checklists that suggested that children should stay home from kindergarten if they couldn't cut with scissors. In the future, national and local assessments should demonstrate the richness of what children do know and should foster instruction that builds on their strengths. Telling a story in conjunction with scribbles is a meaningful stage in literacy development. Reading a story in English and retelling it in Spanish is evidence of reading comprehension. Evidence of important learning in beginning mathematics should not be counting to 100 instead of to 10. It should be extending patterns; solving arithmetic problems with blocks and explaining how you got your answer; constructing graphs to show how many children come to school by bus, by walking, by car; and demonstrating understanding of patterns and quantities in a variety of ways.

In classrooms, we need new forms of assessment so that teachers can support children's physical, social, and cognitive development. And at the level of public policy, we need new forms of assessment so that programs will be judged on the basis of worthwhile educational goals.

1. Lorrie A. Shepard and Mary Lee Smith, "Escalating Academic Demand in Kindergarten: Counterproductive Policies," *Elementary School Journal*, vol. 89, 1988, pp. 135-45.

2. Sue Bredekamp, ed., *Developmentally Appropriate Practice in Early Childhood Programs Serving Children from Birth Through Age 8*, exp. ed. (Washington, D.C.: National Association for the Education of Young Children, 1987).

3. M. Therese Gnezda and Rosemary Bolig, *A National Survey of Public School Testing of Pre-Kindergarten and Kindergarten Children* (Washington, D.C.: National Forum on the Future of Children and Families, National Research Council, 1988).

4. Samuel J. Meisels, "Uses and Abuses of Developmental Screening and School Readiness Testing," *Young Children*, vol. 42, 1987, pp. 4-6, 68-73.

5. Lorrie A. Shepard and M. Elizabeth Graue, "The Morass of School Readiness Screening: Research on Test Use and Test Validity," in Bernard Spodek, ed., *Handbook of Research on the Education of Young Children* (New York: Macmillan, 1993), pp. 293-305.

6. Anne C. Stallman and P. David Pearson, "Formal Measures of Early Literacy," in Lesley Mandel Morrow and Jeffrey K. Smith, eds., *Assessment for Instruction in Early Literacy* (Englewood Cliffs, N.J.: Prentice-Hall, 1990), pp. 7-44.

7. Lorrie A. Shepard, "A Review of Research on Kindergarten Retention," in Lorrie A. Shepard and Mary Lee Smith, eds., *Flunking Grades: Research and Policies on Retention* (London: Falmer Press, 1989), pp. 64-78.

8. Lorrie A. Shepard and Mary Lee Smith, "Academic and Emotional Effects of Kindergarten Retention in One School District," in idem, pp. 79-107.

9. "Guidelines for Appropriate Curriculum Content and Assessment in Programs Serving Children Ages 3 Through 8," *Young Children*, vol. 46, 1991, pp. 21-38.

10. Ibid., p. 32.

11. Kirby A. Heller, Wayne H. Holtzman, and Samuel Messick, eds., *Placing Children in Special Education* (Washington, D.C.: National Academy Press, 1982).

12. "Guidelines," p. 33.

13. Shepard and Graue, op. cit.

14. The Center for Research on Evaluation, Standards, and Student Testing is located on the campuses of the University of California, Los Angeles, and the University of Colorado, Boulder.

15. *Goal 1: Technical Planning Subgroup Report on School Readiness* (Washington, D.C.: National Education Goals Panel, September 1991).

16. Ibid., p. 6.

Transforming Student Assessment

By D. Monty Neill

Illustration by Kay Salem

In a "get tough" environment in which we are seeing an increase in the use of graduation and even grade-promotion tests, more testing seems to be on the agenda. Yet the problems with traditional testing have not gone away, Mr. Neill warns. He suggests a better approach.

IMAGINE AN assessment system in which teachers had a wide repertoire of classroom-based, culturally sensitive assessment practices and tools to use in helping each and every child learn to high standards; in which educators collaboratively used assessment information to continuously improve schools; in which important decisions about a student, such as readiness to graduate from high school, were based on the work done over the years by the student; in which schools in networks held one another accountable for student learning; and in which public evidence of student achievement consisted primarily of samples from students' actual schoolwork rather than just reports of results from one-shot examinations.

D. MONTY NEILL is associate director of the National Center for Fair and Open Testing (FairTest) and co-chair of the National Forum on Assessment, Cambridge, Mass. The views expressed here are the author's own.

From *Phi Delta Kappan*, September 1997, pp. 34-40, 58. © 1997 by Phi Delta Kappa, Inc. Reprinted by permission.

Many would probably dismiss this vision as the product of an overactive imagination. However, these ideas are at the core of *Principles and Indicators for Student Assessment Systems*, developed by the National Forum on Assessment and signed by more than 80 national and local education and civil rights organizations.[1] The widespread support for this document indicates a deep desire for a radical reconstruction of assessment practices, with student learning made central to assessment reform. In this article I draw on *Principles* to outline what a new assessment system could look like and to suggest some actions that can be taken to further assessment reform.

The seven principles endorsed by the Forum are:

1. The primary purpose of assessment is to improve student learning.

2. Assessment for other purposes supports student learning.

3. Assessment systems are fair to all students.

4. Professional collaboration and development support assessment.

5. The broad community participates in assessment development.

6. Communication about assessment is regular and clear.

7. Assessment systems are regularly reviewed and improved.

Classroom Assessment

Assessment for the primary purpose of improving student learning must rest on what the Forum calls "foundations" of high-quality schooling: an understanding of how student learning takes place, clear statements of desired learning (goals or standards) for all students, adequate learning resources (particularly high-quality teachers), and school structures and practices that support the learning needs of all students.

Assessment to enhance student learning must be integrated with, not separate from, curriculum and instruction.[2] Thus assessment reform is necessarily integrated with reform in other areas of schooling. In particular, schools need to ensure the development of "authentic instruction," which involves modes of teaching that foster understanding of rich content and encourage students' positive engagement with the world.

Both individual and societal interests come together in classroom instruction and assessment. Assessment works on a continuum. Helping the student with his or her individual interests and ways of thinking lies at one end. At the other are the more standard ways of knowing and doing things that society has deemed important. In the middle are individualized ways of learning, understanding, and expressing socially important things. There are, for example, many ways for a student to present an understanding of the causes of the U.S. Civil War.

For all these purposes, teachers must gather information. Teachers must keep track of student learning, check up on what students have learned, and find out what's going on with them. Keeping track means observing and documenting what students do. Checking up involves various kinds of testing and quizzing. Finding out is the heart of classroom assessment: What does the child mean? What did the child get from the experience? Why did the child do what he or she did? To find out, teachers must ask questions for which they do not already know the answers.[3]

To gather all this information, teachers can rely on a range of assessment activities. These include structured and spur-of-the-moment observations that are recorded and filed; formal and informal interviews; collections of work samples; use of extended projects, performances, and exhibitions; performance exams; and various forms of short-answer testing. In this context, teachers could use multiple-choice questions, but, as the Forum recommends, they would have a very limited role.

The evidence of learning can be kept in portfolios, which in turn can be used by students and teachers to reflect on, summarize, and evaluate student progress. Documentation systems, such as the *Primary Language Record*, the *Primary Learning Record*, the *California Learning Record*, and the *Work Sampling System*, can be used to organize assessment information and to guide evaluation of student learning.[4]

Following the continuum from individual to societal interests, evaluation should be both "self-referenced" and "standards-referenced."[5] The former evaluates the learner in light of her own goals, desires, and previous attainments and thus helps the student understand and further her own learning. In this way standards for the student's learning emerge from her work, not just from external sources. Standards-referenced evaluation is by now commonly understood. For example, students can be evaluated against the *Curriculum and Evaluation Standards for School Mathematics* of the National Council of Teachers of Mathematics.[6] Standards-based assessment has been mandated in the new federal Title I legislation. Whether standards are established by the school, district, or state, the Forum recommends wide participation in the standards-setting process. However, as the slogan "standards without standardization" suggests, excellence can take many forms. Thus, according to the ideals of *Principles*, "Assessment systems allow students multiple ways to demonstrate their learning."

When students are allowed multiple ways to show what they have learned and can do, evaluation becomes more complex. It becomes essential for educators to define "high quality" in a lucid way and to let students, parents, and the community know what variations on such quality look like. Clear scoring guides and examples of student work of varying kinds and degrees of quality are needed.

An additional objective of classroom performance assessment, supportive of both self-referenced and standards-referenced evaluation, is that students learn to reflect on and evaluate their own work. After all, an important goal of school is for students to be able to learn without relying on teachers. As students become engaged in developing scoring guides and evaluating work, they learn more deeply what good work looks like, and they more clearly understand their own learning processes.

The process of assessment, however, is not just focused on evaluating student accomplishment. Rather, the heart of assessment is a continuing flow in which the teacher (in collaboration with the student) uses information to guide the next steps in learning. The educator must ask, What should I do to help the student progress? This can be a very immediate issue (How can I help him get past a misunderstanding in multiplying fractions?) and thus should be an integrated part of the daily process of instruction. The question can be asked after any significant moment of assessment, such as completion of a project. It can also be asked periodically during the year and at the end of the year, at moments designed for summing up and planning.

The assessment practices outlined above are not common, even though these kinds of approaches are now widely promoted in the professional literature. Substantial professional development for teachers and restructuring of school practices are needed if this kind of assessment is to flourish.

Schools are not likely to make the effort to change merely so that they can use performance assessment. Rather, they will attempt to transform curriculum, instruction, school structures (such as school size and the length of class periods), and assessment, as well as to institute the requisite professional development, as it becomes clear that the changes produce improved learning and more interested and engaged students. Thus this vision of assessment reform flows from a broader vision of what it means to educate young people — what they should learn and be able to do, how they should act, what kinds of people they should become. Assessment, in other words, cannot be divorced from consideration of the purposes of schooling.

Implications for Equity

A powerful concern for equity should underlie all efforts to reform assessment. Traditional tests have presumed that assessing all students in the same format creates a fair situation. However, the process of test construction, the determination of content, and the use of only one method — usually multiple-choice — all build in cultural and educational biases that favor some ways of understanding and demonstrating knowledge over others.[7] Testing's power has, in turn, helped shape curriculum, instruction, and classroom assessment to advantage certain groups. Thus the uniformity and formal equity of the tests contribute to real-world educational inequity.

The solution is to allow diversity to flourish and to do so in ways that neither unfairly privilege some methods of demonstrating knowledge nor excuse some students from learning what society has deemed important. Too often, however, "different" has meant "lesser." For example, to meet the supposed needs of students in vocational education, the curriculum may be watered down. Students of color and those from low-income backgrounds have been most damaged by low expectations and low-level curricula. With regard to assessment, as Norman Frederiksen noted over a decade ago, the "real test bias" is that "multiple-choice tests tend not to measure the more complex

cognitive abilities,"[8] which in turn are not taught, especially to low-income students.[9] This double bias must be overcome.

Students come from many cultures and languages. Instruction and assessment should connect to the local and the culturally particular and not presume uniformity of experience, culture, language, and ways of knowing.

In the context of classroom assessment, perhaps the thorniest issue is whether teachers will be able to assess all their students fairly, accurately, and comprehensively. Such evaluation requires more than that teachers be unbiased; they must also understand their students. Classroom performance assessments can provide a powerful vehicle for getting to know students. For example, the learning records noted above all ask teachers to interview students and their parents at the start of the year, to inquire about the child's learning experiences and interests. Classroom performance assessment requires thinking about the child and about the contexts in which the child is or is not successfully learning. Teachers who do not know their students cannot do self-referenced evaluation.

The hope is that, as teachers make use of instructional and assessment practices that give them more powerful insights into each student's learning processes and styles, they will be more likely to hold high expectations and provide strong support for learning for all their students. At least some evidence is beginning to show that this can happen. The use of clear, strong standards can also help — though standards should be flexible enough to accommodate student diversity. For example, a standard stating that students should understand various interpretations of the separation of powers spelled out in the U.S. Constitution could be met in a variety of ways, such as an essay, an exhibition, a performance by a group of students, or a short story.

Teachers must also help all their students learn the ins and outs of the assessment methods being used. For example, when students select materials for a portfolio, teachers must ensure that all students know what the portfolio is used for, how to construct it, and how it will be evaluated. Students may need help in thinking about choosing work for projects or portfolios so that they will be able to select activities that best show their accomplishments.

Finally, equity requires meeting the needs of all students, including those who

are learning English and those with disabilities or other special needs. Teachers must be able to assess their students in ways that allow them to demonstrate their learning and that provide the information teachers need to guide their future learning. Assessors need to know how to make accommodations and adaptations that are congruent with classroom instructional practices.

Back to Basics?

Some critics have argued that, while performance assessments are useful for assessing more advanced learning, multiple-choice tests are fine for the "basics." Others have even maintained that using performance assessment will undermine teaching of the "basics."[10] These misconceptions are dangerous.

What is meant by the "basics"? Presumably, the term encompasses reading well across a range of subject areas, writing fluently for a variety of purposes, and knowing and understanding math well enough to use it as needed in common educational, social, and employment settings. Rather than opposing such basics, it was largely because so many students were not attaining them that many educators became advocates of performance assessment.

Effective writing, for example, requires feedback on one's actual writing — that is, performance assessment. Writing assessment cannot be reduced to multiple-choice tests. But writing a few paragraphs on a topic about which students may know little and care less provides only minimally useful information. Good writing involves using knowledge and understanding and takes time for reflection and revision. High-quality performance assessment encourages just such practices and is therefore a needed element of learning the "basic" of clear writing.

Another troublesome notion is that first one learns the "basics" — usually defined as being able to do sufficiently well on a low-level multiple-choice test — and then, almost as a reward, one gets to read something interesting or apply math to a real problem. However, denying many students the opportunity to engage in real thinking while they learn some impoverished version of the "basics" only guarantees that the "later" for thinking will never arrive for them.

A somewhat more subtle variant of this idea is that first one learns content and then one learns to apply it. This approach, though discredited by cognitive psychology,[11] now appears to be making a comeback. It is wrong for several reasons. First, humans learn by thinking and doing. The content one thinks about and the thinking itself can and should get more complex as one learns, but one does not learn without thinking.[12] Schooling, however, can narrow and dull the range and intensity of thought by a focus on drill and repetition with decontextualized bits of information or skills. Such narrowed schooling is inflicted most often on children from low-income backgrounds and on students of color. It also reduces the likelihood of connecting schoolwork to the local and cultural contexts of the students.

In the "first know, then do" approach, it could be argued that math has a content knowledge that can be "learned" and then "applied." However, if one does not know how to go about solving the problem (application), knowing the math procedures does not help. More fundamentally, "the distinction between acquiring knowledge and applying it is inappropriate for education."[13] Separating knowing from doing for testing purposes reinforces instruction that isolates these elements, usually with the result that students don't grasp deep structures of knowledge and can't use the procedures and information they supposedly know.[14]

This separation of knowing and doing is used to justify calls, by test publishers and others, for multiple measures — using multiple-choice tests for basic facts and performance assessments for the ability to use knowledge. While it may be true that teachers can separately and efficiently test for declarative knowledge using multiple-choice or short-answer questions, it is critical that educators not allow the occasional use of such tools to reinforce an artificial separation that has had substantially harmful effects on schooling.

These separations also lead to complete confusion in some subjects. For example, multiple-choice reading tests are not described and used as measuring a few limited aspects of "reading skills"; they are erroneously described as measuring "reading."[15] The pervasiveness of these tests makes separating the test from its use a misleading exercise that only serves to disguise the difficulty of using these dangerous products safely.

This version of "basics first" also implies that whether one is excited about or engaged in learning has nothing to do with the results of learning. But if students don't get engaged, they won't think very much or very seriously about their schoolwork, and their learning will suffer.[16] A curriculum organized on "drill and kill" to raise test scores is no way to foster a desire to learn.

This does not mean that attention to particular bits (e.g., phonics) or that repetition in instruction is never acceptable. However, these practices must be subordinate elements of curriculum and instruction, to be used as needed and appropriate for a particular student or group. To determine need, a teacher must understand the particular student or group — which is to say, the teacher must assess students' actual strengths and learning needs, which requires classroom-based performance assessment.

Outside the Classroom

Assessment is, of course, used outside the classroom. Indeed, tests made for such purposes as comparing students to national norms, certifying their accomplishments (or lack thereof), and providing public accountability have come to dominate both public conceptions of assessment and classroom assessment practices. Teachers do use a range of methods, though not often enough and not well enough, but the underlying conceptions of what it means to assess and how to do it are dominated by the model of the external, multiple-choice, norm-referenced test. This domination tends to reduce curriculum and instruction to endless drill on decontextualized bits modeled on multiple-choice questions.[17] Thus assessment beyond the classroom must be changed for two fundamental reasons: to provide richer and fairer means of assessment for these purposes and to remove the control the tests exert over classroom instruction and assessment.

School improvement. If classroom-based assessment is essential for student learning, it is equally essential for school improvement. If teachers talk with one another about student learning, then they will reflect on how to help particular children learn and how to improve the school as a whole.

The Prospect School in Vermont pioneered the use of such a collaborative process. Teachers met regularly to discuss student work.[18] A similar process has been adopted at the Bronx New School, an elementary school in New York City.[19] In a powerfully moving section of *Authentic Assessment in Action*, a teacher describes working with Akeem, a child who seemed destined for school failure, if not worse.

The rich information provided by the Bronx New School's assessment practices enabled his teacher to improve her work with Akeem. But only the process of collaboration among the staff gave her the insights and help she needed to keep struggling to find a way to work successfully with him. Akeem remains in school, is progressing well, and can envision a solid future for himself.

As the examples in this book and a growing body of work on professional development show,[20] talking with one another helps teachers improve their practice and simultaneously work on improving their schools. As with individuals, knowing what works and what does not, figuring out why, and then deciding how to make improvements are essential parts of school progress.

Certification and making decisions. *Principles and Indicators* states that decisions about individuals and schools should be made "on the basis of cumulative evidence of learning, using a variety of assessment information, not on the basis of any single assessment." Neither important individual decisions, such as high school graduation or special placement, nor collective sanctions or rewards for a school should be made on the basis of a test used as a single, required hurdle. The work students actually do should be used to make these decisions.

In many ways this approach is the same one that was used historically: if a student passed his or her courses, that student graduated, perhaps with honors if he or she did well. The problem was that this approach became divorced from high expectations and serious standards, so that some students could graduate knowing very little. The solution often imposed has been the high school exit test, which appears to be enjoying an unfortunate comeback after a decline in the first half of the 1990s. High-stakes exit tests are now used in 17 states,[21] with still more states planning to adopt them. The use of such tests means that some deserving students do not obtain diplomas, in some instances the dropout rates increase, and often schooling is ever more intensively reduced to a test-coaching program.

There is a better way: hold schools, in collaboration with the community, responsible for establishing clear and public criteria for graduation. That way, the community knows what students who graduate actually must know and be able to do. Such requirements can be flexible, with student strengths in one area allowed to balance weaknesses in another.

In this better way, each student compiles a record of achievement through portfolios, culminating projects or exhibitions, or simply doing a good job in a serious course. The record becomes the evidence used for determining readiness for graduation. Independent evaluations of the graduation requirements and of the work students are actually doing can be used to determine the quality of student accomplishments.

It is simply unconscionable — and even violates the quite conservative *Standards for Educational and Psychological Testing*[22] — to allow major decisions to be made on the basis of one-time exams. The testing profession should unite with reformers to educate and pressure policy makers to stop this practice.

Accountability. Key areas of school accountability include student achievement, equity, the proper use of funds, and whether the school provides a supportive environment for its children. My focus here is on student achievement.

Students, their parents or guardians, and their teachers need to know how individual students are doing in terms of the school's curriculum, relevant standards, and the student's previous achievement and interests. This individualized accountability information comes mostly from in-school work: various forms of performance assessment provide substantial information for reporting, through conferences and report cards, on individual student learning.

How should information about schools and districts — evidence of accountability for learning by groups of students — be obtained and presented? Usually, this is done with standardized test results from commercial norm-referenced tests or statewide criterion-referenced tests.[23] Most items on both types are multiple-choice questions. Individual scores are aggregated to provide school and district scores. Unfortunately, aggregation can produce results that are misleading or simply wrong.[24] Extensive evidence also shows that these tests often do not measure much of the curriculum, and scores on them are apt to be inflated by teaching to the tests, thereby invalidating the results.[25] This combination of limited measures and coaching has truly damaging effects on the curriculum. Thus the effort to attain accountability effectively undermines the quality of education. This perverse result needs to be changed.

Principles and Indicators suggests that, for evidence of accountability, states and districts rely on a combination of sampling from classroom-based assessment information (e.g., portfolios or learning records) and from performance exams. In essence, the process could work along the following lines.

Each teacher, using scoring guides or rubrics, indicates where on a developmental scale or a performance standard each student should be placed and attaches evidence (records and portfolio material) to back up the decision. A random sample of the portfolios or learning records is selected from each classroom. Independent readers (educators from other schools, members of the community, and so on) review the records as evidence of student learning and place students on the scale. The scores of teachers and readers are then compared to see whether the judgments correspond. If they do not, various actions, beginning with another independent reading, can be used to identify the discrepancy. A larger sample from the classroom can be rescored. In addition, several procedures can be used to adjust the scores to account for teacher variation in scoring ("moderation"). Initial agreement among readers is usually low to moderate, but it can rise quickly if 1) the readers are well-trained and 2) the guides to what is in the records and how to score them are very clear.[26] Professional development can be targeted to help teachers improve their scoring.

This procedure validates teacher judgments and makes teachers central to the accountability process. It enables independent reviews of teachers' evaluations to check for equitable treatment of the students.

Another advantage of this approach is that it is not necessary to ask all students to enter the same kinds of work. Substantial diversity can be allowed in the records and portfolios, provided that they demonstrate student learning in the domain.

Such models have been used fairly extensively in Britain (and were proposed as the basis for a national assessment system there) and in pilot projects in the U.S.[27] This process is similar to what Vermont does with its portfolios. Developers of the *Primary Language Record*, the *Primary Learning Record*, the *California Learning Record*, and the *Work Sampling System* have begun to explore methods of rescoring. A project in the California Learning Assessment System included the development of an "organic portfolio" for the purposes of accountability; readers scored portfolios for evidence of learning in math and language arts domains derived from the California curriculum frameworks.

Using classroom-based information for accountability involves selecting from a wide range of data rather than trying to generalize from a narrow set of information, as is done in most testing programs. There may be a danger that, in trying to choose from wide data, the requirements for selection of material come to dominate instructional practice. However, allowing diversity in the components of the record or portfolio and rescoring only a sample might prevent such a harmful consequence. In any event, this concern must be considered in any effort to use a valuable classroom assessment for accountability purposes.

As an additional means of checking on the overall accuracy of the portfolio process, the Forum suggests that primarily performance exams can be administered. Using a matrix sample, as is done by the National Assessment of Educational Progress (NAEP), every student in a sample of students is administered one part of the entire exam. The parts are then assembled to provide district or state scores. The results of the exam can be compared at the school level to scores on the sample of portfolios. If a discrepancy exists, further work can be done to find the cause of the difference.

Time and money constraints limit what can be administered in one or a few performance exam sittings, making it difficult to include enough tasks to be able to generalize about student learning in the area being tested. Through sampling, much more can be assessed for the same cost than if every student took an entire test.

Performance exams are often used by states to direct and then measure reforms in curriculum and instruction. These efforts seem to have had mixed results. However, on-demand assessments are limited in their classroom utility, even as a model for classroom assessment practices, because they do not help teachers learn to do continuous classroom assessment. That is, most assessment reform at the state level has involved attempting to find formative, classroom uses for summative, on-demand exams. It is a nearly impossible task, though exam items can be the basis for interesting classroom projects if adapted to involve formative aspects of assessment as well. The on-demand exam approach to overcoming the limitations and dangers of traditional multiple-choice tests will probably prove to be a limited success. These exams make much more sense when used on a sampling basis for assessing achievement at the school or district level and as a complement to classroom-based information. In time, they may prove to be unnecessary.

Beyond scores. A new approach to accountability should involve more than changing the measures of student learning. It should involve alternative ways of using information both to improve schools and to inform the public.

For example, groups of schools in New York City are beginning to form networks in which they share the development of standards for student learning and of means to assess students and faculty.[28] In this way, they work together to improve the schools and to hold one another accountable for, among other things, enhanced student learning. Evidence of learning exists at the school level through portfolios, exhibitions, and other presentations of student work, and one purpose of the networks is to help schools refine these assessment processes. One network has printed a portfolio describing the schools, their procedures, and their accomplishments. Its next step will be to have a group of outsiders evaluate and publicly report on the network. This effort somewhat resembles the school quality review process that has begun in New York State, in which teams of educators and members of the public spend a week closely exploring a school and making a report to that school.

These processes are based on the understanding that improvement and accountability should not be separated, any more than instruction and assessment should be. This approach also proposes to move accountability largely to the communities served by the school. It accepts that real accountability is a human and social process and therefore asks for human engagement in looking at schools and striving to make them better.

Accountability reform can thus take several complementary approaches. One is to revise how assessment is done, shifting from testing every student with a simplistic exam to using a combination of classroom-based information and on-demand performance exams. Both methods should use sampling procedures to report on student achievement in light of agreed-upon standards. This can be done at district or state levels. The second approach is to ask schools to work together in networks to hold one another accountable and to bring the community back into the process of evaluating the schools and networks. These

complementary processes can help improve school practices and ultimately improve student learning.

However, parents, the public, and other social institutions have become conditioned to seeing test scores. Indeed, test scores have become nearly synonymous with accountability. But in order to avoid paying the price of forever narrowing schooling to what can be easily and cheaply measured, parents will have to exchange these narrow statistics for richer local information. They can rely on school-based data about their child's performance in light of standards and then use school-level information, also in relation to standards, to compare schools and districts. Through this procedure, parents can determine how well their child is learning.

What Next?

We are in reactionary times. While far more states include some form of performance testing today than at the start of the decade and more have such assessments in the planning or development stage, California and Arizona have dropped performance exams, and such exams are under attack in Kentucky and elsewhere. A right-wing ideological offensive has been mounted against performance assessment in many locales.[29] The calls for "basics" are often trumpeted together with calls for "basic skills tests." In a "get tough" environment in which we are seeing an increase in the use of graduation and even grade-promotion tests, more testing seems to be on the agenda. This includes President Clinton's proposed mostly multiple-choice exam in reading and math.

Yet the problems with traditional testing have not gone away. Those tests offer no solution to the educational needs of our children. Assessment is thus at a crisis point: the old model is incapable of meeting real needs, and a new approach is not yet clear. In this situation, most states have done little more than tinker at the edge of reform, adding some constructed-response items to mostly multiple-choice tests.[30] Whatever forms of exams are eventually used, they cannot provide much help for teachers in learning to integrate assessment with instruction in a continuous flow — and that is the heart of assessment in the service of learning.

Far better, then, to build an assessment system from the bottom up, relying on teachers and seeking to improve the quality of curriculum and instruction as well as assessment. Construction of this sort

of accountability system will require time and effort, but it is a road worth following. Those who seek to reconstruct assessment should consider uniting around the Forum's *Principles and Indicators for Student Assessment Systems* and taking a number of actions.

First, reform advocates, educators, and researchers must continuously point out the limits of and the harm done by traditional testing. Comparing multiple-choice items to real work in portfolios or even to performance exam tasks and asking parents or community members which option represents the kind of work children should be doing is one powerful educational tool. When shown the alternatives, parents typically prefer performance tasks to multiple-choice items.[31] If parents could consistently get the richer information provided by such assessments, they might be willing to give up their desire for simplistic test scores. We should also expose the limitations of the tests. Few parents, not even many teachers, understand the underpinnings and structures of norm-referenced, multiple-choice standardized tests and therefore understand how narrow and biased they are. In 1994 a slight majority of the public thought that essays would be preferable to multiple-choice tests.[32] This indicates a solid base on which to build public understanding of the need to transform assessment.

Second, educators who understand the harm done by the tests should take all possible steps to block their use. Teachers in Japan boycotted exams for elementary students, forcing the government to drop them.[33]

Third, researchers should shift their emphasis away from a one-sided focus on new exams and toward classroom-based approaches. Foundations and government agencies must be persuaded to apply resources to such approaches.

Fourth, school systems should expand and focus professional development on creating schools as communities of learners that integrate curriculum, instruction, and assessment in ways that are helpful to all students. This approach often requires restructuring the school. Parents and the community must be involved in and educated about the process, as they must be about new assessment practices. Networks of such schools can be a basis for redesigning accountability and explaining it to the public.

Finally, educators can do a lot in their schools and districts, even when faced with external "basic skills" multiple-choice tests.

They can implement high-quality classroom assessments and share them with parents and the community. Widespread use of such assessments can form a base for a renewed effort to curtail traditional standardized tests and to construct assessment systems that support learning.

1. National Forum on Assessment, *Principles and Indicators for Student Assessment Systems* (Cambridge, Mass.: FairTest, 1995). *Principles* can be purchased for $10 from FairTest, 342 Broadway, Cambridge, MA 02139. Note that the idea of "schools in networks" is not included in the Forum document. All references to the Forum are from this document.

2. The discussion on performance assessment draws heavily on D. Monty Neill et al., *Implementing Performance Assessment: A Guide to Classroom, School, and System Reform* (Cambridge, Mass.: FairTest, 1995). See also National Forum on Assessment, op. cit.; and *Selected Annotated Bibliography on Performance Assessment*, 2nd ed. (Cambridge, Mass.: FairTest, 1995).

3. Edward Chittenden, "Authentic Assessment: Evaluation and Documentation of Student Performance," in Vito Perrone, ed., *Expanding Student Assessment* (Alexandria, Va.: Association for Supervision and Curriculum Development, 1991), pp. 22-31.

4. Myra Barrs et al., *Primary Language Record* (Portsmouth, N.H.: Heinemann, 1988); Hillary Hester, *Guide to the Primary Learning Record* (London: Centre for Language in Primary Education, 1993); Mary Barr, *California Learning Record* (El Cajon, Calif.: Center for Language in Learning, 1994); and Samuel J. Meisels et al., "The Work Sampling System: Reliability and Validity of a Performance Assessment for Young Children," *Early Childhood Research Quarterly*, vol. 10, 1995, pp. 277-96.

5. Peter H. Johnston, *Constructive Evaluation of Literate Activity* (New York: Longman, 1992); and Patricia F. Carini, "Dear Sister Bess: An Essay on Standards, Judgment, and Writing," *Assessing Writing*, vol. 1, 1994, pp. 29-65.

6. *Curriculum and Evaluation Standards for School Mathematics* (Reston, Va.: National Council of Teachers of Mathematics, 1989).

7. D. Monty Neill and Noe J. Medina, "Standardized Testing: Harmful to Educational Health," *Phi Delta Kappan*, May 1989, pp. 688-97.

8. Norman Frederiksen, "The Real Test Bias: Influence of Testing on Teaching and Learning," *American Psychologist*, March 1984, p. 193.

9. George F. Madaus et al., *The Influence of Testing on Teaching Math and Science in Grades 4-12* (Chestnut Hill, Mass.: Center for the Study of Testing, Evaluation, and Educational Policy, Boston College, 1992).

10. "KERA: What Works, What Doesn't," *Daily Report Card*, 22 May 1996 (on-line); and Fran Spielman, "Schools Try New Tests, Curriculum," *Chicago Sun-Times*, 22 September 1995.

11. Lauren B. Resnick, *Education and Learning to Think* (Washington, D.C.: National Academy Press, 1987); and Lauren B. Resnick and Daniel P. Resnick, "Assessing the Thinking Curriculum: New Tools for Educational Reform," in Bernard R. Gifford and Mary C. O'Connor, eds., *Future Assessments: Changing Views of Aptitude, Achievement, and Instruction* (Boston: Kluwer, 1992), pp. 37-76.

12. James Hiebert et al., "Problem Solving as a Basis for Reform in Curriculum and Instruction: The Case of Mathematics," *Educational Researcher*, May 1996, pp. 12-21; and Scott G. Paris et al., "The Development of Strategic Readers," in P. David Pearson, ed., *Handbook of Reading Research, Vol. 2* (New York: Longman, 1991), pp. 609-40.

13. Hiebert et al., p. 14.

14. Howard Gardner, *The Unschooled Mind* (New York: Basic Books, 1991); and Resnick and Resnick, op. cit.

15. Deborah Meier, "Why the Reading Tests Don't Measure Reading," *Dissent*, Winter 1982-83, pp. 457-66.

16. John Raven, "A Model of Competence, Motivation, and Behavior and a Paradigm for Assessment," in Harold Berlak et al., eds., *Toward a New Science of Educational Testing and Assessment* (Albany: State University of New York Press, 1992), pp. 85-116; and Thomas Kellaghan, George F. Madaus, and Anastasia Raczek, *The Use of External Examinations to Improve Student Motivation* (Washington, D.C.: American Educational Research Association, 1996).

17. Joan L. Herman and Shari Golan, "The Effects of Standardized Testing on Teaching and Schools," *Educational Measurement: Issues and Practice*, Winter 1993, pp. 20-25, 41; George F. Madaus, "The Influence of Testing on the Curriculum," in Laura N. Tanner, ed., *Critical Issues in the Curriculum: 87th NSSE Yearbook, Part I* (Chicago: National Society for the Study of Education, University of Chicago Press, 1988), pp. 83-121; Thomas A. Romberg et al., "Curriculum and Test Alignment," in Thomas A. Romberg, ed., *Mathematics Assessment and Evaluation* (Albany: State University of New York Press, 1992), pp. 61-74; and Mary Lee Smith, "Put to the Test: The Effects of External Testing on Teachers," *Educational Researcher*, June/July 1991, pp. 8-11.

18. Walter Haney, "Making Tests More Educational," *Educational Leadership*, October 1985, pp. 4-13.

19. Linda Darling-Hammond, Jacqueline Ancess, and Beverly Falk, *Authentic Assessment in Action: Studies of Schools and Students at Work* (New York: Teachers College Press, 1995).

20. See especially Judith Warren Little, "Teachers' Professional Development in a Climate of Educational Reform," *Educational Evaluation and Policy Analysis*, Summer 1993, pp. 129-51.

21. Linda Ann Bond et al., *State Student Assessment Programs Database, School Year 1994-1995* (Washington, D.C., and Oak Brook, Ill.: Council of Chief State School Officers and North Central Regional Educational Laboratory, 1996).

22. American Educational Research Association, American Psychological Association, and National Council on Measurement in Education, *Standards for Educational and Psychological Testing* (Washington, D.C.: American Psychological Association, 1985).

23. Bond et al., op. cit.

24. Walter Haney and Anastasia Raczek, "Surmounting Outcomes Accountability in Education," in *Issues in Educational Accountability* (Washington, D.C.: Office of Technology Assessment, 1994).

25. Thomas M. Haladyna, Susan Bobbit Nolen, and Nancy S. Haas, "Raising Standardized Achievement Test Scores and the Origins of Test Score Pollution," *Educational Researcher*, June/July 1991, pp. 2-7; Robert M. Linn, M. Elizabeth Graue, and Nancy M. Sanders, "Comparing State and District Results to National Norms: The Validity of the Claims That 'Everyone Is Above Average,'" *Educational Measurement: Issues and Practice*, Fall 1990, pp. 5-14; and Lorrie A. Shepard, "Inflated Test Score Gains: Is the Problem Old Norms or Teaching the Test?," *Educational Measurement: Issues and Practice*, Fall 1990, pp. 15-22.

26. Suzanne Lane et al., "Generalizability and Validity of Mathematics Performance Assessment," *Journal of Educational Measurement*, Spring 1996, pp. 71-92; Robert Linn, "Educational Assessment: Expanded Expectations and Challenges," *Educational Evaluation and Policy Analysis*, Spring 1993, pp. 1-16; William Thomas et al., *The CLAS Portfolio Assessment Research and Development Project Final Report* (Princeton, N.J.: Educational Testing Service, 1996); and "Using Language Records (PLR/CLR) as Large-Scale Assessments," *FairTest Examiner*, Summer 1995, pp. 8-9.

27. Myra Barrs, "The Road Not Taken," *Forum*, vol. 36, 1994, pp. 36-39.

28. Deborah Meier and Jacqueline Ancess, "Accountability by Bloated Bureaucracy and Regulation: Is There an Alternative?," interactive symposium at the annual meeting of the American Educational Research Association, New York, April 1996.

29. "Right Wing Attacks Performance Assessment," *FairTest Examiner*, Summer 1994, pp. 1, 10-11.

30. D. Monty Neill, *State of State Assessment Systems* (Cambridge, Mass.: FairTest, 1997).

31. Lorrie A. Shepard and Carribeth L. Bliem, *Parent Opinions About Standardized Tests, Teacher's Information, and Performance Assessments* (Los Angeles: Center for Research on Evaluation, Standards, and Student Testing, CSE Technical Report 367, 1993); and John Poggio, "The Politics of Test Validity: Performance Assessment as a State-Sponsored Educational Reform," interactive symposium at the annual meeting of the American Educational Research Association, New York, April 1996.

32. Jean Johnson and John Immerwahr, *First Things First: What Americans Expect from the Public Schools* (New York: Public Agenda Foundation, 1994).

33. "Japanese Teachers Block Tests," *FairTest Examiner*, Spring 1996, p. 9.

Practicing What We Preach in

Designing Authentic

Designing credible performance tasks and assessments is not easy— but we can improve our efforts by using standards and peer review.

Grant Wiggins

What if a student asked for a good grade merely for handing the paper in? What if student divers and gymnasts were able to judge and score their own performances in meets, and did so based on effort and intent? Naive ideas, of course—yet this is just what happens in schools every day when *faculty* submit new curricular frameworks or design new assessments.

Most faculty products are assessed, if at all, merely on whether we worked hard: Did we hand in a lengthy report, based on lots of discussion? Did we provide students with a test that we happen to like? Only rarely do we demand formal self- or peer-assessment of our design work, against standards and criteria. This not only leads to less rigorous reports and designs but also seems a bit hypocritical: We ask students to do this all the time. We need to better practice what we preach.

But how do we ensure that ongoing design and reform work is more rigorous and credible? At the Center on Learning, Assessment, and School Structure (CLASS) in Princeton, New Jersey, we use design standards and a workable peer review process for critiquing and improving all proposed new curricular frameworks, tests, and performance assessments. At the heart of the work is making adult work standards-based, not process-based or merely guided by good intentions. Using such standards can go a long way in helping parents, students, and the community have faith in locally designed systems.

Standard-Based vs. Process-Based Reform Work

Many new curriculum frameworks and assessment systems produce a significant (and often understandable) backlash. A major reason is that the work is typically produced without reference to specific standards for the proposals and final product.

Think of a typical districtwide curriculum reform project. Twelve teachers and supervisors hold meetings all school year to develop a new mathematics curriculum. Their work culminates in a report produced over a three-week period in the summer, at district behest and with district financial support, resulting in a new local mathematics curriculum framework. They follow a time-tested *process* of scanning national reports, searching for consensus about themes and topics and logical progressions, and summarizing their findings and recommendations. But against what standards is their *product* (as opposed to their process) to be judged? The usual answer is: no legitimate standards at all, other than the implicit one that when the authors deem their work finished, the report is complete.

By contrast, what if all report-writers had to answer these questions: Is the report useful to readers? Does it engage and inform the readers? Does it anticipate the reactions of its critics? Does it meet professional standards of curriculum design or measurement? Does it meet the purposes laid out in a charge to the committee? Most important: *Did the writers regularly self-assess and revise their work in progress against such criteria and standards? Did they regularly seek feedback from faculty affected en route?*—the same writing process questions we properly put to students. Their report would have far greater impact if they addressed such questions. By contrast,

© Susie Fitzhugh

From *Educational Leadership,* December 1996-January 1997, pp. 18-25. © 1997 by the Association for Supervision and Curriculum Development. All rights reserved. Reprinted by permission.

Assessments

© Susie Fitzhugh

with no self-assessment and self-adjustment along the way, the work is predictably ineffective in getting other faculty to change practice or in helping skeptical parents understand the need to do so.

Similarly with new assessments. Almost every teacher designs tests under the most naive premise: "If I designed it and gave it, it must be valid and reliable." Yet we know from research, our own observations, and the process of peer review that few teacher-designed tests and assessments meet the most basic standards for tech-

> **The purpose of assessment is to find out what each student is able to do, with knowledge, in context.**

nical credibility, intellectual defensibility, coherence with system goals, and fairness to students.

When we practice what we preach about self-assessment and adjustment against standards, we can *ensure* more rigorous and effective local teacher products, greater collegiality, and better student performance.

In standards-based reform projects, in short, we must seek a disinterested review of products against standards all along the way—not just follow a process in the hope that our work turns out well. The challenge for school reformers is to ensure that their work has *impact*, like any other performance. Desired effects must be *designed in;* they must inform all our

work from the beginning.[1] As with student performances, then, we will meet standards only by "backwards design"—making self-assessment and peer review against performance standards central to the process of writing and revision—*before* it is too late.

Rather than teaching a lock-step

process of design, we at CLASS teach faculties to see that design is always *iterative*. We constantly rethink our designs, using feedback based on clear design standards. We will likely never revisit our original designs if we lack powerful criteria and a review process with the implicit obligation to critique

> Complex performance tasks focus on understanding as an educational goal, as opposed to mere textbook knowledge.

all work against the criteria. We are often satisfied with (and misled by) our effort and good intentions.

Assessment Design Standards

Standards-based reform work begins with clear standards for eventual products. At CLASS, we instruct faculties involved in performance-based assessment reform in the use of a design template, a design process, and a self-assessment and peer review process based on ultimate-product standards. In addition, we work with leaders to make such standards-based design work more routine in and central to local faculty life (linked to job descriptions, department meetings, and performance appraisal systems, as well as individual and team design work). The template is also the database structure for assessment tasks and rubrics on our World Wide Web site, http://www.classnj.org.

The standards guide all design decisions. The three main criteria for judging emerging tasks are *credibility, user-friendliness,* and *feasibility.* The standards are fixed by specific models that serve to anchor the self-assessment and peer review process (just as in the assessment of student writing). Each criterion is broken down further into subcriteria: Under credibility, for example, the designer (in self-assessing) and the peers (in peer reviewing) ask such questions as:
■ Does it measure what it says it measures? Is this a valid assessment of the intended achievement?
■ Are the scoring criteria and rubrics clear, descriptive, and explicitly related to district goals and standards?
■ Is the scoring system based on genuine standards and criteria, derived from analysis of credible models?
■ Does the task require a sophisticated understanding of required content?

■ Does the task require a high degree of intellectual skill and performance quality?
■ Does the task simulate or replicate authentic, messy, real-world challenges, contexts, and constraints faced by adult professionals, consumers, or citizens?
■ Does the scoring system enable a reliable yet adequately fine discrimination of degrees of work quality?
■ Is the task worthy of the time and energy required to complete it?
■ Is the task challenging—an appropriate stretch for students?

Naturally, in parallel to what we ask of students, there are rubrics for self-and peer-assessment of these questions.

Anticipating Key Design Difficulties

We ask designers to pay particular attention to three crucial, ever-present problems in local assessment design: whether a sophisticated understanding of core content is required by the task, whether the criteria and rubrics used are authentic and appropriate for such a task and target, and whether the tasks really measure the targeted achievement. This last problem can be stated as a single injunction that must be constantly invoked: Beware the temptation of confusing a neat instructional activity with an appropriate performance task.

1. Validity in design. Validity is essential. The purpose of assessment is to find out what each student is able to do, with knowledge, in context. But we must sample from a large domain. In asking students to do a *few* tasks well, we believe we are on solid ground because we view the tasks as apt—at the heart of the subject, and able to

yield more general inferences about achievement in a subject.

When we worry about validity in design, we are thinking backwards from the evidence we need. The task must yield the right kind of information and must enable us to elicit and observe the most salient performance, given the (more general) achievements we seek to measure.

In instruction, our worries are different. We typically try to develop activities that give rise to an educational experience and ask questions that differ from those that apply to assessment design: Will the students be engaged? Will we accommodate different styles, levels, and interests? Will the activity give rise to thinking and learning at the heart of my goal for the unit? Such questions are essential to teaching, but unlikely to ensure that we will have adequate assessment evidence for *each* student when the activity is over.

Easy to say, but what to do? That's where the peer review process comes in. We are now forced to *justify* our design in a nonconfrontational way. In peer review, we often discover that the design does not yet work as a sound assessment. (Eventually, our self-assessment becomes so skilled that we can foresee these kinds of problems without much peer review.)

These are the questions we use in peer review for validity:
■ Does the task evoke the right kind of evidence, given the target? Does the task evoke sufficient evidence?
■ Can a student master the task for the "right" reasons only? Or does the task unwittingly assess for a different outcome than intended by the designer?

Yes, it measures what it's supposed to if the task can only be done well if students are in control of the key achievements.

No, it doesn't measure what it should if students (1) can perform the task well without achieving the intended result or (2) fail to perform the task well for inappropriate reasons, that is, abilities or knowledge unrelated to the target.

■ Are the criteria apt? That is, given the achievements to be assessed and the nature of the task, are these the right traits of performance to assess and the right descriptions of differences in work quality?

■ Is the weighting of the different criteria appropriate, given the nature and purpose of such performance?

■ Do the scoring rubrics discriminate levels of quality appropriately and not arbitrarily?

■ Does the task imply a rich and appropriate understanding of the intended target? Or is the task implicitly based on a questionable or inappropriate definition of the achievement?

■ Do the rubrics honor the criteria and achievement? Or are they implicitly based on questionable or inappropriate definitions of exemplary performance?

2. Assessment for understanding. Because any complex performance tends to focus on fairly general academic skills, performance tasks often unwittingly lack sufficient intellectual rigor and credibility.[2] Many tasks simply reveal whether students can "communicate" or "problem solve"— and often allow great leeway in subject-matter content. Consider the specific knowledge required to perform these complex tasks developed by teachers in North Carolina:

> *Birds and Soldiers.* Wildlife officials and politicians are at odds because of the rare red-cockade woodpecker on the Fort Bragg military base. Fort Bragg officials have to limit military training exercises because of the protection required for the birds under the Endangered Species Act. The Act states that an endangered bird's environment cannot be tampered with. Almost half the

known red-cockade woodpecker population is located on the base. Your task is to propose a workable solution to the problem, based on a careful review of the military's needs and the relevant law. You will write a report and make a speech to a simulated EPA review board.

Federation/Confederation. This task involves three parts: a) the student is asked to assume the role of a resident of North Carolina on the eve of secession and deliver a speech from that person's perspective on whether or not North Carolina should secede from the Union, b) the student then synthesizes the points from all speeches given and writes a letter to the editor of the local newspaper reflecting this person's re-examined point of view, and c) writes a reflective piece in the person's journal, 15 years later, re-examining the wisdom of the earlier stands.

It's Your Choice: Health Insurance. Co-payment? Pretreatment estimate? Deductible? Is health care language a foreign language for you? Students take on the role of a financial analyst and must communicate to each of three different families, in a convincing manner, the best choice of coverage for their needs and budget.

> **FIGURE 1**
>
> **What Does Understanding Mean?**
>
> Complete the following sentence to help construct an authentic, credible performance assessment in any subject matter:
>
> The students *really* understand (the idea, issue, theory, event being assessed) only when they can...
>
> ■ provide credible theories, models, or interpretations to explain ...
> ■ avoid such common misunderstandings as ...
> ■ make such fine, subtle distinctions as ...
> ■ effectively interpret such ambiguous situations or language as ...
> ■ explain the value or importance of ...
> ■ critique ...
> ■ see the plausibility of the "odd" view that ...
> ■ empathize with ...
> ■ critically question the commonly held view that ...
> ■ invent ...
> ■ recognize the prejudice within that ...
> ■ question such strong personal but unexamined beliefs as ...
> ■ accurately self-assess ...

These tasks focus on *understanding* as an educational goal, as opposed to mere textbook knowledge. We at CLASS have developed a complex schema for teaching and assessing understanding, drawing not only on our own research of the past decade but also the fine work of Howard Gardner (1992), David Perkins (1992), and their Project Zero colleagues. As we see it, to assess for understanding means to assess for five related capacities: sophistication of explanations and interpretations; insight gained from perspective; empathy; contextual know-how in knowledge application; and self-knowledge based on knowing our talents, limits, and prejudices.

What is the evidence we need to gather? At CLASS, we use the exercise in Figure 1 as a reminder. As a prompt, we ask teachers to brainstorm ways to complete the sentence stem that reads, "The students understand the idea only when they can..." Then we integrate the brainstormed ideas by building a rubric of sophisticated understanding on a novice-to-expert continuum. For example, take key events in history: What is a novice versus a sophisticated

> Peer review can yield a profound result: the beginning of a truly professional relationship with colleagues.

understanding of the Civil War? What sorts of judgments and discriminations is an expert likely to make that a novice student is unlikely to make? Such questions force us to predict how students are likely to perform.

The most exciting effect of this exercise is to realize that we must be able to predict students' inevitable misunderstandings. Of all the assessment strategies we have used, this is the one that causes the most "Aha!" responses. To teach and assess *mindful of misunderstanding* requires not only rubrics for levels of understanding and misunderstanding, but a new perspective on teaching: If you can now predict student misunderstandings, what are you doing to avoid or aggressively compensate for them in your curriculum and instruction?[3]

3. Critique and revision of rubrics and criteria. The designer of assessments *always* has a blind spot about something. Peers can discover and help to remedy oversights. The following represent typical errors with most rubrics:

■ Turning a quality into a quantity. Thus, students improperly get a higher score for "more" library sources or footnotes, as opposed to "more apt" sources.

■ Using comparative or evaluative language alone, such as "6" or "excellent" and "5" or "good," and so forth, when observable traits of performance are more meaningful.

■ A lack of continuity in the "distance" between score points. Thus, in the descriptors for a 6, 5, and 4, the differences may be slight. Suddenly, a 3 is just awful and not passing, so the score points are bunched at one end and spread out at another, causing misleading results.

Other pitfalls to watch for include combining traits, such as "creative" and "organized," in the same descriptor, and confusing a criterion with its indicators. For example, "asking questions" is an indicator of *good listening,* but silence in church doesn't mean that people aren't listening. Inappropriate questions don't indicate good listening, either. In addition, most rubrics overemphasize content and form of the work and underemphasize or ignore the *impact* of performance—criteria at the heart of what we mean by "performance."

Most of us make these mistakes when we begin writing rubrics. Peer review, based on design standards, ensures that rubrics are debugged of common mistakes.

Peer Review

Besides improving the process of developing performance assessments, peer review can yield a profound result: the beginning of a truly professional relationship with colleagues. In CLASS projects, teachers have termed peer review one of the most satisfying (if initially scary) experiences in their careers. As a 32-year veteran teacher put it, "This is the kind of conversation I entered the profession to have, yet never had. I'm rejuvenated. I'm optimistic."

Peer reviewers serve as consultants to the designer, not glib judges. The process itself is evaluated against a basic criterion in support of that goal: *The designer must feel that the design was understood and improved by the process, and the reviewers must feel that the process was insightful and team building.* As the following guidelines reveal, the reviewers give specific, focused, and useful feedback:

Stage 1: Peers review task without designer present.[4] The designer states issues he or she wishes highlighted, self-assesses (optional), and then leaves. The peers read the materials, referring to the *assessment design criteria.* Working individually, the peers summarize the work's strengths and weaknesses and then report to the group. The group fills out a sheet summarizing the key feedback and guidance, thus rehearsing the oral report to follow. Reviewers rate the task against the task rubric, if appropriate.

Stage 2: Peers discuss review with designer. Appointing a timekeeper/facilitator is crucial. The facilitator's job is to gently but firmly ensure that the designer listens (instead of defending). First, the designer clarifies technical or logistical issues (without elaboration)— *the design must stand by itself as much as possible.* Second, the peers give oral feedback and guidance. Third, the group and the designer discuss the feedback; the designer takes notes and asks questions. Finally, the group decides what issues should be presented to the faculty as a whole—lessons learned and problems evoked.

Criteria for peer review:

1. The core of the discussion involves considering: To what extent is the "targeted achievement" well assessed? To what extent do the task and rubric meet the design criteria? What would make the assessment more valid, reliable, authentic, engaging, rigorous, fair, and feasible?

2. The reviewers should be friendly, honest consultants. The designer's intent should be treated as a given (unless the unit's goal and means are unclear or lack rigor). *The aim is to improve the designer's idea, not substitute it with the reviewers' aesthetic judgments, intellectual priorities, or pet designs.*

3. The designer asks for focused feedback in relation to specific design criteria, goals, or problems.

4. The designer's job in the second session is primarily to listen, not explain, defend, or justify design decisions.

5. The reviewers' job is first to give useful *feedback* (did the effect match the intent?), and only then, useful *guidance.*

Note that we distinguish here between feedback and guidance. The best feedback is highly specific and descriptive of how the performance met standards. Recall how often a music teacher or tennis coach provides a steady flow of feedback (Wiggins 1993). Feedback is *not* praise and blame or mere encouragement. Try becoming better at any performance if all you hear is "Nice effort!" or "You can do better" or "We didn't like it." Whatever the role or value of praise and dislike, they are not feedback: The information provided does not help **you improve. In feedback and guidance,** *what matters is judging the design against criteria related to sound assessment.* Peer reviewers are free to offer concrete guidance—suggestions on how the design might be improved—assuming the designer grasps and accepts the feedback.[5]

Assessment System Criteria

Beyond reviewing specific performance tasks and rubrics, we need to evaluate entire assessment systems. For such systemic assessments, a more complex set of criteria includes credibility, technical soundness, usefulness, honesty, intellectual rigor, and fairness (Wiggins 1996).

Again, a key to credibility is *disinterested* judging—using known and intellectually defensible tasks and criteria—whether we are talking about student or faculty work. A psychometrician may well find a local assessment system not up to a rigid technical standard; but such a system can still be credible and effective within the real-world constraints of school time, talent, and budgets.

Credibility is a concern of the whole school community. We need other feedback—not just from peer reviewers, teacher-designers, or psychometricians, but from parents, school boards, college admissions officers, and legislators. Alas, what one group finds credible, another often doesn't. Clients for our information have differing needs and interests in the data; if we fail to consider these clients, our local assessment systems may be inadequate and provincial. But if we improperly mimic large-scale, audit testing methods in an effort to meet psychometric standards for local assessment design, we often develop assessment systems that are neither authentic nor effective as feedback.

Peer review should always consider the possible customers for the assessment information, to determine whether both the task and the reporting of results are apt and adequate (Wiggins 1996). The primary customer is always the student.

Principles Underlying the Standards and Criteria

When proposing standards and criteria for performance assessments, we need to remember—and clearly state—the

> Consider the possible customers for the assessment information, to determine whether both the task and the reporting of results are apt and adequate.

underlying values of our proposals. Assessment is not merely a blind set of techniques, after all, but a means to some valued end. Effective and appropriate school assessment is based on five principles:

1. Reform focuses on the purpose, not merely the techniques, of assessment. Too many reform projects tamper with the technology of assessment without reconnecting with the purposes of assessment. Assessment must recapture essential educational aims: to help the student learn and to help the teacher instruct. All other needs, such as accountability testing and program evaluation, come second. Merely shifting from multiple-choice questions to performance testing changes nothing if we still rely on the rituals of year-end, secure, one-shot testing.

2. Students and teachers are entitled to a more instructional and user-friendly assessment system than provided by current systems and psychometric criteria. A deliberately instructional assessment makes sure that tests enlighten students about real-world intellectual tasks, criteria, context, and standards; and such an assessment is built to ensure user-friendly, powerful feedback. Conventional tests often prevent students from fully understanding and meeting their intellectual obligations. And teachers are entitled to an accountability system that facilitates better teaching.

3. Assessment is central, not peripheral, to instruction. We must design curriculums backwards from complex and exemplary challenges. A performance-based system integrates curriculum and assessment design,

thereby making the sequence of work more coherent and meaningful from the learner's point of view.

4. Authentic tasks must anchor the assessment process, so that typical test questions play a properly subordinate role. Students must see what adults really do with their knowledge; and all students must learn what athletes already know—that performance is more than just the drill work that develops discrete knowledge and skill. Genuine tasks demand challenges that require good judgment, adaptiveness, and the habits of mind—such as craftsmanship and tolerance for ambiguity—never tested by simplistic test items.

5. In assessment, local is better. Site-level assessments must be of higher intellectual quality—more tightly linked to instruction—than superficial standardized tests can ever be. No externally run assessment can build the kind of local capacity for and interest in high-quality assessment at the heart of all genuine local improvement. But local assessment must be credible—and that means inviting disinterested assessment by people other than the student's teachers, and including oversight of the entire assessment design and implementation system (for case studies in assessment reform, see CLASS 1996).

By keeping these principles in mind, we can continually improve our reform work. Process-driven improvement efforts can become rigid and noncreative; we resort to following the letter of the law only. The real power of standards-based reform is that we are free to innovate and divert from process—if we see a better way to approach the standards and better honor our principles. Thus, our reform efforts, not just our designs, also demand constant self-assessment and self-adjustment, based on comparing emerging work against our principles.[6]

Professionalism depends on standards-based work and peer review. Despite the long-standing habits of schools where teachers are left alone to design assessments, we believe that such practices are counterproductive to both local credibility and professional development. Every school and district ought to require peer review of major assessments, based on sound and agreed-upon standards and criteria of design and use.

[1]For student performance tasks, too, rubric and task writers should emphasize impact-related criteria so that students know the purpose of the task. Thus, instead of just scoring for organization, clarity, and accuracy in essay writing, we should include criteria related to how persuasive and engaging the piece is.

[2]Bob Marzano believes that performance assessment is ill-suited for assessing understanding of subject matter. I disagree: Intellectual understanding is demonstrated by doing well at certain types of performance, but designing such tasks is indeed difficult.

[3]A full development of this schema of understanding will appear in 1997 in a new ASCD book and training program, co-authored by Jay McTighe and myself, and tentatively titled *Understanding by Design*.

[4]Some may wonder about the utility or ethics of discussing the work in the designer's absence. We have found that this first stage gives the peers freedom to express vague concerns and complete criticisms. When the designer is always present, we find that the session bogs down as the designer justifies and explains all decisions.

[5]Video and print material on the peer review process is available from CLASS.

[6]Fairtest (1995) has developed standards and indicators for assessment processes and systems. Contact Fairtest at National Center for Fair & Open Testing, 342 Broadway, Cambridge, MA 02139. Phone: (617) 864-4810; fax: (617) 497-2224; e-mail: FairTest@aol.com.

References

Center on Learning, Assessment, and School Structure (CLASS). (1996). *Measuring What Matters: The Case for Assessment Reform* (video). Princeton, N.J.: CLASS.

Fairtest: National Center for Fair and Open Testing. (1995). *Principles and Indicators for Student Assessment Systems.* Cambridge, Mass.: Fairtest.

Gardner, H. (1992) *The Unschooled Mind.* New York: Basic Books.

Perkins, D. (1992). *Smart Schools: Better Thinking and Learning in Every Child.* New York: Free Press.

Wiggins, G. (1993). *Assessing Student Performance: Exploring the Purpose and Limits of Testing.* San Francisco: Jossey-Bass.

Wiggins, G. (1996). "Honesty and Fairness: Toward Better Grading and Reporting," in *Communicating Student Learning,* edited by T. Guskey. 1996 ASCD Yearbook. Alexandria, Va.: ASCD.

Grant Wiggins is President of the Center on Learning, Assessment, and School Structure (CLASS), 648 The Great Road, Princeton, NJ 08540. He can be reached by e-mail at gpw@classnj.org.

What Happens

Between

Not only assessment needs to change. Curriculums and instructional strategies, too, must reflect a *performance* orientation. Here are seven principles for performance-based instruction.

Jay McTighe

Growing concern over the inadequacy of conventional tests has spurred interest in performance assessments, such as performance tasks, projects, and exhibitions. To many supporters, these performance assessments are better suited than traditional tests to measure what really counts: whether students can apply their knowledge, skills, and understanding in important, real-world contexts. More teachers are using performance assessments in their classrooms, and such assessments are beginning to influence district- and state-level testing programs as well.

Increasing the use of performance assessments—in and of itself—will not significantly improve student performance, however. To borrow the old farm adage: "You don't fatten the cattle by weighing them." If we expect students to improve their performance on these new, more authentic measures, we need to engage in "performance-based instruction" on a regular basis.

But what does it really mean to teach for performance? Working the past six years with hundreds of teachers using performance assessments, I have seen how the development of assessment tasks and evaluative criteria can influence instruction. Based on this experience, I offer seven principles of performance-based instruction, illustrated by vignettes from classrooms in which these principles are being applied.

Establish Clear Performance Targets

As part of a unit on nutrition, a middle school health teacher presents her students with the following performance task.

> You are having six of your friends over for your birthday party. You are preparing the food for the party, but your mother has just read a book on nutrition and tells you that you can't serve anything containing artificial sweeteners or lots of salt, sugar, or saturated fats. Plan a menu that will make your friends happy and still meet your mother's expectations. Explain why your menu is both tasty and healthy. Use the USDA Food Pyramid guidelines and the Nutrition Facts on food labels to support your menu selection.[1]

To teach effectively, we need to be clear about what we expect students to know, understand, and be able to do as a result of our instruction. But performance-based instruction calls for more. We also need to determine *how* students will demonstrate the intended knowledge, understanding, and proficiency. When establishing performance targets, consider Gardner's (1991) contention that developing students' *understanding* is a primary goal of teaching. He defines understanding as the ability to apply facts, concepts, and skills appropriately in new situations.

The principle of *establishing clear performance targets* and the goal of *teaching for understanding* fit together as a powerful means of linking curriculum, instruction, and assessment. A performance-based orientation requires that we think about curriculum not simply as content to be covered but in terms of desired *performances of understanding*. Thus, performance-oriented teachers consider assessment up front by conceptualizing their learning goals and objectives as performance applications calling for students to demonstrate their understanding. Performance assessments, then, become targets for teaching and learning, as well as serving as a source of evidence that students understand, and are able to apply, what we have taught.

Establishing clear performance targets is important for several reasons. Teachers who establish and

Assessments?

communicate clear performance targets to their students reflect what we know about effective teaching, which supports the importance of instructional clarity. These teachers also recognize that students' attitudes and perceptions toward learning are influenced by the degree to which they understand what is expected of them and what the rationale is for various instructional activities. Finally, the process of establishing performance targets helps identify curriculum priorities, enabling us to focus on the essential and enduring knowledge in a crowded field.

Strive for Authenticity in Products and Performances

Fifth graders conduct a survey to gather data about community attitudes toward a proposal that public school students wear uniforms. The students organize the data and then choose an appropriate graphic display for communicating their findings. Finally, students write letters to the editor of the local paper to present their data and their personal views on the proposal. A direct link to the larger world is established when two student letters are published in the newspaper.

Leading reformers recommend that schools involve their students in authentic work. Performance tasks should call upon students to demonstrate their knowledge and skills in a manner that reflects the world outside the classroom. Although diagramming sentences may help students understand sentence structures and parts of speech, this is not really an authentic activity, because few people outside of school diagram sentences. When students engage in purposeful writing (for example, to persuade an identified audience), however, they are using their knowledge and skills in ways much more congruent with the demands of real life.

As in the larger world, authentic work in schools calls for students to apply their knowledge and skills, with the result typically being a tangible product (written, visual, or three-dimensional) or a performance. These products and performances have an

> When students have opportunities to examine their work in light of known criteria and performance standards, they begin to shift their orientation from "What did I get?" to "Now I know what I need to do to improve."

explicit *purpose* (for example, to explain, to entertain, or to solve a problem) and are directed toward an identified *audience*. Because real-world issues and problems are rarely limited to a single content area, authentic work often provides opportunities for making interdisciplinary connections.

Emphasizing authentic work does not lessen the importance of helping students develop basic skills. On the contrary, basic knowledge and skills provide an essential foundation for meaningful application. The "basics" are not ends in themselves, however; they serve a larger goal: to enable students to thoughtfully apply knowledge and skills within a meaningful, authentic context.

Research and experience confirm that when learners perceive classroom activities as meaningful and relevant, they are more likely to have a positive attitude toward them (McCombs 1984, Schunk 1990). In addition, many teachers have observed that when given the opportunity to produce a tangible product or demonstrate something to a real audience (for example, peers, parents, younger or older students, community members), students often seem more willing to put forth the effort required to do quality work.

Remember that what we assess sends

a strong signal to students about what is important for them to learn. When authentic performance tasks play a key role in teaching and assessing, students will know that we expect them to apply knowledge in ways valued in the world beyond the classroom.

Publicize Criteria and Performance Standards

Before beginning a laboratory experiment, a high school science teacher reviews the Science Department's performance list for a lab report with her students. The list, containing the criteria for a thorough report, clearly conveys the teacher's expectations while serving as a guide to the students as they prepare their reports. Before she collects the reports, the teacher allows students to exchange papers with their lab partners, give feedback to one another based on the performance list criteria, and make needed revisions.

Like the problems and issues we confront in the real world, authentic classroom performance tasks rarely have a single, correct answer. Therefore, our evaluation of student products and performances must be based upon judgment and guided by criteria. The criteria are typically incorporated into one of several types of scoring tools: a rubric, a rating scale, or a performance list. With all of these tools, the criteria help to spell out the qualities that we consider to be most significant or important in student work.

Teachers at elementary schools in Anne Arundel County, Maryland, use a "Writing to Persuade" rubric to help students learn the qualities of effective persuasive writing. A large poster of the rubric, containing the criteria in the form of questions, is prominently displayed in the front of the classroom to provide an easy reference for teachers and students. For example: "Did I clearly identify my position?" "Did I fully support my position with facts or personal experiences?" "Did I effectively use persuasive language to convince my audience?"

Evaluative criteria clearly are essential for summative evaluations, but teachers also are recognizing their role in *improving* performance. By sharing the criteria with students, we begin to remove the mystery of how work will be evaluated, while highlighting the elements of quality and standards of performance toward which students should strive. Teachers also can help students internalize these elements of quality by having them use scoring tools themselves to evaluate their own work or that of their peers. When students have opportunities to examine their work in light of known criteria and performance standards, they begin to shift their orientation from "What did I get?" to "Now I know what I need to do to improve."

Provide Models of Excellence

A middle school art teacher displays five examples of well-constructed papier-mâché sculptures of "figures in action." The examples illustrate the criteria by which the sculptures will be evaluated: composition (figure showing action), strength and stability of armature (underlying structure), surface construction (application of papier-mâché), finishing techniques (texture, color, details), and overall effect. The teacher notes that the quality of her students' sculptures has markedly improved since she began sharing and discussing actual models of excellence.

Providing students with lists of criteria or scoring rubrics is a necessary piece of performance-based instruction—but it isn't always sufficient. Not every student will immediately understand the criteria or how to apply them to their own work ("What do you mean by well organized?"). Wiggins (1993) suggests that if we expect students to do excellent work, they need to know what excellent work looks like. Following his idea, performance-based instruction calls for providing students with models and demonstrations that illustrate excellence in products or performances.

This approach, of course, is not unknown in schools. Effective coaches and sponsors of extracurricular activities often involve their club or team members in analyzing award-winning school newspapers or yearbooks, or reviewing videotapes of excellent athletic or dramatic performances. But providing models of quality work is also an essential piece of performance-based instruction in classrooms.

Teachers can use examples of excellent work during instruction to help students understand the desired elements of quality. Some teachers also present students with examples of mediocre and excellent work, asking them to analyze the differences and identify the characteristics that distinguish the excellent examples from the rest. In this way, students learn the criteria of quality through tangible models and concrete examples. In some classrooms, students actually help to construct the scoring tools (rubric, rating scale, or performance list), based on their growing knowledge of the topic and the criteria they have identified in the examples. (The potential benefits of providing students with tangible examples underscore the value of saving examples of student work from performance tasks for use as models in future years!)

Some teachers are wary of providing models of quality, fearing that students may simply copy or imitate the examples. This is a real danger with activities for which there is a single correct answer (or one "best" way of accomplishing the task). With more open-

ended performance tasks and projects, however, we can minimize this problem by presenting students with multiple models. In this way, students are shown several different ways to satisfy the desired criteria, thus discouraging a cookie-cutter approach.

By providing students with criteria *and* models of excellence, teachers are often rewarded with higher quality products and performances. In addition, they are helping students become more self-directed; students able to distinguish between poor- and high-quality performance are more likely to be able to evaluate and improve their own work, guided by a clear conception of excellence.

Teach Strategies Explicitly

An elementary teacher introduces his students to two strategies—summarizing and predicting—to enhance their comprehension of text materials. He describes each strategy and models its use by thinking aloud while applying it to a challenging text. During the lesson, the teacher refers to large posters spelling out a written procedure and visual symbol for each strategy. Following the lesson, he distributes bookmark versions of the posters. Over the next two weeks, each student works with a reading buddy to practice using the strategies with both fiction and nonfiction texts while the teacher monitors their progress and provides guidance.

In every field of endeavor, effective performers use specific techniques and strategies to boost their performance. Olympic athletes visualize flawless performances, writers seek feedback from "critical friends," law students form study groups, coaches share tips at coaching clinics, busy executives practice time management techniques.

Students also benefit from specific strategies that can improve their performance on academic tasks. For example, webbing and mapping techniques help students see connections, cognitive reading strategies boost comprehension (Palinscar and Brown 1984; Haller, Child, and Walberg 1988), brainstorming techniques enhance idea generation, and mnemonics assists retention and recall.

Few students spontaneously generate and use strategies on their own, however, so we need to explicitly teach these thinking and learning strategies. One straightforward approach is to use the direct instruction model, in which teachers

1. introduce and explain the purpose of the strategy;

2. demonstrate and model its use;

3. provide guided practice for students to apply the strategy with feedback;

4. allow students to apply the strategy independently and in teams; and

5. regularly reflect on the appropriate uses of the strategy and its effectiveness.

In addition to direct instruction, many teachers find it helpful to incorporate thinking and learning strategies into tangible products, such as posters, bookmarks, visual symbols, or cue cards (McTighe and Lyman 1988). For example, students in a middle school mathematics class I am familiar with have constructed desktop spinners depicting six problem-solving strategies they have been taught. When working on open-ended problems, the students use the spinners to indicate the strategy they are using. Their teacher circulates around the room, asking students to think aloud by explaining their reasoning and problem-solving strategies. Later, she leads a class discussion of solutions and the effectiveness of the strategies used. The spinners provide students with a tangible reminder of the value of using strategies during problem solving. These and other cognitive tools offer students practical and concrete support as they acquire and internalize performance-enhancing strategies.

Use Ongoing Assessments for Feedback and Adjustment

A middle school social studies teacher notes that the quality of her students' research reports has markedly improved since he began using the writing process approach of brainstorming, drafting, reviewing feedback, and revising. Through the use of teacher and peer reviews of draft reports, students are given specific feedback on strengths, as well as on aspects of their reports that may be unclear, inaccurate, or incomplete. They appreciate the opportunity to make necessary revisions before turning in their final copy.

The Japanese concept of *Kaizen* suggests that quality is achieved through constant, incremental improvement. According to J. Edwards Deming, guru of the Total Quality Management movement, quality in manufacturing is not achieved through end-of-line inspections; by then, it is too late. Rather, quality is the result of regular inspections (assessments) *along the way,* followed by needed adjustments based on the information gleaned from the inspections.

How do these ideas apply in an academic setting? We know that students will rarely perform at high levels on challenging learning tasks on the first attempt. Deep understanding or high levels of proficiency are achieved only as a result of trial, practice, adjustments based on feedback, and more practice. Performance-based instruction underscores the importance of using assessments to provide information to guide improvement throughout the learning process, instead of waiting to give feedback at the end of instruction.

Once again, effective coaches and sponsors of clubs often use this principle as they involve their students in scrimmages, dress rehearsals, and reviews of bluelines. Such activities serve to identify problems and weaknesses, followed by more coaching and opportunities to practice or revise.

The ongoing interplay between assessment and instruction so common in the arts and athletics is also evident in classrooms using practices such as nongraded quizzes and practice tests, the writing process, formative performance tasks, review of drafts, and peer response groups. The teachers in such classrooms recognize that ongoing assessments provide the feedback that enhances their instruction and guides student revision. *Kaizen,* in the context of schools, means ensuring that assessment enhances performance, not simply measures it.

Document and Celebrate Progress

Early in the school year, a middle school physical education teacher has her students analyze their current fitness levels based on a series of measures of strength, endurance, and flexibility. The initial results are charted and used to establish personal fitness goals. The teacher then guides students in preparing individualized fitness plans to achieve their goals. Subsequent fitness tests at the middle and end of the year enable the teacher and her students to document their progress and, if necessary, establish new goals. The teacher believes that the focus on improvement based on a personal benchmark allows every student to achieve a measure of success while cultivating the habits necessary for lifelong fitness.

Perhaps one of the greatest challenges in this current era of school reform is the gap between our goal of higher standards of performance for all and the realization that some students are functioning well below these lofty standards. Many educators struggle daily with this tension: How do we preserve students' self-esteem without lowering our standards? How do we encourage

> Performance-based instruction underscores the importance of using assessments to guide improvement throughout the learning process, instead of waiting to give feedback at the end of instruction.

their efforts without conveying a false sense of accomplishment? Perceptive teachers also recognize that students' own beliefs about their ability to be successful in new learning situations are a critical variable. Confronted with rigorous performance standards, some students may well believe that the target is beyond their grasp and may not, as a result, put forth needed effort.

There are no easy solutions to this dilemma. But reflect for a moment on the natural inclination displayed by parents and grandparents of toddlers and preschoolers. They regularly support new performance by encouraging small steps ("C'mon, you can do it!"), celebrating incremental achievements ("Listen, everyone! She said, 'dada'!"), and documenting growth (witness the refrigerator displays ranging from scribbles of color to identifiable pictures). These celebrations encourage children to keep trying and to strive for greater competence. They focus on what youngsters *can do* and how they have *improved* as a means of spurring continued growth.

Performance-based instruction demands a similar tack. Acknowledging the limitations of one-shot assessments, such as tests and quizzes, as the primary measures of important learning goals, some educators are moving toward creating collections of student work over time. One manifestation of this is the growing interest in and use of portfolios. Consider an analogy with photography. If a test or quiz represents a snapshot (a picture of learning at a specific moment) then a portfolio is more like a photo album—a collection of pictures showing growth and change over time.

Just as portfolios can be extremely useful as a means of documenting student progress, they also provide a tangible way to display and celebrate student work. Grade-level teams at North Frederick Elementary School in Frederick, Maryland, for example, sponsor a "portfolio party" each fall and spring. Parents, grandparents, school board members, central office

> Performance tasks should call upon students to demonstrate their knowledge and skills in a manner that reflects the world outside the classroom.

staff, business partners, and others are invited to review student work collected in portfolios. Before the party, teachers guide students in selecting examples from their portfolios that illustrate progress in key learning areas. During the party, students present their portfolios to the guests, describe their work during the year, highlight the progress they have made, and identify related goals for future improvement.

Principal Carolyn Strum says the school's portfolio program has had at least four benefits: (1) the systematic collection of student work throughout the year helps document student progress and achievement; (2) student work serves as a lens through which the faculty can reflect on their successes and adjust their instructional strategies; (3) school-to-home communication is enhanced as students present and explain their work to their parents and other adults; and (4) students assume greater ownership of their learning and display obvious pride when involved in selecting and showing off their accomplishments and growth.

Developing content standards, creating more authentic performance assessments, and establishing rigorous student performance standards will not—in and of themselves—substantially boost student achievement. But the seven principles above reflect

promising ways that teachers and schools are beginning to rethink their curriculum and instructional strategies to ensure that *performance* is more than something measured at the end of a unit.

[1]This performance task was developed in 1994 by R. Marzano and D. Pickering, Mid-Continent Regional Educational Laboratory Institute, Aurora, Colorado.

[2]For a detailed discussion and examples of classroom performance lists, see M. Hibbard and colleagues, (1996), *Performance-Based Learning and Assessment*, (Alexandria, Va.: Association for Supervision and Curriculum Development).

References

Haller, E., D. Child, and H. Walberg. (1988). "Can Comprehension Be Taught: A Qualitative Synthesis." *Educational Researcher* 17, 9: 5–8.

Gardner, H. (1991). *The Unschooled Mind*. New York: Basic Books.

McCombs, B. (1984). "Processes and Skills Underlying Intrinsic Motivation to Learn: Toward a Definition of Motivational Skills Training Intervention." *Educational Psychologist* 19: 197–218.

McTighe, J., and F. Lyman. (1988). "Cueing Thinking in the Classroom: The Promise of Theory-Embedded Tools." *Educational Leadership* 45, 7: 18–24.

Palinscar, A., and A. Brown. (1984). "Reciprocal Teaching of Comprehension Fostering and Comprehension Monitoring Activities." *Cognition and Instruction* 1: 117–176.

Schunk, D. (1990). "Goal Setting and Self-Efficacy During Self-Regulated Learning." *Educational Psychologist* 25, 1: 71–86.

Wiggins, G. (1993). *Assessing Student Performance: Exploring the Limits and Purposes of Testing*. San Francisco, Calif.: Jossey-Bass.

Jay McTighe is Director of the Maryland Assessment Consortium, c/o Urbana High School, 3471 Campus Dr., Ijarnsville, MD 21754 (e-mail: jmctighe@aol.com).

Lessons Learned About Student Portfolios

By Elizabeth A. Hebert

The idea of going beyond test scores to collect more substantive evidence of a school's curriculum and teaching initiatives seemed innovative to faculty members at Crow Island School a decade ago, Ms. Hebert notes. What they didn't know then was that the process of selecting samples of work and assembling them into a portfolio is profoundly important to children.

A DECADE ago we began a project with student portfolios at Crow Island School in Winnetka, Illinois. Influenced by Howard Gardner's theory of multiple intelligences, our faculty explored the many learning experiences of our students and decided to encourage the children to gather their work over time so that they themselves could see evidence of their learning. During the past 10 years we have learned so much more than we imagined. We now know quite a bit about what a portfolio is and probably more about what a portfolio is not. But what continues to energize our thinking after all this time is what a portfolio can be.

When we started this project, we didn't fully understand the possibilities that portfolios could offer. The notion that there

ELIZABETH A. HEBERT is the principal of Crow Island School, Winnetka, Ill.

Illustration by John Berry

could be some child-centered, qualitative supplement to the single-number characterizations of learning emphasized by our testing culture seemed reason enough to organize our efforts and those of our students. The idea of collecting more substantive evidence of our curriculum and teaching initiatives to counteract narrowly defined test scores seemed innovative at the time. What we didn't know then was that the process of selecting samples of one's own work and assembling them into a

portfolio is profoundly important to children. We also learned that all children have a natural ability and desire to tell their story through the contents of the portfolio. Even now, we remain excited about capturing the individual voices of our students through portfolio collections.

Over the past 10 years we've discussed and rethought many aspects of our understanding of portfolios. Here are some of the lessons we've taken to heart:

• *Don't get too focused on delineating*

From *Phi Delta Kappan*, April 1998, pp. 583-585. © 1998 by Phi Delta Kappa, Inc. Reprinted by permission.

the contents of the portfolio. In the early years of our work, we were far too concerned about the specific contents of the portfolios. Looking back, I believe that discussing this matter is a natural way to explore the purposes of portfolios; however, it's important not to become rigid about what goes into a portfolio. I'm always reminded of the wonderful definition offered by staff developers Pearl Paulsen and Leon Paulsen: "Portfolios tell a story. . . . Put in anything that helps to tell the story." The real contents of a portfolio are the child's thoughts and his or her reasons for selecting a particular entry. That selection process reflects the interests and metacognitive maturity of the child and the inspiration and influence offered by the teachers.

When teachers first get involved with portfolios, they tend to have different ideas and suggestions about what to put on the portfolio "must list." Fortunately, we never committed ourselves to making such a list, and I suspect that is why, in part, we are still so fascinated with this topic. After 10 years we realize that there is no best notion of what goes into a portfolio; rather, portfolios serve as a metaphor for our continued belief in the idea that children can play a major role in the assessment of their own learning. This perspective, rather than a predetermined list of curriculum samples, should be the guideline for placing particular items into a portfolio.

• *The "container" issue.* Initially, most teachers gathered children's work in a wide variety of containers. Hanging file folders became a popular organizing tool. The issue of what work was sent home and what work stayed in the classroom was important in the early years. It took time to establish the expectation that most of the children's work would stay at school. Faculty members spent many hours discussing details: the type and color of containers, the location and labeling of the intermediate gathering folders, the importance of dating all student work, and the directions we would give to the students about selections. Some tensions and anxieties surfaced in response to our open conversations, and there were some disagreements about the contents and purposes of portfolios. Thus the security of knowing we would definitely be using red, yellow, blue, and green legal-sized folders in grades 1-4 and black binders in grade 5 was a source of great comfort. Issues of giving tangible form to the often unwieldy open-

ness of student-centered portfolios need to be addressed but must be secondary to the larger and more fundamental discussions about what a portfolio can represent about a child's learning.

• *Whose portfolio is it?* Because our initial understanding was that portfolios might counterbalance the narrowness of test scores with concrete examples of our students' interests and abilities, we assumed the role of portfolio managers. The notion that children could or should participate in the selection of the contents of the portfolios was intriguing to us, but we didn't have a clear plan to implement that ideal.

How does the child know what to choose? What if a child doesn't select balanced evidence of the teacher's curriculum for his or her portfolio? Is it appropriate for a child to present a portfolio that excludes a major content area? These questions continue to be a part of our ongoing discussions as we discover the ever-growing metacognitive voices of our children — voices that we train to become competent and thoughtful tellers of the stories of their learning.

We now believe that the selection of the contents of the portfolio is an evolving process shared by child and teacher. When children are just beginning to understand what a portfolio is, they require clear scaffolding. We advise students about including certain pieces of work that we feel will be valued — if not now, at a later time. We have discovered that the conversations that take place as portfolios are being compiled give the children the security to suggest additional entries that are more personal or unique to their own school experience. One message about child ownership is very clear: we do not assign a letter grade or evaluation to the portfolio. We honor the child's world that is represented by the portfolio. We want to learn more about that world so that we can more sensitively help each child grow.

• *An archive adds a sense of history to the portfolio.* As children's work was gathered, we were uncertain what to do with it at the close of the school year. Our faculty discussions emphasized how important it was for the children to have access to their work over time so that they could develop a better understanding of their histories as students. We decided to use the term *portfolio* when referring to a single year's selection of works and *archive* for the total collection, which could span up to six years (K-5). Establishing the physi-

cal space to house an archive (in our school, the library/resource center) was an important step: it signaled to all children that each of them was an important part of the history of our school.

• *Defining an audience is crucial.* The notion of gathering work to "tell your story" is far too abstract for young students unless they know who is listening to that story. The question of the contents of a portfolio becomes much clearer once an audience is defined. For our students, the parents were the most natural audience. Other audiences could be siblings, other students from the same or different grade levels, prior teachers in the school, or senior citizens in the community.

• *Attaching meaning to the contents of the portfolio contributes to the child's metacognitive growth.* The collecting of student work was initially overwhelming. Some students saved everything, and others were reluctant to make a decision about what to select for their portfolios. We needed a mechanism to assist students — and ourselves — in managing the size of an individual portfolio and, more important, to inject more thoughtfulness into the selection process. The idea of "reflection tags" quickly worked its way around the building. The basic idea is to consider reasons for including a piece of work in the portfolio, to record these statements of value on a tag of paper, and to attach the tag to the sample of student work. This idea is usually presented in a rug-time discussion with students.

In the early grades, conversations with children focus on the purposes of maintaining a portfolio. In first grade, students are reminded of the baby books that their parents have put together. This example introduces the concepts of purposeful selection, life history, and evidence of change over time. "Now that you're in first grade, you will select some of your first-grade work, and we'll keep it in a portfolio." The first-graders love the sound of this grown-up word and remember that their kindergarten teachers introduced this idea to them last spring. Often fifth-grade student buddies assist the children in sorting through their work and selecting items for their portfolios.

In second grade, children may be asked, "Why would you put something in your portfolio?" "Because it's my best work" is usually the first response. With patience, the teacher elicits further value statements from the students. "Because I'm proud of it." "Because I didn't think I could do this." "Because I worked very hard on it." The teacher records these thoughts on tags of paper and asks the children to affix them to particular entries in their portfolios. "Do you have any blank tags?" asks another student, demonstrating that further ideas have occurred about why one keeps artifacts in a portfolio and indicating that the transfer of ownership from teacher to child has begun. The use of individual reflection tags (or some other open-ended written reflection) about the contents of a portfolio is an important element in portfolio construction. The physical act of attaching meaning to a specific piece of work contributes significantly to the child's metacognitive growth.

• *A celebratory event brings child, portfolio, and audience together.* Trying to balance the micro and macro issues surrounding our portfolio project was no small task. Discussions about contents, containers, file folders, and the location of the archive, together with the philosophical issues of portfolio ownership, the role of portfolios in assessment, and educating parents about the use of portfolios, had us going in many directions at once. What we needed was a unifying experience that would consolidate all our discussions and concerns and that would clearly communicate to both students and parents the value we assigned to portfolios.

Learning is worth celebrating, and children can be competent participants in that celebration. Gradually we have developed structures to express that belief as part of our school culture. By far, the most powerful celebration of student competence has been the Portfolio Evening, an opportunity for children to present their portfolios to their own parents. At one of our regularly scheduled conferences with parents, the children are given the responsibility to present their portfolios individually to their parents and to explain to them the process by which the materials were generated, the self-reflections involved in the selection of the materials, the conversations with the teacher that spurred particular choices, and any other aspects of their "learning stories" they want to share.

To prepare for this event, the children spend several weeks talking about their portfolios and archives with their teachers, with peers, and often with older students. Specific lessons are focused on how to organize selections of work; how to place them in chronological order; how to think about work as evidence of competence in more than one subject area; how to compare earlier work with present work, showing the acquisition of more advanced skills; and, most important, how to reflect on the portfolio as a whole. Students complete portfolio menus called "Ask me about" sheets. On these organizing sheets the students highlight the contents of their portfolios and emphasize learning experiences that are important to their portfolio story.

Another aspect of the Portfolio Evening is the production of a classroom videotape of approximately 15 to 20 minutes in length. This video is intended to portray a day in the life of this particular group of students, including the learning that takes place in special subject areas of art, music, physical education, Spanish, and computers. In addition, many videotapes include recess activities and selected field trips. The project of organizing, scripting, and filming these videotapes is one that the children look forward to with great enthusiasm. Of greater value, however, is the fact that the production of this brief videotape provides an important metacognitive task for each group of children as they reflect on and develop descriptive language for each segment of the school day — as they understand it.

The dates of the Portfolio Evenings appear on the annual school calendar, and parents are also invited by letter. The event takes place over two nights, with half of the class and their parents attending each night for approximately 90 minutes. In the days just prior to the event, the children add final touches to their presentations and select an area of the classroom where they can hold a private conversation with their parents.

• *Parent education is required.* Another lesson we have learned is that we need to deliberately teach the parents about the value of student portfolios — what they mean to us, how we use them as a part of our curriculum, their immeasurable value to the children, and how they fit into an assessment program for our school. It's important to emphasize that portfolios do not replace more standardized measures. Standardized tests address the question "Which child knows more?" whereas portfolios address the question "What does this child know?" One question is not better than the other; posing both questions will provide a more comprehensive perspective of a child's work in school.

For the past three years a panel of eight faculty members representing grades K-5 have presented an informational program for our parents. At this evening meeting, the teachers speak briefly about their understanding of the value and purposes of portfolios for the particular age group they teach. From our years of conversations and direct experience, we are able to provide the scaffolding that enables parents to better understand their children's portfolio presentations and gain a more in-depth view of their children as learners.

These are some of the lessons we've learned about portfolios over the past 10 years. When the adoption of portfolios is first being considered, it's important to begin with a discussion of beliefs about children and learning and the connection between them. And then, of course, there's the question "What is our role in all of this?" More than any book we've read or speaker we've listened to, our own ongoing discussions about portfolios — what they can do and represent — provide direction for our own professional growth. It is important for us to continue to take the time we need to pursue this topic in depth, and we continue to share with one another any new activities and suggestions that might be helpful.

The involvement, the sense of connectedness, and the self-discovery that children demonstrate in compiling their portfolios have taught us that our work over these 10 years has to a large extent fulfilled many of the promises that we thought portfolios held. Of course, we know that there are many more lessons to be learned as we listen intently to the children during this process and learn more about the meaning and value they assign to the development of their portfolios.

Grades: The Final Frontier in Assessment Reform

By Gregory J. Cizek

> **The task of reforming educational assessment has just begun. New forms of assessment cannot provide clearer or more complete information about student achievement unless the ways in which achievement is communicated are refined. The real challenge for assessment reform will be to bring assessment and grading practices into the fold.**

Assessment reform has become a centerpiece of efforts to improve U.S. education (Stiggins, 1988; Wolf, LeMahieu, and Eresh, 1992). The list of innovations is familiar: Students are preparing portfolios of their work to demonstrate complex characteristics like employability skills. Teachers are gathering and synthesizing more information about students involving a greater diversity of valuable educational outcomes. Administrators are evaluating the use of new forms of assessment. Districts are rethinking promotion and retention policies and the measures used to inform those decisions. Professional associations are promulgating new standards for both content and assessment. Test publishers are incorporating a wider variety of alternative assessment formats into their products. Nationally, the importance of assessment can be seen in the Goals 2000 legislation and other federal initiatives.

Gregory J. Cizek is associate professor of educational research and measurement, University of Toledo, Ohio; readers may continue the dialogue on the Internet at gcizek@utnet.utoledo.edu.

One might conclude that assessment reform efforts are making great strides toward a common goal: improving the range and quality of information about educational performance available to students, teachers, parents, administrators, and the public. But, maybe not.

How Performance Is Communicated

Despite all the other changes, a student's educational performance is still primarily reported using grades. Actually, the older term "marks" might be more accurate than grades, because the way achievement is reported does not always involve the use of grades. Instead, the marks *might* be in the form of letters (A, B, C, D, F); numbers (percent correct); symbols (S = Satisfactory, N = Needs Improvement, U = Unsatisfactory); descriptors (Emerging, Developing, Maturing); or other systems.

Regardless of the kinds of marks, however, at the local level, where an individual student's performance matters most to the student, parents, teachers, and others intimately involved in the student's education, grades continue to be relied upon to communicate important information about performance and progress. But they probably don't.

What's Wrong with Grades?

Grades in whatever form are primitive tools for doing the job they are asked to accomplish. As communication devices, they are more like two tin cans and a length of string than a cellular phone. It's an interesting con-

Despite all the other changes, a student's educational performance is still primarily reported using grades.

trast: As bubble sheets whiz through a scanner in a district testing office, a teacher mulls a pile of papers with stickers and happy faces on them, concluding that this student's work merits an A for the marking period.

In a recent study, teachers from midwestern schools were asked about their assessment and grading practices. The findings revealed great differences in what teachers do, and great uncertainty about what they *should* do. For example, teachers were asked

to indicate what factors they consider when assigning marks to assignments and tests. A clear majority (83 percent) indicated they considered the percent or number correct on the assignment; from one-third to one-half the teachers, however, also said they considered the difficulty of the assignment, how the class performed overall, the individual students' ability levels, and the effort a student put into the work.

It appears that nearly *everything* is considered when assigning a mark. There are probably two reasons for this. First, educators want to consider all relevant aspects of a student's classroom experience when assigning a mark. At the same time, there is apparently no clear consensus about which factors *are* relevant to assigning a grade.

What about final grades? To this question, teachers responded that they combined the marks they had assigned to individual assignments and tests—that uncertain mix described above—with three other kinds of information:

- Formal achievement-related measures (attendance, class participation)
- Informal achievement-related measures (answers in class, one-on-one discussions)
- Other informal information (impressions of effort, conduct, teamwork, leadership, and so on).

Unfortunately, this mix of factors is difficult to disentangle. In an attempt to clear things up, teachers were asked to explain how they combine these diverse factors into a single mark. The interviews led to other revealing perspectives on classroom assessment practice.

Deciding on a Grade

Many teachers expressed a clear preference for non-cognitive outcomes. As one elementary teacher said, "Getting the child through the level with a positive attitude and good memories is more important than a raw number grade ... Shaping the kids' minds through group interaction, effort, and participation is more important than averaging tests and quiz scores."

Another teacher reported that "assignments, quizzes, and tests are not crucial in [her] grading policies." This teacher "stresses group interaction and uses several other subjective methods combined with intuition to formulate a final grade." Attendance and participation were also highly valued by the teachers in the study, and these factors were also considered in assigning a final grade.

It was particularly interesting to learn how teachers reported combining the divergent sources of information into the final grade. Although many teachers did not provide much detail regarding how the composite was formed, one teacher said she "considers attendance, participation, effort, conduct,

and teamwork, and adds to this things such as tests and quizzes."

Another teacher was more specific about details. She designs the test she uses herself, and uses "an average of 16–20 grades during the grading period in calculating the final

Attendance and participation were also highly valued by the teachers in the study, and these factors were also considered in assigning a final grade.

grade. However, the lower grades are not factored into the average." To this mix, she adds her "overall impressions of effort and how the class performed."

The practice described by this teacher is apparently not uncommon. Several teachers reported similar practices, throwing out the worst quiz score for each student, considering class performance as a whole, and considering impressions of a student's effort and ability.

The practice of "throwing out" one or more poor scores on formal assessments is apparently quite widespread. Ostensibly, teachers use the practice so that a single low score does not inappropriately affect a student's grade. No teacher, however, reported throwing out a single high score that might inappropriately inflate a student's final grade.

Finally, several teachers made specific mention of taking "extra credit" into account when assigning the final grade.

What Do These Practices Tell Us?

Taken together, these practices point to what might be called a *success orientation* in assigning marks. While educators consider a variety of factors in assigning a final grade, they combine the information in idiosyncratic ways: Not only do different teachers use different factors, they also combine the elements in different proportions within classrooms. The factors considered in arriving at a final grade are weighted in ways that are most advantageous for each student.

In math class, for example, a student who has not mastered fractions may still be awarded a B+ for maintaining a positive attitude, regularly participating in class discussions, and trying hard. On the other hand, an A student who has mastered fractions would usually not be downgraded for being pessimistic, silent during discussions, and "coasting."

Teachers seem to follow the advice our parents gave us: "If you can't say something nice about someone, don't say anything at all." In most cases, they are able to find something good to say.

Although our parents may be happy that we are following their advice, the parents of the students may not be so happy. They assume grades indicate achievement or content mastery. Students themselves are unlikely to be sophisticated enough to understand that their grades are complex composites. Instead, they probably assume—as nearly everyone else does—that their A's and B's mean they have successfully mastered rigorous academic work.

Perhaps the innovations accompanying assessment reform have prompted teachers to gather a more diverse array of information about student performance. The new problems, though, are "What should be done with all this information?" or "How should grades be assigned?" Unfortunately, these are questions that educators are currently not well-prepared to answer. Today many teachers are simply not comfortable with the task of assigning grades.

At least two factors contribute to the problem:

First, little training in educational assessment is available at undergraduate and graduate levels of teacher training, and competence in assessment is not always a prerequisite to licensure.[1]

The research paints an even grimmer picture about the training and experience of administrators with respect to assessment. A recent study sponsored by the National Association of Elementary School Principals (NAESP), the American Association of School Administrators (AASA), and the National Association of Secondary School Principals (NASSP) illustrates the need for educational leaders to become more "assessment literate" (Stiggins, 1991; Impara, 1993).

---

1. These problems have been well-documented for several years. See, for example, Ward (1980), Gullickson (1986), Schafer and Lissitz (1987), O'Sullivan and Chalnick (1991), and Wise, Lukin, and Roos (1991).
2. For one example, see the Standards for Teacher Competence in Educational Assessment of Students, developed by the American Federation of Teachers, National Council on Measurement in Education, and National Education Association, Washington, D.C., 1990.
3. See Cizek and Rachor (1994) for a more detailed description about what such a vision might entail—what the authors refer to as "planned assessment systems."

Second, many educators simply lack an interest in testing and grading (Hills, 1991).

Grades and Report Cards: What Can Be Done?

The lack of knowledge and interest in grading translates into a serious information breakdown in education. A recent study of how the content of report cards facilitates or

> The lack of knowledge and interest in grading translates into a serious information breakdown in education.

hinders parents' understanding of the information they provide was not optimistic. The authors concluded that report cards are not successfully transmitting teachers' intended meaning to parents (Waltman and Frisbie, 1994).

The reform of classroom assessment and grading practices must become a top priority if educational improvement is to be effective. New forms of assessment are welcome, but there will be no educational advantage if the meaning of these measures remains murky. Assessment reforms have introduced a wealth of information to teachers, parents, and students. Our ability to *use* this information, however, has remained essentially unchanged.

At least eight initiatives are warranted; the effort should include all who are interested in reform.

1. All educators must make a commitment to professional development.

Professional development in assessment should become a top priority. There may be different focuses for these efforts: Teachers may be more interested in classroom assessment issues and administrators may be more in need of developing a vision for integrated, planned assessment systems.

2. Training in assessment must be relevant to classrooms.

Even when teachers and administrators receive formal training in assessment, university coursework often focuses on aspects of testing and grading that may not be applicable to those who actually *do* these things. College coursework should be redesigned to provide more relevant training.

3. Professional organizations must promote sound assessment practice.

Professional organizations have become active in this area,[2] although more work is necessary to highlight the need for assessment competence and the benefits of sound assessment practices for both teachers and students.

4. Educational leaders must develop an "assessment vision."

Considering the increasing attention to assessment and all the diverse purposes it serves, it is fair to say the big picture in educational assessment is sometimes chaotic, and is perhaps the most neglected issue in assessment reform. Educational leaders should promote a clear, coordinated conception about the varieties of assessment in classrooms and the purposes and uses they serve.[3] To be effective in promoting reforms, this vision must be communicated to teachers, parents, community members, and students.

5. Grading policies must be developed and applied consistently.

Administrators, parents, and teachers must work together to develop, disseminate, and maintain consistent grading policies. To maximize the utility of grades, developmental efforts should work to build consensus on the policies, listening closely to the information needs of parents, students, employers, and universities. A beginning effort might include discussions about what current policies reveal about the need for assessment reform: for example, many policies simply list percentage ranges for A's, B's, C's, D's, and F's and give teachers little additional guidance about sound evaluation practices.

6. End isolation.

Poor assessment practices flourish in schools where teachers are isolated and do not benefit from interaction about difficult assessment issues. Teachers must take the initiative to collaborate and cooperate on testing and grading practices. Administrators must facilitate collaboration and encourage consistency in grading practices.

7. Students must be initiated into a new grading culture.

Students often see grades and learning as separate, or value grades more than education. A significant educational reform will help students see the link between mastery of knowledge, skills, and abilities, and the grades they receive. We should teach students to value real learning.

8. Assessment experts must lend a hand.

New methods of assessment promise more and better information about student performance, but proliferation of innovative assessment formats has outstripped the development of ways to interpret and report this information. Experts in testing should explore new ways of synthesizing and communicating the information provided by alternative assessments to take full advantage of the innovations.

As the list of challenges implies, the task of assessment reform has just begun. New forms of assessment such as portfolios or performance assessments cannot provide clearer or more complete information about student achievement unless the ways achievement is communicated are refined. The real challenge for assessment will be to make assessment and grading practices part of the reform effort.

References

American Federation of Teachers, National Council on Measurement in Education, National Education Association. *Standards for Teacher Competence in Educational Assessment of Students.* Washington, D.C.: National Council on Measurement in Education, 1990.

Cizek, G. J., and Rachor, R. E. "The Real Testing Bias: The Role of Values in Educational Assessment." *NASSP Bulletin,* March 1994.

Gullickson, A. R. "Teacher Education and Teacher-Perceived Needs in Educational Measurement and Evaluation." *Journal of Educational Measurement* 23(1986): 347–54.

Hills, J. R. "Apathy Concerning Testing and Grading." *Phi Delta Kappan* 72(1991): 540–45.

Impara, J. C. "Joint Committee on Competency Standards in Student Assessment for Educational Administrators Update: Assessment Survey Results." Presented at the Annual Meeting of the National Council on Measurement, New Orleans, La., April 1993.

O'Sullivan, R. G., and Chalnick, M. K. "Measurement-Related Course Work Requirements for Teacher Certification and Recertification." *Educational Measurement: Issues and Practice* 10(1991): 17–19, 23.

Schafer, W. D., and Lissitz, R. W. "Measurement Training for School Personnel: Recommendations and Reality." *Journal of Teacher Education* 38(1987): 57–63.

Stiggins, R. J. "Assessment Literacy." *Phi Delta Kappan* 72(1991): 534–39.

_____. "Revitalizing Classroom Assessment: The Highest Instructional Priority." *Phi Delta Kappan* 69(1988): 363–68.

Waltman, K. K., and Frisbie, D. A. "Parents' Understanding of Their Children's Report Card Grades." *Applied Measurement in Education* 7(1994): 223–40.

Ward, J. G. "Teachers and Testing: A Survey of Knowledge and Attitudes." In *Testing in Our Schools,* edited by L. M. Rudner. Washington, D.C.: National Institute of Education, 1980.

Wise, S. L.; Lukin, L. E.; and Roos, L. L. "Teacher Beliefs About Training in Testing and Measurement." *Journal of Teacher Education* 42(1991): 37–42.

Wolf, D. P.; LeMahieu, P. G.; and Eresh, J. "Good Measure: Assessment as a Tool for Educational Reform." *Educational Leadership* 49(1992): 8–13.

Acknowledgment: The author is grateful for the support of this work provided by the University of Toledo College of Education and Allied Professions.

A

ability goals, motivation and, 156
academic failure, violent behavior and, 186–187
acceleration, of gifted and talented students, 65–68
access, memory and, 93
accommodational learning style, 102
accountability, assessment and, 203
acquisition, memory and, 93
acronyms, as cues, 137
action research, use of, in assessing instruction, 11–14
activity-centered approach, to learning styles, 102
alienation, violent behavior and, 187
alternative education, 47, 48
altruism, 37
American Family, The (Quayle), 28
analogies, as elaboration process, 85, 87
analytic intelligence, 103, 140
anarchic form, of mental self-government, 104, 107–115
anticipatory set, 94
apraxia, 62
arts, brain and, 94
Assertive Discipline (Canter), 168–169, 170–171
assessment, 199–205; authentic, 206–212; of gifted and talented students, 65–66; grades and, 221–224; instructional action research and, 11–14; of mastery motivation, 153; portfolio, 11–12, 196, 203, 204, 217, 218–220
assimilational learning style, 102
at-risk students: high school, 47–51; motivational theory and, 156–158
attachment, parent-infant, 31–33
attention deficit disorder, 62, 63
auditory discrimination, 62
authentic assessment, 202, 206–212
authoritative parenting, 27
autonomy, as developmental task of adolescence, 43, 44, 45

B

back to basics movement, 201–202
Banks, James, 76–77
behavior management: defusing confrontations and, 180–184; goal coordination and, 159–166; in inclusive classrooms, 174–179; in student-centered classrooms, 167–173
behaviorism, 28, 122, 126
benchmark papers, 196
benevolence, prosocial behavior and, 36
Bennett, William, 26, 28
Beyond the Classroom (Steinberg), 27
bias-free curriculum, prosocial behavior and, 38
bibliotherapy, prosocial behavior and, 36
bilingual education, 73
bonding, parent-infant, 31–33

Book of Virtues (Bennett), 26, 28
brain: cognitive psychology and, 90–95; early childhood education and, 20–25

C

cadre approach, conflict resolution and, 187
Call to Character, A (Kohl), 26
Canter, Lee, 168–169, 170–171
caregivers, mastery motivation and, 153
caring quotient (CQ) classroom, 38
Cascio, Wayne, 119, 120
certification, assessment and, 202–203
character education, 28, 29
checklists, procedural, scaffolding and, 135, 136
chief state school officers, predictions of, on future of education, 15–17
choice theory, Glasser's, 144–150
Chugani, Harry, 23, 24
classroom assessment, 196–197
Clinton, Hillary Rodham, 27, 28, 30
cognition, motivation and, 152–153
cognition-centered approach, to learning styles, 101–102
cognitive psychology, brain and, 90–95
Coles, Robert, 93, 140
Common Fire (Daloz), 28
comparative advanced organizers, 85, 87
competence motivation, 151
compliance, as discipline goal, 159–160, 163
conflict resolution, 35, 40, 158; violence prevention programs and, 185–189
confrontations, defusing, 180–184
conservative learning, of mental self-government, 105, 107–115
constructivism, 28, 29, 141
control theory. *See* choice theory
convergent learning style, 102
cooperation, prosocial behavior and, 34–42
cooperative learning groups, 8, 40, 93, 167, 187
corporal punishment, due process and, 175
corpus callosum, 91
cortisol, stress and, 21–22
creative intelligence, 103, 140
CREB gene, 90
credibility, assessment and, 208
criteria: assessment, 210; performance-based assessment and, 214–215
critical periods, brain development and, 22–23
cues, thinking skills and, 135–136
culture: adolescent, high school and, 8–10. *See also* multicultural education
curriculum: bias-free, 38; for gifted and talented students, 66, 67; multicultural, 74, 79–81
Curriculum and Evaluation Standards for School Mathematics (National Council of Teachers of Mathematics), 200

D

Damon, William, 26, 30, 130, 131
Deci, Edward, 119, 120, 124, 127
declarative knowledge, 135
deferred goal coordination strategies, 165
DeFries, John, 63
Developing Minds (Costa), 92
developmental tasks, of middle school adolescents, 43–46
diagnostic testing-prescriptive instruction model, 67
discipline. *See* behavior management
distributive justice, 36
divergent learning style, 102
divorce, choice theory and, 144–150
documentation of progress, performance-based instruction and, 216–217
Doyle, Walter, 162–163
drop outs, and at-risk high school youth, 47–51
due process, 175, 178
dyscalculia, 62
dysgraphia, 62
dyspraxia, 62
dyslexia, 62
dysnomia, 63

E

early childhood education: assessment of, 192–198; brain development and, 20–25; mastery motivation and, 151–155; prosocial behavior and, 34–42
education, predictions of future of, 15–17
Educational Care (Levine), 93
effectance motivation, 151
elaboration process, enhanced knowledge retention and recall through, 84–89
Emotional Intelligence (Goleman), 93, 140
emotions, brain and, 91
empathy, 27, 29
epitome, as elaboration process, 85, 87–88
equity: in assessment, 201; prosocial behavior and, 36
Erikson, Erik, 100, 153
ethics. *See* moral education; prosocial behavior
Evertson, Carolyn, 162–163
executive function, of mental self-government, 104, 107–115
existential intelligence, 97
exit tests, high school, 202
experiential elaborations, 85, 87
experiential intelligence, 140
explicit instruction, performance-based, 215–216
expository advanced organizers, 85, 88
expulsion, due process and, 175, 177

extrinsic rewards, learning and, 117–121, 122–125, 126–128

F

failure, school: choice theory and, 144–150; violent behavior and, 186–187
feasibility, assessment and, 208
feedback, performance-based instruction and, 216
field dependence-independence learning style, 101–102
follow-up, behavior management and, 182, 183
free, appropriate public education (FAPE), special education and, 55
functional analysis, of student behavior, 176
future, of education, predictions of, 15–17

G

Gardiner, Howard, 93, 94, 139, 218; interview with, 96–100
gender differences, in brain structure, 91–92
generality elaborations, 85, 87
general-to-detailed elaboration processes, 85, 87–88
gifted and talented students, 69–71; acceleration of, 65–68; thinking styles of, 101–116
Ginott, Haim, 170, 171
Glasser, William: 170, 172; on quality schools, 144–150
global level, of mental self-government, 105, 107–115
goal coordination, behavior management and, 159–166
Goals 2000, 221
Goleman, Daniel, 93, 140
grades, assessment and, 221–224
graphic organizers, scaffolding and, 135, 136, 141
Greater Expectations (Damon), 30
group assessment, 195

H

"heroes and holidays" approach, to multiculturalism and, 77
hierarchic form, of mental self-government, 104, 107–115
high school: at-risk students in, 47–51; confrontational behavior and, 180–184; exit exams for, 202; successful student teaching in, 8–10; violence prevention programs in, 185–189
honor roll, 157–158
"how-to" memory system, 93
human potential movement, 28

I

identification, as discipline goal, 159–160
impulsivity-reflectivity learning style, 102
inclusion: behavior management and, 174–179; special education and, 54–59
Individualized Education Plan (IEP), 57, 177
Individuals with Disabilities Education Act (IDEA), 55, 175
infants, and bonding with parents, 31–33
integrative goal-coordination strategies, 165
intelligences; multiple, Gardner's theory of, 93, 96–99, 139, 141
internalization, as discipline goal, 159–160
interpersonal intelligence, 93, 99
intrapersonal intelligence, 93, 99
intrinsic rewards, 118
invented spelling, 196–197
IQ (intelligence quotient), 97–98, 193–194
It Takes a Village (Clinton), 28

J

judicial function, of mental self-government, 104, 107–115
justice, distributive, 36

K

keyword method, of transformational elaboration, 85
kindergarten, readiness testing for, 192–198
kinesthetic intelligence, 93, 99
Kohlberg, Lawrence, 27, 29

L

language, development of, 22–23
learnable intelligence, Perkins' theory of, 140
learned helplessness, 152
learning disabilities, 60–64. *See* special needs children
learning goals, motivation and, 156
learning strategies, for special needs students, 84–89
learning style, intelligence and, 100
Learning to Care (Wuthnow), 27
least restrictive environment (LRE), special education and, 54–59, 175
legislative function, of mental self-government, 104, 107–115
Lepper, Mark, 119, 127
Lerner, Barbara, 129, 130, 131
leveling-sharpening learning style, 101
Lewis, Michael, 31, 32, 33
liberal learning, mental self-government and, 105, 107–115

linguistic intelligence, 93, 99
local level, of mental self-government, 105, 107–115

M

macrolevel elaboration processes, 84–89
mainstreaming, 54
manifestation determination, behavior management and, 177
marriage failure, choice theory and, 144–150
mastery motivation, in young children, 151–155
maternal teaching, 39
mathemagenic method, of transformational elaboration, 85
mathematical intelligence, 93, 99
matrix sampling, 195
media, prosocial behavior and, 37
memory, 22, 90, 91, 93–94
mental imagery, as elaboration process, 85, 86
mental self-government, Sternberg's theory of, 102–116
mentors, moral, 38
metacognitive reflection, 135
microlevel elaboration processes, 84–89
middle school: behavior management in, 167–173; developmental tasks of, 43–46; gifted and talented students in, 69–71; multicultural education and, 76–78
mneumonics, as cues, 137
modeling, 130
models of excellence, performance-based instruction and, 215
modified goal-coordination strategies, 165
monarchic form, of mental self-government, 104, 107–115
moral education, 26–30
moral growth, as developmental task of adolescence, 44, 45–46
Moral Intelligence (Coles), 93, 140
motivation: at-risk children and, 156–158; mastery, in young children, 151–155
multicultural education, 8, 72–75, 76–78, 79–81
multiple intelligences, Gardner's theory of, 93, 96–100, 139, 141, 218
music, brain and, 94
musical intelligence, 93, 99

N

National Assessment of Educational Progress (NAEP), 195, 197, 203
National Association for the Education of Young Children (NAEYC), 193, 194, 196
National Education Goals, 197
naturalistic intelligence, 96–97, 99
negotiation, conflict resolution and, 188
neural intelligence, 140
neurological development, brain function and, 91

O

oligarchic form, of mental self-government, 104, 107–115

P

parallel processing, 91
parent-infant bonding, 31–33
peer mediators, 40, 158, 185, 187
peer review, authentic assessment and, 206–212
performance-based assessment, 213–217
performance-contingent rewards, 119
personal identity, as developmental task of adolescence, 44–45
personality-centered approach, to learning styles, 102
Perversion of Autonomy, The (Gaylin & Jennings), 28
Piaget, Jean, 140, 151
Place Called School, A (Goodlad), 117
plasticity, brain, 21–22
portfolio assessment, 11–12, 196, 203, 204, 217, 218–220
practical intelligence, 103, 140
precise conceptual elaborations, 85, 86
prerequisite elaborations, 85, 86–87
prevention, behavior management and, 182
Principles and Indicators for Student Assessment Systems (National Forum on Assessment), 200, 202, 203, 204
problem ownership, goal coordination and, 161
procedural checklists, scaffolding and, 135, 136
process-based assessment, 206–208
process-structured questions, scaffolding and, 135, 136
prosocial behavior, encouraging development of, 34–42
psychological pathology, violent behavior and, 187
punishment, 119–120, 123, 146, 159, 168, 178

Q

quality schools, choice theory and, 144–150
Quayle, Dan, 27, 28
questions, process-structured, scaffolding and, 135, 136

R

readiness testing, kindergarten, 192–198

reading, assessment of, 196
Reclaiming Our Schools (Wynne and Ryan), 28–29
reflective intelligence, 140
registration, memory and, 93
Rehabilitation Act of 1973, 56
reinforcement, behavior management and, 177–178
report cards, 223–224
representational level, of transformational elaboration, 85, 86
required helpfulness, 39
responsibility, prosocial behavior and, 38–39
retention, 193, 194
rewards, extrinsic, learning and, 117–121, 122–125, 126–128
ritual, prosocial behavior and, 40–41
rubrics, assessment, 210
Ryan, Kevin, 28–29

S

scaffolding, thinking skills and, 135–136
school improvement, assessment of, 202
Schools for Learning (Bruer), 94
screening tests, kindergarten, 193
Seedbeds of Virtue (Poponoe), 30
self-esteem, teaching, 129–132
Seligman, Martin, 130, 131
simultaneous goal-coordination strategies, 165
situational elaborations, 85, 86–87
skill level, brian function and, 91
Skinner, B. F., 118, 119–120, 122, 126
social insight, teacher's, high school and, 8–10
social mediation, Vygotsky's theory of, 140
social skills, as developmental task of adolescence, 44, 45
soft virtues, 28
spatial intelligence, 93, 99
special needs children: assessment of, 195–196; least restrictive environment and, 54–59; motivation and, 153; prosocial behavior and, 36–37
spelling, invented, 196–197
standards, performance-based instruction and, 214–215
standards-based assessment, 200, 206–208
Staying Together (Glasser), 145
stern virtues, 28–29
Sternberg, Robert, 93, 140, on thinking styles of gifted and talented students, 101–116
storage memory and, 93
Strange Situation test, 32
stress, cortisol and, 21–22

structural cognitive modifiability, Feuerstein's theory of, 140
student-centered classrooms, behavior management in, 167–173
subskill performance, brain function and, 91
success-contingent rewards, 119
suspension, due process and, 175, 177

T

task-contingent rewards, 119
Taxonomy of Educational Objectives (Bloom), 92
testing. See assessment
textbooks, multicultural, 77, 80
thinking skills, 92, 133–138
thinking styles, of gifted and talented students, 101–116
time out, due process and, 175, 177
total student body approach, conflict resolution and, 187
"tourist" curriculum, multiculturalism and, 80
transfer, memory and, 93
transformational elaboration processes, 85–86
triarchic theory of intelligence, Sternberg's, 93, 101–116, 140

U

understanding, assessment for, 209–210
user-friendliness, assessment and, 208

V

validity, assessment and, 208–209
values clarification, 29
video games, prosocial behavior and, 37
violence prevention programs, 185–189
visual perception disabilities, 62–63

W

"what" memory system, 93
"withitness," teacher's, 176; high school and, 8–10

Z

"zero reject" program, IDEA as, 55

AE Article Review Form

We encourage you to photocopy and use this page as a tool to assess how the articles in **Annual Editions** expand on the information in your textbook. By reflecting on the articles you will gain enhanced text information. You can also access this useful form on a product's book support Web site at ***http://www.dushkin.com/ online/.***

NAME: DATE:
_____

TITLE AND NUMBER OF ARTICLE:
_____

BRIEFLY STATE THE MAIN IDEA OF THIS ARTICLE:
_____

LIST THREE IMPORTANT FACTS THAT THE AUTHOR USES TO SUPPORT THE MAIN IDEA:

_____

WHAT INFORMATION OR IDEAS DISCUSSED IN THIS ARTICLE ARE ALSO DISCUSSED IN YOUR TEXTBOOK OR OTHER READINGS THAT YOU HAVE DONE? LIST THE TEXTBOOK CHAPTERS AND PAGE NUMBERS:

_____

LIST ANY EXAMPLES OF BIAS OR FAULTY REASONING THAT YOU FOUND IN THE ARTICLE:

_____

LIST ANY NEW TERMS/CONCEPTS THAT WERE DISCUSSED IN THE ARTICLE, AND WRITE A SHORT DEFINITION:

ANNUAL EDITIONS revisions depend on two major opinion sources: one is our Advisory Board, listed in the front of this volume, which works with us in scanning the thousands of articles published in the public press each year; the other is you—the person actually using the book. Please help us and the users of the next edition by completing the prepaid article rating form on this page and returning it to us. Thank you for your help!

ANNUAL EDITIONS: Educational Psychology 99/00

ARTICLE RATING FORM

Here is an opportunity for you to have direct input into the next revision of this volume. We would like you to rate each of the 40 articles listed below, using the following scale:

1. Excellent: should definitely be retained
2. Above average: should probably be retained
3. Below average: should probably be deleted
4. Poor: should definitely be deleted

Your ratings will play a vital part in the next revision. So please mail this prepaid form to us just as soon as you complete it. Thanks for your help!

RATING

ARTICLE

1. How Novice Teachers Can Succeed with Adolescents
2. Using Action Research to Assess Instruction
3. What Issues Will Confront Public Education in the Years 2000 and 2020? Predictions of Chief State School Officers
4. New Brain Development Research—A Wonderful Window of Opportunity to Build Public Support for Early Childhood Education!
5. The Moral Child
6. Re-Evaluating Significance of Baby's Bond with Mother
7. Helping Children Become More Prosocial: Ideas for Classrooms, Families, Schools, and Communities
8. Developmental Tasks of Early Adolescence: How Adult Awareness Can Reduce At-Risk Behavior
9. Out of the Mouths of Babes: Voices of At-Risk Adolescents
10. Where to Educate Rachel Holland? Does Least Restrictive Environment Mean No Restrictions?
11. Why Andy Couldn't Read
12. Is It Acceleration or Simply Appropriate Instruction for Precocious Youth?
13. How All Middle-Schoolers Can Be "Gifted"
14. The Goals and Track Record of Multicultural Education
15. Multiculturalism at a Crossroads
16. Multiculturalism: Practical Considerations for Curricular Change
17. Making Information Memorable: Enhanced Knowledge Retention and Recall through the Elaboration Process
18. Brain Basics: Cognitive Psychology and Its Implications for Education
19. The First Seven . . . and the Eighth

RATING

ARTICLE

20. Styles of Thinking, Abilities, and Academic Performance
21. The Rewards of Learning
22. Rewards versus Learning: A Response to Paul Chance
23. Sticking Up for Rewards
24. The Tyranny of Self-Oriented Self-Esteem
25. Improving Student Thinking
26. The Intelligence-Friendly Classroom: It Just Makes Sense
27. A New Look at School Failure and School Success
28. I Think I Can, I Think I Can: Understanding and Encouraging Mastery Motivation in Young Children
29. Using Motivational Theory with At-Risk Children
30. Moving beyond Management as Sheer Compliance: Helping Students to Develop Goal Coordination Strategies
31. Connecting Instruction and Management in a Student-Centered Classroom
32. How to Manage Disruptive Behavior in Inclusive Classrooms
33. How to Defuse Defiance, Threats, Challenges, Confrontations . . .
34. Why Violence Prevention Programs Don't Work—and What Does
35. The Challenges of Assessing Young Children Appropriately
36. Transforming Student Assessment
37. Practicing What We Preach in Designing Authentic Assessments
38. What Happens between Assessments?
39. Lessons Learned about Student Portfolios
40. Grades: The Final Frontier in Assessment Reform

(Continued on next page)

We Want Your Advice

ANNUAL EDITIONS: EDUCATIONAL PSYCHOLOGY 99/00

NO POSTAGE
NECESSARY
IF MAILED
IN THE
UNITED STATES

BUSINESS REPLY MAIL
FIRST-CLASS MAIL PERMIT NO. 84 GUILFORD CT

POSTAGE WILL BE PAID BY ADDRESSEE

Dushkin/McGraw-Hill
Sluice Dock
Guilford, CT 06437-9989

IIIₒₒₒIIₒₒIₒIₒIIₒIIₒₒIIIₒIₒIₒIₒIₒIₒIₒIₒIₒIIIₒIₒIₒI

ABOUT YOU

Name _____ Date _____

Are you a teacher? ☐   A student? ☐
Your school's name _____

Department _____

Address _____ City _____ State ____ Zip ____

School telephone # _____

YOUR COMMENTS ARE IMPORTANT TO US !

Please fill in the following information:
For which course did you use this book?
_____

Did you use a text with this *ANNUAL EDITION*? ☐ yes ☐ no
What was the title of the text?
_____

What are your general reactions to the *Annual Editions* concept?
_____

Have you read any particular articles recently that you think should be included in the next edition?
_____

Are there any articles you feel should be replaced in the next edition? Why?
_____

Are there any World Wide Web sites you feel should be included in the next edition? Please annotate.
_____

May we contact you for editorial input? ☐ yes ☐ no
May we quote your comments? ☐ yes ☐ no
_____

271 P2 FM 115

08/18/99 33780 SKLB

DATE DUE

DEC 1 9 1999			
7/22/00			
GAYLORD			PRINTED IN U.S.A.